School Programs for
Disruptive Adolescents

School Programs for Disruptive Adolescents

Daniel J. Safer, M.D.
with contributors

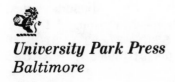

University Park Press
Baltimore

UNIVERSITY PARK PRESS
International Publishers in Science, Medicine, and Education
300 North Charles Street
Baltimore, Maryland 21201

Typeset by University Park Press, Typesetting Division.
Manufactured in the United States of America by
The Maple Press Company.

Library of Congress Cataloging in Publication Data

Safer, Daniel J.
School programs for disruptive adolescents.

Includes index.
1. Problem children—Education.   I. Title.
LC4801.S23   371.93   81-16446
ISBN 0-8391-1698-5   AACR2

Contents

Contributors

Richard P. Allen, Ph.D.
Senior Psychologist
Baltimore City Hospitals
Baltimore, Maryland 21224

Winton Ahlstrom, Director
Technical Assistance—Information
  Univ. Affil. Facility
University of Missouri—
  Kansas City
Kansas City, Missouri 64110

Simon Dinitz, Ph.D., Professor
Department of Sociology
Ohio State University
Columbus, Ohio 43210

Burton D'Lugoff, M.D., M.P.H.
Director
Department of Community
  Medicine
Baltimore City Hospitals
Baltimore, Maryland 21224

James Filipczak, Director
Center for Applied Studies in
  Education
Institute for Behavioral Research
Silver Spring, Maryland 20910

Antoine Garibaldi, Ph.D.
National Institute of Education
Washington, D.C. 20208

Howard Garner, Ph.D.
Associate Professor
School of Education
Virginia Commonwealth University
Richmond, Virginia 23284

Robert J. Havighurst, Ph.D.
Professor Emeritus
Departments of Education and
  Human Development
University of Chicago
Chicago, Illinois 60637

Ronald C. Heaton, Ph.D.
Clinical Psychologist
Overlea Mental Health Services
Baltimore, Maryland 21206

Charles Lawrence, Ph.D., M.P.H.
Private practice
Baltimore, Maryland

Mark Litynsky, Ph.D.
Staff Psychologist
Veterans' Administration Hospital
San Francisco, California

Frank C. Parker, Ph.D.
Department of Medicine and
  Psychiatry
Louisiana State University
  Medical Center,
New Orleans, Louisiana 70112

Daniel J. Safer, M.D., Director
Youth Services, ECMHC
Baltimore County Department of
  Health
Rosedale, Maryland 21237
and Associate Professor
Division of Child Psychiatry
Johns Hopkins University
Baltimore, Maryland 21205

Ashton D. Trice, M.A.
Benedum Fellow in Educational
  Psychology
West Virginia University
Morgantown, West Virginia

John S. Wodarski, Ph.D.
Director
Research Institute
University of Georgia
Athens, Georgia 30602

Foreword

Disruptive youth have presented clearly increasing problems for school personnel during the last three decades, particularly in urban areas. This increase is the result of no single cause and may be largely the product of family problems and student failure to learn the basic school subjects. We can expect no simple solution.

On the educational scene today, a major consideration in setting up school programs for disruptive and alienated students is cost. With limited educational budgets, public school educators are quite reluctant to initiate new programs and school boards generally seem unwilling to target their declining resources for the disruptive and the disadvantaged. The long-range outcome of such policies will be known only in time. But with little new in the way of programmatic endeavors for these populations, studies from the 1960s and 1970s on the subject will probably remain quite up-to-date throughout the 1980s.

School Programs for Disruptive Adolescents is the most comprehensive book on this subject to date. It provides an extensive review of all the major facets of school disruption and in addition describes numerous controlled intervention projects designed to ameliorate the problem. The book offers a scholarly analysis of the field from educational, psychological, and sociological perspectives, leaving almost no stone unturned. It sheds much light on this very sensitive and often tender area for education.

To those who work with this troubled and troublesome population, the need for imaginative, practical, and successful school programs is obvious. This book fills a vital need by conveying an abundance of general information and programmatic data on this subject. I highly recommend it, advise that it be carefully read by involved professionals and hope that it will ultimately spur new developments in the field.

Robert J. Havighurst

Preface

In late 1976, two of my colleagues, Dick Allen and Ron Heaton, and I decided to organize a symposium on the subject of school programs for disruptive youth. Dr. Robert Havighurst agreed to be our keynote speaker, and I began to search for other presenters. The task developed into a formidable one because I attempted to limit symposium speakers to investigators who had done controlled studies in the field. The search for qualified speakers and the symposium led to some interesting discoveries, a few of which were that:

1. Controlled studies of secondary school programs for disruptive youth are so few they can be counted on one's fingers.
2. The subject of school disruption is of great interest to educators. (Over 475 people paid to attend our 1977 and 1979 one-day symposia).
3. Educators as a group prefer how-to-do-it workshops to a discussion of the issues and the possibilities.

In my search in 1976/77, I was referred to Drs. John Wodarski and Charles Lawrence, who were engaged in controlled studies of educational programs for disruptive adolescents. Papers on their programs, a synopsis of the Ahlstrom-Havighurst study *(400 Losers)* and a report on our on-going research (from 1972 to 1980) became the basis of this book.

To these papers, a number were added. Dr. Howard Garner delivered the most popular presentation at one of our symposia, in part because positive peer culture (PPC) has great appeal. His paper thoughtfully reviews PPC and related programs. Dr. Antoine Garibaldi organized a symposium on in-school suspension (for the National Institute of Education) in 1978 and the results of his field survey and his review of the literature logically merited inclusion. Next, I came across the book *The Prevention of Delinquency,* which like *400 Losers* summarized a very large-scale school program for disruptive students, a vital work for anyone in this field. Fortunately, Dr. Simon Dinitz, its co-author, agreed to condense it for this volume. Another well evaluated, investigational study that deserved inclusion was the PREP program; this 1969–1976 multi-site, in-school program for disruptive students has been one of the most comprehensive efforts to date. It is cogently summarized by Mr. James Filipczak, its administrator.

In our 1979 symposium on this subject, we included a 50-page how-to-do-it manual based on our own in-school program for disruptive students. The manual was judged to be very useful by program participants, and is available for $4 from the Essex Book Service, P.O. Box 7754, Essex, Maryland 21221.

This book covers a good deal of territory. Background material on the problem, population, options, philosophy, results, and the role of special education is included (in detail) for those who believe that thorough exploration must precede project initiation. The behavior modification section contains both a detailed discussion of classroom support possibilities as well as of the methods and outcomes of comprehensive, behavioral school programs for disruptive youth. One chapter discusses funding possibilities, and in addition, material is presented in a number of chapters on program design, research difficulties, likely program complications and personnel issues.

Generally, my chapters and my editing reflect a bias for in-school programs, even though this is presently against the tide. A second characteristic of my editorial comments and my chapters is a certain degree of cynicism, generated perhaps by reading so many anecdotal and self-serving reports on program interventions. Third, my writing in this volume is not gentle. I am aware that teaching disruptive adolescents is very trying and that most secondary school teachers routinely attempt, often for extended periods of time, to work with one or more of these youth. Nonetheless, most *official* secondary school responses to student disruption stress exclusion and punishment strategies, and I would be amiss not to point out their serious limitations and to propose alternatives.

I truly hope that this book stirs some feelings and some controversy. I believe that both are needed.

D. J. S.

Acknowledgments

Without my lengthy and direct involvement in a secondary school program for disruptive students, I would not have developed a personal familiarity with this subject and would not have become motivated to write and compile this volume. Therefore, I wish to first acknowledge those in the Baltimore County Board of Education and Department of Health who supported me in our joint school based venture. Key administrative support from the Board of Education came from Mr. Nick Spinnato, Mr. John Jedlicka, Dr. Phil Rhoads, and Mr. Fred Prumo. In the Health Department, vital top-level support came from Dr. Mehdi Yeganeh, Dr. Gene Ostrom, and Dr. John Krager. Necessary program assistance (generally of a less administrative nature) was provided by Dr. Ron Heaton, Dr. Richard Allen, Dr. Frank Parker, Mr. Ashton Trice, Mrs. Connie Caplan, Mrs. Shirley Thorpe, Mr. Kim Dismukes, Mrs. Margaret Iwata, Mrs. Martha VanDenHeuvel, Mrs. Dottie Dowling, Mr. Joe Gentile, Mrs. Virginia Homberg, and Mr. Bill Brown.

Assisting with valuable textual advice for my chapters in the book were Dr. Frank Parker, Dr. Linda Meade, Mr. Ashton Trice, Dr. David Sabatino, Dr. Ron Heaton, and Dr. Michael Bender. The typing was very capably done by Mrs. Lillian Burke and Mrs. Shirley Thorpe.

School Programs for
Disruptive Adolescents

I

Serious student misconduct in secondary schools

INTRODUCTION TO CHAPTERS 1 AND 2

Simple causal assumptions abound to explain school disruption. Teachers commonly emphasize the home circumstances of misbehaving pupils; some researchers stress differences in the atmosphere of schools; and still other observers emphasize sociological or cultural factors influencing student misconduct. A similar wide-ranging set of theories has evolved to explain delinquency.

To sort out the possible effect of *each* influence or factor, mathematical analyses can be applied. A more useful approach is to assess the impact of *multiple* factors on school disruptiveness, because risk appears to be cumulative. Reaching firm conclusions from such analyses is difficult, though, in part because factors such as grade failure and alienation appear to be both cause and effect.

Simply identifying seriously and persistently disruptive students is easily accomplished by the early junior high school years, if not before. After this identification, successful intervention then becomes a major challenge. How much the intervention needs to reverse the impact of adverse influences on student conduct in order to be successful is debatable. Nonetheless, to ignore obvious circumstances increasing student vulnerability to disruptive behavior is both narrow-minded and downright foolish. (Imagine school administrators ignoring knife possession, alcohol abuse, gangs, outside intruders and the like.) Hence these chapters.

1

Some factors influencing school misconduct

Daniel J. Safer

Numerous factors ranging from the genetic to the societal are known to influence adolescent misconduct. The relative importance of each factor in the causation of school disruption has not yet been determined, but headway is slowly being made in these assessments.

The listing of factors influencing student disruption that follows is by no means complete and the sketchy discussion reflects to a great extent the limited amount of information from good research data presently available on the subject.

DEVELOPMENTAL HYPERACTIVITY, ORGANIC FACTORS, AND TEMPERAMENTAL DEVIANCE

Approximately 6% of all students manifest persistent and serious school conduct problems that exist with most teachers, for most years, and in most schools (1). Approximately 25% to 40% of these disruptive students are developmentally hyperactive (2–4), reflecting the obvious fact that, as a group, hyperactive children are more aggressive (2, 5). Another factor increasing the risk for school misconduct is a genetic disposition to aggressive behavior (6–8).

The rate of conduct disorder is also sizably increased by the presence of chronic physical disorders (9), neuroepileptic conditions (9), language delays (10), mental retardation (11), and the experience of moderate to severe perinatal stress (12). Being male additionally increases the risk of physical aggressiveness, a finding that is true cross-culturally (13).

5

The positive relationship between some deviant temperamental patterns in early infancy and later misconduct decreases over time (14), but temperamentally "difficult" infants exhibit a *threefold* greater rate of conduct disorder in later life than do temperamentally "easy" infants (15). Similarly, destructiveness and nonsubmissiveness to authority at age three are significant predictors of delinquency in adolescence (16).

LACK OF ACADEMIC SUCCESS

It is clear that serious school misbehavior is far more prevalent in low track academic sections and that misbehavior and nonpromotion are highly correlated. This does not prove that low achievement and failing grades cause misbehavior. (Indeed, most low track students do not have serious misconduct problems.) Nevertheless, the least one can conclude from this and related information is that continued lack of success academically leads to demoralization, impaired motivation, the aggravation of existing behavior problems, and an increased likelihood of drop-out.

EMOTIONAL DISABILITY

From the phenomenological perspective, disruptive youth often have impulse control difficulties revealed by the severity and duration of their "over-response" or by the apparently mild provocation required to induce an outburst (17, 18). Additionally, many aggressive adolescents have a distrust of others, a ready ability to project responsibility (i.e., to externalize the locus of control), and an increased need for stimulation (17, 19). To what degree impulsive behavior is a reflection of emotional difficulty is a matter of semantics and terminology. In the present psychiatric classification (DSM-III) (20), persistently aggressive patterns of misconduct are considered emotional disorders. However, poor impulse control is not a misconduct pattern per se and its character has yet to be clearly elucidated and quantified.

Marked coping skill deficits, deviant thought patterns, and customary features of adult psychiatric illness occur *occasionally* among delinquent and disruptive adolescents, but primarily for those few classified as violent offenders (21). Lewis and Balla evaluated the most deviant 5% of juvenile court offenders and found that "approximately ⅓ of [delinquent] children referred to [a] juvenile court [psychiatric] clinic demonstrated clear evidence of serious psychopathology" (22).

Although only a small percentage of disruptive adolescents present such evidence of major psychiatric illness, those who do *and* have poor impulse control have a greater relative degree of behavioral deviance (22, 23). Furthermore, serious emotional deviance appears at an increased rate and in more characteristic patterns as misbehaving youth grow into adulthood. In 20- and 30-year follow-up studies, it has been found that aggressive youth experience a 9%–11% rate of psychiatric hospitalization (approximately half that for schizophrenia) and an 8% rate of chronic alcoholism, both of which represent a rate two to three times that of the population as a whole (21, 24).

GANG INFLUENCES

Student gangs are perceived as having a substantially disruptive influence in secondary schools, as attested to in 54% of the questionnaire responses of high school juniors and seniors (25). In inner city schools, 38% of high school juniors and seniors rated the disruptive impact of student gangs as serious. The percentage rating the effect of the gang as serious dropped to 18% in suburban schools and to 13% in small town schools (25). As would be expected, members of student gangs are far less successful in their academic and school behavioral adjustment than are nongang members (26).

ALCOHOL AND DRUG ABUSE

Illicit drug use by junior and senior high school students is quite common (27, 28). At least 12% of high school students smoke marijuana daily or seriously abuse alcoholic beverages weekly (29, 30). Furthermore, in questionnaire responses, 37%–47% of secondary school students reported that beer, wine, and marijuana were readily available within the school building (27).

The influence of illicit drug use on student disruptiveness has not, unfortunately, been well documented. One report, though, lists 5% of student/faculty altercations as caused by alcoholic intoxication by students (31). In studies of adults, it has been consistently reported that marijuana does not increase aggressive behavior, whereas alcohol often does (32).

FACULTY MANAGEMENT LIMITATIONS
AND THE IMPACT OF TEACHING STYLE

Although the term *teacher incompetence* is used, its definition is inexact and its rate is not established. Estimates of academic incompetence by teachers range from 10%–50% (33). Assessing incompetence in classroom management is an even less objective process, and its rate also has not been reliably measured. Nonetheless, 74% of teachers report that poor administrative control within the classroom is a major cause for disciplinary problems (34, Note A).

Teaching styles that have been reported in comparative evaluative studies to *improve* classroom behavior include: 1) preparing the class lesson in advance; 2) arriving on time; 3) directing attention to the class as a whole (35); 4) spotting disruptive behavior early and dealing with it appropriately, firmly, and with a minimum of interference to the lesson (27, 36, 37); 5) praising student work; 6) keeping class interest high; 7) communicating behavioral expectations effectively (36); 8) keeping students engaged in productive work most of the class period (38); 9) using fewer and less extreme punishments (35, 36); 10) emphasizing student success more than student shortcomings; and 11) increasing student responsibility (35).

GRADE LEVEL AND INCREASING AGE

Serious school disruption and student victimization occur at least three times more often in secondary than in elementary schools (27). Furthermore, the junior high school rate is about twice that of senior high school (27). In all, approximately 50% of major, troublesome student behaviors occur at the junior high school level.

One distinctive feature of secondary schools (compared to elementary) schools is that students receive instruction from many more teachers. Gottfredson and Daiger found that the greater the rotation of students through classes taught by different teachers, the greater the degree of teacher victimization (37, Note B). Likewise, the NIE report on school violence noted that when many different teachers are involved in the education of students, disruptiveness increases and the educational climate becomes more impersonal (27). Blyth et al. specifically compared 7th grade experiences in a K–8 school and in a junior high school and found that the level of victimization was 25% in the K–8 school compared to 42% in the junior high school. Also, anomie (i.e., rootlessness) was higher and participation lower in the junior high school (39).

The striking increases in reported misconduct upon entry into the 7th grade in junior high school appears to be caused primarily by the junior high school environment and not by the increase in age from 11 to 12 (or 12 to 13). This is supported by the fact that in one middle school, at least, the misconduct rate did not increase from the 6th to the 7th grade (40).

School misconduct is most common from ages 12 to 16, which approximate the ages (13–17) of greatest overall prevalence of delinquency (41). The decrease in the rate of student disruptiveness after age 16 in large measure is due to the great increase in school drop-out by disruptive students then. Nonetheless, it is noteworthy that the highest level of teacher victimization occurs at the senior high school level (27). This is probably due to the increase in body size during the late teens, making aggression then more potentially dangerous. In studies of delinquency, also, body size and build have an influence; those boys with a muscular (mesomorphic) body build tend to be the most aggressive (16).

SCHOOL SIZE AND STRUCTURE

The issue of the effect of school size on student conduct has been debated for some time. McPartland and McDill recently reviewed the literature and concluded that smaller school size had a "slight" effect on decreasing student violence (42). Likewise, Gottfredson and Daiger found that teacher victimization was less in smaller secondary schools (37). Nonetheless, there is still a sizable literature that finds no significant relationship between small school size and satisfactory behavioral management (35, 43, 44). More agreement exists for the conclusion that there is no relationship between modestly reduced student *class* enrollment and improved classroom control (37, 45–47).

The open classroom, an educational experiment that was prominent during the mid and late 1970s, did not benefit classroom discipline (48). If anything, there is evidence that open classrooms can adversely affect classroom control (49, 50).

Thus, simply changing school size, classroom numbers, and classroom architecture are not likely to reduce student disruption even moderately. It is important to note, though, that nearly two-thirds of violent acts in secondary schools occur in the halls, stairs, restrooms, gyms, locker rooms, and the cafeteria (27). Consequently, decreasing the use of or controlling the access to or within these areas should measurably lessen student violence.

SCHOOL ATMOSPHERE

Rutter et al. (35) and Rutter (51) found in an inner city area that some schools maintain certain personnel patterns (e.g., high teacher and student turnover rate, low pupil/teacher ratio, high student absenteeism) and certain processes (e.g., low academic emphasis, more punitive discipline, loose staff organization) that are highly correlated to and probably partly causative of high levels of student academic and behavior problems. Furthermore, Rutter (51) and Power et al. (52) believe that these kinds of school patterns and processes can increase the rate of adolescent delinquency. In effect, they conclude that school "culture" is the major characteristic separating problem from nonproblem schools. Farrington (53) on the other hand, believes that differences in delinquency rates between schools are "primarily due to differences among the boys entering them."

Although Farrington's finding accounts for most of the difference in delinquency rates between schools, it is also very likely that the rate of school misconduct is appreciably influenced by school personnel patterns and processes. In this respect, one major influence on school milieu and morale is its administrative leadership. Several observers and investigators have, in fact, specified that the principal exerts a major influence on the development of school morale and in the maintenance of a relatively safe and law abiding school (27, 54–58, Note C).

PARENTAL AND HOME INFLUENCE

Family variables have an important impact on the child's academic outcome, far exceeding that of school variables (59). Likewise, in relation to the child's conduct outcome, family variables are probably more important than school influences. This latter conclusion, however, has not been scientifically demonstrated.

Rutter reported that 61% of the children of hostile or neurotic parents were found to be deviant on teacher rating scales compared to only 10% of the children of nonsymptomatic parents (60, Note D). Likewise, Quinton et al. reported that an average of 46% of children whose parents had "very poor" marriages showed behavioral deviance; this compared to an average of 28% for the "poor" marriage and only 13% for the "good" marriage populations (61). Following a lengthy study, Miller et al. (62) even more strongly concluded that "maladjustment at school nearly always indicates maladjustment at home." Rutter's listing of parent and home influences that significantly and sizably (generally by twofold or more) increase the risk that a child will have a conduct disorder included the following home-related factors: maternal psychiatric disorder, parental criminality, large family size, low socioeconomic status, and marital discord (63, Note E).

From the perspective of organizational management, parents of aggressive adolescents have been found in comparative studies to exhibit the following differences in their home patterns: less unity in authority (64, 65), more parental rejection and less nurturance (66, 67), functional permissiveness in child rearing in an atmosphere of intermittent punitiveness (64, 68, 69), more encouragement of aggression (70), lax supervision (71), and less clear communication patterns (68).

SOCIOECONOMIC AREA DIFFERENCES

There are sizable differences between "economically deprived" and middle-class area schools in the number and character of their students with disciplinary problems. Inner city schools, compared to suburban and rural schools, have approximately double the number of conduct-disordered students (72). In comparative reports on the frequency of student aggression, inner city *secondary* schools have a two to three times greater violence rate than do suburban secondary schools (37, 73–75). Likewise, a far greater amount of teacher time is spent controlling the classroom in underprivileged sociocultural areas than in middle-class environs (76, 77).

Rutter reports, too, that schools in poor areas have different features and characteristics, all of which correlate significantly to the presence of conduct disorders. Economically poorer, inner city schools, compared to schools in middle-class areas, have shorter teacher and student tenure, more students on free meals, greater absenteeism, and more non-indigenous children (78).

Although low socioeconomic status correlates highly to school drop-out (79), grade retentions (80), and persistent absenteeism (81), as well as to school disadvantage, it is not among the major *independent* high-risk factors for antisocial behavior (79, 82), and psychiatric illness in children (including conduct disorders) (83). Other factors, particularly family pathology and low academic achievement, positively relate far better to adolescent misconduct (79, 83–86). Furthermore, Wilson presents some evidence to support the conclusion that minor and moderate reductions in social disadvantage do not decrease school violence (87).

REGIONAL DIFFERENCES

In the United States, disruptive and delinquent offenses against teachers, students, and school property are most frequent in large cities, followed by small cities, suburban areas, and rural areas in that order (27). School offense rates are also generally higher in the northeastern and western regions of the United States than in the southern and north central areas (27). These regional differences do not demonstrate a consistent economic pattern, as evidenced particularly by the low frequency of student disruption found in rural locales and in the South, neither of which are (compared to the others) *relatively* affluent areas.

RACIAL TENSION

The NIE survey, published in 1978, found that "being under a court order to desegregate" is associated with a slight but significant increase in school violence when other factors are taken into account (27). Gottfredson and Daiger (37) and Bailey (88) reported similar findings. Much of the disruptive effect ascribed to school busing to achieve racial balance is probably due to the sizable influx of under-achieving and disorderly students into previously less "disrupted" schools, and not the effect of relocation or racial tension as such (see 27). Nonetheless, some increase in disruption is also due to increased racial tension following school based racial integration. In a 1979 student survey in a suburban Maryland junior high school with a 9% minority enrollment, 37% ranked "problems between the races" as a major problem for the school. In a somewhat related 1969 survey, secondary school principals ascribed an average of 14% of disruptive student behavior to racial conflicts (88).

The finding that white students are twice as likely to be attacked and robbed in schools enrolling primarily nonwhite students (27) might be explained adequately by environmental factors. However, such factors do not explain the fact that, comparatively, *nonwhite* students are somewhat more likely to be attacked and robbed in schools that enroll primarily white students (28). This more strongly suggests the influence of racial tension.

INTRUDERS

Unauthorized nonschool persons coming into secondary schools account for about 11%–18% of all disruptive and destructive school incidents (excluding mere trespassing) (88, 89). In 1973/74 in schools in New York City, intruder offenses accounted for 16% of all assaults, 61% of the *major* robberies, and approximately 50% of the reported sex offenses (89). Generally similar findings have been reported in the NIE "Safe Schools" study (27).

THE AVAILABILITY OF WEAPONS

In many urban secondary schools, the carrying of knives—mainly for protection—is commonplace. In 1965, 8% of teachers reported that they confiscated one or more dangerous weapons during the previous year (75). Even more striking is the report that during the school year 1979/80, New York City school officials confiscated 130 handguns from students (90).

The major problem with the ready availability of weapons is that it increases the likelihood that they will be used. In fact, in 4 of 6 studies on the subject cited by Berkowitz, access to weapons was found to have significantly increased the level of aggressive response (91). More telling evidence on this point comes from statistics on comparative handgun use. In the United States, where handguns can be readily purchased, there were 13,070 gun murders in 1973. In England and Wales, where handguns cannot easily be obtained, there were only 35 such murders that year (67).

CONCLUSION

The problem of student disruptiveness, like that of alcoholism, appeared simpler and more unidimensional 20 years ago. Now that we are more willing to grapple with behavior problems, student conduct is acknowledged (like alcoholism) to be a far more complex matter. Pupils differ from one another predominantly with respect to temperament and proneness to misconduct; students also vary markedly in home conduct and in attitude toward authority; school student bodies differ a great deal in sociocultural values and in motivation for academic learning; teachers vary notably in class management skills; and schools differ measurably in administrative organization and in faculty morale.

The list of factors influencing student misconduct that was presented in this chapter is only a partial one. Other influences on conduct disorders, such as child abuse, labeling, parental neglect, and violence shown on television could have been added as could have countless others.

Having more than one adverse influence or factor may sizably compound the risk of adolescent misconduct. Rutter reported that the presence of two or more (of six) high risk factors quadrupled the risk of child behavioral deviancy (63), and that having four (of six) increased the risk tenfold (92). Likewise, West and Farrington (93) found that having three or more (of five) "adverse features" increased the delinquency risk sixfold. Other investigators have reported similar findings (22, 82, 94).

NOTES

Note A. In naturalistic studies of teacher interaction with pupils within the classroom, rates of teacher disapproval average three times the rate of teacher approval (independent of student misconduct) (95, 96). This can influence the frequency of classroom misconduct because research findings show that an increase in appropriately contingent teacher praise will generally increase student on-task classroom behavior (45).

Note B. It was hoped that smaller middle schools (grades 6–8) would decrease the disruption so prevalent in junior high schools (grades 7–9). Instead, the NIE study found the comparative rates of student victimization in these two types of schools to be very similar in the 7th and 8th grades (which they have in common) (27). On the other hand, the NIE team found that junior-senior high schools (grades 7–12) had lower rates of student victimization in their 7th and 8th grades (27).

Note C. Coleman concludes that effective control by school authorities is greater in the South than in the North, in private more than in public schools, in elementary more than in secondary schools, in small towns more than in large cities, in small schools more than in large ones, and where the student population is stable rather than rapidly changing (97).

Note D. The influence of the parents on the occurrence of truancy is particularly striking. Robins reported that the risk of truancy went from 8%, when neither parent had been truant as a child, to 27% when one parent had been truant, to 78% when both parents had been truant (82), and that the pattern began, in most instances, in the 1st and 2nd grades (98). There has been some doubt that schizophrenogenic parents exist, but there should be none about "school avoidogenic" parents.

Note E. The familial transmission of delinquency certainly does exist even though its cause is probably a composite one. Robins et al. reported that there was a 9% rate of delinquency if neither parent had an arrest record, a 37% rate if one parent had been arrested, and a 57% rate if both parents had been arrested. Furthermore, if both grandparents had antisocial records as adults, the childhood arrest rate rose to 80% (99).

   In an adoptive study attempting to partially sort out factors contributing to the familial transmission of criminal behavior,

Hutchings and Mednick reported that if neither the adoptive or biological father had a criminal record, the criminal rate for the youth was 11%. If only the biological father had a criminal record, the rate rose to 21%. When both the biological and adoptive fathers had a criminal record, then the rate jumped to 36% (100).

REFERENCES

1. Rubin, R. A., & Balow, B. Prevalence of teacher identified behavior problems: A longitudinal study. *Exceptional Children,* 1978, *45,* 102–111.
2. Safer, D. J., & Allen, R. P. *Hyperactive children: Diagnosis and management.* Baltimore: University Park Press, 1976.
3. York, R., Heron, J. M., & Wolff, S. Exclusion from school. *Journal of Child Psychology and Psychiatry,* 1972, *13,* 259–266.
4. Lyons, D. J., & Powers, V. Follow-up study of elementary school children exempted from Los Angeles City schools during 1960–1961. *Exceptional Children,* 1963, *30,* 155–162.
5. Patterson, G. R., Littman, R. A., & Bricker, W. Assertive behavior in children: A step toward a theory of aggression. *Monograph of the Society for Research in Child Development,* 1967, *32* (5).
6. Christiansen, K. O. A review of studies of criminality among twins. In S. A. Mednick & K. O. Christiansen (Eds.), *Biosocial Bases of Criminal Behavior.* New York: Gardner Press, 1977, pp. 45–88.
7. Matheny, A., Dolan, A. B., & Wilson, R. S. Twins with academic learning problems: Antecedent characteristics. *American Journal of Orthopsychiatry,* 1976, *46,* 464–469.
8. Crowe, R. R. An adoptive study of antisocial personality. *Archives of General Psychiatry,* 1974, *31,* 785–791.
9. Rutter, M. L., Graham, P., & Yule, W. A neuropsychiatric study in childhood. *Clinics in Developmental Medicine,* 1970, 35/36.
10. Stevenson, J., & Richman, N. Behavior, language, and development in three-year-old children. *Journal of Autism and Childhood Schizophrenia,* 1978, *8,* 299–313.
11. Rutter, M. L. Psychiatry. In J. Wortis (Ed.), *Mental retardation: An annual review,* Vol. 3. New York: Grune & Stratton, 1971, pp. 186–221.
12. Werner, E. E., & Smith, R. S. *Kauai's children come of age.* Honolulu: University of Hawaii Press, 1977.
13. Whiting, B., & Edwards, C. P. A cross cultural analysis of sex differences in the behavior of children aged three through eleven. *Journal of Social Psychology,* 1973, *91,* 171–188.
14. Carey, W. B., & McDevitt, S. C. Stability and change in individual temperament diagnoses from infancy to early childhood. *Journal of the American Academy of Child Psychiatry,* 1978, *17,* 331–337.
15. Thomas, A., & Chess, S. *Temperament and development.* New York: Brunner/Mazel, 1977.
16. Glueck, S., & Glueck, E. *Unraveling juvenile delinquency.* New York: Commonwealth Fund, 1950.
17. Quay, H. C. Classification. In H. C. Quay & J. S. Werry (Eds.), *Psychopathological disorders in childhood,* 2nd Ed. New York: Wiley, 1979.

18. Longworth-Dames, S. M. The relationship between personality and behaviour to school exclusion. *Educational Review,* 1977, *29,* 163–177.
19. Zuckerman, M. *Sensation seeking: Beyond the optimal level of arousal.* New York: Wiley, 1979, p. 307.
20. *Diagnostic and statistical manual of the American Psychiatric Association,* (DSM-III). Washington, D.C.: *American Psychiatric Association,* 1980.
21. Lewis, D. O., Shanok, S. S., Pincus, J. H., & Glaser, G. H. Violent juvenile delinquents: Psychiatric, neurological, psychological, and abuse factors. *Journal of the American Academy of Child Psychiatry,* 1979, *18,* 307–319.
22. Lewis, D. O., & Balla, D. A. *Delinquency and psychopathology.* New York: Grune & Stratton, 1976.
23. Offord, D. R., Sullivan, K., Allen, N., & Abrams, N. Delinquency and hyperactivity. *Journal of Nervous and Mental Disease,* 1979, *167,* 734–741.
24. Robins, L. N. *Deviant children grown up.* Baltimore: Williams & Wilkins, 1966.
25. Gallup, G. H. Sixth annual gallup poll of public attitudes toward education. *Phi Delta Kappan,* 1974, *56,* 20–32.
26. Short, J. F., & Strodbeck, F. L. *Group process and gang delinquency.* Chicago: University of Chicago Press, 1965, p. 236.
27. *Violent schools—safe schools: The safe school study report to the Congress.* Washington, D.C.: National Institute of Education, 1978.
28. Wynne, E. A. Behind the discipline problem: Youth suicide as a measure of alienation. *Phi Delta Kappan,* 1978, *59,* 307–315.
29. *Alcohol and health: New knowledge.* 2nd special report to the U.S. Congress, Washington, D.C.: U.S. Department of HEW, Government Printing Office, June, 1974.
30. Students' marijuana use has leveled off: Decriminalization doesn't seem to affect use. *Phi Delta Kappan,* 1980, *61,* 443.
31. *Challenge for the third century: Education in a safe environment.* Final report on the nature and prevention of school violence and vandalism. Report of the Subcommittee to Investigate Juvenile Delinquency, Sen. Bayh, Chairman. Washington, D.C.: Government Printing Office, February 1977, p. 31.
32. Carr, R. R., & Meyers, E. J. Marijuana and cocaine: The process of change in drug policy. In B. M. Webster (Ed.), *The facts about "drug abuse."* New York: Free Press, 1980, p. 175.
33. Elam, S. M. Some observations on incompetence. *Phi Delta Kappan,* 1979, *60,* 337.
34. Lufler, H. S. Discipline: A new look at an old problem. *Phi Delta Kappan,* 1978, *59,* 424–426.
35. Rutter, M., Maughan, B., Mortimore, P., & Ouston, J. *Fifteen thousand hours: Secondary schools and their effects on children.* Cambridge, Mass.: Harvard University Press, 1979.
36. Kounin, J. S. *Discipline and group management in classrooms.* New York: Holt, Rinehart & Winston, 1970.
37. Gottfredson, G. D., & Daiger, D. C. *Disruption in Six Hundred Schools.* Center for the Social Organization of Schools, Report 289. Baltimore: Johns Hopkins University, November 1979.

38. Brophy, J. E., & Evertson, C. M. *Learning from teaching: A developmental perspective.* Boston: Allyn & Bacon, 1976.
39. Blyth, D., Simmons, R., & Bush, D. *The transition into early adolescence: A longitudinal comparison of children in two educational contexts.* Paper presented to the Biennial Meeting of the Society for Research in Child Development, New Orleans, March 17–20, 1977.
40. Ferguson, H. Personal communication, April 1979.
41. Zimring, F. E. American youth violence: Issues and trends. *Crime and Justice: Annual Review of Research,* 1979, *1,* 67–107.
42. McPartland, J. M., & McDill, E. L. Research on crime in schools. In J. M. McPartland and E. L. McDill (Eds.), *Violence in schools: Perspectives, programs and positions.* Lexington, Mass.: Lexington Books, 1977, pp. 23–33.
43. Rogeness, G. A., Bednar, R. A., & Diesenhaus, H. The social system and children's behavior problems. *American Journal of Orthopsychiatry,* 1974, *44,* 499–502.
44. Campbell, L. P., & Williamson, J. A. Teacher control and school size. *ERIC (Educational Research Information Center),* 11:201 (ED 120-108), July 1976.
45. Marlowe, R. H., Madsen, C. H., Bower, C. E., Reardon, R. C., & Logue, P. E. Severe classroom behavior problems: Teachers or counselors. *Journal of Applied Behavior Analysis,* 1978, *11,* 53–66.
46. Little, A., Mabey, C., & Russell, J. Do small classes help a pupil? *New Society,* 1971, *18,* 769–771.
47. Asher, K. N., & Erickson, M. T. Effects of varying child teacher ratio and group size on day care children's and teachers' behavior. *American Journal of Orthopsychiatry,* 1979, *49,* 518–521.
48. Horwitz, R. A. Psychological effects of the "open classroom." *Review of Educational Research,* 1979, *71,* 86.
49. Bennett, N., Jordan, J., Long, G., & Wade, B. *Teaching styles and pupil progress.* Cambridge, Mass.: Harvard University Press, 1976.
50. Solomon, D., & Kendall, A. J. *Children in classrooms: An investigation of person-environment interaction.* New York: Praeger, 1979.
51. Rutter, M. Family area and school influences in the genesis of conduct disorders. In L. A. Hersov and M. Berger (Eds.), *Aggression and Antisocial behaviour in childhood and adolescence.* Oxford: Pergamon Press, 1978, pp. 95–113.
52. Power, M. J., Alderson, M. R., Phillipson, C. M., Schoenberg, E., & Morris, J. N. Delinquent schools? *New Society,* October 1967, *10,* 542–543.
53. Farrington, D. Delinquency begins at home. *New Society,* 1972, *21,* 495–497.
54. McKerrow, S. Many problems found in city's junior highs. *Baltimore Evening Sun,* April 25, 1977, pp. A-1 and A-4.
55. Clegg, A., & Megson, B. *Children in distress.* Middlesex: Penguin Books, 1968.
56. Ianni, F. A. J. A positive note on schools and discipline. *Educational Leadership,* 1980, *37,* 457–458.
57. Conant, J. B. *Education in the junior high school years.* Princeton, New Jersey: Princeton Educational Testing Service, 1960.
58. Sarason, S. B. *The culture of the school and the problem of change.*

Boston: Allyn & Bacon, 1971.
59. Rutter, M., & Madge, N. *Cycles of disadvantage: A review of research.* London: Heinemann Educational Books, 1976, p. 125.
60. Rutter, M. Prospective studies to investigate behavioral change. In J.S. Strauss, H. M. Babigan, & M. Roff (Eds.), *The origins and course of psychopathology: Methods of longitudinal research.* New York: Plenum Press, 1977, pp. 223-248.
61. Quinton, D., Rutter, M., & Rowlands, O. An evaluation of an interview assessment of marriage. *Psychological Medicine,* 1976, *6,* 577-586.
62. Miller, F. J., Court, S. D., Knox, E. G., & Brandon, S. *The school years in Newcastle upon Tyne: 1952-1962.* London: Oxford University Press, 1974.
63. Rutter, M. Early sources of security and competence. In J. S. Bruner, & A. Garton (Eds.), *Human growth and development.* Oxford: Clarendon Press, 1978, pp. 33-61.
64. Glueck, S., & Glueck, E. *Family environment and delinquency.* Boston: Houghton Mifflin, 1962.
65. McCord, W., McCord, J., & Howard, A. Familial correlates of aggression in non-delinquent male children. *Journal of Abnormal and Social Psychology,* 1961, *62,* 79-93.
66. Rutter, M. Other family influences. In M. Rutter and L. Hersov (Eds.), *Child psychiatry: Modern approaches.* Oxford: Blackwell Scientific Publications, 1977, pp. 74-108.
67. Lefkowitz, M. M., Eron, L. D., Walder, L. O., & Huesmann, L. R. *Growing up to be violent: A longitudinal study of the development of aggression.* New York: Pergamon Press, 1977.
68. Andry, R. G. *Delinquency and parental pathology.* London: Methuen, 1960.
69. Sears, R. R., Maccoby, E. E., & Levin, H. *Patterns of child rearing.* Evanston, Ill.: Row & Peterson, 1957.
70. Bandura, A., & Walters, R. H. *Adolescent aggression.* New York: Roland, 1959.
71. Wilson, H. Parents can cut the crime rate. *New Society,* December 4, 1980, *54,* (942), 456-458.
72. Rutter, M., Cox, A., Tupling, C., Berger, M., & Yule, W. Attainment and adjustment in two geographical areas. I. Prevalence of psychiatric disorder. *British Journal of Psychiatry,* 1975, *126,* 493-509.
73. DeCecco, J. P., & Richards, A. K. *Growing pains: Uses of school conflict.* New York: Aberdeen, 1974.
74. Teacher opinion poll. *Today's Education,* September-October 1974, *63,* 105.
75. Iwamoto, D. Student violence and rebellion. *NEA Journal,* December 1965, *54,* 10-13.
76. Deutch, M. Minority group and class status as related to social and personality factors in scholastic achievement. *Society for Applied Anthropology:* Monograph No. 2, 1962, pp. 25-26.
77. Roberts, I. *Scene of the battle: Group behavior in urban classrooms.* Garden City, N.Y.: Doubleday & Co., 1970.
78. Rutter, M., Yule, B., Quinton, D., Rowlands, O., Yule, W., & Berger, M. Attainment and adjustment in two geographical areas. III. Some factors accounting for area differences. *British Journal of Psychiatry,* 1975, *126,* 520-533.

79. Elliott, D. S., & Voss, H. L. *Delinquency and drop out.* Lexington, Mass.: Lexington Books, 1974.
80. Sexton, P. C. *Education and income.* New York: Viking Press, 1961.
81. Galloway, D. Size of school, socio-economic hardship, suspension rates and persistent unjustified absence from school. *British Journal of Educational Psychology,* 1976, *46,* 40–47.
82. Robins, L. N. Sturdy childhood predictors of adult antisocial behavior: Replication from longitudinal studies. *Psychological Medicine,* 1978, *8,* 611–622.
83. Rutter, M., Tizard, J., & Whitmore, K. *Education, health and behaviour: Psychological and medical study of childhood development.* New York: Wiley, 1970.
84. Kelly, D. H. Status origins, track position and delinquent involvements: A self report analysis. *Sociological Quarterly,* 1975, *16,* 264–271.
85. Weinberg, C. Achievement and school attitudes of adolescent boys as related to behavior and occupational status of families. *Social Forces,* 1964, *42,* 462–466.
86. Frease, D. E. Delinquency, social class, and the schools. *Sociology and Social Research,* 1973, *57,* 443–457.
87. Wilson, J. Q. Crime in society and schools. In J. M. McPartland and E. L. McDill (Eds.), *Violence in schools: Perspectives, programs and positions.* Lexington, Mass.: Lexington Books, 1977, pp. 43–50.
88. Bailey, S. K. *Disruption in urban public secondary schools.* Washington, D.C.: National Association of Secondary School Principals, 1970.
89. Marvin, M., Connolly, J., McCann, R., Tempkin, S., & Henning, P. *Planning Assistance Programs to Reduce School Violence and Disruption.* Washington, D.C.: U.S. Department of Justice, January 1976.
90. New York, N.Y., It's a . . . . *Time Magazine,* August 18, 1980, p. 19.
91. Berkowitz, L. Situational and personal conditions covering reactions to aggressive cues. In D. Magmusson and N. S. Endler (Eds.), *Personality at the crossroads: Current issues in interactional psychology.* New York: Wiley, 1977, pp. 165–183.
92. Rutter, M. Invulnerability or why some children are not damaged by stress. In S. J. Shamsie (Ed.), *New directions in child mental health.* New York: S. P. Medical and Scientific Books, 1979, pp. 53–75.
93. West, D. J., & Farrington, D. P. *Who becomes delinquent?* London: Heinemann Educational Books, 1973.
94. Safer, D. J. A familial factor in minimal brain dysfunction. *Behavior Genetics,* 1973, *3,* 175–186.
95. Thomas, J. D., Presland, I. E., Grant, M. D., & Glynn, T. L. Natural rates of teacher approval and disapproval in grade-7 classrooms. *Journal of Applied Behavioral Analysis,* 1978, *11,* 91–94.
96. O'Leary, S. G., & O'Leary, K. D. Behavior modification in the school. In H. Leitenberg (Ed.), *Handbook of behavior modification and behavior therapy.* Englewood Cliffs, N.J.: Prentice-Hall, 1976, pp. 475–515.
97. Coleman, J. S. Social and cultural integration and educational policy. In H. J. Walberg and A. T. Kopan (Eds.), *Rethinking urban education.* San Francisco: Jossey-Bass, 1972.
98. Robins, L. N. Antecedents of character disorder. In M. Roff and D. F. Ricks (Eds.), *Life history research in psychopathology,* Vol. 1. Minneapolis: University of Minnesota Press, 1970, pp. 226–239.

99. Robins, L. N., West, P. A., & Herjanic, B. L. Arrests and delinquency in two generations: A study of black urban families and their children. *Journal of Child Psychology and Psychiatry,* 1975, *16,* 125–140.

100. Hutchings, B., & Mednick, S. A. Registered criminality in the adoptive and biological parents of registered male criminal adoptees. In S. A. Mednick, F. Schulsinger, J. Higgins, & B. Bell (Eds.), *Genetics, environment and psychopathology.* Amsterdam: North Holland/ American Elsevier, 1974.

2

Characteristics, school patterns, and behavioral outcomes of seriously disruptive junior high school students

Daniel J. Safer and Ronald C. Heaton

Adolescents with a pattern of serious and repeated school misconduct can understandably be viewed simply as "bad kids" by victims and by observers. From a broader perspective, however, the group of seriously disruptive youth includes many who are handicapped academically and emotionally. When seriously disruptive youth are compared to nondisruptive youth, this becomes evident—even though the disruptive student category is a fairly heterogeneous one.

In a 1972 survey based on an examination of school records, 75 junior high school (JHS) students who were multisuspended (MS) for behavioral reasons were compared to 75 age-, sex-, and area-matched controls who were not multisuspended (1, Note A). Both groups attended junior high schools in working class areas. Sizable differences between the groups with respect to academic achievement, IQ, school grades, etc. were found. The MS students showed significant deficits in nearly all dimensions even during their early school years. Their *elementary* school differences are summarized in Table 1.

This chapter presents material on the characteristics of multisuspended, junior high school (MS-JHS) students gathered from this and similar surveys. Traditional categories of behaviorally and academically deviant youth are then compared to the category of school disruptive youth. Finally, customary behavioral outcomes for seriously disruptive students are presented and assessed.

Table 1. A comparison of elementary school data on multisuspended and nonmultisuspended junior high school boys

Elementary school data	Multi-suspended ($N=75$)[a] (in %)	Non-MS control ($N=75$)[a] (in %)	X^2[b]
Moderate or severe classroom misconduct in the 5th and 6th grades	46.3	4.3	31.9
Classroom misbehavior (Teacher notes)	48.0	11.0	24.3
Hyperactivity (Teacher notes)	14.7	1.4	8.8
Grade average of D or below in the 5th and 6th grades	44.0	13.3	17.2
Suspensions	14.7	0.0	11.9
Retentions	65.3	30.7	18.1
IQ < 100	60.8	33.3	11.3
Broken homes	41.3	9.3	20.3
Absent 45 days for both 5th and 6th grades	21.1	13.7	1.4
> 2 years behind academically on the 3rd grade Iowa test (Reading)	27.0	9.6	7.0
> 2 years behind academically on the 5th or 6th grade Iowa test (Reading)	52.3	23.6	12.0

[a]Data on all subjects was not available, but each cell reflects data on at least 63 students.

[b]All chi-square results, except the comparison of absence rates, are statistically significant, $P < 0.005$.

CHARACTERISTIC AND HIGH RISK PATTERNS OF MULTISUSPENDED STUDENTS

Grade Failure

Sixty-five percent of multisuspended junior high school students were retained in at least one grade during their elementary school years compared to only 31% of non-MS students (Table 1). By age 14½, over 85% of the MS students had experienced nonpromotion. Bowman likewise reported that 94% of behavior problem 8th graders had a history of grade failure (2). In still another study of students aged 6–18 who received one or more suspensions, 52% had experienced grade retention (3).

For school populations as a whole, the rate of retention is usually highest in the 1st, 2nd, and 7th grades (4); yet for seriously disruptive students, the rate climbs to its highest point during the 8th and 9th grades. In two junior high schools in the mid-1970s, MS students averaged a 52% *annual* rate of grade failure (5)—although a small number of these youth were later socially promoted (Note B).

Academic Underachievement

On group achievement tests given in the 5th grade, the average MS-JHS student was 2 years academically retarded relative to local grade norms (Table 1). At age 14, he was 3½ years below his age and area norms in achievement on individual achievement tests. In a 1976 individual evaluation of 24 MS-JHS students, 42% were 5 or more years academically retarded, 29% were 2–5 years behind and only 29% were within 2 years of their age-expected level (6). In a later evaluation (1979) of a 14–15-year-old MS student population, the median age-expected achievement deficit was 4 years (6). In a Chicago school for socially maladjusted youth, the average academic deficit relative to age-expected levels was 5 years at age 14–15 (7). In the New York so-called "600" schools (for disruptive students), it was 4 years (8). Similarly, others have reported that 43% and 50% of seriously disruptive students have "extreme" academic deficiencies (9, 10), a relationship frequently described (11–14). Evidence further supporting the significant relationship between teacher-rated misconduct and low achievement scores is the finding on group data that the greater the misbehavior, the greater the underachievement (15).

Lower IQ

On group intelligence tests, MS students had an average IQ score of 97 (1), whereas the non-MS group average was 102 (1). Other studies of behavior-problem youth have reported average IQ scores of from 91 to 96 (13, 16, 17). In general, the degree of school misconduct has been shown to be inversely related to IQ (18).

Prior Difficulties in School Behavior, Temperament, Grades, and Attendance

Compared to non-MS-JHS students, MS-JHS students in the 5th and 6th grades had a higher prevalence of serious classroom misconduct (46% versus 4%), excessive absenteeism (21% versus 14%), suspensions (15% versus 0%), and low (D and E) grades (44% versus

13%). Before junior high school, MS students also had a greater prevalence of teacher-rated hyperactivity (15% versus 1%) (Table 1). Ahlstrom and Havighurst similarly reported that approximately 50% of JHS behavior-problem youth were rated as poor in deportment and achievement in the 6th grade (13).

School Absenteeism

Prior to junior high school, MS students demonstrated only a mildly elevated rate of excessive absenteeism (Table 1). Nonetheless, in junior high school, MS student absenteeism *averaged* approximately 30% (5) to 35% (19), nearly four times the 8% comparison rate for non-MS-JHS students. The MS-JHS rates are quite close to the 32% rate of absenteeism reported for disruptive adolescent students in the New York City "600" school program (20).

If an MS-JHS student manifests a 30% absenteeism rate, it means he misses 54 days out of the 180-day school year. Of these 54 days, an average of 4 to 7 can be considered authentic sick days (21, 22). Short school suspensions (averaging 2–3 per year) account for only an additional 8 days. Official long suspensions and expulsions average 6–10 additional days per year (due in large measure to the fact that one-fifth of all MS-JHS students are expelled annually (5)). Unofficial and semiofficial exclusion policies keep MS-JHS students out of school an average of 4–5 more days. These include: 1) end of the year recommended exclusions with parental acceptance ("he's failing anyway"), and 2) procedural delays by administrative school personnel during and after long suspensions. Unexcused absenteeism—when the child is not at home—accounts for about 11% of (unofficial) school absence, in this case about 4–5 days (23). Parent-sanctioned or parent-condoned school avoidance—wherein the child is at home—represents approximately 50% of (unofficial) school absence (23), and thus accounts for the lion's share of the remaining 28 days. Parent-sanctioned or parent-condoned school avoidance includes the following: 1) not getting to suspension conferences as soon as possible, 2) keeping the student home because of minor complaints, 3) keeping the child home so he won't get into trouble in school, 4) using the student to babysit at home, and 5) having a callous or hostile attitude with respect to school attendance.

Social Disadvantage

MS students tend to come from large families, and have parents with less formal education and a higher rate of divorce (24). In 1972, 41%

of MS students were found to come from broken homes as opposed to 9% of the controls (1). Since then, the prevalence of MS students coming from broken homes has risen. In a 1979 survey of MS students from the same junior high schools sampled in the 1972 report, a 61% rate of MS students from broken homes was reported (25). In an off-site day school program for disruptive students in Sacramento, less than one-third of the students lived with their natural parents (26). Further details of the social disadvantage that disruptive students experience have been reported elsewhere (27–29).

Racial Minority

Blacks are suspended twice as frequently as whites on average nationally (29). In the New York City "600" schools day-school program for disruptive youth, black and Puerto Rican enrollment was approximately double their representation in the school system (20). This same degree of minority overrepresentation also characterized the enrollment in the Sacramento Opportunity program for disruptive students with respect to black and Chicano youth (26).

Male Sex

Suspensions occur 2 to 3 times more frequently for boys than girls (6, 29). Multiple suspensions occurred in 1972 at a 5:1 male/female ratio. In 1979, the ratio of MS males to MS females was 4:1 (6). In other studies of suspension and multisuspension, the male/female ratio has ranged from 5:1 (30) to nearly 15:1 (7).

Office Referrals

The average MS junior high school student is referred to the office for misconduct an average of 9 (19) to 12 (6) times per year. Non-MS-JHS students are referred an average of 0.9 times per year (31).

Suspensions

Nearly 15% of students who were multisuspended in junior high school in a 1972 assessment were previously suspended in the *elementary* school (Table 1). This compares with 0% (0 of 75) for non-MS-JHS controls. During the year following their identification in

JHS, MS students average 2-3 suspensions per year (5). Whereas approximately 12%-15% of students in junior high school are suspended per year, only about 3%-4% become multisuspended while in JHS for *behavioral* reasons (6). (Behavior reasons primarily exclude suspensions for smoking and for absenteeism.)

Disciplinary Withdrawal

Approximately 20% of MS students are expelled annually from their junior high school for the remainder of the term (5). Most who are over 16 are dropped subsequently from the rolls. Of the others, some are transferred to other regular schools, some to special schools, and some to home teaching.

School Drop-out

In a 4-year follow-up study of suburban MS-JHS students, only 40% made it to the 10th grade (senior high school) and only 10% graduated from senior high school (5). In similar surveys in the same area, the high school graduation rate for MS students was only 12% in 1972 and 17% in 1977-1980 (32). In the Ahlstrom and Havighurst report, only 18% of disruptive JHS students graduated from high school (13). These figures compare to an approximately 70% high school graduation rate for students in suburban working class areas (Note C).

Delinquency

By age 14, 53% of MS students have become known to the local Department of Juvenile Services for delinquency. This compares to the non-MS group rate of 5% (33). By age 17, the delinquency rate of MS students increases to 77% (33). Ahlstrom and Havighurst reported a delinquency rate of 55% for 14-15-year-old disruptive students and a nondisruptive student rate of 10% (13). Similar high delinquency rates for *disruptive* students have been reported by Berleman et al. for 7th graders—46% (34), by Bowman for 8th graders— 41% (2), and by Tait and Hodges, by age 17—65% (35).

Havighurst et al. in their River City study reported that aggressiveness in the 6th grade correlated very highly with an official later record of delinquency. Of the 18 most aggressive youth, 15 became delinquent. This compares to a 6 out of 15 rate for moderately aggressive youth and a 15 out of 137 rate for the nonaggressive (36).

OVERLAP OF BEHAVIORALLY AND
ACADEMICALLY DEVIANT ADOLESCENT CATEGORIES

Numerous books have been written identifying and grouping behaviorally and academically deviant adolescent youth as *truant, underachiever, drop-out, learning disabled,* and *delinquent.* As might be expected, these groupings cover a good deal of similar ground. Therefore, questions arise whether the identification of the *seriously disruptive student* as an entity is useful and to what degree this category overlaps with the others. To clarify these issues, the five overlapping categories mentioned above are considered in relation to school disruptive youth (often also referred to here as MS students).

Truants

Persistent truancy (defined broadly as school refusal of more than 20–35 days/year for reasons other than a clear-cut physical illness or school phobia) occurs in JHS students at a reported prevalence of over 15% in the inner city (37), over 7% in working class suburbs (6), and 1%–2% in middle-class areas (38, Note C). The rate of persistent truancy in junior high schools is over two times that of behavioral multisuspension. Further evidence that the categories, although overlapping, are distinctive is the fact that even though most MS-JHS students are truant, most JHS truants are not seriously disruptive (39).

Underachievers

In an unpublished 1974 academic and behavioral analysis of the three lowest track regular 7th grade sections in one junior high school, it was found that over 6% of the *total regular* 7th grade enrollment were achieving at or below the 3rd-grade level on individual achievement tests (40). Of these low achieving students, approximately 30% had behavior problems of sufficient magnitude to warrant repeated office referrals and/or a behavioral suspension. This finding matches that of Rutter, who reported that one-third of reading disabled students had notable conduct problems (41). Thus, even though most MS students exhibit a major degree of academic underachievement, most underachievers do not manifest major behavior problems. Of course, this is not to say that the two are unrelated. Underachievers have more than the average degree of conduct disorder and their underachievement tends to increase their proneness to school misconduct.

Drop-outs

Approximately 25% of students drop out of school nationally, whereas only 3%–4% experience JHS multisuspension for behavioral reasons. Of those who drop out, only about 11% to 24% are pressured to do so for disciplinary reasons (12, 42–44). In effect, then, whereas the majority of MS students drop out largely because of misconduct, only one-fifth of all drop-outs do so for that reason.

Junior High School Students
in Learning Disability Classes

In two separate group studies in 1974 (45) and 1978 (6), JHS students in a learning disability class were compared to multisuspended (MS) junior high school students on behavior and learning characteristics. The two populations did not differ appreciably or significantly on the following: 1) elementary school retentions, 2) elementary school conduct grades, 3) junior high school absences and suspensions, or 4) sex ratio. Although the two groups had a similar median degree of academic deficit, the special education group was far more uniform in its underachievement pattern. The two groups measurably differed in that learning-disabled students had a two- to three-fold greater history of hyperactivity and a twofold greater frequency of referral to a mental health center.

Thus, aside from minor differences, 50%–65% of MS students have individual characteristics that closely match students in junior high school learning-disabled classes. The close match is understandable because serious misconduct is a major determinant in the special education referral of learning-disabled children (see Chapter 6) (Note E).

Delinquents

Of all the five overlapping categories, delinquents are the most closely matched to multisuspended students. Most delinquents are truants, underachievers, drop-outs, and have persistent school misconduct (46–55). The great majority of MS junior high school students have these same patterns, in part because over 75% of their number become officially delinquent by age 17. It is no wonder, therefore, that most early intervention or "prevention" programs for delinquent youth are educationally oriented for youth with serious school behavior problems (56).

Because of the large overlap between delinquents and school disruptive youth, one would hope that by identifying MS-JHS students, one might identify most future delinquents. Unfortunately, such screening efforts—although surprisingly accurate over time—identify only about 40% of all delinquents (33).

In summary, the category of serious school disruption overlaps the other five listed categories of adolescent behavioral and academic deviancy to various degrees. Although the match is greatest for delinquency, even then a slim majority (52%–60%) of delinquents do not experience multisuspension in junior high school (33, 57). School disruptiveness, then, is both an independent and an overlapping category. Indeed, all the six listed categories are useful, and none is in any way sufficient to reflect the totality of adolescent behavior deviancy and school maladjustment. In effect, this argues for a multiaxial classification, one with various kinds or levels of informational input.

OUTCOME OF YOUTH WITH BEHAVIOR DISORDER

Prevalence and Persistence of School Misbehavior

Classroom misconduct in the elementary school years is a common experience, particularly for boys. At one time or another in elementary school anywhere from 25% to 50% of all boys are identified as having classroom behavior problems worthy of mention (58–60). However, when counting only serious and persistent cases, the prevalence of elementary school misconduct decreases to only 6%–8% of all students (61–63).

On follow-up 2 to 16 years after identification, 15%–37% of those who had *mild* elementary school classroom misconduct maintained their antisocial pattern (64–66). On the other hand, children with *serious* behavior problems and adolescents with *moderate to serious* degrees of misconduct had a 72%–84% frequency of behavioral deviancy on follow-up 1 to 4 years later (63, 64, 66–68, Note F). Longer term (6–30 year) follow-ups of serious behavior problem youth produced a smaller, but still impressive, 41% to 51% rate of major misconduct in late adolescence or adulthood (66, 68, 69 Note G).

School History of Behavior Problem JHS Students

In a retrospective 1972 school folder appraisal of MS-JHS students, 41% (14/34) had recorded school behavior problems during their first 3 years in school, as judged by low conduct grades and descriptive teacher comments (6). However, by the time of admission to junior

high school, only 21% (7/34) of these JHS students had a clean behavioral record. A total, then, of over 75% of those who became MS-
JHS students had school folder evidence of repeated behavioral difficulties in elementary school. As is suggested in Table 1, elementary
school misconduct is most common in the 5th and 6th grades, when
46% of the MS-JHS students were rated as having moderate to serious degrees of misconduct, a rate over 10 times greater than that of
non-MS-JHS students. Academic grades followed a similar pattern;
in the 5th and 6th grades, 44% of MS-JHS students maintained a D
average or worse (Table 1).

In a similar assessment done on 36 behavior problem 6th grade
students, Kraus reported that 13 had had "adjustment" problems in
kindergarten, 20 in the 1st grade, and 28 in the 4th grade. Furthermore, 13 of the 36 had notable classroom adjustment problems during at least 6 of their first 7 years in school (70).

Ahlstrom and Havighurst (13) also reported that approximately
30% of JHS behaviorally deviant boys were notably below average
in deportment and aptitude in the 1st grade. The number rose to approximately 40% by the 3rd grade. A related finding by Craig and
Glick (53) was that 80% of those who later became delinquent had
classroom misconduct ratings during their first three years in
school, compared to a 27% rate for those who did not become delinquent. (Other studies of aggressive and delinquent youth similarly
show that the onset of behavioral difficulty occurs before age 10 in
60%–85% of cases (66, 69).)

Thus, although behavior problem JHS students did not show a
uniform early school behavior problem pattern, about half of them
evidenced *prominent* misconduct during their late elementary school
years. Of these, over half started out that way in the 1st grade.

Some Prognostically Different
Subgroups of Misbehaving Youth

In general, the more varied the features of behavioral deviancy the
youth exhibits, the more likely it is that his behavior difficulty will
be prolonged (69). Also, the total number of instances of misconduct
has a greater relationship to poor behavioral outcome than the occurrence of any given type of misconduct (69). Nonetheless, there are
certain subgroups of misbehaving youth with poor behavioral prog-
noses. Some are given below.

Hyperactive-Aggressive Youth   Although the behavioral outcome of
hyperactive-aggressive youth is primarily determined by the aggressive component (71), the combination of these patterns is particu-

larly problematic and additive (72). In a retrospective chart survey of MS-JHS students in 1978, it was found that 7 of the 27 students (26%) had been hyperactive in the elementary school (6). Of these seven MS-JHS students who had been hyperactive, all had a record of *repeated* misconduct during their elementary school years (compared to a 56% rate for the nonhyperactive). In addition, of the seven, five (71%) had been suspended in their elementary school years compared to a 23% rate for the rest of the group. (These suspension rates differ moderately from those in Table 1 and reflect the greater than 50% increase in suspension rates during the 1970s. See Chapter 3.)

Similarly, Rutter reported that two-thirds of pervasively hyperactive behavior-problem 10-year-old youth continued their behavioral difficulties through age 14, compared to a 40% rate for situationally hyperactive and an 8% rate for nonhyperactive behavior-problem youth (73).

Youth Who Steal   Children who steal in childhood have a subsequent juvenile court record approximately three times greater than youth whose parents do not report stealing as a problem (74). Similarly, Reid and Hendricks (75) found that behavioral treatment was only half as successful with stealers as with other "pre-delinquents."

Youth with Serious School and Home Misconduct   There is evidence that youth with both school *and* home behavior problems have higher delinquency rates than do youth who misbehave at home but not at school (76). Similarly, we found that MS-JHS delinquent students had recidivism rates over two times those of non-MS-JHS delinquent students (33).

Youth with an Early Age of Onset of Symptoms   Some data on the specific impact of an *early onset* of misconduct are negative relative to differential school and home behavioral outcomes (64, 66), but two studies suggest that an earlier onset of school misconduct leads to greater neighborhood rates of delinquency (27, 77). Since greater severity and repeated instances of misconduct are known to relate to a worse overall behavioral outcome, these factors must be taken into consideration before simply assuming the deleterious effect of an early onset of misconduct. Therefore, more comprehensive assessments on this subject are awaited.

Youth with Prominent Academic Underachievement   The co-existence of prominent academic underachievement and a conduct disorder is associated with a heightened risk of *persistent* behavioral difficulty (67, 73, 78). However, the mechanism behind this association is unclear. It may be that antisocial behavior and many learning deficiencies are an outgrowth of a common social disadvantage or biological limitation, and that they do not *causally* interact. Indeed, the presence or absence of a conduct disorder does not affect the academic progress of reading-disabled youth (67), and it has been reported that antisocial youth with and without academic retardation have similar characteristics (79, 80).

Youth Who Abuse Drugs   Youth who abuse drugs show appreciably more behavioral deviance during *adolescence* than do non-drug abusers. Furthermore, they are far more likely than are other delinquents to be arrested (three or more times) as *adults* for drug abuse. Such evidence in fact led Robins and Ratcliff to conclude that drug abuse is a "more powerful prediction of the level of adult deviance than (is) any other juvenile behavior" (81).

WHY SUBDIVIDE STUDENT DISRUPTIVENESS?

The process of subdividing school behavior disorders is at an early stage and the practical value of such grouping is certainly open to question at this time. Nonetheless, a categorization based upon age of onset or severity could lead to useful intervention strategies.

Rutter et al. (82), for example, reported that adolescents who show school misconduct for the first time in adolescence do not as a rule have academic problems. Indeed, it may be that the group who show serious behavioral disorders for the first time upon entry into junior high schools are reacting largely to the impersonal nature of the junior high school environment. On the other hand, it may be useful to view the restless, immature, impulsive, and academically slow children who begin elementary school with misconduct as developmentally disabled. It may also be the case that certain behavior-problem youth with limited ability and interest in developing abstract skills increasingly turn off to classroom expectations as the curriculum becomes less concrete in the 3rd and 4th grades.

If by chance these hypotheses were true, one could reasonably emphasize a transitional class in the early elementary grades (83) for the immature group, a more mechanistic curriculum for those whose conduct problems develop during the later elementary school period, and core teaching for the newly disruptive JHS student.

NOTES

Note A. The 75 multisuspended students accumulated 263 suspensions ($X=3.5$) over their first 1½ to 2 years in junior high school. Seven (9.3%) of the control students received a single suspension in junior high. Smoking and class cutting suspensions were not included.

Note B. The rate of grade failure is strongly related to socioeconomic status (4, 84). Grade failure in elementary schools averages 3%–5% per year nationally (85), but the cumulative rate of nonpromotion in elementary schools averages around 30% (4). Inner city junior high school students average a 19%–23% annual rate of nonpromotion (21, 37).

Note C. The rate of high school drop-out is about 25% nationally. In other words, about 75% of students who enroll in the 9th grade graduate high school. Not all students, however, drop out of school during their senior high school years. In one study in Maryland, of all students who left school before graduating, 36% did so while in junior high school (in the 8th and 9th grades) (86). The rate of drop-out in New York City is nearly three times greater for Puerto Ricans and blacks than for whites (87).

About 40% of all those who drop out have serious learning problems (21). As would be expected, the greater the academic deficit, the greater the rate of drop-out (88). Also over 50% who drop out have a record of grade retention (88), and it is quite unusual to see an adolescent or young adult two years "overage" stay on to finish high school.

Note D. Truancy has been defined by some as school avoidance wherein the child is not at home. Since in most instances of school avoidance the child remains home, viewing the problem in that way is simply too limiting. Truancy can alternatively be defined as unexcused absenteeism (other than school phobia). This is clearly more encompassing, but the term *unexcused* is too vague. What if the parent finds the sniffles or a headache excusable?

Because no definition of truancy is completely satisfactory, it is important to consider that each definition results in different rates of "truancy." Consequently, the rates presented here should be considered as only general estimates.

In any event, absenteeism that is unofficial, unexcused, or illegal accounts for the majority of urban secondary school nonattendance. One report estimates that two-thirds of absences in these schools are illegal (21). Another finds that three-quarters are "illegitimate" (89).

Note E. The fact that only one-third of prominently underachieving students have serious behavior problems but that a clear majority of learning-disabled (special class) junior high school students do, reflects on the behavior-weighted selection criteria used for JHS classes for the learning disabled (Chapter 6).

Note F. The rate of recidivism (over a period of a few years) for serious delinquent offenders is quite similar, averaging approximately 75% to 80% (46, 77).

Note G. Serious misconduct patterns in boys persist to a greater degree than do other personality characteristics. Olweus (90) notes that the "across time stability of aggressive behavior was not much lower than that typically found in the intelligence domain." Furthermore, he points out that the "behavior of highly aggressive boys . . . is often maintained irrespective of considerable environmental variations and in opposition to forces acting to change this same behavior." For example, "change of school did not seem to appreciably affect . . . (this) degree of stability over time."

REFERENCES

1. Heaton, R. C., & Safer, D. J. Characteristics of multisuspended junior high school students. Unpublished manuscript, 1977.
2. Bowman, P. H. Effects of a revised school program on potential delinquents. *Annals of the American Academy of Political and Social Science,* 1959, *322,* 53-61.
3. *Suspensions and expulsions: Current trends in school policies and programs.* Arlington, Va.: National School Public Relations Association, 1976.
4. Safer, D. J., Heaton, R. C., & Allen, R. P. Socioeconomic factors influencing the rate of non-promotion in elementary schools. *Peabody Journal of Education,* 1977, *54,* 275-281.
5. Safer, D. J., Heaton, R. C., & Parker, F. C. A behavioral program for disruptive junior high school students: Results and follow-up. *Journal of Abnormal Child Psychology,* 1981, *9,* 483-494.
6. Safer, D. J. Unpublished data, 1973-1980.
7. Stullken, E. H. Chicago's special school for social adjustment. *Federal Probation,* 1956, *20,* 31-36.
8. Rhodes, W. C. Delinquency and community action. In H. C. Quay (Ed.), *Juvenile delinquency: Research and theory.* Princeton, N.J.: Van Nostrand, 1965, pp. 209-262.
9. Annesley, F. R. A study of the relationship between normal and behaviour problem children on reading achievement, intelligence, self-concept and locus of control. *Slow Learning Child,* 1974, *21,* 185-196.
10. Glavin, J. P., & Annesley, F. R. Reading and arithmetic correlates of conduct-problem and withdrawn children. *Journal of Special Education,* 1971, *5,* 213-219.
11. Weinberg, C. Achievement and school attitudes of adolescent boys as related to behavior and occupational status of families. *Social Forces,* 1964, *42,* 462-466.
12. Feldhusen, J. F., Thurston, J. R., & Benning, J. J. Classroom behavior, intelligence and achievement. *Journal of Experimental Education,* Winter 1967, *36,* 82-87.
13. Ahlstrom, W. M., & Havighurst, R. J. *400 losers: Delinquent boys in high school.* San Francisco: Jossey-Bass, 1971.
14. Kelly, D. H. Track position, school misconduct, and youth deviance. *Urban Education,* 1976, *10,* 379-388.
15. Graubard, P. S. The relationship between academic achievement and behavior dimensions. *Exceptional Children,* 1971, *37,* 755-757.

16. Kauffman, J. M. *Characteristics of children's behavior disorders.* Columbus, Ohio: Charles Merrill, 1977.
17. Reckless, W., & Dinitz, S. *The prevention of juvenile delinquency.* Columbus, Ohio: Ohio State University Press, 1972.
18. Blatz, W. E., & Bott, E. A. Studies in mental hygiene of children: Behavior of public school children—a description of method. *Pedagogical Seminary and Journal of Genetic Psychology*, 1927, *34*, 552–582.
19. Heaton, R. C., Safer, D. J., Allen, R. P., Spinnato, N. C., & Prumo, F. M. A motivational environment for behaviorally deviant junior high school students. *Journal of Abnormal Child Psychology*, 1976, *4*, 263–275.
20. Mackler, B. A report on the 600 schools: Dilemmas, problems, and solutions. In R. A. Dentler, B. Mackler, & M. E. Warshauer (Eds.), *The urban R's: Race relations as the problem in urban education.* New York: Praeger, 1967, pp. 288–302.
21. Block, E. E., Covill-Servo, J., & Rosen, M. F. *Failing students—failing schools: A study of dropouts and discipline in New York State.* Rochester, N.Y.: New York Civil Liberties Union, 1978.
22. Davis, C. F., & Gozali, J. *School work program.* Milwaukee, Wisconsin. Mimeo, 1972.
23. Galloway, D. Size of school, socio-economic hardship, suspension rates and persistent unjustified absence from school. *British Journal of Educational Psychology*, 1976, *46*, 40–47.
24. Swift, M., & Spivak, G. The assessment of achievement-related classroom behavior. *Journal of Special Education*, 1968, *2*, 137–149.
25. Trice, A. D. Unpublished data, 1980.
26. Parker, H. K., & Masuda, R. Opportunity schools. *NASSP Bulletin*, April 1971, *55* (354), 37–55.
27. Glick, S. J. Identification of predelinquents among children with school behavior problems as a basis for multi-service treatment program. In S. Glueck & E. Glueck (Eds.), *Identification of predelinquents.* New York: Intercontinental Medical Book Corp., 1972, pp. 84–90.
28. Davies, J. G., & Maliphant, R. Refractory behaviour at school in normal adolescent males in relation to psychopathy and early experience. *Journal of Child Psychology and Psychiatry*, 1971, *12*, 35–41.
29. Edelman, M. W., Beck, R., & Smith, P. V. *School suspensions: Are they helping children?* Cambridge, Mass.: Children's Defense Fund, 1975.
30. *"600" Schools: Yesterday, today and tomorrow: A report to the superintendent of schools.* New York: New York City Board of Education, February 1965.
31. *Disruptive youth: Causes and solutions.* Reston, Va.: National Association of Secondary School Principals, 1977.
32. Heaton, R. C., & Safer, D. J. Secondary school outcome following a junior high school behavioral program, *Behavior Therapy*, in press.
33. Safer, D. J., Heaton, R. C., & Allen, R. P. A comprehensive approach to multisuspended students. LEAA grant proposal. Unpublished manuscript, 1974.
34. Berleman, W. C., Seaborg, J. R., & Steinburn, T. W. The delinquency prevention experiment of the Seattle Atlantic Street Center: A final evaluation. *Social Service Review*, 1972, *46*, 323–346.
35. Tait, C. D., & Hodges, E. F. Follow-up study of the Glueck table applied

to a school population of problem boys and girls between the ages of five and fourteen. In S. Glueck and E. Glueck (Eds.), *Identification of pre-delinquents.* New York: Intercontinental Medical Book Corp., 1972, pp. 49–59.

36. Havighurst, R. J., Bowman, P. H., Liddle, G. P., Matthews, C. V., & Pierce, J. V. *Growing up in River City.* New York: Wiley, 1962.

37. McKerrow, S. Major problems in city junior highs. *Baltimore Evening Sun,* April 25, 1977, p. A-1.

38. Nielsen, A., & Gerber, D. Psychosocial aspects of truancy in early adolescence. *Adolescence,* 1979, *14,* 313–326.

39. Roberts, J. L. Factors associated with truancy. *Personnel and Guidance Journal,* 1956, *34,* 431–436.

40. Young, P., & Safer, D. J. Unpublished data, 1974.

41. Rutter, M. L. Psychosocial disorders in childhood and their outcome in adult life. *Journal of the Royal College of Physicians,* London, 1970, *4,* 211– 218.

42. Schreiber, D. Juvenile delinquency and the school dropout problem. *Federal Probation,* 1963, *27* (3), 15–19.

43. Elliott, D. S., & Voss, H. L. *Delinquency and dropout.* Lexington, Mass.: Lexington Books, 1974.

44. Anduri, C. Our concern: They dropped out of our local high schools. In J. C. Gowan & G. D. Demos (Eds.), *The disadvantaged and potential dropout: Compensatory educational programs.* Springfield, Ill.: Charles C Thomas, 1966, pp. 454–462.

45. Safer, D. J. Position paper on special educational needs of multisuspended junior high school students. Unpublished manuscript, 1974.

46. Glueck, S., & Glueck, E. *Unraveling juvenile delinquency.* Cambridge, Mass.: Harvard University Press, 1950.

47. Tennent, T. G. School non-attendance and delinquency. *Educational Research,* 1971, *13,* 185–190.

48. Kvaraceus, W. C. *Juvenile delinquency and the school.* Yonkers, N.Y.: World Book Company, 1945.

49. Margolin, J. B., Roman, M., & Harari, C. Reading disability and the delinquent child. *American Journal of Orthopsychiatry,* 1955, *25,* 25–27.

50. Silberberg, N. E., & Silberberg, M. C. School achievement and delinquency. *Review of Educational Research,* 1971, *41,* 17–33.

51. Jessness, C. F. Comparative effectiveness of behavior modification and transactional analysis programs for delinquents. *Journal of Consulting and Clinical Psychology,* 1975, *43,* 758–779.

52. Mulligan, G., Douglas, J. W. B., Hammond, W. A., & Tizard, J. Delinquency and symptoms of maladjustment: The findings of a longitudinal study. *Proceedings of the Royal Society of Medicine,* 1963, *56,* 1083–1086.

53. Craig, M. R., & Glick, S. J. School behavior related to later delinquency and non-delinquency. *Criminologia,* 1968, *5,* 17–27.

54. Robins, L. N., & Hill, S. Y. Assessing the contributions of family structure, class and peer groups to juvenile delinquency. *Journal of Criminal Law, Criminology, and Police Science,* 1966, *57,* 325–334.

55. Robins, L. N., & Lewis, R. G. The role of the antisocial family in school completion and delinquency: A three generational study. *Sociology Quarterly,* 1966, *7,* 500–514.

56. Lundman, R. J., & Scarpitti, F. R. Delinquency prevention: Recommendations for future projects. *Crime and Delinquency,* 1978, *24,* 207-220.

57. Barton, W. H., & Sarri, R. Where are they now? A follow-up study of youth in juvenile correction programs. *Crime and Delinquency,* 1979, *25,* 162-176.

58. Wood, F. H., & Zabel, R. H. Making sense of reports on the incidence of behavior disorders/emotional disturbance in school-aged populations. *Psychology in the Schools,* 1978, *15,* 45-51.

59. Rubin, R. A., & Balow, B. Prevalence of teacher identified behavior problems: A longitudinal study. *Exceptional Children,* 1978, *45,* 102-111.

60. Cox, T. Children's adjustment to school over six years. *Journal of Child Psychology and Psychiatry,* 1978, *19,* 363-371.

61. Werner, E. E., Bierman, J. M., French, F. E., Simonian, K., Connor, A., Smith, R. S., & Campbell, M. Reproductive and environmental casualties: A report of the ten year follow-up of the children of Kauai pregnancy study. *Pediatrics,* 1968, *42,* 112-127.

62. Kelly, T. J., Bullock, L. M., & Dykes, M. K. Behavioral disorders. Teachers' perceptions. *Exceptional Children,* 1977, *43,* 316-318.

63. Olweus, D. *Aggression in the schools: Bullies and whipping boys.* New York: Halsted Press, 1978.

64. Cummings, J. D. A follow-up study of emotional symptoms in school children. *British Journal of Educational Psychology,* 1946, *16,* 163-177.

65. Shepherd, M., Oppenheim, B., & Mitchell, S. *Childhood behaviour and mental health.* New York: Grune & Stratton, 1971.

66. Thomas, A., & Chess, S. Evolution of behavior disorders into adolescence. *American Journal of Psychiatry,* 1976, *133,* 539-542.

67. Safer, D. J., & Allen, R. P. Factors associated with improvement in severe reading disability. *Psychology in the Schools,* 1973, *10,* 110-118.

68. Kohn, M. *Social competence, symptoms and underachievement in childhood: A longitudinal perspective.* Washington, D.C.: Winston & Sons, 1977.

69. Robins, L. N. Sturdy childhood predictors of adult antisocial behavior: Replications for longitudinal studies. *Psychological Medicine,* 1978, *8,* 611-622.

70. Kraus, P. E. Yesterday's children: A longitudinal study of children from kindergarten into the adult years. New York: Wiley, 1973.

71. Milich, R., & Loney, J. The role of hyperactive and aggressive symptomatology in predicting adolescent outcome among hyperactive children. *Journal of Pediatric Psychology,* 1979, *4,* 93-112.

72. Offord, D. R., Sullivan, K., Allen, N., & Abrams, N. Delinquency and hyperactivity. *Journal of Nervous and Mental Disease,* 1979, *167,* 734-741.

73. Rutter, M. *Changing youth in a changing society.* Cambridge, Mass.: Harvard University Press, 1980, p. 68.

74. Moore, D. R., Chamberlain, P., & Mukai, L. H. Children at risk for delinquency: A follow-up comparison of aggressive children and children who steal. *Journal of Abnormal Child Psychology,* 1979, *7,* 345-355.

75. Reid, J. B., & Hendricks, A. F. Preliminary analysis of the effectiveness of direct home intervention for the treatment of the predelinquent boys who steal. In L. Hamerlynck, L. C. Hardy, & E. J. Mash (Eds.), *Behavior change: Methodology, concepts, and practice.* Champaign, Ill.:

Research Press, 1973.
76. Elliott, D. S., Dunford, F. W., & Knowles, B. A. Diversion—a study of alternative processing practices: An overview of initial study findings. Behavioral Research Institute, Mimeo, July 1978.
77. West, D. J., & Farrington, D. P. *The delinquent way of life.* New York: Crane Russak, 1977.
78. Rutter, M., Tizard, J., Yule, W., Graham, P., & Whitmore, P. Isle of Wight Studies: 1964–1974. *Psychological Medicine,* 1976, *6,* 313–322.
79. Critchley, E. Reading retardation, dyslexia, and delinquency. *British Journal of Psychiatry,* 1968, *114,* 1537–1547.
80. Offord, D. R., Poushinsky, M. F., & Sullivan, K. School Performance, I.Q. and Delinquency. *British Journal of Criminology,* 1978, *18,* 110–127.
81. Robins, L. N., and Ratcliff, K. S. Childhood conduct disorder and later arrest. In L. N. Robins, P. J. Clayton, and J. K. Wing (Eds.), *The social consequences of psychiatric illness.* New York: Brunner/Mazel, 1980, pp. 248–263.
82. Rutter, M., Graham, P., Chadwick, O., & Yule, W. Adolescent turmoil: Fact or fiction? *Journal of Child Psychology and Psychiatry,* 1976, *17,* 35–56.
83. Dunn, L. An overview. In L. M. Dunn (Ed.), *Exceptional children in the schools: Special education in transition,* 2nd Ed. New York: Holt, Rinehart & Winston, 1973, pp. 3–62.
84. Sexton, P. C. *Education and income.* New York: Viking Press, 1961.
85. Rubin, R., & Balow, B. Learning and behavior disorders: A longitudinal study. *Exceptional Children,* 1971, *38,* 293–299.
86. Schreiber, D. The school dropout. In P. A. Witty (Ed.), *The educationally retarded and disadvantaged.* Chicago: University of Chicago Press, 1967, pp. 211–236.
87. Hentoff, N. *Does anyone give a damn?: On education.* New York: Alfred Knopf, 1977, p. 161.
88. Meacham, J. A., & Mink, E. B. Characteristics of and programs for the school dropout: Some research findings. In O. G. Mink and B. A. Kaplan (Eds.), *America's problem youth: Education and guidance of the disadvantaged.* Scranton, Penn.: International Textbook Co., 1970, pp. 64–78.
89. Reynolds, D., & Murgatroyd, S. Being absent from school. *British Journal of Law and Society,* 1974, *1,* 78–81.
90. Olweus, D. Stability of aggressive reaction patterns in males: A review. *Psychological Bulletin,* 1979, *86,* 852–875.

II

General intervention issues

INTRODUCTION TO CHAPTERS 3 THROUGH 5

Designing, introducing, and maintaining school programs for disruptive adolescents take a good deal of thought and planning. Involved are considerations such as: 1) How costly will it be and how cost-effective can it be? 2) Can and should the program be an adjunct to existing school services? 3) What will be its specific goals? 4) Should it stress both school *and* home interventions? 5) Can the return of disruptive students to the mainstream be built in initially? 6) Where will the program's natural sources of support be? 7) Will resistance to such a program ultimately doom it to failure? and 8) What can be achieved in the short and in the long run?

The following three chapters provide much of the necessary background information to enable a school staff to consider more knowledgeably these and other vital issues and to design their own intervention plan for disruptive youth. Although some programs are indeed more measurably successful than are others, no single approach appears applicable to most schools.

In the 1980s, the greatest immediate concern relative to public school disruptive student programs is cost. Naturally, more funds, shifts within the budget, and additional staff time are quite helpful in systematically beginning new school services. But school programs for disruptive students do not require federal or state grants. (Nearly half of all sizable secondary school programs for disruptive students are financed with local funds; see Chapter 19.) Furthermore, many useful school approaches to this problem do not require more or new funding. These include: selective teacher and aide assignments, positive peer group programs, resolving staff morale problems, in-service training for teachers to improve their classroom management efforts, more parent contracting by guidance counselors, limiting the access of intruders to the school building, decreasing student access to abused drugs, and providing group contingencies to support improved behavior.

3

Varieties and levels of intervention with disruptive adolescents

Daniel J. Safer

Interventions to deal with disruptive student behavior can take place in the school environment, at home, in a social agency, or elsewhere. Because remediation approaches in the school setting predominate, they are discussed first and at great length. School interventions are subdivided into: 1) customary administrative practices, approaches that commonly use punitive and exclusion responses, and 2) other school actions, a listing of less frequent, primarily faculty- and school-wide responses to student misconduct. Following this is a very brief discussion of non–school-based interventions.

SCHOOL-BASED INTERVENTIONS

Customary School Administrative Practices

Office Referrals   In secondary schools, teachers send students to the office for a variety of reasons including not doing the work, not having classroom materials, repeated lateness, back talk, excessive calling out, vulgarity, and fighting with peers. The office referral expresses the teacher's message to both the student ("I won't tolerate this") and to the assistant principal ("straighten him out"). The assistant principal, after getting the particulars on the disciplinary incident, usually responds in one of four ways: 1) chastising the student and threatening him with suspension if the behavior persists, 2) giving the child one or more days of after-school detention, 3) notifying a parent and possibly also suspending the student, or 4) calling the parent, finding a witness, and inflicting corporal punishment. Naturally, the nature of the offense and the frequency of offenses influence the administrative decision (Note A).

In junior high schools, office referrals are quite common. The average number in junior high schools with an enrollment of 1,000–1,500 students is 1,200–2,400 per school year, or 7–13 per day (1–3). In Maryland junior high schools in 1975, 39% to 46% of the total student population (varying with the grade level) were referred to the office for misconduct during a school year (3). As would be expected, some students receive more than their share. In one school, for example, 6% of the student body received five or more office referrals and amassed 57% of the total number of referrals (2).

After-School Detention   The use of after-school detention as a minor form of discipline has decreased since busing has become the dominant mode of transportation to and from school. Nonetheless, it is still used in most schools (4, 5). Failure to serve detention is sometimes a reason for suspension.

Other Forms of School Discipline   Other school disciplinary measures include: extra assignments, more study halls, grade reduction, work detail, exclusion from extracurricular activities, and disciplinary transfer (4). Three modifications of formal suspension procedures that do not result in time lost from the classroom include: 1) a 3-hour after-school suspension on a weekday evening from 6 to 9 P.M. (6); 2) required attendance at a 1½-hour movie on smoking for suspensions resulting from smoking (7); 3) a requirement that the parent of a suspended student attend all his classes with him for one day (8).

Suspensions   Suspensions are actions of the principal to exclude a student from school for periods up to 10 days pending a parent conference. With the Goss decision (9), principals or their designates are required to conduct an informal hearing on the charge without undue delay. The mini-hearing is set up to: 1) present the nature and basis of the charge against the student, 2) hear the apprehended student's version, and 3) obtain additional information on the offensive act if necessary (10). The average duration of a suspension is 3–4 days (11), and the action is characteristically terminated by a parent conference.

1. *Reasons for suspension* The reasons for suspension vary widely from school to school, from school district to school district, and from state to state. Most are given for nonviolent disruptive or uncooperative acts (including class cutting, truancy, and smoking). Major student suspension infractions and their approximate frequencies are presented from six recent surveys in Table 1.

2. *Suspension likelihood in relation to the offense* A survey of principals to determine the likelihood of suspension relative to the offense resulted in the following probability estimates: 1) fighting (100%), 2) possession of a weapon (98%), 3) insubordination (95%), 4) extortion (95%), 5) possession of drugs (80%), 6) smoking (78%), 7) class cutting (55%), 8) truancy (44%) (4).

3. *Rate of recurrence of suspensions* The National Association of Secondary School Principals (NASSP) survey of 1975 (10) found that 52% of suspended students had been suspended previously. This rate has been found by others to be 16% (4), 22% (12), 37% (13), and 40% (11)—a broad range indeed. The 37%–52% figures are probably most representative. Furthermore, the Children's Defense Fund report noted that 24% of those suspended had been suspended 3 or more times previously (11).

4. *Rate of suspensions according to grade level* The percentage of students suspended at least once annually has conservatively been estimated to be 0.9% in the elementary school and 8% in secondary schools (11). Since 60% to 75% of all suspensions occur in the junior high school (14, 15), the rate in junior high is at least 12%–15%. Other sources corroborate this estimate (16–19, Note B).

5. *Rate of suspension according to race and ancestry* The suspension rate for black youths averages approximately two times that for whites, Spanish Americans, and Native Americans, with the latter three sharing a nearly identical rate (11, 20). Children of Asiatic ancestry have approximately one-third the rate of whites and nearly one-sixth the black rate (11). For expulsions, the rate for blacks is two to three times that for whites (10, 21, 22). In general, blacks have a higher suspension rate for fighting, although whites have a relatively high rate for truancy (13). Although the evidence is mixed (23), the high suspension rate for black youth could in small part be racially discriminatory (24–26). In comparative analyses, suspensions correlate far better to low achievement than to racial background (17, Note C).

Table 1.   Major reasons for student suspension

CM-HSA Report (126)[a]	NASSP State Survey (10)[b]	Children's Defense Fund (11)
1. Defiance, noncompliance, and fighting (40%)	1. Attendance problems (50%)	1. Fighting with peers (35%)
2. Absence related (e.g., class cutting and truancy (20%))	2. Smoking	2. Truancy and tardiness (25%)
3. Smoking (14%)	3. Nonviolent acts	3. Disruptive to class routine (14%)
	4. Violation of school rules	4. Verbal confrontation (9%)
	5. Assault	5. Smoking (6%)
	6. Drugs	6. Not complying with punishment (4%)
		7. Criminal activity (3%)
		8. Fighting with school staff (1.5%)

[a]Central Maryland Health Systems Agency.
[b]National Association of Secondary School Principals.

6. *Rate of suspensions according to sex*   The number of males suspended exceeds females by approximately a 2–3:1 ratio (11, 27). Since teachers generally are more likely to respond to male aggression (28), they probably tend to discriminate against male students in disciplinary referrals to the office. This is likely to apply more to female teachers who, compared to male teachers, more readily interpret the behavior of male students as aggressive (26).

7. *Recent increases in the suspension rate*   Suspension rates are now more systematically reported because of requirements of the Office of Civil Rights. This may in part account for some of the recent increases in the reported rate, but there are too many indicators that reveal that the major reason is simply a real increase in the number of suspensions/student enrollment. On the average, the increase in the rate nationally has been over 5% per year for the last 10 years, even in the face of an enrollment decline of 30% over that period (29). Increases in excess of 10% per year during the 1970s have been reported in Los Angeles (10), East Baton Rouge (10), St. Petersburg (16), Baltimore (30), St. Louis (31), and New York City (32).

Williams (a four-school study) (13)	Ohio 1977 Secondary Schools Report (19)	Prince George's County, Maryland, 1973/74 Report (11)
1. Disruptive classroom behavior (36%–51%)	1. Attendance problems (33%)	1. Absence-related (34%)
2. Attendance problems (10%–45%)	2. Fighting or abusive language (28%)	2. Disrespect for rules (20%)
3. Fighting with peers (10%–29%)	3. Failure to comply (17%)	3. Fighting (19%)
4. Law violations and smoking (8%–15%)	4. Disruption of school (9%)	4. Smoking (12%)
	5. Smoking (7%)	5. Class disruption (6%)
	6. Weapon, drugs, ~~alcohol, and theft~~ (4%)	6. Destruction of school property (2%)

Although there is much variability, overall average increases in the school suspension rate nationally in all likelihood reflect increases in school disruption in recent years. During the 1970s, rates of student violence have increased over 50% and in many locales in excess of 100% (see Chapter 19).

8. *Evaluations of suspension*   Not much has been written on the effectiveness of suspension as a disciplinary tool. Strunk (12) provides data indicating that suspensions for truancy lead mainly to drop-out, suspensions for class cutting lead mainly to increased attendance followed by more classroom misconduct, suspensions for insubordination do not change the number of office referrals for misconduct, and suspensions for smoking lead to a decreased rate of office referrals for smoking (which the author ascribes to students being more careful not to be caught) (Notes D and E).

Expulsions   Expulsions are disciplinary removals from school on a permanent basis or for an indefinite period of time. Commonly, expulsions given to students under age 16 result in an exclusion (or transfer) for a semester or a school year. Offenses that can result in expulsion include behavior in the school building that is judged to endanger person or property, possession of drugs or alcohol, and persistent and serious school disruptiveness (33).

Expulsions require a hearing chaired by a designate of the local school district superintendent for adjudication and eventually for reinstatement. The hearing team also includes other school system officials (4). The number of students expelled annually varies from 0.2% to .6% of the student enrollment (22, 34). Of course, most expelled students are from secondary schools, so that the rate there is closer to 1% (35).

In New York state, the expelled student is legally entitled to an alternative education (4); in Maryland, he is not. Nonetheless, in New York state, Block et al. maintain that this legal entitlement is ignored (4).

Push Out   Around age 16, most repeatedly disruptive students are nudged to drop out of school officially following a suspension, expulsion, grade failure, or an office referral for misconduct (4). Frequently, unofficial school actions lead to the school withdrawal of these youth. Of all students who are withdrawn from the rolls before graduation, 17%-24% are pushed out because of their misconduct (4, 21, 36, 37).

Grade Retention   Grade retention in urban junior high schools is quite common. In the late 1970s in Baltimore, 23% of the students in city junior high schools failed to pass and 19% were retained annually (14). Particularly vulnerable are behavior problem students, over 70% of whom experience grade failure prior to age 14 (see Chapter 2). Grade failure in secondary schools is a common prelude to drop-out (38), notably among males.

The experience of grade failure and retention is quite demoralizing, particularly the second time around. Students who are male have serious academic deficits, lose much school time because of suspensions, have poor motivation, and have family difficulties are at a higher risk for grade retention (39).

If one considers that multisuspended junior high school students are absent an average of 33 days per school year because of suspensions, expulsions, and unofficial exclusions (including delays by parents in attending a reinstatement conference) and that repeated absence is a common and major reason for grade failure, then retention can be more readily seen as one (albeit, somewhat indirect) school response to misconduct.

Corporal Punishment Corporal punishment is a common form of discipline in U.S. schools. Forty-seven states allow it in schools, and the Supreme Court in the *Ingraham* vs. *Wright* case (40) recently upheld its use. Furthermore, the majority of the public and teachers favor corporal punishment (41). In the 1960s and probably in the 1970s, in the *majority* of schools in the U.S., some students who misbehaved were paddled each year by a school administrator.

Data on the use of paddling by school staff are incomplete, although available reports reveal its frequent use. In Houston and Dallas in 1972, there was a combined average of 6,100 reported instances of paddling by school staff per month (41). In approximately one-half of the school districts in California in 1972/73, there were 46,000 instances of corporal punishment on the school records, 65% of which occurred at the junior high school level (42). In one survey of high school principals from Georgia in 1974, 60% reported the use of corporal punishment in their school (5). In another survey by the National Institute of Education, 61% of rural junior high schools reported the use of paddling within a given month, and 36% of all secondary schools reported the practice during a given month (35). In one junior high school, of the 1,395 students referred to the office for misconduct, 428 received a paddling (2). Finally, in a 1968 survey in Pittsburgh, 68% of teachers reported that they had used corporal punishment (42, 43, Note F).

Looking at corporal punishment from an international perspective, it is in most common use in English-speaking countries. In England, Highfield and Pinsent's 1952 survey revealed that 89% of teachers supported the use of corporal punishment (44). They also reported that over one-third of difficult children had been caned (hit with a cane) during their public school experience (44). In a New Zealand book on the subject of caning, Mercurio (45) reported an average of five canings per day per high school. In contrast, few of the countries of continental Europe and none of the Communist countries allow corporal punishment in schools (42).

Corporal punishment appears to have an immediate, although temporary, effect in decreasing certain types of misconduct (42, 44, 45). Its use does not, however, positively correlate to longer term measures of improved student behavior (46, 47, Note G). Specifically, corporal punishment has *not* been shown to decrease the need for suspensions (41). Particularly where it does not have parental support, it has been shown to be "of little value" (44, Note H).

Other School Actions or Policies to Cope with Student Misconduct

Remedial Efforts before an Office Referral   In a typical elementary school, a teacher will not send a disruptive student to the office before trying on a number of occasions and in a number of different ways to settle him or her down. If this doesn't work, the teacher will talk to the parents one or more times. In addition, the teacher will probably bring in the counselor to help.

At the elementary school level, one teacher generally has the primary responsibility for a given student. If the child acts up in the hall, in minor subjects, or in the cafeteria, this teacher will be notified of the child's transgressions by his or her colleagues and will be expected to deal with them. In elementary schools, behaviors like frequent drug use and recurrent misbehavior in the halls are quite uncommon.

The milieu in urban junior high schools is quite different. Students there routinely have seven different teachers. Even in the 9th grade, most of the 70 or so teachers in the school will not know the name or grade of most of the students. In junior high, the halls are in chaos eight times a day (for a total of over 40 minutes) and the lavatories (those declared available), the cafeteria, the busing areas, and the playground are actively guarded by teachers and possibly also by a security guard. When a student acts up in any of these areas, he is sent to the office by a teacher who usually does not have him in his or her classes. If the child has a scheduling problem, the guidance counselor, not a teacher, is the one to see. When the student seriously acts up in class, it is commonly the assistant principal who is expected to make the threats and call the parents.

Some junior high school administrators have tried to alter the impersonal nature of junior high school disciplinary practice. They have tried to stem the tide of office referrals by demanding that more be done beforehand by the faculty. This effort is usually not popular with teachers, a high proportion of whom are afraid to deal directly with disruptive youth. (In one survey, 28% of teachers in big city secondary schools said that they hesitated to confront misbehaving students for fear of their own safety (35); in another survey, 17% of secondary school faculty members reported that they daily feared physical assault by students (48).) Other reasons for the unpopularity of increased teacher responsibility in response to misconduct at the secondary level are that it takes extra effort, space, an available telephone, and occasionally unpaid overtime work. Furthermore, most junior high school teachers view an increase in faculty requirements before punitive action as a sign of administrative weakness. They prefer firm and immediate action by the "front office" (Note I).

In any event, a few junior high school administrators report some success in increasing faculty responsibility for discipline and thereby decreasing office referrals. In one school in Prince George's County, Maryland (10), the teacher is expected to attempt or to arrange for one or more of the following before an office referral: 1) teacher-student conference, 2) teacher-parent conference, 3) counselor-student conference, and/or 4) counselor-parent conference. The third and fourth options in dealing with serious student misconduct are uncommon in most secondary schools because they firmly put the counselor into the disciplinary field (49).

In a junior high school in Green Bay, Wisconsin (10), the teacher must check what initial steps were tried before making an office referral. The check-off list includes: 1) none, 2) checked student's folder, 3) held conference with student, 4) sent report home, 5) detained student after school, 6) consulted counselor, 7) telephoned parents, 8) held conference with parents, 9) changed student's seat, section, or classroom.

In most instances, these procedures are difficult to enforce upon a secondary school faculty and if tried will undoubtedly make the assistant principal quite unpopular. Not only that, but some teachers simply will not stand for them. In many areas, teachers have the right, by way of clauses in their negotiated contracts, to go over the head of their school administrators and to exclude a disruptive child from their classroom (10, 50). Because of faculty resistance, then, it is likely that the procedure described for the two junior high school faculties in Prince George's County and in Green Bay are being applied primarily by teachers for students in their classrooms who exhibit nonviolent disruptiveness.

A Code of Student Conduct   The effect of instituting a formal code of student conduct on the disciplinary management within schools has not been systematically evaluated. Nonetheless, a code can make school policy in regard to discipline fairly explicit. In this way, it can help students and their parents know their options and possibly influence them to be less suspicious that school administrators are "pulling a fast one" on them.

Presently, over 75% of schools have some form of printed disciplinary code. In general, student codes of conduct clarify the following matters (4):

1. The right to an education for students
   a. from 5–21
   b. with special needs
   c. who want to leave and return
   d. who leave pregnant

2. The school discipline policy relative to
   a. prohibited acts
   b. specific consequences of the commission of such acts
   c. due process entitlement
   d. types of discipline (detention, short and long suspensions, disciplinary transfer, corporal punishment, other)
3. Freedom of expression in regard to
   a. the right to association and to chose speakers
   b. the right to distribute literature
   c. personal appearance
4. Police in school—searches
5. Access to student records
6. Extracurricular activities
7. Student government
8. Prohibition of racial and sexual discrimination

Writing and enforcing a stricter code of conduct can lead to an increased rate of student exclusions and to a lessening of obvious school infractions. Some high schools, for example, report the implementation of new firm school rules tying a fixed number of class cuts and truancies to nonpromotion (51–53). As a result, class cutting decreases and the attendance of *remaining* students increases. However, drop-out, grade failure, and exclusion also increase. In respect to smoking and drug use, there is no evidence to suggest that the implementation of tighter school rules decreases such behavior within schools. Tougher school rules on smoking and drug use primarily serve to increase exclusion of open and clumsy offenders and to push drug use further underground, that is, make its use in school less apparent to the faculty.

Increasingly the number of expellable offenses can obviously increase the frequency of student expulsions. In one school district in Maryland, doubling the number of listed offenses in the code of conduct that required expulsion reportedly doubled the expulsion rate during the following year (1979) (34, Note J).

Security Guards   Since 50% to 65% of all "security incidents" occur in junior high schools, it is quite understandable that schools at this level have the most security guards (55, 56). In Baltimore, nearly every junior high school has at least one security guard, and there is a security force of 111 for 140,000 students (56). New York City had, in 1981, 1,600 school security guards (57). In 1973, Los Angeles hired 235 new security guards to "control crime in the schools" (58). In Atlanta, Lexington, Los Angeles, Washington, D.C., Chicago, Philadelphia, Minneapolis, and Indianapolis, security guards carry weapons (58).

The impact of security guards on student violence has not been formally evaluated, but presumably their presence within the school building reassures anxious teachers and parents (56). Security hardware and devices can decrease after-hours school vandalism (35, 59), but the effectiveness and cost-effectiveness of security patrols have been seriously challenged (35, 60).

Alternative Schools   Alternative schools in the United States have clearly been on the increase for over 20 years. In 1976, they numbered over 5,000. Their admission emphasis, however, is on alienated, not disruptive students (61). Most are small, offer a shorter day, and have a more varied curriculum. Their results on achievement (61) and on absenteeism have been mixed. A frequently mentioned example of an alternative school is the Parkway School of Philadelphia (62, 63).

The Ombudsman   The idea behind hiring an ombudsman is to have an adult advocate for the student in trouble. The ombudsman is one who would be willing to understand and support the deviant student (primarily using investigation, mediation, and compromise) and to try to steer him or her to achieve practical results within the system. Essentially, the role is that of an intelligent, sympathetic go-between (64), a role which overlaps with that of the guidance counselor. In a critical analysis, Hollingsworth notes that specially funded persons in this position are "outsiders," have no real power, and cannot address system change (49).

The concept of an in-school student advocate has received funding support for several trials during the 1970s. In one unpublished report, the effort failed to achieve significant changes (65). In nearly all instances, when outside funding for ombudsman positions eroded, the positions were not maintained (66).

Teacher Training and Selective Assignment   Reports on training to improve a teacher's classroom management skills suggest that *didactic* instruction in this regard is of no practical benefit (67, 68), but that behaviorally programmed on-the-job classroom training is often useful (67, 69–74).

Overall, there are striking differences between teachers in their classroom management skills. Successful teachers learn, mainly by trial and error, to manage the job of education with the greatest degree of productive student involvement and the least amount of friction. Therefore, one ostensibly easy way to lessen student misconduct is to selectively use teachers who are successful with most of these students. An alternative and far more practical approach is to assign such successful teachers to classes with a greater number of troublesome students. The selective assignment of such teachers has its drawbacks, though, in terms of maintaining teacher interest, teacher incentives, faculty competitiveness, and administrative headaches, so it is an approach that is infrequently used.

Peer Pressure   Peer pressure can obviously be influential in producing classroom misconduct (74). (Indeed, the great majority of adolescent delinquent acts and truancies are committed in groups (75–77).) However, aside from some small-scale group contingency programs (78), channeling peer influence to limit disruptive behavior in schools is in this country mostly a consideration for the future. In the Soviet Union, on the other hand, observers consistently report that quasi-political youth discipline committees inhibit rebelliousness in students (79, 80). Naturally, these committees in the USSR are given a good deal of authority by the involved adults to ostracize, chastise, and punish the disruptive deviants.

In China, students who observe behavioral infractions are trained to feel obligated to report them to those in authority. Strong social pressure by peers is also utilized in China to decrease deviance (81).

In the United States, student disciplinary committees having far less coercive influence have been attempted in secondary schools. In the opinion of most principals, they have been unsuccessful (82). Furthermore, Gottfredson and Daiger reported that in the Baltimore area, greater degrees of student influence on school "governance" correlated significantly to *increased* student victimization and overall student disruption (83).

A responsibility-directed peer approach has been tried in a number of locations in public secondary schools in the U.S. and has had some success. It is called Positive Peer Culture and is described in Chapter 17.

School-Based Counseling   School-based individual and group counseling to lessen disruptive behavior has been tried for decades. Controlled studies of its impact have yielded disappointing results (84–86).

Medication   In 1977, 0.7% of public junior high school students received stimulant medication to control their hyperactive and impulsive behavior (87), making medication a common intervention for school misconduct. In controlled studies on hyperactive youth, stimulant drug treatment usually reduces restlessness and classroom misconduct (88). As a result, it probably reduces the office referral and suspension rate of most drug-responsive hyperactive students. These particular effects have not, however, been formally evaluated.

Other Methods The following methods are discussed at greater length in separate chapters:

In-school suspension (See Chapter 16.)
Work experience programs (See Chapter 5.)
Special education referrals (See Chapter 6.)
Behavior management programs (See Chapters 9–13.)
Comprehensive in-school programs (See Chapters 10 and 12.)

NON–SCHOOL-BASED INTERVENTIONS

Non–school-based interventions can improve student conduct. Of these, the most successful to date have been parent-focused efforts.

Parent Support for Good School Behavior

Of all parent counseling studies reported, most aim primarily to improve the child's home behavior (89–91). As a group, the more successful ones have focused on: 1) young children (usually ages 6–10), 2) motivated parents who sought treatment, 3) behaviorally oriented parent counseling, and 4) children with *at most* a moderate degree of conduct disturbance. For the involved children, the results of behavioral intervention have been measurably successful at home, but have not persisted much beyond the termination of treatment (91–93). Treatment results with poorly motivated parents are distinctly less successful (91, 94).

Programs using parents to improve their child's motivation in school have become increasingly numerous and have generally reported some success (95, 96). To attain school results from parent intervention, one must program this into the total treatment program (90, 97). One way is to request that parents give home reinforcers based on daily and/or weekly school reports. If the program is systematic and the incentives are attractive to the child, the result can be improved school conduct (95, 96, 98).

A major nonbehavioral parent intervention program, initiated by Reverend Jessie Jackson, has been Push to Excellence. This group program aims to motivate parents to reinforce greater academic effort by their children (99). Its effectiveness in the 30 schools (in 6 cities) where it is being tried has not been evaluated (100).

Neighborhood Intervention

Although neighborhood political and social pressures have reportedly been successfully used in China and Cuba to increase conformity in youth (101), the control required to achieve such ends would in all likelihood make it unacceptable in the United States. In this country, voluntary neighborhood programs designed to redirect or control community misconduct in youth have been tried. These include recreational efforts, street workers, and vigilantes. Generally such efforts have been unsuccessful with delinquent youth (102).

Community Child Guidance Clinic Counseling

Professional individual counseling programs for deviant youth have generally emphasized a supportive relationship and a focus on insight. Such efforts have consistently had no positive impact on antisocial conduct (e.g., delinquency and recidivism) (103, 104).

Juvenile Justice System Involvement

The juvenile justice system has not had a major influence in controlling juvenile misconduct (105). Most obviously this system locks up some serious offenders in penal institutions, which at the very least keeps them out of community circulation for a while (106). The deterrent effect of such punishment is for the most part lost on repeat offenders, for reasons not generally agreed upon; its effect on other youth is at best only slightly greater (107).

Of late, there has been an acceptance of the proposition that punishing most juvenile offenders within the juvenile justice system probably does them more harm than good (108, 109). Consequently the recent aim of the juvenile justice system has been to divert the bulk of nonviolent youthful law violators from the system (110).

Whereas repeated truancy or severe school misconduct (along with major home complaints of incorrigibility) could have sent a juvenile to training school 20 years ago, status offenders (people in need of supervision (PINS) or children in need of supervision (CINS)) are far less frequently brought to juvenile court or to Juvenile Services Administrations today. The juvenile justice system is thus only rarely available of late to support attempts to decrease student disruptiveness, a fact attested to by 92% of big city school principals (35).

CONCLUSIONS

Present secondary school policies commonly emphasize two major responses to seriously disruptive student behavior: exclusion and punishment. Exclusion includes office referrals, suspension, disciplinary transfer, and expulsion. Punishment includes detention and corporal punishment. The first (exclusion) aims to keep the school's usual programs on course. The second (punishment) expresses the anger and retaliatory feelings of the victims and their natural allies (student victims, their parents, teachers, and administrators) and aims to create a fear that they hope will deter the culprit and others from similar acts.

Other school efforts to cope with disruptive student behavior include tactics and responses that are generally broader in scope. Suppressive methods include security guards, some peer pressure tactics, in-school suspension (also an exclusion effort), and, to a great extent, the use of medication for those classified as hyperactive. Another tactic is program transfer. This includes transfers to special education and to work-experience school programs. A third involves the use of counseling intermediaries, such as school-based counselors and ombudsmen. The fourth consists of motivational efforts. This includes the offering of school and home incentives to students if they achieve agreed upon academic and behavioral goals. A fifth can be called minor system modifications. Included in this are teacher training, programs matching difficult students with competent teachers who personally view their educational needs as important, and training or replacing principals (when needed) to achieve tighter administrative organization.

Efforts outside the school to decrease student misconduct in this country involve mainly enlisting parent support. In addition, support from neighborhood groups and governmental agencies (such as the juvenile or district court) merit inclusion here.

Of all these, a number of interventions have clearly led to improved student behavior. These include: some peer pressure efforts, parent contracting, behavior modification classroom programs, some minor system modifications (such as tighter administrative organization and matching problem students with competent and interested teachers), and stimulant drug treatment for hyperactive youth. None of these are strikingly effective with serious behavior problem students, but combinations can be additive in their effects. Hopefully, in the not too distant future, the list of successful strategies and programs will significantly increase.

NOTES

Note A. The transaction wherein members of the school staff chastise a student for his misconduct can be viewed from a generational or role perspective. School personnel (including secretaries, the nurse, and the janitor) take the authoritative, critical adult position with the student who is out of line. Lectures and threats are the rule. The student—even though perhaps 14, tall, and 140 pounds—is clearly and immediately put in the position of the child who transgressed.

Chesler et al. call this a "coalition of adults against the young" (50). Woods characterizes such transactions as deliberate shaming (111). Such an approach is also used liberally in the USSR, but in Russia the major social pressure to change student misconduct is reportedly applied not by adults, but by peers (79).

Note B. There has been great administrative variation in the reporting of suspensions. In Ohio, for example, 18 of 82 districts suspended (at least once) fewer than 2% of their students in 1976, whereas 18 other districts suspended over 21% of their students (19). This difference was not primarily due to the big city "influence" because the three districts with the highest suspension rates were small city areas. Larkin (20) reports junior high school suspension *totals* in the same school district ranging from 2% to 105% of the student body (in 1976) and ascribes this great variation primarily to differences in reporting. He states that schools with low suspension rates routinely send their students home for misconduct without reporting these interventions as suspensions. The extent of this practice certainly warrants a more detailed investigation.

Note C. Racial discrimination does not appear to explain much of the high suspension rate of black youth any more than reverse discrimination can generally explain the unusually low suspension rate of Asiatic Americans. Cultural and family factors appear to be far more important. Partially supporting this proposition are low rates of delinquency in Japanese children (112), high rates of "behavioral deviancy" and aggressiveness by black children (113, 114), the six- to tenfold greater adult homocide rate for blacks (compared to whites) (115, 116), and a very low rate of homocide among Japanese adults (117).

Note D. Dr. Tegarden, a high school principal in Maryland, probably conveys the general feeling (with some overstatement) about the value of suspension for the disciplined student. He says, "We know for certain that suspension from school has been totally ineffective in disciplining youngsters . . . . It's like sending kids out on a three day vacation. They come back the same" (18). Obviously, for those remaining in the classrooms and in the school building, the temporary exclusion of seriously disruptive youth is a relief. It results in increased order and tranquility, and allows for a more concerted emphasis on academic instruction.

Note E. The adverse consequences of suspension include: 1) labeling the student within the school as bad, 2) nudging him to drop out, 3) not allowing him to complete assignments during the period, 4) affording him a vacation from school, 5) decreasing state educational funds to his school district if they are provided in relation to attendance, 6) further alienating the youth's parents (119), and 7) increasing the hostility of the student (4, 13).

Note F. Although the use of corporal punishment in the United States has been slowly declining over the past few decades (5), particularly in major cities, the process has not been uniform. Los Angeles, with over 500,000 pupils, abolished corporal punishment in 1975 only to reinstate it in 1980 as "another means of dealing with classroom disruption" (110).

Note G. Physical punishment by parents *by itself* does not appear to have a uniform effect on the behavior of youth. In a fascinating study, Lefkowitz et al. found that paternal punishment reduced aggressive behavior in youths who strongly identified with their fathers, but when such positive identification was not present, paternal physical punishment was strongly and positively associated with increased aggression (121).

In general, though, there is a highly positive correlation between parental physical punishment and aggression in youth (122). The relationship is particularly close for violent youth (123).

Note H. Corporal punishment is more commonly used on the poor and on minorities (124). Boys are recipients of corporal punishment more than girls by a ratio reported by one investigator to be 18:1 (41).

Note I. The 1973 report of the National Commission on the Reform of Secondary Education viewed the matter this way: "Because of the increase in physical assaults in recent years, many teachers are afraid of their students and have turned over their role in school discipline to building administrators and school security officers" (125).

Note J. Codes of school conduct and school discipline hearings are only distantly related to laws and civil court procedures that apply to adults in the United States. At best, school policy for student misconduct is quasijudicial. Although the vast majority of students referred to the office are guilty as charged, such students are generally assumed from the start to be guilty. Their mini-hearings frequently take less than a minute and the assistant principal who judges the case is usually under strong pressure to back up his teachers. Furthermore, if an appeal procedure exists, it is seldom made explicit to the students (49).

REFERENCES

1. Pardon our solecism. *Creative Discipline,* November 1977, *1,* 2.
2. Ainsworth, L., & Stapleton, J. C. Discipline at the junior high school level. *NASSP Bulletin,* February 1976, *60,* 54–59.
3. *Disruptive youth: Causes and solutions.* Reston, Va.: National Association of Secondary School Principals, 1977.
4. Block, E. E., Covill-Servo, J., & Rosen, M. F. *Failing students—failing*

schools: *A study of dropouts and discipline in New York State.* New York: New York Civil Liberties Union, 1978.

5. Kingston, A. J., & Gentry, H. W. Discipline problems in Georgia Secondary Schools: 1961 and 1974. *NASSP Bulletin,* February 1977, *61* (406).

6. A Spring Valley innovation: After school suspensions. *Creative Discipline,* April 1978, *1,* 5.

7. An alternative to suspensions for smoking. *Creative Discipline,* August 1977, *1,* 7.

8. Bass, A. Another approach to suspension. *NASSP Bulletin,* May 1980, *64* (436), 109–110.

9. *Goss* vs. *Lopez,* 419 US, 565, 1975.

10. *Suspensions and expulsions: Current trends in school policies and programs.* Arlington, Va.: National School Public Relations Association, 1976.

11. Edelman, M. W., Beck, R., & Smith, P. V. *School suspensions: Are they helping children?* Cambridge, Mass.: Children's Defense Fund, 1975.

12. Strunk, W. P. Exclusion from school as a disciplinary tool. *NASSP Bulletin,* October 1961, *45* (267), 136–144.

13. Williams, J. In-school alternatives: Why bother? In A. M. Garibaldi (Ed.), *In-school alternatives and suspensions: Conference report.* Washington, D.C.: National Institute of Education, 1979, pp. 1–22.

14. McKerrow, S. Many problems found in city's junior highs. *Baltimore Evening Sun,* April 25, 1977, pp. A-1 and A-4.

15. The crisis in pupil personnel services. *The Clarion for Mental Health,* March 1973, *15,* 1.

16. Bailey, R. E., & Kackley, J. C. *Positive Alternatives to Student Suspension: An Overview.* St. Petersburg, Fla., 1975, Mimeo.

17. Osborne, D. L. Race, sex, achievement and suspension. *Urban Education,* 1977, *12,* 345–347.

18. Goldberg, E. Black students get suspended more. *Baltimore Sun,* March 10, 1977, p. D-7.

19. Kaeser, S. C. Suspensions in school discipline. *Education and Urban Society,* 1979, *11,* 465–484.

20. Larkin, J. School desegregation and student suspensions. *Education and Urban Society,* 1979, *11,* 485–495.

21. Elliott, D. S., & Voss, H. L. *Delinquency and dropout.* Lexington, Mass.: Lexington Books, 1974.

22. *The student pushout: Victim of continued resistance to desegregation,* Washington, D.C.: The Robert F. Kennedy Memorial and the Southern Negro Council, 1973.

23. Kraus, P. E. *Yesterday's children: A longitudinal study of children from kindergarten into the adult years.* New York: Wiley, 1973.

24. Duncan, B. L. Differential social perception and attribution of intergroup violence: Testing the lower limits of stereotyping Blacks. *Journal of Personality and Social Psychology,* 1976, *34,* 590–598.

25. Eaves, R. C. Teacher race, student race and the behavior problem checklist. *Journal of Abnormal Child Psychology,* 1975, *3,* 1–9.

26. Kelly, T., Bullock, M., & Dykes, M. K. Behavioral disorders: Teachers' perceptions. *Exceptional Children,* 1977, *43,* 316–318.

27. Safer, D. Unpublished data.
28. Serbin, L. A., O'Leary, K. D., Kent, R. N., & Tonick, I. J. A comparison of teacher responses to the pre-academic and problem behavior of boys and girls. *Child Development,* 1973, *44,* 796–804.
29. Kleinman, D. Keeping discipline in the schools is the no. 1 educational headache. *New York Times,* October 28, 1979, p. 6-E.
30. Sadler, J. E. Suspensions up by 100% in school; 91% are Blacks. *Baltimore Sun,* December 4, 1975, p. C-1.
31. Allen, T. W. The evaluation of a program of special classes for "disruptive children" in an urban school system. *Community Mental Health Journal,* 1970, *6,* 276–284.
32. LoCicero, J. *Another choice—another chance: A survey of alternative public school programs in New York City.* New York City: Community Service Society of New York, 1976, pp. 7, 11.
33. *Student Behavior Handbook,* Towson, Md.: Baltimore County Board of Education, September 1979.
34. Olmstead, L. Expelled youth lose on funds. *Baltimore Evening Sun,* February 29, 1980, p. D-3.
35. National Institute of Education. *Violent Schools—Safe Schools.* Washington, D.C.: Author, 1978.
36. Schreiber, D. Juvenile delinquency and the school dropout problem. *Federal Probation,* September 1963, *27* (3), 15–19.
37. Anduri, C. E. Our concern: They dropped out of our local high schools. In J. C. Gowan & C. D. Demos (Eds.), *The disadvantaged and potential dropout: Compensatory educational programs.* Springfield, Ill.: Charles C Thomas, 1966, pp. 454–462.
38. Robins, L. Follow-up studies. In H. C. Quay and J. S. Werry (Eds.), *Psychopathological disorders of childhood,* 2nd Ed. New York: Wiley, 1979, pp. 483–513.
39. Safer, D., Heaton, R., & Allen, R. P. Socioeconomic factors influencing the rate of non-promotion in elementary schools. *Peabody Journal of Education,* 1977, *54,* 275–281.
40. *Ingraham* vs. *Wright, 430,* U.S., 651, 1977.
41. Hyman, I. A., & McDowell, E. An overview. In I. A. Hyman & J. H. Wise (Eds.), *Corporal punishment in American education.* Philadelphia: Temple University Press, 1979, pp. 3–21.
42. Hyman, I. A., McDowell, E., & Raines, B. Corporal punishment and alternatives in the schools: An overview of theoretical and practical issues. In J. H. Wise (Ed.), *Proceedings: A conference on corporal punishment in the schools: A national debate.* Washington, D.C.: National Institute of Education, February 1977, pp. 1–13.
43. Rothman, E. P. *Troubled teachers.* New York: David McKay, 1977.
44. Highfield, M. E., & Pinsent, A. *A survey of rewards and punishments in schools.* London: National Foundation for Educational Research, 1952.
45. Mercurio, J. A. *Caning: Educational rite and tradition.* Syracuse, N.Y.: Syracuse University Press, 1972.
46. Clegg, A., & Megson, B. *Children in distress.* Middlesex: Penguin Books, 1968.
47. Rutter, M., Maughan, B., Mortimore, P., & Ouston, J. *Fifteen thousand hours: Secondary schools and their effects on children.* Cam-

bridge, Mass.: Harvard University Press, 1979.
48. O'Toole, P. Casualties in the classroom. *New York Times Magazine*, December 10, 1978, pp. 59, 78–90.
49. Hollingsworth, E. J. Exploring remedies from within. *Education and Urban Society*, 1979, *11*, 511–526.
50. Chesler, M., Crowfoot, J., & Bryant, B. I. Organizational context of school discipline. *Education and Urban Society*, 1979, *11*, 496–510.
51. Suprin, R. N. Cutting down on student cutting. *NASSP Bulletin*, February 1979, *63* (424), 27–31.
52. Childs, M. L. Making students accountable for absences. *NASSP Bulletin*, April 1979, *63* (426), 119–120.
53. Garcia, E. J. Instant quarter-credit concept—An answer to class cutting? *NASSP Bulletin*, February 1979, *63* (424), 39–43.
54. Marvin, M., Connolly, J., McCann, R., Tempkin, S., & Henning, S. *Planning assistance programs to reduce violence and disruption.* Washington, D.C.: U.S. Department of Justice, January 1976.
55. Discipline ranges from strong to weak, even in the same school. *Baltimore Evening Sun*, April 26, 1977, p. A-1.
56. Mothers protest school security conditions. *Baltimore Sun*, October 12, 1978, p. C-1.
57. Haberman, C. Reagan budget forcing region to rethink goals. *New York Times*, March 22, 1981, p. 1.
58. Rubel, R. J. *The unruly school: Disorders, disruptions and crimes.* Lexington, Mass.: Lexington Books, 1977.
59. Furno, O. F., & Wallace, L. B. Vandalism: Recovery and prevention. *American School and University*, July 1972, *44*, 19–22.
60. Dentler, R. A. School violence: Building an R and D agenda. In J. M. McPartland and E. L. McDill (Eds.), *Violence in schools: Perspectives, programs and positions.* Lexington, Mass.: Lexington Books, 1977, pp. 137–152.
61. Deal, T. E., & Nolan, R. R. Alternative schools: A conceptual map. *School Review*, 1978, *87*, 29–49.
62. Cox, D. W. *The city as a schoolhouse.* Valley Forge, Pa.: Judson Press, 1972.
63. Bremer, J., & Von Moschzisker, M. *The school without walls.* New York: Holt, Rinehart & Winston, 1971.
64. Koltveit, T. H. Counselor-consultant as quasi-ombudsman. *Personnel and Guidance Journal*, 1973, *52*, 198–200.
65. *The Northampton county social restoration program.* Philadelphia: Social Research Associates, October 1974.
66. Frees, J. W. *Alternatives to litigations: Ombudsman and others.* Madison, Wisconsin: Center for Public Representation, March 1978.
67. Borg, W. R., Langer, P., & Wilson, J. Teacher classroom management skills and pupil behavior. *Journal of Experimental Education*, 1975, *44*, 52–58.
68. Nietzel, M. T., Winnett, R. A., MacDonald, M. L., & Davidson, W. S. *Behavioral approaches to community psychology.* New York: Pergamon, 1977, p. 50.
69. Marlowe, R. H., Madsen, C. H., Bowen, C. E., Reardon, R. C., & Logue, P. E. Severe classroom behavior problems: Teachers and counselors. *Journal of Applied Behavioral Analysis*, 1978, *11*, 53–66.

70. Randolph, P. L., & Hardage, N.C. Behavioral consultation and group counseling with potential dropouts. *Elementary School Guidance and Counseling,* 1973, *7,* 204–209.

71. Miller, T. L., & Sabatino, D. A. An evaluation of the teacher consultant model as an approach to mainstreaming. *Exceptional Children,* 1978, *45,* 86–91.

72. Rollins, H. A., McCandless, B. R., Thompson, M., & Brassell, W. R. Project success environment: An extended application of contingency management in inner-city schools. *Journal of Educational Psychology,* 1974, *66,* 167–178.

73. Brown, J. C., Montgomery, R., & Barclay, J. R. An example of psychologist management of teacher reinforcement procedures in the elementary classroom. *Psychology in the Schools,* 1969, *6,* 336–340.

74. Solomon, R. W., & Wahler, R. C. Peer reinforcement control of classroom problem behavior. *Journal of Applied Behavioral Analysis,* 1973, *6,* 49–56.

75. West, D. J., & Farrington, D. P. *Who becomes delinquent?* London: Heinemann, 1973.

76. Empey, L. T. Delinquency theory and recent research. *Journal of Research in Crime and Delinquency,* 1967, *4,* 28–42.

77. Nielsen, A., & Gerber, D. Psychosocial aspects of truancy in early adolescence. *Adolescence,* 1979, *14,* 313–326.

78. Medland, M. B., & Stachnik, T. J. Good behavior game: A replication and a systematic analysis. *Journal of Applied Behavioral Analysis,* 1972, *5,* 45–51.

79. Bronfenbrenner, U. Response to pressure from peers versus adults among Soviet and American school children. *International Journal of Psychology,* 1967, *2,* 199–207.

80. Haltmeyer, N. No discipline problems for the teacher? *Educational Leadership,* October 1972, *30,* 61–62.

81. Kessen, W. *Childhood in China.* New Haven: Yale University Press, 1975, pp. 151–172.

82. Duke, D. L. How administrators view the crisis in school discipline. *Phi Delta Kappan,* 1978, *59,* 325–330.

83. Gottfredson, G. D., & Daiger, D. C. *Disruption in six hundred schools.* Report No. 289. Baltimore, Md.: Center for the Social Organization of Schools, Johns Hopkins University, 1979.

84. Meyer, H. J., Borgatta, E. F., & Jones, W. C. *Girls at vocational high: An experiment in social work intervention.* New York: Russell Sage Foundation, 1965.

85. Sarri, R. C., & Vinter, R. D. Group work for the control of behavior problems in secondary schools. In D. Street (Ed.), *Innovation in mass education.* New York: Wiley, 1969, pp. 91–119.

86. Gildea, M. C., Glidewell, J. C., & Kanton, M. B. The St. Louis mental health project: History and evaluation. In E. L. Cowen, E. A. Gardner, & M. Zax (Eds.), *Emergent approaches to mental health problems.* New York: Appleton-Century-Crofts, 1967, pp. 290–306.

87. Krager, J. M., Safer, D., & Earhart, J. Follow-up survey results of medication used to treat hyperactive school children. *Journal of School Health,* 1979, *49,* 317–321.

88. Safer, D. J., & Allen, R. P. *Hyperactive children: Diagnosis and man-*

agement. Baltimore: University Park Press, 1976.
89. Atkeson, B. M., & Forehand, R. Parent behavioral training for problem children: An examination of studies using multiple outcome measures. *Journal of Abnormal Child Psychology,* 1978, *6,* 449–460.
90. Patterson, G. R. The coercive child: Architect or victim of a coercive system. In E. J. Mash, L. A. Hamerlynck, & L. C. Handy (Eds.), *Behavior modification and families.* New York: Brunner/Mazel, 1976, pp. 267–316.
91. Wahler, R. G. The insular mother: Her problems in parent-child treatment. *Journal of Applied Behavioral Analysis,* 1980, *13,* 207–219.
92. Ferber, H., Keeley, S. M., & Shemberg, K. M. Training parents in behavior modification: Outcome of and problems encountered in a program after Patterson's work. *Behavior Therapy,* 1974, *5,* 415–419.
93. Kent, R. N., & O'Leary, K. D. A controlled evaluation of behavior modification with conduct problem children. *Journal of Consulting Clinical Psychology,* 1976, *44,* 588–596.
94. Wahler, R. G., Leske, G., & Rogers, E. S. The insular family: A deviance support system for oppositional children. In L. A. Hamerlynck (Ed.), *Behavioral systems for the developmentally disabled. I. School and family environments.* New York: Brunner/Mazel, 1979, pp. 102–127.
95. Bailey, J. S., Wolf, M. M., & Phillips, E. L. Home-based reinforcement and the modification of predelinquent classroom behavior. *Journal of Applied Behavioral Analysis,* 1970, *3,* 223–233.
96. Clark, H. B. A program of delayed consequences for the management of class attendance and disruptive classroom behavior of 24 special education children. In G. Semb (Ed.), *Behavior analysis and education.* Lawrence, Ks.: University of Kansas, 1972.
97. Wahler, R. G. Setting generality: Some specific and general effects of child behavior therapy. *Journal of Applied Behavior Analysis,* 1969, *2,* 239–246.
98. Barth, R. Home based reinforcement of school behavior: A review and analysis. *Review of Educational Research,* 1979, *49,* 436–458.
99. Sheppard, N. Schools like Jackson's "push" but they ask, "What is it?" *Baltimore Sun,* March 6, 1979.
100. Bennett, A. Jackson's EXCEL gets mixed grade. *Baltimore Sun,* January 28, 1980, p. C-1.
101. Cuba's caderista's fight crime, dissidents. *Baltimore Sun,* October 20, 1976, p. B-5.
102. Dixon, M. C., & Wright, W. E. *Juvenile delinquency prevention programs.* Nashville, Tenn.: Peabody College for Teachers, 1975.
103. Powers, E., & Witmer, H. *An experiment in the prevention of delinquency: The Cambridge-Somerville youth study.* New York: Columbia University Press, 1951.
104. McCord, J. A thirty-year follow-up of treatment effects. *American Psychologist,* 1978, *33,* 284–289.
105. Wolfgang, M. E., Figlio, R. M., & Sellin, T. *Delinquency in a birth cohort.* Chicago: University of Chicago Press, 1972.
106. Wilson, J. Q. *Thinking about crime.* New York: Basic Books, 1975.
107. Teevan, J. J. Subjective perception of deterrence (continued). *Journal of Research in Crime and Delinquency,* 1976, *13,* 155–164.

108. Farrington, D. P., Osborn, S. G., & West, D. J. The persistence of labelling effects. *British Journal of Criminology,* 1978, 18, 277–284.
109. Paternoster, R., Waldo, G. P., Chiricos, T. G., & Anderson, L. S. The stigma of diversion: Labeling in the juvenile justice system. In P. L. Brantingham & T. G. Blomberg (Eds.), *Courts and diversion: Policy and operations studies.* Beverly Hills, Ca.: Sage Publications, 1979, pp. 127–142.
110. Lemert, E. M. *Instead of court: Diversion in juvenile justice.* HEW Publication No. 76-59, Washington, D.C., NIMH, 1971.
111. Woods, P. "Showing them up" in secondary schools. In G. Chanan & S. Delamont (Eds.), *Frontiers in classroom research.* Sussex: NFER Publishing Company, 1975, pp. 122–145.
112. Vogel, E. F. *Japan as number one: Lessons for America.* Cambridge, Mass.: Harvard University Press, 1979.
113. LaPouse, R., & Monk, M. A. Behavioral deviations in a representative sample of children. *American Journal of Orthopsychiatry,* 1964, *34,* 437–447.
114. Miller, L. C., Hample, E., Barrett, C. L., & Noble, H. Children's deviant behavior within a general population. *Journal of Consulting and Clinical Psychology,* 1971, *37,* 16–22.
115. Homocide ranked fourth as killer of black males. *New York Times,* April 27, 1980, p. 54.
116. Dennis, R., & Lockert, E. *Homocide in young black males.* Read at the 133rd annual meeting of the American Psychiatric Association, San Francisco, May 8, 1980.
117. Barth, A. Tokyo—the lowest crime rate. *Washington Post,* November 23, 1971, p. A-18.
118. Clark, M. J. Unruly Wilde Lake students need a contract. *Baltimore Sun,* November 13, 1978, p. C-3.
119. Safer, D. Factors affecting outcome in a school mental health service. *Community Mental Health Journal,* 1974, *10,* 24–32.
120. Despite doubters, spanking revived. *Baltimore Evening Sun,* February 5, 1980, p. A-3.
121. Lefkowitz, M. M., Eron, L. D., Walder, L. O., & Huesmann, L. R. *Growing up to be violent: A longitudinal study of the development of aggression.* New York: Pergamon, 1977.
122. Welsh, R. S. Delinquency, corporal punishment and the schools. *Crime and Delinquency,* 1978, *24,* 336–354.
123. Farrington, D. P. The family backgrounds of aggressive youths. In L. A. Hersov & M. Berger (Eds.), *Aggressive and anti-social behaviour in childhood and adolescence.* New York: Pergamon, 1978, pp. 73–93.
124. Mauer, A. All in the name of the last resort. In J. H. Wise (Ed.), *Proceedings: A conference on corporal punishment in the schools: A national debate.* Washington, D.C.: NIE, 1977, pp. 43–47.
125. Brown, B. F. *The reform of secondary education: A report to the public and the profession.* New York: McGraw-Hill, 1973, p. 123.
126. *Children's mental health,* 2nd draft. Central Maryland Health Systems Agency Report on Mental Health, Alcoholism and Alcohol Abuse, 1979.

4

Dimensions and issues of school programs for disruptive youth

Daniel J. Safer

Public secondary schools that have implemented programs for disruptive students have reported positive outcomes in most respects. Generally, studies without control groups have reported substantial improvements relative to a baseline (pre-intervention) rate. Programs with matched control groups have had far more modest claims.

This chapter first presents the dimensions of reported program impact. These are, for the most part, improvements in conduct and academic achievement during the program operation. Second is a listing and discussion of areas where intervention results are marginal at best. These exist primarily in the long-term results sphere. Last, a loosely fitting set of programmatic issues is presented in question form and discussed. These range from philosophical to technical matters.

DIMENSIONS OF POSSIBLE IMPACT

Improved Attendance

School programs designed to manage disruptive youth more effectively have generally reported increases in attendance ranging up to 100% improvement (1-9). Many of these programs have utilized inidvidual or group rewards, contingent upon the achievement of improved attendance (1, 3, 6, 9). These and other reports in the literature (10, 11) suggest that behavioral programs have had more consistently positive and well-documented results in this area than have other approaches.

There are of course other, more direct approaches to the general problem of school absence. Given the finding that over 50% of unexcused student absences are parent-sanctioned or parent-condoned (12), one strategy is to enlist adult volunteers or school staff to call the parents of the absent students daily. This method has resulted in a 2% to 3% decrease in absenteeism by an entire junior high school (13, 14). Another simple means of improving the attendance rate for enrolled students is to tighten the attendance requirements needed for the attainment of grades and credits (15, 16). In senior high schools, this process can decrease the rate of absenteeism (although it also accelerates the drop-out of chronic non-attenders).

Still other approaches to improve attendance have been found to be less useful. Among these, referrals of persistent non-attenders to court and to child guidance clinics have been reported to be particularly unrewarding (17). Home visits by school staff can somewhat decrease truancy rates, but the improvement is not great and the cost in personnel time is high.

Improved Academic Achievement

Achievement gains in reading and arithmetic have been reported by many school programs for disruptive adolescents (1-3, 6, 9, 18) although others have reported no significant achievement gains relative to comparison groups (8, 9, 19, 20). Those programs reporting gains have noted improvements from 0.6 grade levels/year to 2.0 grade levels/6 months, with the bulk of academic improvement appearing in the first 6 to 12 months of intervention (3). These data are often difficult to interpret because most programs only report achievement changes relative to baseline, do not use control groups, do not use independent (blind) assessment, and do not consider the effect of the students' familiarity with a test when he is retested using the same assessment instrument.

In appraising the total effort to improve the achievement of academically deficient adolescents, the following findings should be considered:

1. Individualized instruction and task analytic approaches tend to yield better results. (See Chapter 6.)

2. Improvement in academic achievement is more dependent upon basic cognitive abilities than on other *measurable* factors (21).
3. Motivation to learn can be appreciably influenced by the curriculum (22).
4. Efforts to improve motivation probably have a more influential effect on the achievement of academically slow secondary school students than an emphasis on improving formal instruction techniques.
5. The vast majority of follow-up studies on remedial instruction show that after the treatment, a gradual washout of benefits occurs. (See Chapter 6.)
6. Improvement in reading skills does not necessarily lead to gains in reading comprehension (23).

Reduced Suspensions

Programs designed to reduce the number of out-of-school suspensions of disruptive youth report 5% to over 200% decreases (1, 3, 9, 24). The official suspension rate, however, can be fairly easily manipulated by school administrative staff. For instance, some suspension type offenses can be alternatively handled by parent contacts without exclusion from school, or by the placement of the student in an in-school holding room in association with parent telephone contacts. Thus, administrative procedures alone can appreciably decrease the *recorded* rate of suspensions for minor school offenses (see Chapter 3, Note B).

In any event, out-of-school suspensions characteristically have many untoward effects on involved students, and decreasing the number and duration of such suspensions by any method can be beneficial for both these students and for their parents. As a result of suspension, parents are commonly alienated from the school (25) and students lose much of the time required to obtain passing grades (see Chapter 3, Note E).

Increase in Passing Grades

Of the classroom programs for disruptive students reporting changes in grades, all reported an improvement (2, 9, 20). However, like suspension rates, student grades can be appreciably influenced by the criteria determined by a program's teaching staff. For example, good grades can be tied exclusively to the successful completion of individualized, school-based assignments.

Nonetheless, improved grades give all students who receive them a genuine morale boost. In addition, improved grades increase the number of students who pass to the next grade. Failing grades and grade retention, on the other hand, constitute the strongest predictors of school drop-out (26, 27) and nonpromotion is one of the most stressful experiences possible for the school-aged child (28).

Greater Progress toward High School Graduation

Whereas some report an increased duration of matriculation by disruptive adolescents because of special school programs (2, 9), others report no such change (4, 8, 18, 19, 29, 30). In the programs reporting an increased period of matriculation, if it is averaged, it comes to less than a 1-year gain. This seemingly negligible gain is nonetheless of value, because *some* disruptive youth benefit from their relative success in school and continue to slowly accumulate credits toward high school graduation. Also, those who drop out from more personalized educational programs usually experience less trauma and rancor in the process and appear more ready to re-enter school. Thus, in one behavioral resource room program in a Baltimore County high school, 8 of 12 students who dropped out in the 10th and the 11th grades (in 1978/79) re-entered school the following September (31).

Decreased Delinquency

Formal efforts to decrease the likelihood of delinquency by adolescent "pre-delinquents" or disruptive students using school programs have been tried for over 35 years. Two controlled school program studies have reported modest or partial decreases in delinquency (32, 33), but the great majority of educational endeavors have shown no impact on community misconduct (18, 29, 30, 34, 35). Of the two programs with some positive results, Parker et al. reported that school program youth—compared to control youth not receiving special school support—had fewer first offenses in delinquency, but no significant changes in the recidivism rate (32). Lawrence et al., on the other hand, found a mild decline in recidivism (33). (See Chapter 9.) In both the Parker et al. and the Lawrence et al. reports, the control and experimental groups were not well matched (at baseline) in terms of delinquency. In any event, Parker et al. described possible changes in the delinquency rate as by-products of their school program intervention, since such programs do not deal with community misconduct as a primary target behavior (32).

WHAT SCHOOL PROGRAMS FOR
DISRUPTIVE YOUTH HAVE NOT SHOWN

Although school programs for disruptive youth have usually produced measurable benefits, their overall impact is by no means striking. Particularly, they have not demonstrated positive results in the following areas.

Long-Term Achievement Gains

Since long-term achievement gains have not been assessed for remedial programs involving underachieving disruptive adolescents, the results of other educational programs for underachieving younger children are cited here. Becker and Engelmann have reported that, when used with early elementary school children, the DISTAR remedial reading program produces greater achievement gains than for controls, and that these differences persist for up to 3 years (36). Likewise, in an even younger population, Palmer and Andersen reported similar long-term benefits following Project Head Start (37). Nonetheless, the great majority of other studies have not demonstrated the persistence of academic gains beyond 1 year after the termination of treatment (38–40).

Long-Term Behavioral Change

Although Safer et al. (9) report that school programs for disruptive youth slightly improve school behavior during the year following the termination of treatment, others report either that there are no significant behavioral gains following treatment or that the behavioral gains wash out within a few months after treatment ceases (41–43). Certainly, in respect to neighborhood delinquency, the clear weight of evidence is that school programs for disruptive youth have had at most a minimal impact.

Significant Increases in School Holding Power

Safer et al. (9) and Friedman et al. (3) report that school programs for disruptive adolescents produced some generalizations and maintenance effects as measured by improved student grades. However, the evidence is clear that at least 70% of seriously disruptive secondary school students drop out before the end of the 11th grade and that special programs have not as yet appreciably increased the motivation of such students to continue their formal education much beyond the age required by compulsory attendance laws.

Program Success with Disruptive
Youth Using a Vocational Curriculum

If anything, in public schools an academically weighted program is more operationally feasible and successful for disruptive adolescents than one utilizing a vocational curriculum (29). (See Chapter 5.)

Better Outcomes in Off-Site Educational Environments

As the data presented in Chapter 5 show, except for decreased delinquency during institutional or residential care, off-site educationally oriented facilities have not been shown to have better results than comprehensive, on-site programs. Relative to on-site programs, the return to school rate from off-site programs is lower and their cost is far greater.

Program Maintenance at the Local
Level after Grant Funding Stops

Most *large* school programs for disruptive youth are initiated with state or federal money (such as Title IV–C or LEAA). After the outside dollars cease to arrive, the great majority of new programs customarily terminate (44), although some are maintained at the local level on a far smaller scale. In effect, it has not been demonstrated that most school systems will support programs for disruptive youth with local funds (45).

One school program for disruptive youth received millions of federal dollars in the late 1960s and early 1970s. It produced a well-run school program, but never had firm high level, school system support. Not only is that program not operative at this time, but its innovations have had no sizable impact on the schools it served. In another instance, a state-financed program was set up for disruptive youth in a public junior high school in the 1970s. It was directed by non-school-based specialists who were viewed by the faculty as outsiders. The program was in operation for only part of 1 year and over $100,000 was spent on it (mainly to pay for teacher salaries and workshop expenses) before it folded.

In contrast, a few small-scale projects begin with and continue to receive local support (46). One program that began locally and remains in existence with local funding after 12 years is the Anne Arundel County Learning Center in Annapolis, Maryland. This program is unusual in that it has always received the active and personal support of the county superintendent of schools.

In effect, it has not been demonstrated that most school systems want and will support major programs for disruptive youth with local funds.

SOME VITAL ISSUES FOR DISRUPTIVE YOUTH PROGRAMS

Why Not Let Disruptive Youth Drop Out of School?

Arguments given *for* the responsibility of the public schools to provide for the educational needs of disruptive students until age 18 or graduation are:

1. Many drop-outs have serious academic deficiencies (46% read at or below the 6th grade level) (47). The longer these students can be encouraged to attend, the more academic material they will master.
2. On the whole, the greater the duration of formal schooling, the greater will be the average adult income (48).
3. Drop-out before age 18 is a bleak experience in the 1980s mainly because of the limited employment opportunities for non–high school graduates.

In 1950, nearly 35% of all *advertised* jobs were available to applicants without a high school degree or a GED, whereas in 1970, only 9% of advertised job openings were for applicants without a high school diploma or its test equivalent (49). Related to this is the report that employment of youth aged 14–17 was ten times greater in 1920 than in 1961 (50). Furthermore, the employment disadvantage for young people continues to grow. Unemployment for youth aged 16–19, for example, rose in New York City from 25% in 1978 to 34% in 1979 (51). Contributing to the disadvantage of youth on the labor market is the continuing increase in the federal minimum wage; one economics professor, in fact, calculated that the rise in the minimum wage in 1979/80 increased minority youth unemployment by nearly 40% (52). An additional risk for drop-outs is that the percentage of new blue collar jobs will continue to decline in the 1980s and is expected to account for only 25% of new jobs during that decade (53).

The proponents of the "benign" acceptance of early drop-out can argue:

1. Programs for disruptive youth are expensive and have shown limited results (over time).
2. Disruptive and other alienated students who drop out are usually not attracted to most secondary school courses (29, 54, 55).
3. Unlike those who complete high school, the delinquency rate of high school drop-outs decreases *after* they reach age 16 and drop out, suggesting that school requirements had an adverse effect on the general behavior of drop-outs before their departure from school (56).
4. Most school administrators (24), school board members (57), and probably most high school teachers, parents, and diligent students want disruptive youth out of school at age 16 or before (Note A).

Simply breathing a sigh of relief when disruptive students drop out or are pushed out of school at the legal age is probably more appealing to most people, particularly those of a conservative bent, than struggling to provide alternative educational programming for them. However, many also want some school programming available for these students out of a sense of fairness. As a result, local, state, and federal government officials have attempted to at least partially satisfy the proponents of both positions. Governments have: 1) allowed school administrators to exclude students as they see fit, 2) taken the teeth out of most truancy laws, 3) financed a small number of alternative schooling opportunities (mostly with special education funding and particularly for the children of persistent parents), 4) financed large, poorly defined, compensatory education programs for the poor and poorly achieving (e.g., Title I), and 5) given temporary government employment (e.g., CETA) to many drop-outs, particularly those from minority groups.

Thus, the government has tried not to step on anyone's toes. Its programs have spent money, cut dissatisfaction, and have given the aura (and occasionally the reality) of progressive action.

Why Not Use More Punishment with Disruptive Students?

Over the last two decades, punitive discipline has modestly decreased in U.S. public schools, whereas violence within the schools has measurably increased. One may argue that these two trends are casually related, but before this proposition is accepted, one should consider that neighborhood delinquency has increased even more than has school violence, that there are numerous alternative explanations for student disruptiveness (see Chapter 1), and that many more students with marginal enthusiasm for abstract learning are now matriculating in secondary schools.

Nonetheless, it can still be argued that more punitive and restrictive discipline will decrease the general level of disruptive student behavior, and this is probably true. A major school policy emphasis in this direction is often resisted, though, because it runs counter to recent civil rights trends, affirmative action, handicapped rights decisions, and egalitarian pressures.

In appraising the question of the degree of needed school disciplinary practice, one should consider the following arguments.

1. Although restrictive and physical punishment can usually produce temporary submission to authority, the weight of evidence is that in the long run an emphasis on aversive control procedures tends to reinforce aggressiveness in disruptive youth (58– 60).

2. Teachers are a heterogeneous population with respect to student management. Approximately 20% of secondary school teachers (particularly women) are constantly fearful of assault and respond to student provocations by immediately referring the offending student to the office. At the other extreme are a sizable number of authoritarian teachers who aggressively attempt to put rowdy students "in their place" by firm, often physical, acts, comments, and threats.

3. Although restrictive and punitive management is now utilized somewhat less in secondary schools, it is still a common practice. DeCecco and Richards, after an in-school assessment, reported that school personnel used "force" (e.g., physical force, suspension, property damage, restraint, and coercion) in 11% of their conflicts with students, and that students initiated "force" in only 3% of their conflicts with teachers (and in only 5% of their conflicts with their fellow students) (61). Rubel, following his own survey, came to somewhat parallel conclusions about teacher provocations, although he didn't present his findings numerically. He writes, "Pupils did not often assault teachers, but when they did, it was judged objectively to be the result of some kind of provocation by the teacher" (62). Other information relative to these points can be found in the section on corporal punishment in Chapter 3.

Why Not Modify the Secondary School Curriculum or the Duration of the School Day for Disruptive Students?

The major modification of the curriculum that has been consistently suggested over the last few decades for disruptive youth stresses a vocational orientation. However, career-oriented programs have not proliferated for these students for the following reasons: 1) disruptive students as a group are at least as much of an anathema to shop teachers as they are to English teachers, 2) if placed in work-experience jobs in a community setting, these students usually lose the jobs quickly, and, in the process, usually lose long-sought job openings for subsequent youth as well, 3) disruptive adolescents drop out of school at least as readily in vocational as in academic programs (29). A broader discussion of the comparative merits of an academic versus a vocational curriculum for disruptive youth can be found in Chapter 5.

As to implementing a shorter school day for disruptive youth in secondary schools, it is certainly utilized in many alternative programs (5, 9, 24, 29). Also, 47% of principals reported in a survey that they frequently shorten the school day for individual disruptive students (24). When disruptive students are scheduled to take all their major subjects in four consecutive school periods in the morning and walk home soon thereafter (assuming they have done their work properly and behaved well), the shortened day is viewed as a blessing by both the students and their teachers. Of the people involved in the logistics of a shortened day, only a small portion of working mothers and some apprehensive educators object. It is of interest, in this respect, that one of the recommendations of the National Panel on High School and Adolescent Education is that the duration of compulsory school attendance for adolescents be reduced "to an academic day of 2–4 hours" (63, Note B).

Why Not Prevent Adolescent Student Disruptiveness Beforehand by Successful Elementary Intervention?

Preventive intervention in primary schools to curb later misbehavior is a very attractive concept to secondary school personnel, but it represents a romantic notion. First, disruptive school behavior becomes a serious problem primarily after admission to junior high school. Second, no elementary school program for disruptive students to date has produced a positive, behavioral carry-over into the secondary school years.

Can a Comprehensive Integrated In-School Junior High School Program for Disruptive Students Succeed and Survive?

The two comprehensive, in-school, behavior management, regular education programs for disruptive junior high school school youth that are described in this book both attained good results. (See Chapters 10 and 13.) One utilized a resource room for two periods a day, along with a behavioral management system to reward good behavior and academic effort during the other periods. The second operated from specially designated regular sections for four periods a day; its staff arranged for the reward of good school behavior and achievement occurring throughout the school day. Both programs ran a multischool operation for a total of 6 to 7 years. Both accepted referrals of students with serious behavioral problems.

Thus, it is possible for comprehensive, partially self-contained, integrated, regular education, in-school programs to succeed with serious conduct-problem youth. However, both programs received outside funding and neither was in large measure adopted by its school system after its funds dried up. Furthermore, these two programs are unusual compared to others nationally. Almost all other in-school programs for disruptive students emphasize an in-school suspension or one of its variations. (See Chapter 16.)

Although many faculty members will tolerate integrated, successful, in-school programs for disruptive youth, they will do so only under the best of circumstances. When problems develop, faculty pressures for total self-containment, expulsion, or transfer of seriously disruptive students will be strong, and if exclusion type options are available within the system, most faculty members will seek these out and support them.

The advantages of low cost and increased success in mainstreaming, which clearly favor integrated, in-school programs, are not major issues with cautious school administrators. Faculty flak is far more important and immediate.

Can and Should Schools Take the Primary Community Responsibility to Educate Disruptive and Alienated Adolescents?

The majority of youth aged 14 to 18 whose behavior is seriously disruptive or who feel alienated when in school are unlikely to be found in a public school classroom on any given school day. The major reasons for these high rates of non-attendance are suspension, expulsion, class cutting, truancy, and drop-out, with truancy and drop-out

accounting for most of the time not in school. Chronic truancy (defined by some as over 30 unexcused absences/year) characterizes
over 15% of inner city junior high school students (64). Persistent
truancy in junior high school is, in effect, an unofficial drop-out; it
becomes official at age 16 for the majority (30).

Responses by school personnel to persistent school absenteeism
by adolescents who are 14 years of age and older include: 1) letting it
be, using the philosophy that, after all, schools are not for everyone,
2) trying to pressure truants to attend school, and 3) referring
truants and their parents for counseling. "Letting it be" avoids the
fact that most chronic truants have had moderate to serious academic problems since their early school years (65) and that school experiences have been consistently unrewarding for them. Trying to
force chronically non-attending (non-school-phobic) adolescents back
into secondary school classes produces on average only marginal and
temporary increases in their rate of return. Furthermore, when these
students do return, their classroom behavior often worsens (66).
Counseling recommendations are rarely followed up by truants or by
their parents.

If one takes the position that it is the responsibility of the public
schools to meet the educational needs of all students, including the
disruptive and the disenchanted, then the large number of students
who are not attending school cannot be reasonably ignored. However, America tolerates a high degree of handgun abuse, petty delinquency, crowded jails, alcoholism, unwed motherhood, inefficiency
and waste in the military, and white collar crime, and it also seems to
tolerate having many adolescents engaged in no productive activity
from ages 14 to 18.

Is There an Increasing Sensitivity of Late to the
Needs of Biosocially Disadvantaged Adolescent Students?

Although work experience programs for adolescents with marginal
academic interests are slowly expanding and special education is
slowly taking a larger role in programming for biosocially disadvantaged adolescents, a more sizable trend in regular secondary education is to rid itself of slow-learning students. Peculiarly, minimum
competency laws are used to support this push. These laws affect
the mildly learning impaired, the low achieving, the dull normal
and many minority students as well as callous students (for whom
the law was intended) and increase their rates of nonpromotion and
drop-out.

The numbers that will be affected are large. In California, for example, 10% of graduating seniors failed a high school competency test geared to the 6th grade level (67). In New York City, over 7,000 students per year are likely to fail, according to the testing chief of the city schools (68). Nationally, an estimated 12% of students are still considered functionally illiterate by age 17 (69).

Emphasizing a concern about student competency, public schools in the late 1970s increased their rates of nonpromotion. In New York City, School Chancellor Frank Macchiarola recently initiated "an end to social promotion" and mandated that all students whose test scores revealed academic retardation of over 1 to 2 years "be held back" after the 4th and the 7th grades (70, 71). Likewise, in Baltimore City public *elementary* schools, because of the "new proficiency guidelines," the annual grade retention rate rose from 5.8% in 1976, to 7.0% in 1977, to 12.2% in 1978 (72).

Since grade failure is a major predictor of school drop-out (26, 27), one would expect that increasing the rate of nonpromotion will ultimately increase the rate of drop-out and this has consistently occurred. Former U.S. Commissioner of Education, Harold Howe, II, some years ago, also linked grade failure and drop-out together when he stated, "Attempts to coax or persuade potential dropouts to stay in school when the school continued to fail them accomplishes absolutely nothing" (73).

The steep climb in the New York City high school drop-out rate from 39% in 1978 to 45% in 1979 even shocked New York City School Chancellor, Frank Macchiarola, who publicly admitted, "There is no question that our responsibilities to these young people have been grievously unfulfilled" (74, 75). Nonetheless, he didn't take the opportunity to alter his stand halting social promotion (Note C).

Do Other Countries Have Fewer Disruptive Secondary School Students or Do They Handle Them More Successfully?

Before meaningful comparisons can be made between approaches to managing disruptive students here and abroad, differences in enrollment patterns must be considered. In the United States, 78% of its students remain in school until the 12th grade, whereas only 20% in England, 13% in the Netherlands, and 29% in Australia remain in school through age 17 (76). Cuba increased its compulsory education requirement to the 9th grade only as late as 1977 (77). Greece had a compulsory education requirement of only 6 years throughout the 1970s (78). In China, only 20% graduate from "senior middle school"

(79), and in 1970, over one-half of the population of the Soviet Union had no formal education beyond the 7th grade (80). In all fairness, it must be added that 88% of Japanese 15-year-olds entered high school in 1973 (81) and that compulsory education until age 17 was mandated during this past decade in Russia (82). Nonetheless, the point is that the United States has led in the "mass production" of secondary educational opportunities and therefore has kept far more students in school whose motivations to succeed academically were less than overwhelming.

Second, comparatively more U.S. students from working class and poor homes enter and complete secondary schools. In the United States, 14% of 12th graders come from families of unskilled parents versus 1% in West Germany and 5% in England (76).

A third point is that elementary student misconduct appears to be similar in various industrialized countries. Swift et al. gave a student behavior checklist to French and American teachers and found similar patterns (83). Also, German, American, and New Zealand scores on the Conners' Student Behavior Checklist are comparable (84, 85). Furthermore, estimates of serious and persistent conduct problems in pre-adolescent students consistently range from 5%– 10% in a number of countries (86).

Thus, although industrialized countries appear to have similar numbers of disruptive youth in the elementary schools, there are more problem students in U.S. secondary schools in part because the American educational system advances proportionally more "low academic track" students into secondary schools and because proportionally more students from lower working class backgrounds matriculate in secondary schools. There is, of course, a strong positive relationship between low track sectioning, low socioeconomic status, and disruptive student behavior (87), so that U.S. secondary schools kept precisely those students whose risk is high for disruptive behavior.

The matter of whether other countries handle their disruptive adolescent students more effectively than the U.S. has not been evaluated objectively. However, it deserves note that all school systems have problems with disruptive student behavior and that all have developed methods to cope with them. West Germany, for example, had 127 schools for behaviorally difficult students in 1959 (88). French school officials use detention halls and expulsion (89, 90). The English occasionally resort to strapping defiant students (90) and the Russians socially and politically ostracize deviant students and sometimes confine them to special schools (91).

Obviously school management mirrors a society's attitude to youth and to deviance, and this to some extent explains international differences in control within secondary schools. Also, as has been suggested, it is difficult to compare student behavior management practices in schools that have few working class and low track students and where education is considered a privilege (more than a right) with schools in countries, such as the U.S., which implement, to a moderate degree, egalitarian views.

Can School Programs for Disruptive Youth Be Well Evaluated?

School programs for disruptive youth can be well evaluated, but the procedure is fraught with complexities and obstacles. Some aspects of a thorough evaluation follow.

Random Assignment to Different Interventions Random assignment to different interventions or to treatment and nontreatment groups is very difficult to arrange with school officials. Of all researchers, only Reckless and Dinitz (18), Meyer et al. (19), and Davis (20) were able to use this approach in disruptive student research. Some others have used equivalent or matched control groups (3, 9, 29). Most have simply reported a change from baseline. (For example, there has been no controlled evaluation of in-school suspension.)

Use of Evaluative Measures Independent of the Intervention If an assistant principal is the gatekeeper to an in-school suspension program, he can, for example, use his position to reduce out-of-school suspensions. In this instance, "harder," more independent outcome measures (such as grades or attendance rate) would more generally reflect changes that resulted from the program intervention.

Independent Assessment Even in the best of circumstances, the proponent of a program is not likely to be an objective rater. An evaluator of a program can, for example, compare only youth who remain in an intervention program with a recognized comparison rate and minimize the fact that by excluding program drop-outs, the comparison is seriously biased (92). Likewise, the evaluator can present mainly the positive aspects of his data. If renewed funding requires positive results, it would be hard for the director of a continuing grant-funded program not to find these within the data. Clearly, the more independent the assessment, the less likely it is that the treatment will be shown to be of benefit.

Researchers whose livelihood and pride do not depend upon positive results and who desire to produce quality studies in order to do the best job possible and to publish in good journals are more willing to use independent measures, independent assessment, random assignment, a controlled outcome evaluation, and follow-up.

Need for Parental Consent   In these days of the Buckley Amendment and the Privacy Act, one needs to obtain written parental permission to specially test a child or to have the child receive a *novel* educational intervention. Nonetheless, the law allows for evaluative studies of educational programs using school records if the reports do not contain personally identifiable information (93). Stated differently, parental consent is needed for all novel educational or testing interventions (such as giving an individual achievement test), but not for the analysis of existing school data (such as group test scores, grades, and rates of suspensions and expulsions).

Control Group Problems   Finding an equivalent comparison population is not difficult in school program evaluation because most school districts have schools or school populations that are similar. However, it is necessary to gain official access to this information and that requires the support of top school system administrators. Such support is particularly hard for outsiders to obtain, possibly even more so of late.

Control group problems do not end there. If one needs to test the program and comparison groups individually (for example, on individual achievement tests), one needs written informed consent from the parents of the involved youth. This rarely presents a problem for parents of adolescents assigned to a beefed up school program, but it doesn't sell as well with parents of the control group. Even if 60% of the control group parents eventually sign, one is still left with a biased comparison sample because the most uncooperative parents usually have the least cooperative children and by not signing, their children (the greatest deviants) are then not represented in the control group population (94–99).

The resulting skew then requires new analyses for mismatched samples, which is anything but clean (100). (This problem of a skewed comparison group is similar to that encountered when one counts only the "surviving" intervention population in an evaluation analysis, and not the initial treatment sample.) In long-term follow-up studies, difficulties created by informed consent requirements are even greater and have had a very chilling effect generally on the process of outcome evaluation (101).

Who Will Reinforce School Staff in
Programs to Better Manage Disruptive Youth?

At this time, parent lobby groups have not directed their attention to better school programs for disruptive adolescents, and the relative emphasis for such programs is at the discretion of school administrators and school boards. Most give it a low priority.

Because there has been so little support for programs for disruptive youth in secondary schools, the Office of Juvenile Justice and the Prevention of Delinquency has recently taken it upon itself to financially entice public schools (through grant awards) to initiate projects for disruptive youth. In 1980/81, eleven million dollars was spent on this endeavor (102).

Other inducements have been used. In New York City from 1946 to 1967, extra salary payments ($480 to $600/year) were used to recruit teachers and principals to work exclusively with problem youth (103). Alternative reinforcers for interested teachers include: more recognition by the principal, more consultative support, more paid workshops, more preparation time, and a classroom aide.

Can School Programs for Disruptive
Adolescents Be Cost-Effective?

To confront the issue of program utility, those approaches that produce measurable beneficial results in controlled studies and those which are the least costly must be ascertained. Then, a favorable cost-benefit ratio can be attained.

In regard to program effectiveness, comprehensive, well-run school programs for disruptive adolescents generally show positive results on less independently assessed measures. For example, they can reduce out-of-school suspensions and office visits, improve grades, and increase student and parent satisfaction (3, 9). However, their effect on more independently obtained measures (as attendance and achievement scores) is far less impressive. On follow-up, *after termination of the treatment,* no independently replicated, controlled evaluation of a program for antisocial, truant, runaway, or drug-abusing adolescents has produced even moderately beneficial, significant results.

As to the cost of programs, it would be difficult to run a comprehensive on-site school program for disruptive adolescents for much under $4,000/student/year (double the usual cost of public education), an off-site comprehensive day school for under $10,000/student/year, and residential treatment for under $20,000/student/

year. For the most part, the cost of alternative programs goes up in proportion to the number and the professional training of its staff, its separate program maintenance expenses, and its length of student stay.

Another way of looking at cost is to consider cost per successful case. If a program's short-term gains are distinct and sizably exceed the results of a comparison group (for example, 56 out of 100 adolescents instead of 42 out of 100 succeed in attaining 1 year of sobriety, nondelinquency, or the like), the cost per successful case can be computed. If the intervention is an outpatient program costing $125,000 for 100 youth per year (a conservative estimate in 1981), then the program's short-term result—its success *above* the control rate (i.e., 14 cases)—costs $9,000/case/year. When an employment, group home, or inpatient program is evaluated in this manner, then the cost per successful case/year increases seven- to twentyfold.

The cost-effectiveness issue involving programs for disruptive students is probably better put: Is the cost worth the modest gains?

Is the Cost Worth the Modest Gains?

For behavior problem, adolescent students, the cost of comprehensive school programs is more justifiable than the cost of counseling and of residential treatment. But, is it worth $2,000 more per student year?

Worth is, of course, relative. If a county or city government budget is tight, should the money go instead to programs for the gifted? (Gifted students probably show less relative gain in special programs than disruptive youth.) Should no money be spent so that taxes can be lower? Should no money be spent on this because the results are modest? Is some additional and newer nuclear weaponry worth more than these programs? Will we be spending money on these students later in an even less efficient way? Aren't such costly interventions as social security disability, alcohol detoxification, methadone programs, Youth Employment and Demonstration Project Acts (YEDPA), and Comprehensive Employment Training Act (CETA) even less effective for their clients?

NOTES

Note A.   Forty percent of all teachers in fact have gone on record as suggesting that compulsory education laws should be modified to enable chronic disciplinary problem youth to leave school before age 16 (104). Furthermore, 17% of school superintendents and

21% of school board members feel that *all* 14- and 15-year-old students should be legally able to drop out of school (57).

Note B.   The prospect of a shortened school day touches again on the issue of compulsory education. In the United States, formal education is usually required until age 16. In big cities, however, attendance laws are rarely enforced for adolescent students. Since approximately 20% of big city junior high school students miss 40 or more days of school per year (64), one can readily understand why police tolerate this primarily truant behavior in most instances.

Although school drop-out is common unofficially before age 16 and officially at 16, jobs are not generally available until age 18. This limited availability of employment below the age of majority is reinforced by a multitude of age-biased government regulations and laws, employers' insurance restrictions, and union requirements.

Thus, the total effect of the above-mentioned restrictions and laws and their differential enforcement is to keep available mid-adolescent youths out of the job market, but not in schools.

Note C.   The myth embodied within stopping social promotions (and fulfilling minimum competency requirements) is that it raises academic standards. It does not, although skewed data based on grade and not age level could lead one to that conclusion. If anything, grade retention is academically disadvantageous to the involved student (105, 106). As Wrightstone, the former Director of Research of the New York City Board of Education, wrote, "Research on nonpromotion over the past 40 years has shown that it is generally ineffective. . . . Actually, most [nonpromoted students] make less progress in learning subject matter than if they . . . [were] promoted to the next grade" (107). Undoubtedly, nonpromotion was not established to meet student needs. When not in use as a penalty, it serves mainly to facilitate group instruction by classroom teachers.

In secondary schools, grade retention reinforces truancy and drop-out patterns. Tracking (or streaming) students into *achievement-based* sections on a given grade level has its limitations (87, 108), but it is a far more fair and equitable practice than nonpromotion based upon national norms of achievement. Similarly, another more equitable practice than arbitrary promotion requirements is to return to awarding different "levels" of high school diplomas (such as academic, vocational, and general).

REFERENCES

1. Heaton, R. C., Safer, D. J., Allen, R. P., Spinnato, N. C., & Prumo, F. M. A motivational environment for behaviorally deviant junior high school students. *Journal of Abnormal Child Psychology,* 1976, *4,* 263–275.
2. Walizer, M. H., Erickson, E. L., Bournazos, K., & Sonnad, S. R. *The Wallbridge Academy: Final evaluation report.* Grand Rapids, Mi., 1975.

3. Friedman, R. M., Filipczak, J., & Fiordaliso, R. Within school generalization of the preparation through response educational programs (PREP) academic project. *Behavior Therapy*, 1977, *8*, 986–995.
4. Filipczak, J., Archer, M. B., Neale, M. S., & Winett, R. A. Issues in multivariate assessment of a large-scale behavioral program. *Journal of Applied Behavioral Analysis*, 1979, *12*, 593–613.
5. Davis, C. F., & Gozali, J. *School-work programs*. Milwaukee, Wis., 1972, Mimeo.
6. Phillips, E. L., Phillips, E. A., Fixen, D. L., & Wolf, M. M. Behavior shaping works for delinquents. *Psychology Today*, June 1973, *6*, 75–79.
7. *Suspensions and expulsions: Current trends in school policies*. Arlington, Va.: National School Public Relations Association, 1976.
8. Bowman, P. H. Effects of a revised school program on potential delinquents. *Annals of the American Academy of Political and Social Science*, 1959, *322*, 53–61.
9. Safer, D. J., Heaton, R. C., & Parker, F. C. A behavioral program for disruptive junior high school students: Results and follow-up. *Journal of Abnormal Child Psychology*, 1981, *9*, 483–494.
10. Barber, R. M., & Kagey, J. R. Modification of school attendance for an elementary population. *Journal of Applied Behavioral Analysis*, 1977, *10*, 41–48.
11. Brooks, B. D. Contingency management as a means of reducing school truancy. *Education*, 1975, *95*, 206–211.
12. Galloway, D. Site of school, socio-economic hardship, suspension rates and persistent unjustified absence from school. *British Journal of Educational Psychology*, 1976, *46*, 40–47.
13. Carson, L. Reports, follow-ups help center combat attendance. *Baltimore Evening Sun*, May 3, 1977, p. A-4.
14. Fiordaliso, R., Lordeman, A., Filipczak, J., & Friedman, R. M. Effects of feedback in absenteeism in the junior high school. *Journal of Educational Research*, 1977, *70*, 188–192.
15. Childs, M. L. Making students accountable for absences. *NASSP Bulletin*, 1979, *63* (426), 119–120.
16. Garcia, E. J. Instant quarter credit concept—An answer to class cutting? *NASSP Bulletin*, 1979, *63* (424), 39–43.
17. Roberts, J. L. Factors associated with truancy. *Personnel and Guidance Journal*, 1956, *34*, 431–436.
18. Reckless, W., & Dinitz, S. *The prevention of juvenile delinquency: An experiment*. Columbus, Ohio: Ohio State University Press, 1972.
19. Meyer, H. J., Borgatta, E. F., & Jones, W. C. *Girls at vocational high*. New York: Russell Sage Foundation, 1965.
20. Davis, D. A. An experimental study of potential dropouts. *Personnel and Guidance Journal*, 1962, *40*, 799–802.
21. Safer, D. J., & Allen, R. P. Factors associated with improvement in severe reading disability. *Psychology in the Schools*, 1973, *10*, 110–118.
22. Fader, D. N., & McNeil, E. G. *Hooked on books: Program and proof*. New York: Putnam, 1968.
23. Lahey, B. B. Research on the role of reinforcement in reading instruction: Some measurement and methodological deficiencies. *Correc-*

tional and Social Psychiatry, 1977, *23*, 27-32.
24. Block, E. E., Covill-Servo, J., & Rosen, M. F. *Failing students—failing schools: A study of dropouts and discipline in New York State.* Rochester, N.Y.: New York American Civil Liberties Union, 1978.
25. Safer, D. Factors affecting outcome in a school mental health service. *Community Mental Health Journal*, 1974, *10*, 24-32.
26. Robins, L. N. Follow-up studies. In H. C. Quay & J. S. Werry (Eds.), *Psychopathic disorders in childhood*, 2nd Ed. New York: Wiley, 1979, pp. 483-493.
27. Kelly, D. H., & Pink, W. T. Academic failure, social involvement, and high school drop out. *Youth and Society*, 1972, *4*, 47-59.
28. Yamamoto, K. Children's ratings of stressfulness of experiences. *Developmental Psychology*, 1979, *15*, 581-582.
29. Ahlstrom, W. M., & Havighurst, R. J. *400 losers: Delinquent boys in high school.* San Francisco: Jossey-Bass, 1971.
30. Longstreth, L. E., Stanley, F. J., & Rice, R. E. Experimental evaluations of a high school program for potential dropouts. *Journal of Educational Psychology*, 1964, *55*, 228-236.
31. Trice, A. D. Unpublished data, 1980.
32. Parker, F. C., Trice, A. D., Marriott, S. A., Iwata, M. M., & Safer, D. J. Some products and by-products of a public, school-based program for disruptive adolescents. Paper presented at the annual meeting of the American Association of Behavior Therapists. San Francisco, December 15, 1979.
33. Lawrence, C. Remedial education and counseling for truant and delinquent youth. Paper presented at the annual meeting of the American Orthopsychiatric Association, Washington, D.C., April 4, 1979.
34. Hackler, J. C. Boys, blisters, and behavior: The impact of a work program in an urban central area. *Journal of Research in Crime and Delinquency*, 1966, *3*, 155-164.
35. Berleman, W. C., Seaberg, J. R., & Steinburn, T. W. The delinquency prevention experiment of the Seattle Atlantic Street Center: A final evaluation. *Social Service Review*, 1972, *46*, 323-346.
36. Becker, W., & Engelmann, S. *Analysis of achievement data on six cohorts of low income children from 20 school districts with the University of Oregon direct intervention follow through model. Technical Report 76-1, Eugene, Ore.: University of Oregon, 1976.*
37. Palmer, F. H., & Andersen, L. W. Long term gains from early interventions: Findings from longitudinal studies. In E. F. Zigler and J. Valentine (Eds.), *Project Head Start: A legacy of the war on poverty.* New York: Free Press, 1979, pp. 433-466.
38. Silberberg, N. E., Iverson, I. A., & Gorn, J. T. Which remedial reading method works best? *Journal of Learning Disabilities*, 1973, *6*, 547-556.
39. Rutter, M. Prevalence and types of dyslexia. In A. L. Benton and D. Pearl (Eds.), *Dyslexia: An appraisal of current knowledge.* New York: Oxford University Press, 1978, pp. 5-28.
40. Williams, J. Reading instruction today. *American Psychologist*, 1979, *34*, 917-922.
41. Glavin, J. P. Behaviorally oriented resource rooms: A follow-up. *Journal of Special Education*, 1974, *8*, 337-347.

42. Vacc, N. A. Long term effects of special class intervention for emotionally disturbed children. *Exceptional Children*, 1975, *39*, 15–22.
43. Kent, R. N., & O'Leary, K. D. A controlled evaluation of behavior modification with conduct problem children. *Journal of Consulting and Clinical Psychology*, 1976, *44*, 586–596.
44. Whittington, R. R., & Brand, C. R. Defunct grants—Special considerations for termination effectiveness. *Adolescence*, 1980, *57*, 201–210.
45. Berman, P., & McLaughlin, M. W. Factors affecting the process of change. In M. M. Milstein (Ed.), *Schools, conflict, and change*. New York: Teachers' College Press, 1980, pp. 57–71.
46. *Alternative disciplinary programs and practices in Pennsylvania schools*. Harrisburg, Pa.: Pennsylvania Department of Education, April 1977.
47. Williams, P. V. School dropouts. *NEA Journal*, February 1963, *52*, 11–13.
48. Jencks, C. *Who gets ahead: The determinants of economic success in America*. New York: Basic Books, 1979.
49. Carter mounts campaign to wipe out functional illiteracy. *The Baltimore Sun*, January 10, 1980, p. A-10.
50. Havighurst, R. J., & Neugarten, B. L. *Society and education*, 3rd Ed. Boston: Allyn & Bacon, 1967, pp. 332–359.
51. Shanker, A. Unemployed teens: Target of U.S. *New York Times*, January 6, 1980, p. E-9.
52. Loeb, M. Climbing that first job rung. *Time*, January 21, 1980, p. 66.
53. White collar jobs seen likely to rise. *New York Times*, December 30, 1979.
54. Stinchcombe, A. L. *Rebellion in a high school*. Chicago: Quadrangle Books, 1964.
55. Anduri, C. E. Our concern: They dropped out of our local high schools. In J. C. Gowan & G. D. Demos (Eds.), *The disadvantaged and the potential dropout: Compensatory educational programs*. Springfield, Ill.: Charles C Thomas, 1966, pp. 454–462.
56. Elliott, D. S., & Voss, H. L. *Delinquency and dropout*. Lexington, Mass.: Lexington Books, 1974.
57. Violence in the schools: Everybody has solutions. *American School Board Journal*, 1975, *162*, 27–37.
58. Lewis, D. O., Shanok, S. S., Pincus, J. H., & Glaser, G. H. Violent juvenile delinquents: Psychiatric, neurological, psychological and abuse factors. *Journal of the American Academy of Child Psychiatry*, 1979, *18*, 307–319.
59. Eron, L. D., Walder, L. O., & Lefkowitz, M. M. *Learning of aggression in children*. Boston: Little, Brown & Company, 1971.
60. Farrington, D. P. The family backgrounds of aggressive youths. In L. A. Hersov & M. Berger (Eds.), *Aggression and anti-social behaviour in childhood and adolescence*. New York: Pergamon, 1978, pp. 73–93.
61. DeCecco, J. P., & Richards, A. K. *Growing pains: Uses of school conflict*. New York: Aberdeen Press, 1974.
62. Rubel, R. J. *The unruly school: Disorders, disruptions and crimes*. Lexington, Mass.: Lexington Books, 1977.
63. *The education of adolescents: The final report and recommendations of the National Panel on High School and Adolescent Education*. Washington, D.C.: U.S. Department of HEW, 1976.

64. Saddler, J. E. School attendance up 4% in September. *Baltimore Sun*, November 17, 1976, p. C-2.
65. Tennent, T. G. Truancy and stealing: A comparative study of education act cases and property offenders. *British Journal of Psychiatry*, 1970, *116*, 587-592.
66. Strunk, W. P. Exclusion from school as a disciplinary tool. *NASSP Bulletin*, October 1961, *45* (267), 136-144.
67. Winter, B. California dropouts have to be smarter. *Baltimore Sun*, March 17, 1977, p. A-3.
68. Stiff 4th year test in high school set. *New York Times*, January 21, 1979, pp. 1-2.
69. Deninger, M. L. Minimum competency testing: Benefits and dangers for the handicapped student. *NASSP Bulletin*, December 1979, *63* (431), 43-48.
70. City reading levels slip farther back. *New York Times*, January 6, 1980, p. E-5.
71. Back to basics in New York schools. *New York Times*, June 29, 1980, p. E-6.
72. 12% of city primary pupils denied grade promotions. *Baltimore Sun*, January 11, 1980, p. C-4.
73. Dauw, E. G. Individual instruction for potential dropouts. *NASSP Bulletin*, September 1970, *54* (347), 9-21.
74. School dropouts at epidemic level. *New York Times*, October 21, 1979, p. E-6.
75. New York City's dropout rate hits 45%. *Phi Delta Kappan*, 1980, *61*, 307.
76. Shanker, A. No reason for separate education department. *New York Times*, March 4, 1979, p. E-9.
77. Cogan, J. J. Cuba's schools in the countryside: A model for the developing world? *Phi Delta Kappan*, 1978, *60*, 30-32.
78. Psacharopoulos, G. Economic implications of raising the school leaving age. *Comparative Educational Review*, 1978, *22*, 71-79.
79. Tyler, R. W. Some observations on Chinese education. *Phi Delta Kappan*, 1978, *60*, 26-29.
80. Jacoby, S. *Inside Soviet schools*. New York: Hill & Wang, 1974.
81. Duke, B. C. Statistical trends in postwar Japanese education. *Comparative Educational Review*, 1975, *19*, 252-266.
82. Jahr, H. R. U.S.A.: Two worlds apart? *Comparative Educational Review*, 1975, *19*, 451-467.
83. Swift, M., Spivak, G., DeLisser, O., Danset, A., Danset-Leger, J., & Winnykamen, F. Children's disturbing classroom behavior: A cross cultural investigation. *Exceptional Children*, 1972, *38*, 492-493.
84. Eichlesder, W. The MBD/LD problem as it is seen in Munich. In L. Oettinger (Ed.), *The psychologist, the school, and the child with MBD/LD*. New York: Grune & Stratton, 1978, pp. 197-201.
85. Werry, J. S., & Hawthorne, D. Conner's teacher questionnaire— Norms and validity. *Australian and New Zealand Journal of Psychiatry*, 1976, *10*, 257-262.
86. Jonsson, G. Delinquent boys, their parents and grandparents. *Acta Psychiatrica Scandinavica*, Supplement, 1967, *95*, 227-256.
87. Hargreaves, D. H. *Social relations in a secondary school*. London: Routledge & Kegan Paul, 1967.

88. Huebener, T. *The schools of West Germany.* New York: New York University Press, 1962.
89. Schonfeld, W. R. *Obedience and revolt: French behavior toward authority.* Beverly Hills, Cal.: Sage Publications, 1976.
90. Magnuson, R. P. Pupil control in English and French schools. *Educational Forum,* January 1970, *34,* 251–257.
91. Haltmeyer, N. No discipline problems for the teacher? *Educational Leadership,* 1972, *30,* 61–62.
92. Lerman, P. Evaluative studies of institutions for delinquents: Implications for research and social policy. *Social Work,* July 1968, *13,* 55–64.
93. Federal Register, Vol. 41, No. 118, p. 21073, May 17, 1976.
94. Patterson, G. R., & Fleishman, M. J. Maintenance of treatment effects: Some considerations concerning family systems and follow-up data. *Behavior Therapy,* 1979, *10,* 168–185.
95. West, D. J., & Farrington, D. P. *Who becomes delinquent?* London: Heinemann, 1973.
96. Rutter, M. Prospective studies to investigate behavioral change. In J. S. Strauss, H. M. Babigian, & M. Roff, *The origins and course of psychopathology: Methods of longitudinal research.* New York: Plenum Press, 1977, pp. 223–248.
97. Dubey, D. R., Kaufman, K. F., & O'Leary, S. G. *Training parents of hyperactive children in child management: A comparative outcome study.* Unpublished manuscript, SUNY at Stony Brook, 1977.
98. Gibson, H. B. The measurement of parental attitudes and their relationship to boys' behaviour. *British Journal of Educational Psychology,* 1968, *38,* 233–239.
99. Empey, L. T., & Erickson, M. L. *The Provo experiment: Evaluating community control of delinquency.* Lexington, Mass.: Lexington Books, 1972.
100. Reichardt, C. S. The statistical analysis of data from non-equivalent group designs. In T. D. Cook and D. T. Campbell (Eds.), *Quasi-experimentation: Design and analysis issues for field settings.* Chicago: Rand McNally, 1979, pp. 147–205.
101. Robins, L. N. Problems in follow-up studies. *American Journal of Psychiatry,* 1977, *134,* 904–907.
102. Federal Register, Vol. 45, No. 31, pp. 9830–9837, February 13, 1980.
103. Smith, C. C. The "600" schools. *Education,* 1959, *80,* 215–218.
104. Levin, J. Lay vs. teacher perception of school discipline. *Phi Delta Kappan,* 1980, *61,* 360.
105. Chansky, N. M. Progress of promoted and repeating grade 1 failures. *Journal of Experimental Education,* Spring 1964, *32,* 225–237.
106. Safer, D., Heaton, R., & Allen, R. P. Socioeconomic factors influencing the rate of non-promotion in elementary schools. *Peabody Journal of Education,* 1977, *54,* 275–281.
107. Wrightstone, J. W. *Class organization for instruction.* Washington, D.C.: National Education Association, 1957.
108. Schaefer, W. E., Olexa, C., & Polk, K. Programmed for small class: Tracking in high school. *Transaction,* October 1970, *7* (12), 39–46.

5

Major comparative features of alternative programs for disruptive adolescents

Daniel J. Safer

Programs for disruptive youth differ appreciably and meaningfully from one another in a number of ways. One difference is where the program is located. Whether it is on-site (in the student's assigned regular public school) or off-site has a great influence on such factors as cost and the rate of mainstreaming. A second distinguishing dimension is the program's theoretical orientation. Because the behavioral approach has been so prominent a psychological orientation since the 1970s, it was deemed best to divide school programs for disruptive youth into those following behavioral and nonbehavioral approaches. Such a dichotomy is surprisingly useful in comparing the short-term outcome of intervention projects. A third important differentiating feature of these programs is their vocational versus academic emphasis. This difference in curriculum has thus far been of only limited value in respect to the outcome of programs for disruptive secondary school students, but it continues to be of considerable interest to program planners. A discussion of each of these discriminating features of programs for disruptive students follows.

ON-SITE VERSUS OFF-SITE

Removal

To most school staff, off-site programs (day therapeutic and residential) have one unequivocal advantage over on-site programs. They remove the disorderly child. Removal is viewed favorably not only by most parents of nondisruptive youth, but also by the majority of teachers (1, Note A). Gallagher, speaking of special education placements in general observed, "In too many instances, general educators ask only one thing of special educational programs—that they take troublesome youth and not give them back" (2). Budnick and Andreacchi, administrators of the off-site "600" schools program, saw a major function of their program to be "removing constantly disruptive children" (3). Abrahamsen also commenting on that program says, "The benefit is much more of isolation than of correction" (4), and Donahue and Nichtern describe the program's placement approach as "internal exclusion" (5). Long et al. share these opinions of off-site placement stating, "The schools and the community are ridding themselves of those they cannot tolerate and then forgetting them" (6).

Most government officials have also gone on record as desiring the exclusion of seriously disruptive students. In Baltimore in the mid-1970s, the school board fired its superintendent partly because he opposed creating a special school for disruptive youth. In New Jersey, in 1979, a state committee listed as its *top* recommendation the setting up of special regional schools for disruptive students. (*The New York Times* appropriately titled the news article about the proposal, "Segregation Urged for Unruly Pupils") (7).

Therefore, it is no surprise that most programs for disruptive students are located off-site. In Pennsylvania, for example, 14 of the 21 listed school programs for disruptive youth in 1975 were off-site and two of the seven that were on-site were after regular school hours (8). Howard, in a 1978 publication, reported that the Los Angeles system operated 12 separate school facilities for "delinquent and near delinquent youth" (9). Even many "in-school" suspension programs are located outside the main school building (8, Notes B and C).

Return Rate from Off-Site

Akin to exclusion is the matter of return to the regular school setting. In this regard, off-site educational programs for disruptive adolescents return few. Although the exact number of returnees from the N.Y.C. "600" schools (off-site, day school) program was not consistently reported, it was uniformly low. In its final report, the committee on the "600" schools reported that only 25% of the students who left these day schools were actually sent back to public school (regular or special education) classrooms (10). How many of these youth actually returned is not known. In a 1957 report on the "600" schools program, the return rate to public school and the graduation rate combined to add up to only 12.6% of the total enrolled (11). A still lower figure in this regard was reported by Rhodes. He noted that in 1955, only 7% returned from the "600" schools to regular schools (12).

Other annual return rates of disruptive youth from off-site programs to public school classes are: 18% from the Wallbridge Academy (13), 17% from the Alternative Learning Center (14), 29% from the Individualized Study Center (15), a potential of 37% from the Opportunity School of Sacramento (16), and 10% from a school described in an unpublished study by Irvine (1, Note D). Burchill reported that about 30% of his off-site, work experience students returned to regular classes but that only 11% (17/150) did so successfully (17). In effect, most disruptive adolescent students leaving off-site educational facilities officially drop out, unofficially drop out (become persistent truants), are expelled, or go to other institutions (penal and residential) (Notes E and F).

After looking at much of these data, one could make a good case for the proposition that the closer the treatment program is to the community, the more likely is school re-entry. At one extreme, Safer et al. reported that 80% of seriously disruptive 8th grade students in an on-site intervention setting completed 9th grade in fully mainstreamed classes and entered senior high school the following September (18). At the other extreme are three reports indicating a quite low community re-entry rate for conduct-problem youth following residential treatment. These are as follows: 1) Wolkind and Renton followed 92 disturbed, primarily antisocial, children admitted to a residential facility and found that 68 (74%) were still in institutional care 4 years later (19). 2) Barker found that 8 of 12 (67%) conduct-disordered youth admitted to an off-site treatment setting were in treatment or shelter care institutions 3 to 4 years after discharge (20). 3) Davids et al. reported that one-half of the "passive-aggressive" youths in residential care were still in such institutions 6 years later (21). The on-site and off-site populations in the studies alluded to were no doubt moderately different, but their reported or suggested school return results are at opposite poles.

Cost

Major financial disadvantages of off-site schools are the cost of separate maintenance and the cost of busing. In one nonpublic day school for 65 students, maintenance and administrative costs in 1979 were over $300,000 per year. Special education bus requirements and busing to distant locations can also be quite costly. In one suburban public school system, the average cost of busing for special education students in 1978/79 was nearly $1,500 per student year, over 10 times greater than the average school year cost for busing non-special education students. This is because special education busing requires another adult in addition to the driver, and special features, such as a lift for wheel chairs. Furthermore, these buses usually carry fewer students and travel far greater distances.

The total per capita cost of public off-site programs is often difficult to ascertain in its entirety because it is usually high enough to cause official embarrassment. Most off-site public program administrators give out estimates of the cost by simply adding up staff salaries and dividing by the number of students enrolled. In so doing, they avoid including the following:

1. *Fringe benefits on salaries*   This can be 18%–20% on top of the salary.
2. *Staff development expenses, supplies, travel expenses, and consultant services.*
3. *Extra busing*   In one large, public off-site program, this totaled (in 1978) over $700 per student per school year, nearly five times the average cost of public school busing in N.Y.C. and in Illinois (22).
4. *Cost per student year*   In many off-site day therapeutic programs, students stay an average of 6 months. Since regular programs determine costs "per student year," alternative programs should use the same measure to allow comparison.
5. *Maintenance, depreciation, and overhead*   A separate building for disruptive students is costly to maintain. In 1977, it cost an average of over $200,000 per year in one educational jurisdiction in Maryland to physically maintain one elementary school building.

Overall, off-site facilities are quite expensive. Residential treatment centers cost from $20,000 to $60,000/student year (in 1979/80), day schools cost $9,000 to $15,000/student year, and group homes cost from $7,000 to $12,000/year. These costs compare to the average cost of education in regular classes of $1,700 to $2,300/student year in 1978/79, and $4,000 to $6,000/student year in (on-site) special education classes (23, 24, Notes G and H).

Administrative Management

Directors of nonpublic programs for disruptive youth have the advantage of *not* having to deal with the restrictions imposed by teachers' unions. This is administratively advantageous because: 1) teacher union clauses frequently provide options for the faculty to exclude belligerent students from their classes over the heads of school-based administrators, 2) teacher union clauses spell out tenure and strongly limit an administrator's freedom to fire, and 3) salaries negotiated by teacher unions add appreciably to the cost of educational programs. In two nonpublic, off-site facilities, for example, teachers in 1979/80 were paid $9,000–$14,000 per school year (not $11,000–$25,000) and aides $4,000–$6,000 (not $5,000–$11,000). The salary fringe was kept as low as 7% (not 20%) and the staff was paid on the basis of a 180-day (not a 210-day) school year.

Being off-site provides program administrators the benefit of not having to deal with a majority of on-site teachers who (for the most part understandably) want serious behavior-problem youth excluded from their classes. Being both off-site and nonpublic gives program directors the greatest flexibility and the least programmatic restrictions. Managers of such programs have the freedom to sort out and assemble a cohesive, sympathetic, and like-minded staff who are united by common goals.

The major disadvantage faced by all off-site program administrators is that they generally encounter substantial resistance when they attempt to return their wards to regular education, on-site classes. In attempting this return, nonpublic program directors experience the greatest difficulty.

Enrollment Bias

Enrollment biases in the alternative educational placement of deviant students, for the most part, follow socioeconomic lines. The often preferred and costliest substitutive education programs (e.g., residential treatment) are utilized more frequently by the middle and upper class. The less desirable programs (e.g., EMR classes) take a disproportionate number of poor and minority children. Browne et al. (25) found that public schools had the poorest children, day schools had the middle group, and residential centers had the richest. Conners likewise reported a significant positive relationship between residential treatment and high socioeconomic status (26). In Maryland, in 1978, nearly 40% of all excess cost funds for off-site special education placements were given to children from the wealthiest county (Montgomery) (27), which has only one-eighth of the state's population. In Massachusetts, Weatherly reported that "affluent parents are more successful in placing their children at public expense in the more costly private residential and day schools" (28). In

New York state, the Fleishman report of 1972 noted that "comparatively fewer children in minority groups were receiving the benefits of state funding for residential special schooling" (29).

This should come as no surprise. Those who are well placed, well-to-do, and well educated get there first when extra public funds are available for the taking. The aspect of class privilege in special education funding of residential programs seems to be true nationwide (30, Note I).

Enrollment in off-site programs that are viewed as undesirable is overrepresented by minorities and the poor. In New York City, 15 day schools were set aside for seriously disruptive and/or expelled students in the "600" schools program. The program served over 2,000 students/year and ran from 1946 to 1967. Referral to the program was made primarily by the principal. In the early 1960s, when over 50% of the New York City public school enrollment was white (3), 87% of the "600" schools enrollment was nonwhite (28% Puerto Rican, 57% black, and 2% other) (31). Another very similar off-site public day school program for expelled students is the Opportunity School program of California, which began in the 1960s. Sacramento's Opportunity School population was 65% black and Chicano in 1971, when over two-thirds of the public school enrollment was white (16).

In juvenile justice programs, also, the most undesirable placements (e.g., training school) have a disproportionate number of minority and poor children, while the more desirable ones (e.g., forestry camps) have a far greater percentage of white and middle-class children (32, 33).

Home teaching, not often a preferred off-site educational program, is frequently used for undesirable, disruptive students. When it is prescribed for emotional-behavioral reasons, disadvantaged students are overrepresented. In New York City from 1972–1974, those on home teaching who were placed because of "emotional" disturbances were more often poor, black, and male (34). Furthermore, 75% of those placed on home teaching for emotional disturbance remained on home teaching "in spite of academic gains" compared to 23% of physically (health) impaired (34).

Overall, the greatest overrepresentation of minority groups and the disadvantaged occurs in educably mentally retarded (EMR) special education classes (26, 35, 36). In Utica, New York, for example, blacks comprised 16% of the school population in the early 1970s but 41% of students in EMR classes (35). Generally, whites with prominent academic difficulties appear to be selectively assigned to learning-disabled classes and blacks to EMR classes (37, 38). In England, a somewhat similar pattern appears to exist. West Indian immigrant children are overrepresented fivefold in special programs for the educationally "subnormal" (39).

Effectiveness

Usually, the immediate behavioral results of programs for disruptive youth are on the positive side as long as the child is in treatment, but the gains made during treatment dissipate by the time of moderate to long-term follow-up. This discouraging long-term outcome appears to be equally true for off-site and on-site programs. Since there is little reported on the mid- and long-term outcomes of conduct disordered youth from day therapeutic centers, the off-site outcomes reported here are exclusively from residential (live-in, off-site) programs.

During the period of off-site placement, residential programs have generally reported that their wards have experienced beneficial changes in conduct and motivation. Wahler et al. reported "large behavioral gains in residence" (40). Braukmann et al. documented the increased diligence and responsibility of youth while at Achievement Place (41), and Davidson and Wolfred reported that at 3 and 9 months, the behavioral treatment group in residential treatment behaved better in the classroom than did controls (42).

One would expect that restrictive residential or group home supervision would also decrease the delinquency rate while youth are in residence and this beneficial result is supported by data (43–46). The mild decrease in delinquency during placement represents a major advantage of off-site over on-site programs for disruptive adolescents. Once these youth leave the institution, however, their delinquency rate climbs again essentially to the rate of the "untreated" comparison group. Such results have been reported by every off-site program (41–46), and thus, in the long run, both off-site and on-site programs (see Chapters 4, 11, and 13) are generally comparable in their failure to effect a reduction in delinquency.

The long-term effect of residential placement on nondelinquent, but aggressive behaviors also appears to be negligible. Wahler reports that before the end of the first year (after termination of residential treatment), 25 of 30 (83%) behaviorally deviant children "regressed" to their presenting status (40). Wolkind and Renton found that 24 of 27 antisocial youth were judged to have similar problems 4 years after entry into residential care (19). Similarly, Groeschel reported that 3 years after residential treatment, which lasted an average of 31 months, 10 of 16 aggressive youth (63%) were rated as having a very poor behavioral adjustment and 4 others (25%) as having a poor adjustment (47, Note J).

The effectiveness of both off-site and on-site programs for disruptive youth is thus relatively good while disruptive adolescents receive structured intervention, but at best marginal at the time of follow-up. In possibly the only controlled assessment of the therapeutic effectiveness of residential versus community care for behavior problem youth, the findings clearly favored the community treatment effort during and 2 years following treatment. However, the 2-year follow-up findings were still moderately discouraging for both groups (48).

BEHAVIORAL VERSUS NONBEHAVIORAL

Compared to other social system treatments, behavioral management programs are generally more systematic and data-based. During the 1970s behavioral therapy approaches became the predominant psychosocial treatment intervention used by American psychologist investigators. Of the five programs for disruptive students reported in some detail in this book, three are behavioral in orientation; understandably, they were begun in the 1970s. Not surprisingly, the two nonbehavioral projects described in this book were begun in the 1960s.

Encouraging short-term results have been reported for *all* intervention approaches for disruptive students, perhaps because in large measure, dedicated, able teachers (49) and administrators contribute so much to outcome (Note K). Nonetheless, behavioral programs as a group produce relatively better short-term results (43, 50-53).

This is probably because they: 1) pinpoint goals, monitor behavior, and channel the program's energies exclusively in specific directions, 2) emphasize the development of motivation, a vital issue with disruptive students, and 3) provide more structure, a weakness of which will risk program disaster when disruptive adolescents are involved.

After termination of all program interventions, the benefits fade. This is true for both behavioral and nonbehavioral programs and for psychosocial change efforts generally. The loss of the improvement gains for student conduct is a fairly rapid phenomenon (51, 54, 55), usually a matter of a few weeks or months. Comparatively, the decline in program benefits in achievement is slower (43, 54, 56), usually a matter of a year or so.

VOCATIONAL VERSUS ACADEMIC

Because most disruptive adolescents do not graduate from or do well in secondary school, it is reasonable to view a part-time vocational curriculum as most feasible for them. It is hoped that with work training and experience they will be better prepared for later employment (Note L).

Although it is likely that school-based work experience could benefit some disruptive youth, the current evidence does not support the view that it is generally useful. In the most comprehensively described and intensively evaluated program covering this issue, Ahlstrom and Havighurst (57) found that not only were the relative results of a 3-year, work-study, secondary school program for disruptive adolescents discouraging (in terms of high school graduation and delinquency prevention), but also that *only* 30% of the parents of youth in this program expressed positive views on it.

Other reports have been as discouraging. Longstreth et al. (58) found paying jobs in the afternoon for 75 potential drop-outs during their high school years and had almost completely negative results in comparison to the outcome of controls. Robin (59), Burchill (17), Hackler (60), Hackler and Hagen (61), and Jeffery and Jeffery (62) all reported negative results for adolescent work experience programs in relation to school and GED training outcomes. Furthermore, Jeffery cites three additional vocational program studies for disadvantaged youth with negative school and/or community adjustment outcomes (63), and Sabatino cites four others showing that vocational training had no effect on recidivism (64, Note M).

The Jeffery and Jeffery report is cited often because the authors did not find a decrease in delinquency even when students were successfully supported to complete their work- and school-related objectives (62). Those youth who completed their work experience and obtained their GED had a surprisingly higher rate of delinquency than those who dropped out. Furthermore, academic progress in the GED preparation program had no relationship to passing the GED exam. Hackler and Hagen found equally discouraging results; they reported that 14- and 15-year-old boys in a work experience program showed a relative increase in delinquency recidivism during the 4-year postintervention follow-up period compared to the group that had received teaching machine training and compared to a no-treatment control group (61, Note N).

Countering these overwhelmingly negative results are three reports with positive outcomes resulting from work experience programs for disruptive adolescents. A report by Shore and Massimo, which indicates positive results from vocational counseling and work experience, covers the evaluation of only 10 experimental and 10 control youth (65). Another by Mills and Walter, supporting the merits of vocational programming, has a serious design weakness, an inequitable control population (66). A third, the study by O'Dell, indicates a significant decrease in recidivism for the work experience youth at 3 and 6 months—compared to casework treatment controls—but not at 9 months (67).

Thus, the outcome of vocational intervention for seriously disaffected and disruptive adolescents remains largely negative. There is, in fact, some evidence to suggest that disruptive youth as a group do better when the curriculum is academically rather than vocationally weighted (57, 61). One could explain this (post hoc) by noting that high schools are best at and primarily set up to teach academic courses rather than provide work experience.

NOTES

Note A. Highfield and Pinsent point out that the greatest agreement among teachers asked to evaluate reforms for disruptive students was for more special schools for them (68).

Teachers often support their recommendation for exclusion on the grounds that it is very difficult to successfully engineer a group instructional format for 30 students in a classroom when there are one or more seriously and persistently disruptive students present. The argument has merit and cannot be answered simply by suggesting that the teacher individualize her instruction. However, expanding off-site educational placement is about as far-sighted a solution to this problem as building more training schools for delinquents.

Note B. The same resistance to community placement of mental patients and to neighborhood group home placement of delinquents exists to keeping unruly students in regular schools. Who wants them in our neighborhood, in our children's classes, in our school?

Note C. The number of youth in residential, shelter care, and penal institutions in the U.S. in 1972 was estimated to be one-half million by the Bureau of the Census. This number represents about 1% of American youth. In breaking down this total, Hobbs estimates that it includes 150,000 delinquent youth in detention centers and training schools, 80,000 mentally retarded in residential settings, and 100,000 emotionally ill children in live-in treatment facilities (69).

Note D. Follow-up studies of the rate of return from off-site programs for emotionally disturbed (ED) children yield surprisingly similar results. Stotsky reported that 31% of ED youngsters "successfully completed schooling after placement in a residential school for an average of 27 months" (70), and Gold and Reisman reported that over a 4-year period, 11 of 48 (23%) ED children admitted to a day therapeutic facility returned to regular classes (71).

Note E. Expulsion of disruptive youth from off-site special schools and from on-site special education classes is by no means a rarity. In England, 32% of all expelled students in one school district were expelled from special schools (72). In a Maryland off-site program for expelled students, the re-expulsion rate was 17% over an 8-month period (73). A relatively lower but still high rate of exclusion has been reported for special education (on-site) classes. In Los Angeles, 15% of all expulsions were from on-site EMR classes, a rate over six times that expected by their enrollment numbers (74).

Note F. On-site, self-contained special education classes in elementary schools have a higher rate of re-entry to regular classes than do off-site facilities. Their rate of return to regular classes is approximately 30%–45%, although their successful return rate is about one-third to one-half of this (75, 76).

Note G. Archbishop Sheehan, commenting on the $30,000 annual per capita cost of residential treatment in Boys Town, said in 1978, "It is certainly within the standards of child care institutions across the country" (77). A similar estimate is given by the New York State Director of Probation for the cost of training school/year/detainee (78).

Note H. Personnel costs tend to be highest when programs are separate and small. One day-therapeutic (off-site) program with a student enrollment of 20 had, in 1976, a full-time staff of 9 and a part-time staff of 2. The full-time staff included 3 teachers, 2 aides, an administrator, a psychologist, a social worker, and a secretary. Another off-site day school reported 18 faculty positions for 70 students, a 1:4 ratio, and still another had 15 faculty for 95 students (79). In respect to teacher-student ratios, larger programs probably are more economical. Horan reported a staff of 240 teachers for 2,045 students in the "600" schools day school program, nearly a 1:9 teacher-pupil ratio (80).

Note I. A general inequity in funds for public education exists in most areas of the United States. For example, in 1977 in New York state, one school district spent $8,092 annually per pupil whereas, at the other extreme, another spent only $1,054 (81).

Note J. Residential treatment centers are seldom a popular placement for those sent there. In an extensive study of the issue, Bush found that to a prominent degree "children living in institutions at the time they were interviewed were less comfortable, loved, looked after, trusted, cared about and wanted than children in any other form of surrogate care." Approximately 70% of children placed in group homes, foster care, and with relatives wished to stay in their placement versus 30% of those in institutions (82).

Note K. The relative influence of teacher support versus tangible behavioral incentives on student behavior is not clear at this time. Broden et al. found token reinforcement to have more powerful effects on student behavior than teacher attention (51), but Marlowe et al. found positive, selective teacher attention contributed more to on-task behavior improvement than tangible reinforcers (49). Understandably, Fo and O'Donnell found these effects to be additive; they also reported that the addition of a material reinforcer (money) was significantly more effective in producing behavior change than social reinforcement alone (83).

Note L. School drop-outs have a very high rate of unemployment in their teens. At age 16–17, their unemployment rate is 4–5 times that of adults (84). In Italy, youth unemployment is said to be 9 times the adult rate (85). In China, the unemployment rate for youth is reported to be over 15% (86). The problem is being viewed so seriously in Belgium that the government provides private employers a subsidy of $800 for every young employee hired (87).

In the United States, the rate of unemployment of youth—relative to adults—has risen sharply over the last 50 years. In the 1930s, it was only 1.5 times the adult rate (88). In the 1960s it rose to 3 times the adult rate (88). In 1979, it stood at 4 to 5 times the adult rate in New York City (89).

Note M. Mattick, summarizing the 6-year multimillion dollar comprehensive YMCA "Action in the Streets" project (1960–1966), writes discouragingly, "Despite the successful efforts of staff in finding jobs, in returning school dropouts, and intervening in formal legal processes, the youth employment rate remained about the same level; the school dropout rate increased slightly, and the arrest rate in the project area increased over time, with a lesser proportion of them being disposed of by station adjustment" (90).

Note N. Most disruptive youth cannot be enticed to stay on the job even though the pay is good. Jeffery and Jeffery (62) reported that paying $20–$40/week in the late 1960s wasn't enough to motivate 75% of the youth to stick to the job and continue GED classes. Amos likewise reported that most of his paid inner city, work-experience youth dropped out within 2 months (91).

Students' quitting their jobs creates practical problems for the work experience teacher who has to round up private employers to take a chance on these youth. When irresponsible youth are placed on these jobs, work-experience placement positions soon disappear.

REFERENCES

1. Nelson, C. M., & Kauffman, J. M. Educational programming for secondary school delinquent and maladjusted pupils. *Behavior Disorders,* 1977, *2,* 102–113.
2. Gallagher, J. J. The special education contract for mildly handicapped children. *Exceptional Children,* 1972, *32,* 527–535.
3. Budnick, A., & Andreacchi, J. Day schools for disturbed boys. In P. H. Berkowitz & E. P. Rothman (Eds.), *Public education for disturbed children in New York City.* Springfield, Ill.: Charles C Thomas, 1967, pp. 57–77.
4. Abrahamsen, D. *The psychology of crime.* New York: Columbia University Press, 1967.
5. Donahue, G. T., & Nichtern, S. *Teaching the troubled child.* New York: Free Press, 1968.

6. Long, N. J., Morse, W. C., & Newman, R. G. Postscript. In N. J. Long, W. C. Morse, & R. G. Newman (Eds.), *Conflict in the classroom,* 2nd Ed. Belmont, Cal.: Wadsworth Publishing Company, 1971, p. 551.

7. Segregation urged for unruly pupils. *New York Times,* April 1, 1979, p. 6-E.

8. *Alternative disciplinary programs and practices in Pennsylvania schools.* Harrisburg, Pa.: Pennsylvania Department of Education, April 1977.

9. Howard, E. R. *School discipline desk book.* West Nyack, N.Y.: Parker Publishing Company, 1978.

10. 600 Schools: Yesterday, today and tomorrow. Committee Study 6/24-2/65, New York City Public Schools, 1965, Mimeo.

11. MacIver, R. M. *Juvenile delinquency evaluation project of the city of New York,* Interim Report No. III, The "600" Day Schools. New York: New York City Public Schools, April 1957.

12. Rhodes, W. C. Delinquency and community action. In H. C. Quay (Ed.), *Juvenile delinquency: Research and theory.* Princeton, N.J.: Van Nostrand, 1965, p. 242.

13. Walizer, M. H., Erickson, E. L., Bournazos, K., & Sonnad, S. R. *The Wallbridge Academy: Final evaluation report.* Grand Rapids, Mi., 1975.

14. 20% of disruptive pupils readjust. *Baltimore Sun,* August 4, 1978, p. C-6.

15. Suspensions and expulsions: Current trends in school policies. Arlington, Va.: National School Public Relations Association, 1976.

16. Parker, H. K., & Masuda, R. Opportunity schools. *NASSP Bulletin,* April 1971, *55* (354), 37–55.

17. Burchill, G. W. *Work-study program for alienated youth: A casebook.* Chicago: Science Research Associates, 1962.

18. Safer, D. J., Heaton, R. C., & Parker, F. C. A behavioral program for disruptive junior high school students: Results and follow-up. *Journal of Abnormal Child Psychology,* 1981, *9,* 483–494.

19. Wolkind, S., & Renton, G. Psychiatric disorders in children in long-term residential care: A follow-up study. *British Journal of Psychiatry,* 1979, *135,* 129–135.

20. Barker, P. The results of inpatient care. In P. Barker (Ed.), *The residential psychiatric treatment of children.* London: Crosby, 1974, pp. 294–309.

21. Davids, A., Ryan, R., & Salvatore, P. D. Effectiveness of residential treatment for psychotic and other disturbed children. *American Journal of Orthopsychiatry,* 1968, *38,* 469–475.

22. School bus costs highest in nation, Albany audit says. *New York Times,* April 30, 1978, p. 44.

23. Venetoulis budget unites county factions. *Baltimore Sun,* January 16, 1978, p. C-2.

24. Shanker, A. Special education needs more U.S. dollars. *New York Times,* January 18, 1978, p. E-7.

25. Browne, T., Stotsky, B. A., & Eichorn, J. A. A selective comparison of psychological, developmental, social, and academic factors among emotionally disturbed children in three treatment settings. *Child Psychiatry and Human Development,* 1977, *7,* 231–242.

26. Connors, J. E. *Special education needs for emotionally disturbed children.* Boston, Mass.: Department of Mental Health, 1969.
27. *State of the state: Special education in Maryland.* Baltimore: Maryland State Department of Education, September 1, 1979.
28. Weatherley, R. A. *Reforming special education: Policy implication from state level to street level.* Cambridge, Mass.: MIT Press, 1979.
29. *New York State Commission on quality, cost, and financing of elementary and secondary education.* Fleishman Report. Albany, N.Y.: State Education Department, 1972, Chapter 9.
30. Wooden, K. *Weeping in the playtime of others.* New York: McGraw-Hill, 1976.
31. Mackler, B. A report on the "600" schools: Dilemmas, problems and solutions. In R. A. Dentler, B. Mackler, & M. E. Warchauer (Eds.), *The urban R's: Race relations as the problem in urban education.* New York: Praeger, 1967, pp. 288–302.
32. Taliaferro, P. *Children in need of supervision.* Report No. 3. Baltimore: Citizens' League of Baltimore, April 1979.
33. Wheeler, G. R. *Counter-deterrence: A report on juvenile sentencing and effects of prisonization.* Chicago: Nelson-Hall, 1978.
34. Baker, J. W. Locus of conrol: Characteristics of a homebound population. *Exceptional Children,* 1978. *45,* 208–210.
35. Block, E. E., Covill-Servo, J., & Rosen, M. *Failing students—failing school: A study of drop out and discipline in New York State.* Rochester, N.Y.: New York Civil Liberties Union, April 1978.
36. Slade, M. Bias in labeling the handicapped. *Psychology Today,* October 1978, *12,* 31–32.
37. Franks, D. J. Ethnic and social status characteristics of children in EMR and LD classes. *Exceptional Children,* 1971, *37,* 537–538.
38. Kealy, J., & McLeod, J. Learning disability and socioeconomic status. *Journal of Learning Disabilities,* 1976, *9,* 596–599.
39. Townsend, H. E. R. *Immigrant pupils in England.* London: National Foundation for Educational Research, 1971.
40. Wahler, R. G., Leske, G., & Rogers, E. S. The family: A deviance support system for oppositional children. In L. A. Hamerlynck (Ed.), *Behavioral systems for the developmentally disabled. I. School and family environments.* New York: Brunner/Mazel, 1979, pp. 102–127.
41. Braukmann, C. J., Kirgin, K. A., & Wolf, M. M. *Achievement place: The researcher's perspective.* Paper read at the American Psychological Association Annual Meeting, Washington, D.C., 1976.
42. Davidson, W. S., & Wolfred, T. R. Evaluation of a community-based behavior modification program for prevention of delinquency: The failure of success. *Community Mental Health Journal,* 1977, *13,* 296–306.
43. Jones, R. R. First findings for the national evaluation of the teaching family model. Presented to the National Teaching Family Association, Boys' Town, Nebraska, October 25, 1978.
44. Hackler, J. C., & Hagen, J. L. Cited in M. R. Haskell & L. Yablonsky, *Juvenile delinquency,* 2nd Ed. Chicago: Rand McNally, 1978, p. 12.
45. Clarke, R. V., & Cornish, D. B. The effectiveness of residential treatment for delinquents. In L. A. Hersov & M. Berger (Eds.), *Aggression and antisocial behaviour in childhood and adolescence.* Oxford: Pergamon, 1978, pp. 143–159.

46. Empey, L. T., & Erickson, M. L. *The Provo experiment: Evaluating community control of delinquency.* Lexington, Mass.: Lexington Books, 1974.

47. Groeschel, B. J. Social adjustment after residential treatment. In D. F. Ricks, A. Thomas, and M. Roff (Eds.), *Life history research in psychopathology* (Vol. 3). Minneapolis: University of Minneapolis Press, 1974, pp. 259-274.

48. Winberg, B. G., Bialer, I., Kupietz, S., Botti, E., & Balka, E. B. Home vs. hospital care of children with behavior disorders. *Archives of General Psychiatry*, 1980, *37*, 413-418.

49. Marlowe, R. H., Madsen, C. H., Bowen, C. E., Rearden, R. C., & Logue, P. E. Severe classroom behavior problems: Teachers or counselors. *Journal of Applied Behavior Analysis*, 1978, *11*, 53-66.

50. Bailey, J. S., Wolf, M. M., & Phillips, E. L. Home-based reinforcement and the modification of pre-delinquent classroom behavior. *Journal of Applied Behavioral Analysis*, 1970, *3*, 223-233.

51. Broden, M., Hall, R. V., Dunlap, A., & Clark, R. Effect of teacher affection and a token reinforcement system in a junior high school special education class. *Exceptional Children*, 1970, *36*, 341-349.

52. Friedman, R. M., Filipczak, J., & Fiordaliso, R. Within school generalization of the preparation through response education programs (PREP) academic project. *Behavior Therapy*, 1977, *8*, 986-995.

53. Heaton, R. C., Safer, D. J., Allen, R. P., Spinnato, N. C., & Prumo, F. M. A motivational environment for behaviorally deviant junior high school students. *Journal of Abnormal Child Psychology*, 1976, *4*, 263-275.

54. Kent, R. N., & O'Leary, K. D. A controlled evaluation of behavior modification with conduct problem children. *Journal of Consulting and Clinical Psychology*, 1976, *44*, 586-596.

55. O'Leary, S. G., & Schneider, M. R. Special class placement of conduct problem children. *Exceptional Children*, 1977, *44*, 24-30.

56. Glavin, J. P. Behaviorally oriented resource rooms: A follow-up. *Journal of Special Education*, 1974, *8*, 337-347.

57. Ahlstrom, W. M., & Havighurst, R. J. *400 losers: Delinquent boys in high school.* San Francisco: Jossey-Bass, 1971.

58. Longstreth, L. E., Shanley, F. J., & Rice, R. E. Experimental evaluation of a high school program for potential dropouts. *Journal of Educational Psychology*, 1964, *55*, 228-236.

59. Robin, G. D. Anti-poverty programs and delinquency. *Journal of Criminal Law, Criminology, and Police Science*, 1966, *60*, 323-331.

60. Hackler, J. C. Boys, blisters and behavior: The impact of a work program in an urban central area. *Journal of Research in Crime and Delinquency*, 1966, *3*, 155-164.

61. Hackler, J. C., & Hagen, J. L. Work and teaching machines as delinquency prevention tools: A four-year follow-up. *Social Service Review*, 1975, *49*, 92-106.

62. Jeffery, C. R., & Jeffery, I. A. Delinquents and dropouts: An experimental program in behavior change. *Canadian Journal of Correction*, 1970, *12*, 47-58.

63. Jeffery, C. R. *Crime prevention through environmental design.* Beverly Hills: Sage Publications, 1977.

64. Sabatino, D. A. Institutionalization: History, influence and the problems of recidivism. In D. A. Sabatino & A. J. Mauser (Eds.), *Specialized education in today's public schools.* Boston: Allyn & Bacon, 1978, pp. 181–211.

65. Shore, M. F., & Massimo, J. After ten years: A follow-up study of comprehensive vocationally oriented psychotherapy. *American Journal of Orthopsychiatry,* 1973, *43,* 128–132.

66. Mills, C. M., & Walter, T. L. Reducing juvenile delinquency: A behavioral employment program. In J. S. Stumphauser (Ed.), *Progress in behavior therapy with delinquents,* 2nd Ed. Springfield, Ill.: Charles C Thomas, 1979, pp. 287–301.

67. O'Dell, B. N. Accelerating entry into the opportunity structure: A sociologically-based treatment for delinquent youth. *Sociology and Social Research,* 1974, *58,* 312–317.

68. Highfield, M. E., & Pinsent, A. *A survey of rewards and punishments in schools.* London: National Foundation for Educational Research, 1952.

69. Hobbs, N. *The futures of children.* San Francisco: Jossey-Bass, 1975.

70. Stotsky, B. A., Browne, T., & Philbrick W. A. A study of outcome of special schooling of emotionally disturbed children. *Child Psychiatry and Human Development,* 1974, *4,* 131–150.

71. Gold, J., & Reisman, J. An outcome study of a day treatment school in a community mental health center. Paper presented at the Annual Meeting of the American Psychiatric Association, San Francisco, May 1970.

72. York, R., Heron, J. M., & Wolff, S. Exclusion from school. *Journal of Child Psychology and Psychiatry,* 1972, *13,* 259–266.

73. Burlingame, K. Personal communication, 1980.

74. Lyons, D. J., & Powers, V. Follow-up study of elementary school children exempted from Los Angeles City schools during 1960/1961. *Exceptional Children,* 1963, *30,* 155–162.

75. Morse, W. C., Cutler, R. L., Fink, A. H. Public school classes for the emotionally handicapped: A research analysis. In N. J. Long, W. C. Morse, & R. G. Newman (Eds.), *Conflict in the classroom,* 2nd Ed. Belmont, Cal.: Wadsworth Publishing Company, 1971, pp. 539–547.

76. Koppitz, E. M. *Children with learning disabilities: A five year follow-up study.* New York: Grune & Stratton, 1971.

77. Archbishop denies Boys' Town overcharges. *Wilmington Morning News,* November 24, 1978, p. 6.

78. Silver, R. R. Restitution plan seeks to cut juvenile jail terms. *New York Times,* March 11, 1979, p. C-35.

79. Tobin, D. D. Overcoming crude behavior in a "600" school. In N. J. Long, W. C. Morse, & R. E. Newman (Eds.), *Conflict in the classroom,* 2nd Ed. Belmont, Cal.: Wadsworth Publishing Company, 1971, pp. 465–468.

80. Horan, E. M. Special education programs in New York City public school system. In M. V. Jones (Ed.), *Special education programs within the United States.* Springfield, Ill.: Charles C Thomas, 1968, pp. 311–314.

81. Shanker, A. School finance reform demands debate. *New York Times,* April 22, 1979, p. E-7.

82. Bush, M. Institutions for dependent and neglected children: Therapeutic option or last resort? *American Journal of Orthopsychiatry,* 1980, *50,* 239–255.

83. Fo, W. S. O., & O'Donnell, C. R. The buddy system: Relationship and contingency conditions in a community intervention program for youth with professionals as behavior change agents. *Journal of Consulting and Clinical Psychology,* 1974, *42,* 163-169.

84. Schreiber, D. Work experience programs. In W. W. Wattenberg (Ed.), *Social deviancy among youth.* Chicago: University of Chicago Press, 1966, pp. 280-314.

85. Europe hunting jobs for its youth. *Baltimore Sun,* March 1, 1978, p. A-2.

86. Parks, M. China starts huge jobs program. *Baltimore Sun,* July 30, 1979, pp. 1-2.

87. Raskin, A. H. The system keeps the young waiting. *New York Times,* December 5, 1976, section 4, p. 1.

88. Evans, R. N. *Foundations of vocational education.* Columbus, Ohio: Charles Merrill Company, 1971, pp. 16-17.

89. Shanker, A. Unemployed teens: Target of U.S. $. *New York Times,* January 6, 1980, p. E-9.

90. James, H. *Children in trouble.* New York: David McKay Company, 1970, pp. 236-237 & 252.

91. Amos, W. E. Job adjustment problems of delinquent, minority group youth. *Vocational Guidance Quarterly,* Winter 1964, *13,* 87-90.

INTRODUCTION TO CHAPTER 6

This chapter is not written by a special educator and, therefore, suffers from some limitations in depth. However, an outsider has potential advantages that can, in part, offset this disadvantage. The outsider may be more free to reject assumptions that are too readily accepted by practitioners in the field. He also may have a broader perspective.

What may upset special educational practitioners even more about this chapter is its irreverence for some of the present categories within special education. It is obviously necessary for authors of special education texts, high level school administrators, and lawmakers to present fairly tight definitions of learning, behavior, emotional and intellectual handicaps. Nonetheless, in 1980, the definitions and incidence levels of the "minor" special education handicaps are so variable from state to state (1, 2), and so many children assigned to a particular handicapping category do not fit the defining criteria (3–6), that the author has chosen to use "working" more so than "accepted" definitions and has not hesitated to overlap categories as he deems fit.

1. Brewer, G. D., & Kakalik, J. S. *Handicapped children: Strategies for improving services.* New York: McGraw-Hill, 1979.
2. Hirschonen, A., & Heller, G. G. Programs for adolescents with behavior disorders: The state of the art. *Journal of Special Education,* 1979, *13,* 275–281.
3. Garrison, M., & Hammill, D. D. Who are the retarded? *Exceptional Children,* 1971, *38,* 13–20.
4. Slade, M. Bias in labelling the handicapped. *Psychology Today,* October 1978, *12,* 31–32.

5. Werner, E. E., & Smith, R. R. *Kauai's Children Come of Age.* Honolulu, University of Hawaii Press, 1977.
6. Smith, M. D., Coleman, J. M., Dokecki, P. R., & Davis, E. E. Intellectual characteristics of school labeled learning disabled children. *Exceptional Children, 1977, 43,* 352–357.

6

Special education and programs for behavior problem youth

Daniel J. Safer

During the first half of the 20th century, public special education primarily served handicapped youth with obvious intellectual and sensorimotor limitations. Beginning in the early 1960s, special education added separate classes for learning-disabled (LD) and emotionally disturbed (ED) children. The number of LD students given special education services was small in the 1960s, but it rapidly expanded to include up to 8% of some school populations by 1980. Enrollment of ED students in special education programs was and remains miniscule by comparison.

SPECIAL EDUCATION AND BEHAVIOR DISORDERED STUDENTS

Generally accepted special education criteria for the identification of LD students include primarily developmental, achievement, and perceptual delays and deficits. The criteria used to identify ED students include mainly evidence of a thought disorder or gross deficiencies in coping skills. Regardless of those formal criteria, however, the major impetus for referral from regular to both LD and ED classes is serious misbehavior. Consequently, most LD and ED children selected for special classes not only fit special education criteria, but also have prominent behavior disorders (BD).

111

It was not that special educators wanted BD youth that caused so many to be enrolled in special education classes. Rather, special educators were less averse to them than were regular educators and were unable to reject most such referrals successfully. After all, most seriously BD children have bona fide LD and/or ED features (2, 3).

Before the 1950s, most nonretarded BD youth were sent to vocational schools during their teenage years. The referral process could have remained that way had not two circumstances intervened. One was that vocational schools became more interested in educating capable tradespeople and technicians; the other was that special educators received a broader mandate and more funds. With the rejection of disciplinary-problem youth by vocational schools and the wider acceptance of the less obviously handicapped by special education, special educators took an increasing responsibility in this area.

When PL 94-142 (Education for All Handicapped Children Act) was written in the early 1970s, the final version of the bill was worded so as to sort out special education services from compensatory educational assistance to disadvantaged students (Note A) and to control the number of chronic behavior problem referrals. Indeed, allowing more disruptive youth ready access to special education classes and services would clearly add unpleasant pressures to already over-committed special education teachers and aides. Consequently, under PL 94-142, BD was not made a bona fide special education category. If the BD child also had LD, he or she could be referred (as had been the practice) with learning disabilities being the handicapping condition. An alternative approach was to assign the BD child the diagnostic label "severely emotionally disturbed" (ED) and in that way qualify him for special education. However, the ED classification could only be applied if the disorder were serious, persistent and marked, such as in the case of childhood schizophrenia, the specific example mentioned in the law.

While it is obvious that most regular education, secondary school staff as a group have demonstrated little flexibility and have had little success in managing and teaching BD youth, special educators have not done appreciably better with their BD/LD or BD/ED students. Furthermore, special education as a separate educational subdivision has serious limitations in dealing independently with this problem.

The entire issue of the role of special education with disruptive adolescents is complicated by fairly rigid patterns of special education services, questions of efficacy in their interventions, often ill-fitting descriptions of educational handicap, and oft-times prominent degrees of overlap and selectivity in special educational practice. Consequently, an attempt will be made in the next four sections of this chapter to review these matters briefly before going further.

SPECIAL EDUCATION: PLACEMENT AND METHODS

Self-Contained Classes

For handicapped youth (excluding the speech-impaired), self-contained classes have been and remain a bulwark for special education services (4). Under optimal conditions, these classes provide shelter and some temporary support for the remediation of learning disabilities. On the negative side, however, they customarily offer—for involved students—no relative advantages educationally or socially over regular classes and they have serious maintenance drawbacks.

The evidence from the mental retardation literature clearly suggests that educably mentally retarded (EMR) children do as well or somewhat better academically and as well socially in regular classes (5–13). Likewise, for ED (and BD) youth, special class on-site placement—although popular with referring teachers (14–16)—is of marginal value academically (17, 18) and has no moderate- to long-term benefits (18, 19). Furthermore, re-entry to regular classes after a self-contained (on-site) experience is frequently problematic. In a 3-year follow-up study by Morse et al. (19) only 46% of ED (special class) students returned to regular classes. Other 4- to 5-year outcome studies of elementary school special education ED classes also note that a total of only 24% to 56% of the enrolled students return to regular classes (20, 21).

The return rate from special class (on-site) placement for LD children is similar. Although these students are somewhat more likely to return to regular classes from self-contained classes than from off-site programs, the five-year return total is only about 30% (22). Furthermore, in the long-term follow-up of LD special class students by Koppitz (22), the number who returned "fairly successfully" to regular classes was only 17%.

Resource Rooms

The outcome of behaviorally oriented resource rooms has been reported to be more successful than the outcome of special class placement in regard to achievement and social behavior (23, 24), but not in regard to the maintenance of gains (25).

Remediation of Learning Disabilities

Remediation efforts for LD students have consistently been reported to cause temporary gains, but no long-term benefits (26). Some approaches have never established their merit (e.g., perceptual training and prescriptive teaching) (5, 27–29), whereas other approaches have frequently demonstrated comparative advantages (e.g., individualized instruction (30, 31) and task-analytic remedial efforts focusing on improving academic skills (32, 33)).

LEARNING DISABILITY: DEFINITIONS AND EXCLUSIONS

Categorical Boundaries

In their criteria for learning disability, some states emphasize low academic achievement, requiring a 50% to 65% achievement deficit relative to age expected levels (40, 41). This is undoubtedly the most useful single measure. Other states also require an early onset (or developmental evidence) for the determination of learning disability (Note B). Although developmental data are obviously useful in assessing the total clinical picture, these data are not of primary diagnostic value. For example, in a study by Satz et al. (42), a full 39% of children with only a mild reading delay when tested in the second grade were judged to be "severely reading disabled" when tested again in the sixth grade.

Still other identifying requirements stress perceptual limitations as necessary for the diagnosis of learning disability (34). Whereas perceptual data can be relatively clear cut, their value in the identification of learning disability is limited because the correlation between perceptual delays and academic deficits is quite low (5, 31, 43, 44). Furthermore, the existence of an earlier perceptual deficit becomes characteristically marginal in the teens (45, 46), whereas the academic deficit usually remains.

In an attempt to resolve these dilemmas, some professionals require multiple kinds of evidence to define learning disability. Others, as it has been suggested, feel that prominent academic underachievement should be the primary guide. Because of this sizable lack of agreement, the upper boundary for learning disability is quite fluid and many marginal cases exist. Some experts further complicate the picture by separating reading disability from learning disability (34, 35) (a practice which has only minimal utilitarian value (36)), and mild mental retardation from learning disability (an often clinically detrimental practice based primarily on an arbitrary IQ cut-off point) (20, 37-39).

Exclusions

A major means of excluding students from the LD category under PL 94-142 is by assuming that their disability had a nonphysical etiology. Learning disability ostensibly caused by environmental, cultural, or economic disadvantage is, under the new law, excluded from special education services. On the pragmatic level, this distinction is difficult to support. First, it is exceedingly difficult to separate the seriously academically underachieving population into "true" and "false" LD children, because most children living in deprived urban environments who have serious academic deficits have overlapping reasons for their handicap (50, 51). Second, there is no evidence that different educational services are necessary for different subgroups of LD children (37, 39, 52, 53).

The primary reason for the arbitrary nature of the inclusion and exclusion criteria in special education is numbers. In urban elementary schools, approximately 6% of the 6th grade students are 3 or more years below the national norm in achievement (54). In secondary schools, the extent of such achievement deficits is far more prevalent (55, 56). (In fact, 112 (15%) of 740 10th graders in one middle-class area senior high school scored below the 6th grade level on achievement testing (57).) In order to cope with the potential flood of referrals of such children, an initial 2% LD quota and an overall maximum 12% special education limit were established under PL 94-142.

The use of quotas has created major debates within the special education field. Estimates of the number of LD students in schools range from 2% up to 15%, with the vast majority of survey results indicating LD percentages three to seven times greater than the LD student estimate of 2% from the U.S. Office of Education (48, 54, 58-63). Obviously, the exclusionary nature and narrowness of the LD definition represents a political and/or tactical compromise (Note C).

EMOTIONAL DISTURBANCES: DEFINITIONS AND EXCLUSIONS

PL 94-142 is entitled "Education for All Handicapped Children Act," and yet for ED children the pace of formal identification has been very slow. By 1979, only 20% of the 2% estimated to belong in this category were identified as emotionally disturbed for special education services (64). This underidentification is in large measure a result of the narrowness of the ED criteria. The ED category is qualified with the descriptive term "serious" and is the only category so restricted. Also, the etiology of the emotional disturbance is an important consideration in the law because one cause, social maladjustment, is specifically excluded, obviously an attempt to keep neighborhood rowdies out of ED classes.

OPERATIONAL SELECTIVITY IN LD
AND ED CLASSES: AGE, SEX, AND RACE

In practice, special education programs have given priority to the inclusion of elementary over secondary school students. Dunn estimated that over three-fourths of special education students served were in elementary schools (1). Similarly, Scranton and Downs found that over 80% of LD classes were in the primary grades (65). Sex and race have also been represented outside the expected percentage in special education classes, with males selected preferentially (64%–83%) (19, 62, 66) and minorities selected out of proportion to their numbers for EMR classes (38, 55, 66, 67).

Providing the bulk of special education services for LD and ED students at the elementary school level is very difficult to justify empirically. No one has demonstrated that LD and ED students make more progress or adjust better when the intervention is early (59, 68, 69). If anything, the major problems for these youth occur at the secondary school level—regardless of time of intervention (19, 20). The marked selection bias for males in special education is equally unjustifiable because in group testing for learning defects, rate differences attributable to gender are usually minor (62).

BEHAVIOR DISORDERS

Formal Exclusion

Even though the majority of ED and, in most settings, LD students have serious behavior disorders (2, 14, 20, 59, 70–80) and misbehavior is commonly the critical factor in a special education referral (80–82, Note E), persistently disruptive behavior is not a formal category or major criterion under PL 94-142. The formal exclusion of conduct disorder as a special education entity is difficult to justify on scientific grounds because BD is the most serious and most prevalent of the major child mental health disorders (83). (Moderate and severe mental retardation and childhood psychosis are more serious but very uncommon.) BD youth as a group have an exceedingly poor social adjustment outcome in adulthood, the worst among the major categories (84). Thus, the formal exclusion in PL 94-142 of BD youth from among the handicapped population makes a mockery of the law's formal title, Education for All Handicapped Children Act. It makes no educational sense either, because BD children have the least successful secondary school outcome of any deviant group.

Persistence of Behavioral Deviance and School Difficulties

Approximately 30% to 40% of disruptive secondary school students begin the 1st grade exhibiting serious conduct disorders, and these behavior problems persist throughout their school careers (59, 85–87).   Generally, they have the same misconduct patterns from teacher to teacher and from grade to grade. Also, the majority of this persistent BD population regularly demonstrate a restless temperament and/or learning disability (2, 3, 76, 88).

Although children with persistent behavior disorders are viewed by mental health experts as disturbed and/or maladapted, they are frequently judged by regular classroom teachers to be simply culprits and rowdies. Much as alcoholics were viewed 20 years ago as having weak morals and poor self-control, so are most persistently misbehaving children appraised by regular classroom teachers. Special educators tend to be far more sensitive than their regular education counterparts in appreciating that BD children have complex problems that merit concerted remedial efforts.

Who Speaks for BD Children: Can One Be
Idealistic in an Educational Bureaucracy?

Educators (regular more so than special) tend to justify existing school policy when many LD and ED students in regular or in special classes are retained or are suspended to a fair degree because of their behavioral disability. They often ignore the biased placement of an inappropriate number of minority youth in classes for the mentally retarded. They minimize the unfair discrimination in vocational education—such that only 2% of those selected are handicapped (89). They rationalize as commonplace the selection bias supporting the placement of more well-to-do behaviorally deviant students in costly residential treatment. They often back away from mainstreaming plans for BD students because they know that most regular class-room educators do not want these children in their classes (and will not make the necessary accommodations for them). They accept semi-autonomous special education programming even though they suspect that a tight integration with regular education might lead to better results. They mislead themselves into believing that an emphasis on the academic curriculum (and on "normal" discipline) for BD, LD, and ED students is more important than a structured motivational emphasis because it is easier to relate to, deal with, and publicly support.

Unfair discriminations and weak attempts at justification occur within all organizations; they are certainly no less common in the health field than in education.

SHOULD ALL LD AND ED CHILDREN BE
WITHIN SPECIAL EDUCATION TERRITORY?

Since PL 94-142 became operational in 1978, more LD and ED students have been identified and referred to special education. However, it is unlikely that *most* children in need of LD and ED services will receive special educational support during the 1980s, in part because of the 12% maximum special education student enrollment specified under PL 94-142. In the large-scale Kauai population survey and evaluation, only 36% of the LD children were known to special education, 23% were evaluated for special classes, and 9% were placed in such classes (59). In other surveys of LD students (also done during the 1970s), only 13% to 30% received special educational support (61, 90–93). Consequently, because of legal limits and limited funds (Note F), only 30% to 50% of LD students during the early 1980s will receive special education services at any given time. Instead, most will receive their education in low track, regular education classes and will be retained in grade at least once.

For ED children, the problem is similar. An estimated 7% to 10% of school children have emotional problems serious enough to require intervention (82, 94), but far less than 1% of such children receive special educational services.

Obviously, special education is not likely to cover most of the LD/ED territory in the foreseeable future. Furthermore, there is another argument against the formal transfer of major programming for LD and ED children to special education. Special educators have shown no "special" treatment success with these children. Special educators can teach the deaf to use sign language and total communication, the blind to read braille, and the physically handicapped to better compensate for their disabilities, but in the case of LD and ED students, special educators have demonstrated no greater success than talented regular education teachers, and they have shown no special skill in handling BD youth (Notes G and H). Special education certainly has no monopoly on good teachers, and competence in teaching is far more important in handling emotionally deviant students than is advanced academic training (95).

WHO SHOULD CONTROL LD AND ED PROGRAMS?

Whereas it would certainly be advantageous if regular educators received consultation on learning disabilities and behavior management from well-qualified special educators, there are disadvantages when most LD and ED services are provided primarily through a separately funded, separately supervised program within the public school system. One disadvantage of this separate programming is in relation to mainstreaming. Not being regular education teachers, special educators have the misfortune of being outsiders when they attempt to place their children back into the mainstream (7, 96, 97). Second, by using special education academic training more than excellence in teaching as the major professional prerequisite for employment, the opportunity is missed to put the priority where it belongs, on teachers with an established record of successful teaching. (Specialized courses can always be taken later.) Third, putting the final and major special class and off-site placement decisions and special class supervision into the hands of special education administrators restricts the school principal in his usual position of authority. Such restrictions can hurt cohesive leadership within the school. A fourth disadvantage to separately run special education classes is their stigma of being "special education" (98). If special education services were a flexible offshoot of regular education, assigned children might feel somewhat less stigmatized, and in any event would be less stigmatized officially. Fifth, in special education placement decisions, many arbitrary, all-or-none decisions having questionable clinical utility are made. For example, a child is 12, is 3 years academically deficient, and is failing. Under the present system, before the child is eligible for special education services, it must be determined whether or not he is "handicapped." (Most students with these characteristics are *not* so identified.) If special education services were a part of the regular program, there would be fewer such problematic and arbitrary decisions. Likewise, the inflexibility applies to minimum competency tests. In Maryland, for example, if a student is in special education, there is at this time no competency test requirement for graduation. However, students enrolled in regular classes will soon be required to pass this test. The test can be a real problem for slow-learning, non–special education students who constitute at least 10% of the population of many schools (99, 100). Sixth, special education funds are now allocated under PL 94-142 regulations on a fairly rigid schedule and a sizable percentage of these funds go into off-site (day therapeutic and residential) services (Note I). If there were more local control over special educational expenditures, the school team could decide, for example, that it would prefer two educational resource rooms and one holding resource room rather than (comparably priced) out-of-school placements for three students.

PL 94-142 AND ITS IMPACT ON PRIORITIES

Another major problem with PL 94-142 is that even though the "least restrictive environment" concept is written into the law, an independent (outside) enforcement of this provision is not mandated (Note J). In Massachusetts, for example, data revealed that under the first year of the "least restrictive law," special educational assignments were by and large *more* restrictive (e.g., less in regular classes) (80). Furthermore, as the number of LD and ED referrals increase, a greater *percentage* of such children will be receiving off-site day therapeutic and residential treatment services (Note K). No doubt, attempts to mainstream handicapped students into regular education will increase, but these efforts will be most consistently evident for the physically impaired and the retarded, not for BD youth (Note L).

With the cost of off-site therapeutic placements ranging from $9,000 to $30,000 per individual per school year, the total expenditures for such services are sizable. In Massachusetts, in 1969, approximately $10 million was spent in off-site public and nonpublic placements for ED children (80). In Maryland, in 1978, 12% of all those enrolled in special education programs were served in off-site (public and nonpublic) day therapeutic or residential programs (101) and costs for these 12% totaled over 40% of all the state's special educational expenditures for the year (Note M). No wonder the average annual, per student cost of special education in New York City rose in 1979 to $8,180 (102).

Spending such a large amount of the total education budget on relatively few is a highly questionable practice, yet those parents who receive the funds for their children generally don't complain, and those who do not receive this funding generally don't know about its availability. Furthermore, public school teachers who are in a position to know about these funds are the last to complain about their relative cost. As a rule, they want more excess cost, off-site placements for the BD children who would otherwise be in their classes.

A more general problem with channelling federal and state money for LD and ED services through the special education bureaucracy is that the responsibility is taken off regular education to support mainstreaming, to ensure that most LD and ED children succeed in regular classes, and to enrich instruction in low track classes. Regular educators can then more readily transfer responsibility to special education. After they make a special education referral, they can feel it is not their function to make an effort to serve educationally those who drop out prior to 16 and those who turn off to education while in junior high school. Reger et al. view this issue similarly; they maintain that "special education faces a critical danger of becoming a vehicle for preventing change in the general curriculum. It is becoming easier...to remove children who do not fit...than to make changes in the general curriculum" (103, Note N).

THE PREFERRED SYSTEM MESH

No one denies that many LD and ED students need additional and often special education program support. What is at issue is the preferred means of delivering these services. By routing the extra services through special education—with its customary reliance on special classes and off-site programs (for LD and ED children)—the emphasis is placed away from the regular school operation. A preferable approach for LD and ED students would be a required regular education-special education program mesh, such that regular education would be required to upgrade its services with special education staff assisting them primarily in academic areas (96).

Regular education needs to provide better, more useful and more attractive services for the LD, ED, BD, failing, and the very low track students who account for the vast majority of those who are unsuccessful in school. This entire population is at high risk for every unfortunate school consequence, including grade failure, drop-out, and suspension. Their school adversity usually starts during the elementary school years and rapidly accelerates while in junior high school. In secondary school, as age 16 nears, drop-out pressures increase. At that point, educational program modifications are seldom attempted to reverse this trend, and in fact, the drop-out process is often covertly encouraged (55).

PARENT PRESSURE AND OUTCOME

Parent lobby groups (such as the Association for Children with Learning Disabilities) have successfully pressured legislators, public education administrators and school boards during the 1960s and 1970s to offer programs which would provide their LD, ED, and BD children a more successful school experience. For vocal and well-placed parents who obtained extra services for their children the immediate results seemed moderately satisfactory. Their third-grade children (for example) were taken out of classes of 32 and placed into nongraded classes of nine, given more individual instruction and a few years later given a chance at mainstreaming. Although these moves were comforting, they were also somewhat deceiving. In the long run, the "separate and remediate" approach did not produce the significant benefits that were expected (17–20).

An analogous situation exists in mental health intervention. The anxious deviant is taken out of the community and placed in an accredited mental hospital with good professional care. In theory, the results of this intervention strategy should be highly successful. However, in most instances, an alternative mental health treatment effort within the community was possible and would have been at least as effective, less expensive, and probably longer lasting (104, 105).

Parent groups should look beyond the individual, immediate desires of their members and demand from schools long-term educational outcome results. They should more seriously question the often self-serving and rarely data-based claims of most residential institutions. Also, they should seriously question why they have to accept labeling and nonregular education in order to get needed educational services for their children.

SPECIAL EDUCATION AND BD: POSSIBILITIES

Special education can lead the way to integrative school programming for BD children. Special education has shown an appreciation for behavior management techniques (32) and a sensitivity to individual educational needs far more than has regular education (Note O). Special education has far more vocal parent support, advocacy groups, and parent involvement than does regular education. Furthermore, it has a number of energetic, nationally recognized leaders who have strongly advocated the need to integrate educational services (2, 14).

Special education thus has the potential to successfully promote the education of BD youth. To do so, however, it should more squarely and more openly face the many sensitive issues involved and require integrative arrangements with regular education.

NOTES

Note A. Elementary and Secondary Education Act (ESEA) Title I provides compensatory educational assistance to academically deficient students whose educational handicaps appear in large measure to stem from poverty, neglect, delinquency, or cultural or linguistic isolation. The program is massive and has been in existence since 1965. In 1977, it served over 4 million students, and cost nearly 2 billion dollars. The program's federal money is given to each school district in proportion to its number of economically disadvantaged students (106). The target in these areas are those students whose academic achievement is low, presumably in large part because of environmental disadvantage.

The bulk of Title I money (80%) is spent at the elementary school level (107), usually to pay aides (or teachers) who provide educational support services for children in grades K through 3.

Travis documents an attempt by the General Electric Company (under an Office of Education contract) to do a cost-benefit analysis of Title I. Reportedly, the investigators found it difficult to find a successful program (108). Substantive research on Title I programs is minimal at best (55), achievement data are usually unreliable, and negative results have been common in the unpublished reports that have been done (109). Kirst concludes that "Title I ESEA remains shrouded in conflicting and unattainable data in both the cognitive and affective domains." He adds also that Title I has not influenced the educational process within public schools (110). Similarly, but more cautiously, Madaus et al. (11) conclude in their 1980 overview that "Title I programs . . . appear to have had little effect in narrowing the achievement gap between advantaged and disadvantaged children."

Note B. With each state setting its own definition for the term *learning-disabled* under PL 94-142, there can be a great deal of unevenness in the field (106). One example of this is the fact that the LD:EMR ratio in Wisconsin is three times greater than that in Minnesota (112).

Note C. The total number of school-age academic underachievers is easily identifiable. This is not the problem. Profound academic under-achievement (in non-EMR children) represents a minimum of 6% of the student population in most studies (52). The disagreement of course lies in the number of these students included as LD children. Whereas many investigators include within the LD group the most profoundly underachieving children (48, 59–63) (e.g., those whose academic achievement is less than 50% of the age expected norm), others do not. They require developmental, educational, and perceptual evidence as well, and these additional requirements serve to reduce the numbers considerably.

Note D.   In Maryland, in 1979, a majority of those identified formally as handicapped by special education are in the LD category (113). Obviously, *learning-disabled* is a far more palatable label for parents than is *emotionally disturbed*.

Note E.   Although serious misconduct increases the priority for the acceptance of a special education referral at the elementary school level, it works against it in the high school (55). When the child reaches that age, it is easier to exclude him from regular classes by allowing or furthering the process of drop-out.

Note F.   The limitations in federal funding of PL 94-142 are becoming obvious in the 1980s. Although the law planned to have 40% of the excess cost of special education covered by federal funds by 1982, it appears that Congress will at most authorize a 12½% expenditure. To cope with this insufficient funding, students will either be put on waiting lists or limited programs will be financed with state funds (102).

Note G.   In two separate and informal comparisons of the school outcome of junior high school LD (special class) students and a grade-matched group of multisuspended students in typical regular education programs, the populations had a *comparable* annual rate of suspensions, expulsions, and absenteeism (114). (See chapter 2.)

Note H.   Indeed, the percentage of regular *or* special education teachers who are comfortable and clearly successful with most behaviorally deviant students is small. My estimate on this is 5%–10% in regular education and 10%–25% in special education.

Note I.   In the mental health field, the bulk of state human services money goes to inpatient programs. In fact, nearly 75% of the operating budget of the state of Maryland Mental Hygiene Administration goes to support state hospital services (116). This degree of emphasis on institutional placement fortunately is not as extreme in special education.

Note J.   PL 94-142 mandates: 1) appropriate special education assistance, classes, or placement for all children handicapped in educational pursuits who have a specified handicapping condition (such as LD), 2) the same opportunities in extracurricular activities and nonacademic activities for the "handicapped" as for the nonhandicapped, 3) educational placement in the least restrictive environment to the maximum extent appropriate, 4) a due process procedure for identification and educational placement, and 5) an individualized educational plan (IEP) for each identified handicapped child. The IEP is drawn up by the school staff, optimally in conjunction with the parents, and signed by the parent. The IEP includes an assessment of the child's individual needs, a statement of goals, specific timetables, and methods to achieve the goals. It must be reviewed annually. Priorities under PL 94-142 are: 1) the handicapped not receiving any education, and 2) the most severely handicapped whose education is inadequate (116). There is a numerical limitation in the number of special education students who can be served and financed under the law: 12% of children ages 3 through 17. However, beginning in 1980, all children qualified for special education, ages 3–21, were ostensibly eligible for service. Each state defines its own criteria for handicap, and plans must be approved at the federal level. For example, Virginia includes as major criteria for learning disabilities both of the following: 1) an IQ over 85, and 2) an achievement lag greater than 65% below the age-expected level in any basic academic area (40).

Note K. Bridgeland reported that 1,199 maladjusted children were awaiting placement for residential care within Great Britain in 1965. By 1967, he noted that "...despite the addition of 1494 places, the waiting list had, in fact, increased to 1209." Bridgeland concluded not surprisingly that "the number of maladjusted children appears to increase proportionately to the number of places" (117).

In New York City, parents formally petitioned for off-site special educational placement for over 50,000 school children in 1979/80. In part because of a 55 million dollar New York City school budget deficit and "high threshold" admission criteria for special education programs, less than 20% of these student applicants were placed. However, stringent special education criteria have come under legal attack by groups of parents in New York City, and in a 1980 New York City court case involving LD guidelines, a federal judge ruled that the school system had to alter the criteria and in effect "lower the threshold" (118).

Note L. An interesting finding along this line is that in the 1978 book, "Readings in Mainstreaming" (119), there was *nothing* on the mainstreaming of emotionally or behaviorally disturbed youth.

Note M. In Maryland in 1977/78, 1,399 students (1.6% of those identified as handicapped) received nonpublic off-site educational placements (120). Most so placed had a history of serious behavior problems. About seven times more students (over 9,700) received public day-therapeutic educational placements.

Note N. Johnson puts it this way: "Special education is helping the regular school maintain its unspoiled identity when it creates special programs for the 'disruptive child' and the 'slow learner'" (38). Gallagher echoes the above comments with the statement, "Special education for the mildly handicapped has tended to be an exclusionary process masquerading as a remedial one" (14).

Note O. There are notable forces of resistance to the development of integrated, in-school programs for BD youth: 1) most parents do not want BD children in their child's school, 2) most teachers do not want them either, 3) school administrators work hard to decrease complaints and BD programs can stir up more trouble than having no such program at all, and 4) even reporting school data on BD youth can cause problems for school administrators.

With such pressure to transfer the problem or keep it submerged, it is no wonder that an outside, non-affiliated group, the Children's Defense Fund (CDF), came out with two of the most important and influential books on alienated and disadvantaged students: *School Suspensions: Are They Helping Children* (121) and *Children Out of School in America* (122). With its reports, the Children's Defense Fund clearly delved into areas not thoroughly explored by involved professional groups (such as the National Association of Secondary School Principals) and institutionally protective agencies (such as the National Institute of Education and the Bureau for the Education of the Handicapped).

REFERENCES

1. Dunn, L. An overview. In L. M. Dunn (Ed.), *Exceptional children in the schools: Special education in transition*, 2nd Ed. New York: Holt, Rinehart & Winston, 1973, pp. 3–63.
2. Rubin, E. Z. Cognitive dysfunction and emotional disorders, in H. R. Myklebust (Ed.), *Progress in learning disabilities*, Vol. 2. New York: Grune & Stratton, 1971, pp. 179–195.
3. Kauffman, J. M. *Characteristics of children's behavior disorders.* Columbus, Ohio: Charles Merrill, 1977.
4. *Annual education summary.* Albany, N.Y.: New York State Educational Department, 1977, p. 17.
5. Egeland, B., & Schrimpf, V. Approaches to the understanding and treatment of learning-disabled children. In A. P. Goldstein (Ed.), *Prescriptions for child mental health and education.* New York: Pergamon, 1978, pp. 175–271.
6. Budoff, M., & Gottlieb, J. Special class EMR children mainstreamed: A study of an aptitude (learning potential)×treatment interaction. *American Journal of Mental Deficiency*, 1976, *81*, 1–11.
7. Corman, C., & Gottlieb, J. Mainstreaming mentally retarded children: A review of research. In N. R. Ellis (Ed.), *International Review of Research in Mental Retardation*, 1978, *9*, 251–275.
8. Carroll, A. W. The effect of segregated and partially integrated school programs on self concept and academic achievement of educable mental retardates. *Exceptional Children*, 1967, *34*, 93–99.
9. Macy, D. J., & Carter, J. L. Comparison of a mainstream and self contained special education program. *Journal of Special Education*, 1978, *12*, 303–313.
10. Haring, N. G., & Krug, D. A. Placement in regular programs: Procedures and results. *Exceptional Children*, 1975, *41*, 413–417.
11. Johnson, G. O. Special education for the mentally handicapped—A paradox. *Exceptional Children*, 1962, *29*, 62–69.
12. Sheare, J. B. Social acceptance of EMR adolescents in integrated programs. *American Journal of Mental Deficiency*, 1974, *78*, 678–682.
13. Gampel, D. H., Gottlieb, J., & Harrison, R. H. Comparison of classroom behavior of special class EMR, integrated EMR, low IQ and non-

retarded children. *American Journal of Mental Deficiency*, 1974, *79*, 16–21.

14. Gallagher, J. J. The special education contract for mildly handicapped children. *Exceptional Children*, 1972, *38*, 527–535.
15. Nelson, C. M., & Kauffman, J. M. Educational programming for secondary school age delinquent and maladjusted pupils. *Behavior Disorders*, February 1977, *2*, 102–113.
16. Gickling, E. E., & Theobald, J. T. Mainstreaming: Affect or effect. *Journal of Special Education*, 1975, *9*, 317–328.
17. O'Leary, S. G., & Schneider, M. R. Special class placement of conduct problem children. *Exceptional Children*, 1977, *44*, 24–30.
18. Vacc, N. A. Long term effects of special class intervention for emotionally disturbed children. *Exceptional Children*, 1972, *39*, 15–22.
19. Morse, W. C., Cutler, R. L., & Fink, A. H. Public school classes for the emotionally handicapped: A research analysis. In N. J. Long, W. C. Morse, & R. G. Newman (Eds.), *Conflict in the classroom*, 2nd Ed. Belmont, Cal.: Wadsworth, 1971, pp. 539–547.
20. Marrone, R. T., & Anderson, N. Innovative public school programming for emotionally disturbed children. *American Journal of Orthopsychiatry*, 1970, *40*, 694–701.
21. Woodward, C. A., Johnson, Y., Santa-Barbara, J., Roberts, R. S., & Pipe, M. A collaborative special education program for emotionally disturbed children: Philosophy, design and outcomes. In S. J. Shamsie (Ed.), *New directions in children's mental health*. New York: S. P. Medical & Scientific Books, 1979, pp. 41–51.
22. Koppitz, E. M. *Children with learning disabilities: A five year follow-up study*. New York: Grune & Stratton, 1971.
23. Glavin, J. P., Quay, H. C., Annesley, F. R., & Werry, J. S. An experimental resource room for behavior problem children. *Exceptional Children*, 1971, *38*, 131–137.
24. Sindelar, P. T., & Deno, S. L. The effectiveness of resource programming. *Journal of Special Education*, 1978, *12*, 17–28.
25. Glavin, J. P. Behaviorally oriented resource rooms: A follow-up. *Journal of Special Education*, 1974, *8*, 337–347.
26. Silberberg, N. E., Iversen, I. A., & Gorn, J. T. Which remedial reading method works best? *Journal of Learning Disabilities*, 1973, *6*, 547–556.
27. Rutter, M. Prevalence and types of dyslexia. In A. L. Benton & D. Pearl (Eds.), *Dyslexia: An appraisal of current knowledge*. New York: Oxford University Press, 1978, pp. 5–28.
28. Ysseldyke, J. E. Diagnostic-prescriptive teaching: The search for aptitude-treatment interactions. In L. Mann & D. Sabatino (Eds.), *The first review of special education* (Vol. 1). Philadelphia: JSE Press, 1973, pp. 5–32.
29. Arter, J. A., & Jenkins, J. R. Differential diagnosis-prescriptive teaching: A critical appraisal. *Review of Educational Research*, 1979, *49*, 517–555.
30. Jenkins, J. R., Mayhall, W. F., Peschka, C. M., & Jenkins, L. M. Comparing small group and tutorial instruction in resource rooms. *Exceptional Children*, 1974, *40*, 245–250.
31. D'Annunzio, A., & Steg, D. R. Effects of individualized learning procedures on children with specific learning disabilities. *Developmental*

Medicine and Child Neurology, 1974, 16, 507–512.
32. Gardner, W. I. Learning and behavior characteristics of exceptional children and youth. Boston: Allyn & Bacon, 1977.
33. Ysseldyke, J. E., & Salvia, J. Diagnostic-prescriptive teaching: Two models. Exceptional Children, 1974, 41, 181–185.
34. Lerner, J. W. Remedial reading and learning disabilities: Are they the same or different? Journal of Special Education, 1975, 9, 119–131.
35. Kirk, W. D. The relationship of reading disabilities to learning disabilities. Journal of Special Education, 1975, 9, 133–137.
36. Rice, D. B. Learning disabilities: An investigation in two parts. Journal of Learning Disabilities, 1970, 3, 149–155.
37. Hallahan, D. P., & Kauffman, J. M. Introduction to learning disabilities: A psycho-behavioral approach. Englewood Cliffs, N.J.: Prentice-Hall, 1976.
38. Johnson, J. L. Special education in the inner city. Journal of Special Education, 1969, 3, 241–251.
39. Neisworth, J. T., & Greer, J. G. Functional similarities of learning disability and mild retardation. Exceptional Children, 1975, 42, 17–21.
40. Trice, O. A., & Trice, A. D. Special education: Programmed manual for regular classroom teachers. Waynesboro City Public School, Waynesboro, Va., 1977.
41. Office of Education. Assistance to states for education of handicapped children: Notice of proposed rule making. Federal Register, Vol. 41 (No. 230) 52404–52407, November 29, 1976.
42. Satz, P., Taylor, H. G., Friel, J., & Fletcher, J. M. Some developmental and predictive precursors of reading disabilities: A six year follow-up. In A. L. Benton & D. Pearl (Eds.), Dyslexia: An appraisal of current knowledge. New York: Oxford University Press, 1978, pp. 315–347.
43. Rutter, M., & Yule, W. Reading difficulties. In M. Rutter & L. Hersov (Eds.), Child psychiatry: Modern approaches. New York: Oxford University Press, 1977, pp. 556–580.
44. Larsen, S. C., & Hammill, D. D. The relationship of selected visual-perceptual abilities to school learning. Journal of Special Education, 1975, 9, 281–291.
45. Goodman, L., & Mann, L. Learning disabilities in the secondary school: Issues and practices. New York: Grune & Stratton, 1976.
46. Silver, A. A., & Hagin, R. A. Specific reading disability: Follow-up studies. American Journal of Orthopsychiatry, 1964, 34, 95–102.
47. Meichenbaum, D. Cognitive-functional approach to cognitive factors as determinants of learning disabilities. In R. M. Knights & D. J. Bakker (Eds.), The neuropsychology of learning disorders. Baltimore: University Park Press, 1976, pp. 423–442.
48. Larsen, S. C. The learning disabilities specialist: Role and responsibilities. Journal of Learning Disabilities, 1976, 9, 498–508.
49. Danielson, L. C., & Bauer, J. N. A formula-based classification of learning disabled children. Journal of Learning Disabilities, 1978, 11, 163–176.
50. Herrick, M. J. Disabled or disadvantaged, what's the difference? Journal of Special Education, 1973, 7, 381–386.
51. Hartman, R. K. Differential diagnosis: Assets and liabilities. Journal of Special Education, 1973, 7, 393–397.

52. Hallahan, D. P., & Kauffman, J. M. Labels, categories, behaviors: ED, LD, and EMR reconsidered. *Journal of Special Education,* 1977, *11,* 139-149.

53. O'Grady, D. J. Psycholinguistic abilities in learning-disabled, emotionally disturbed and normal children. *Journal of Special Education,* 1974, *8,* 157-165.

54. Eisenberg, L. Reading retardation: Psychiatric and sociologic aspects. *Pediatrics,* 1966, *37,* 352-365.

55. Block, E. E., Covill-Servo, J., & Rosen, M. *Failing students: A study of dropouts and discipline in N.Y. State.* Rochester, N.Y.: N.Y. Civil Liberties Union, April 1978.

56. Winters, B. California dropouts have to be smarter. *Baltimore Sun,* March 17, 1977, p. A-3.

57. Wiseman, D. E., Hartwell, L. K., & Kros, P. Child service demonstration center for secondary school age learning disability. Title VII-E, End of year report: 1977/1978, Arizona State University, August 1978.

58. Rutter, M., Tizard, J., Yule, W., Graham, P., & Whitmore, K. Isle of Wight Studies: 1964-1974. *Psychological Medicine,* 1976, *6,* 313-332.

59. Werner, E. E., & Smith, R. R. *Kauai's children come of age.* Honolulu: University of Hawaii Press, 1977.

60. Mykelbust, H. R., & Boshes, B. *Minimal brain damage in children.* Washington, D.C.: U.S. Department of HEW, 1970.

61. Gaddes, W. H. Prevalence estimates and the need for definition of learning disabilities. In R. M. Knights and D. J. Bakker (Eds.), *The neuropsychology of learning disorders.* Baltimore: University Park Press, 1976, pp. 3-24.

62. Lambert, N. M., & Sandoval, J. The prevalence of learning disabilities in a sample of children considered hyperactive. *Journal of Abnormal Child Psychology,* 1980, *8,* 33-50.

63. Hammer, S. L. School underachievement in the adolescent. *Pediatrics,* 1967, *40,* 373-381.

64. Vlasak, J. Mental health services and PL 94-142: What kind of marriage. Symposium presented at the meeting of the American Orthopsychiatric Association, Washington, D.C., April 4, 1979.

65. Scranton, T. R., & Downs, M. L. Elementary and secondary learning disabilities programs in the U.S.: A survey. *Journal of Learning Disabilities,* 1975, *8,* 394-399.

66. Gilhool, T. K. Education: An inalienable right. *Exceptional Children,* 1973, *39,* 597-609.

67. Burke, A. A. Placement of black and white children in educable mentally handicapped classes and learning disability classes. *Exceptional Children,* 1975, *41,* 438-439.

68. Frauenheim, J. G. Academic achievement characteristics of adult males who were diagnosed as dyslexic in childhood. *Journal of Learning Disabilities,* 1978, *11,* 476-483.

69. Palmer, F. H., & Andersen, L. L. Long-term gains from early intervention: Findings from longitudinal studies. In E. Zigler & J. Valentine (Eds.), *Project Head Start: A legacy of the war on poverty.* New York: Free Press, 1979, pp. 433-466.

70. Wilson, M. D., Evans, M. B., Dawson, R. L., & Kiek, J. S. Disturbed

children in special schools. *Special education: Forward trends,* June 1977, *4* (2), 8–10.

71. Rogen, L., & Lukans, J. Education administration and classroom procedure. In *Minimal brain dysfunction in children: Educational, medical, and health related services,* Phase Two. Public Health Publication No. 2015, Washington, D.C., U.S. Department of HEW, 1969, pp. 21–30.

72. Browne, T., Stotsky, B. A., & Eichorn, J. A selective comparison of psychological, developmental, social and academic factors among emotionally disturbed children in three treatment settings. *Child Psychiatry and Human Development,* 1977, *7,* 231–253.

73. Olweus, D. *Aggression in the schools: Bullies and whipping boys.* New York: Halsted Press, 1978.

74. Parashar, O. D. Disturbed classroom behaviour: A comparison between mentally retarded, learning disabled and emotionally disturbed children. *Journal of Mental Deficiency Research,* 1976, *20,* 109–120.

75. McIntosh, D., & Dunn, L. Children with major specific learning disabilities. In L. M. Dunn (Ed.), *Exceptional children in the schools: Special education in transition,* 2nd Ed. New York: Holt, Rinehart & Winston, 1973.

76. Wright, L. S. Conduct problem or learning disability? *Journal of Special Education,* 1974, *8,* 331–336.

77. Stevenson, J., & Richman, N. Behavior, language, and development in three year old children. *Journal of Autism and Childhood Schizophrenia,* 1978, *8,* 299–313.

78. Quay, H. C., Morse, W. C., & Cutler, R. L. Personality patterns of pupils in special classes for the emotionally disturbed. *Exceptional Children,* 1966, *32,* 297–301.

79. Grieger, R. M., & Richards, H. C. Prevalence and structure of behavior symptoms among children in special education and regular classroom settings. *Journal of School Psychology,* 1976, *14,* 27–38.

80. Weatherley, R. A. *Reforming special education: Policy implication from state to street level.* Cambridge: M.I.T. Press, 1979.

81. Slade, M. Bias in labelling the handicapped. *Psychology Today,* October 1978, *12* (5), 31–32.

82. Kolvin, I., Garside, R. F., Nicol, A. R., Leitch, I., & Macmillan, A. Screening school children at high risk of emotional disorder. *British Journal of Psychiatry,* 1977, *131,* 192–206.

83. Werner, E. E., & Smith, R. S. An epidemiologic perspective on some antecedents and consequences of childhood mental health problems and learning disabilities: A report from the Kauai longitudinal study. *Journal of the American Academy of Child Psychiatry,* 1979, *18,* 292–306.

84. Robins, L. *Deviant children grown up.* Baltimore: Williams & Wilkins, 1966.

85. Ahlstrom, W., & Havighurst, R. J. *400 losers: Delinquent boys in high school.* San Francisco: Jossey-Bass, 1971.

86. Thomas, A., & Chess, S. Evolution of behavior disorders into adolescence. *American Journal of Psychiatry,* 1976, *133,* 539–542.

87. Kraus, P. E. *Yesterday's children: A longitudinal study of children from kindergarten into the adult years.* New York: Wiley, 1973.

88. Safer, D. J., & Allen, R. P. *Hyperactive children: Diagnosis and management.* Baltimore: University Park Press, 1976.
89. Stacts, E. B. *Training educators for the handicapped: A need to redirect federal programs.* Washington, D.C.: U.S. General Accounting Office, 1976.
90. Kirk, S. A. *Educating exceptional children,* 2nd Ed. Boston: Houghton Mifflin Co., 1972.
91. Sabatino, D. A. The seriously handicapped. In D. A. Sabatino & T. L. Miller (Eds.), *Describing learner characteristics of handicapped children and youth.* New York: Grune & Stratton, 1979, pp. 497–519.
92. Education for the handicapped today: From the 1976 annual report of the National Advisory Commission on the Handicapped. In H. Goldstein (Ed.), *Readings in special education.* Guilford, Conn.: Special Learning Corp., 1978, pp. 14–16.
93. Spreen, O. Neuropsychology of learning disorders: Post-conference review. In R. M. Knights & D. J. Bakker (Eds.), *The neuropsychology of learning disorders.* Baltimore: University Park Press, 1976, pp. 445–467.
94. Bower, E. M. *Early identification of emotionally handicapped children in school,* 2nd Ed. Springfield, Ill.: Charles C Thomas, 1969.
95. Kounin, J. S., & Obradovic, S. Managing emotionally disturbed children in regular classrooms: A replication and an extension. *Journal of Special Education,* 1967, *2,* 129–135.
96. Newcomer, P. L. Special education services for the "mildly handicapped": Beyond a diagnostic and remedial model. *Journal of Special Education,* 1977, *11,* 153–165.
97. Milosfsky, C. *Special education: A sociological study of California programs.* New York: Praeger Publications, 1976, p. 70.
98. Jones, R. L. Student views of special placement and their own special classes: A clarification. *Exceptional Children,* 1974, *41,* 22–29.
99. Olson, L. School prognosis: Work, standards, parents are the key. *Baltimore Sun,* March 29, 1979, p. A-11.
100. Stiff 4th year test in high schools set. *New York Times,* January 21, 1979, pp. 1, 42.
101. Lineberg, L. Personal communication, 1979.
102. Shanker, A. Carter, Congress renege on a promise. *New York Times,* February 3, 1980, p. E-11.
103. Reger, R., Schroeder, W., & Uschold, K. *Special education: Children with learning problems.* New York: Oxford University Press, 1968, p. 13.
104. Dinitz, S. Home care treatment as a substitute for hospitalization: The Louisville experiment. *New Directions for Mental Health Services,* 1979, *1,* 1–13.
105. Pasamanick, B., Scarpitti, F. R., & Dinitz, S. *Schizophrenics in community: An experimental study in the prevention of hospitalization.* New York: Appleton-Century-Crofts, 1967.
106. Brewer, G. D., & Kakalik, J. S. *Handicapped children: Strategies for improving services.* New York: McGraw-Hill, 1979.
107. Shanker, A. Unemployed teens: Target of U.S. $. *New York Times,* January 6, 1980, p. E-9.
108. Travis, C. Compensatory education. *Psychology Today,* September

1976, *10* (4), 63–64.
109. Hill-Scott, K., & Grigsby, J. E. Some policy recommendations for compensatory education. *Phi Delta Kappan*, 1979, *60*, 443–446.
110. Kirst, M. W. The growth of Federal influence in education. In C. W. Gordon (Ed.), *Uses of the sociology of education*. Chicago: University of Chicago Press, 1974, pp. 448–477.
111. Madaus, G. F., Airasian, P. W., & Kellaghan, T. *School effectiveness: A reassessment of the evidence*. New York: McGraw Hill, 1980, p. 40.
112. Sabatino, D. A., & Miller, T. L. The dilemma of diagnosis in learning disabilities: Problems and potential directions. *Psychology in the Schools*, 1980, *17*, 76–86.
113. Hammes, R. Personal communication, 1979.
114. Safer, D. Unpublished data, 1972–1979.
115. Karahassan, A. Personal communication, 1979.
116. *An analysis of PL 94-142: The Education for All Handicapped Children Act*. Washington, D.C.: National Association of State Directors of Special Education, 1977.
117. Bridgeland, M. *Pioneer work with maladjusted children: A study of the development of therapeutic education*. London: Staples Press, 1971.
118. Redefining the handicapped may cost millions. *New York Times*, July 6, 1980, p. 6-E.
119. Goldstein, H. (Ed.) *Readings in mainstreaming*. Guilford, Conn.: Special Learning Corp., 1978.
120. *State of the state: Special education in Maryland, MSDE Report—1978*. Baltimore, Md.: State Department of Education, September 1979.
121. Edelman, M. W., Beck, R., & Smith, P. V. *School suspensions: Are they helping children?* Cambridge, Mass.: Children's Defense Fund, 1975.
122. Edelman, M. W. *Children out of school in America*. Cambridge, Mass.: Children's Defense Fund, 1974.

III

Management aspects
of behavioral interventions

INTRODUCTION TO CHAPTERS 7 AND 8

The following chapters by Parker and Trice and Trice and Parker cover vital school issues that should be considered if disruptive students are to be managed more successfully in schools. The chapters center on helping teachers to structure their classroom time and energies more productively so that disruption is less likely, less intense, and less prolonged. The second chapter involves more complex strategies using primarily positive classroom interventions to improve student motivation and academic effort.

The classroom is the school's front line. Having only one persistently disruptive student in a class represents a major stress for teachers, but having two or more is undoubtedly a real chore. Furthermore, the distractive and provocative interaction caused by serious, behavior-problem students can detrimentally change the entire character of a classroom. Nonetheless, good teacher management can significantly lessen this adversity, and the converse is equally true. As 74% of teachers report, poor administrative control within classrooms is a major cause for disciplinary problems (1).

One must acknowledge that reading these chapters will not by itself improve teaching, but hopefully it can spur interest in variations and experimentations in teaching that, if successful, will do so.

REFERENCES

1. Lufler, H. S. Discipline: A new look at an old problem. *Phi Delta Kappan*, 1978, *59*, 424–426.

7

Teaching disruptive youth in the mainstream:
I General behavioral strategy

Frank C. Parker and Ashton D. Trice

Although this volume describes numerous school programs for disruptive students, few disruptive adolescents are currently enrolled in such programs (1). Most are assigned to regular classrooms where they are the responsibility of regular instructional and resource personnel. Only a small number of school districts have created special programs for this population. Still fewer have made permanent commitments to this group of troubled and troublesome students.

Practically, the problem of disruptive students is of real concern to all classroom teachers at the secondary level. As many as 7% of a school district's secondary population may be classified as chronically disruptive (2), making it probable that most teachers will encounter such students daily. Many other students engage in serious forms of misbehavior from time to time. Increasingly, legal barriers are being erected to make it more difficult to remove such students from the classroom, either informally or by suspension or expulsion (3), although this has not yet been reflected in national suspension rates. Thus, it is vital for teachers to use what is known about preventing and controlling disruption.

Most alternative programs for disruptive youth control behavior and influence academic productivity by a large megastructure, such as a group-wide point system or a social skills training class. Whereas this is generally useful and has contributed to our knowledge of how to educate groups of these youth, it is not usually pertinent for regular teachers who have the responsibility of managing uncooperative individuals within the context of the normal classroom environment. Regular teachers have a greater need for more specific information to develop individualized programs for disruptive students.

This chapter and the next attempt to meet this need. The first presents the general principles of behavior management for application by regular classroom teachers. The subsequent chapter examines in some detail more intensive and more complex efforts to alter student conduct and initiative in classrooms.

A BASIC PARADIGM OF CLASSROOM MANAGEMENT

The student who is labeled seriously disruptive misbehaves *despite* normal school disciplinary procedures. Since the majority of students behave appropriately most of the time, it is tempting to view repeatedly disruptive students as grossly abnormal, not only undisciplined but undisciplinable.

Many recent investigations, however, have made it clear that these students are manageable, but that more powerful and/or more consistent procedures are necessary. Madsen, Becker, and Thomas (4) have provided what may be the classic formula for this point of view. For these authors, successful classroom management consists of three components: 1) a clear statement of rules, generally ex· pressed positively in terms of what should be done, 2) ignoring dis ruptive behavior whenever possible, and 3) praising, frequently and consistently, those behaviors which the teacher wishes to develop. This technique, known widely by the slogan, "Rules, Ignore, Praise," or the acronym RIP, has found its way into the educational literature as *the* general behavioral strategy for classroom management. This procedure was developed to deal with fairly minor forms of disruption among primary school-aged children. Although the paradigm must be expanded to take into account the more serious forms of disruption which are the major concerns of the secondary school (5), the RIP approach does outline the basic requirements of behavioral classroom management.

Rules

Most classrooms have rules at least by virtue of the fact that they are in schools and school districts that have published codes of conduct. Most of these codes, however, do not meet the criteria of formal rules, that is, *clearly specified descriptions of the consequences for the commission or omission of certain well-defined behaviors.* To meet the formal criteria, rules must be consistently enforced. That is, the consequence should always follow the behavior, unless the rule specifies circumstances under which the consequence will not be applied. "You will be sent to the principal's office if you get out of your seat during a lecture" and "If you answer all the items on the test correctly, you will get an A+" are examples of rules, while "Misconduct will not be tolerated" and "Students shall refrain from cheating" are not: the first because of imprecisely defined behavior and consequence, and the second because no consequence is stated.

Most codes of conduct fail the definition because they are not well defined. Consider the following example from a recent public school handbook:

> A student may be suspended for violent interference with the normal school operation or other behavior in which an individual is unable to assume responsibility for his or her behavior resulting in disruption of or interference with the normal academic process or a substantial danger to persons or property (6).

Here, what is not readily apparent is what constitutes a violation (vandalism, threats, substance abuse, theft, and assault were specifically mentioned in previous rules). Furthermore, the paragraph does not describe the specific circumstances when students will or will not be suspended or what will happen if they are not.

The second problem with codes of conduct is that they are inconsistently enforced. Lufler (7) presents data showing the disparity of ways in which teachers deal with instances of truancy. Over 46% of the senior high teachers surveyed maintained that truancy was an infraction of the disciplinary code and must be reported to the school principal, yet nearly 33% dealt with truancy themselves. Informal observation in several secondary schools strongly indicates that individual teachers set radically different standards of conduct and academic behaviors, even when such behaviors are ostensibly covered by formally articulated school policy. In working with disruptive secondary school students, we have frequently noted that significant problems develop when students are punished by teachers for behaviors tolerated or encouraged by other teachers. "Disruptive talking out" for one teacher may be "class participation" for others and "honest self expression" may be "vulgarity," depending on the individual classroom.

A third problem arises from the first two: students are frequently unaware of what the rules are. In a survey conducted in 1979 among multisuspended 10th and 11th grade students, 76% of the students identified at least one unacceptable reason for absence as a legitimate excuse; and 44% maintained that as long as they stayed home or their parents knew where they were it was all right to miss school (8). This problem is further complicated by school districts that couch these codes in legal jargon to meet potential challenges.

It may be useful to conceptualize classroom behaviors as forming a continuum from those that are highly desirable (orderly participation in class discussions and superior achievement) to those that are highly inappropriate (refusing to follow directions or aggression). Between these extremes lies a variety of behaviors that are more or less appropriate for the classroom. Goffman (9) has suggested that this continuum can be divided into behaviors that are encouraged, behaviors that are tolerated, and behaviors that are not tolerated.

Rules are concerned with behaviors that are either encouraged or are not tolerated. The consequences for encouraged behaviors are positive (reward, privilege, reprieve, or praise). The consequences for behaviors that are not tolerated are negative (reprimand, punishment, penalty, or loss of privilege) (Note A). There are usually no disciplinary consequences for tolerated behaviors.

The recommended strategy is to state rules in terms of encouraged behaviors and positive consequences, as it seems reasonable that granting students rewards or privileges for good performance is more productive than taking privileges away when students misbehave. By concentrating on behaviors incompatible with misbehavior, it is possible to build a set of rules that will minimize disruptive behavior. For example, the junior high school teacher who is overwhelmed with students calling out may choose to reward students who raise their hands before speaking. Likewise, the teacher confronted with a class tardiness problem may wish to schedule open discussion time at the beginning of the period or begin each period with a brief graded quiz that cannot be made up.

Ignoring

Teacher attention serves as a powerful stimulus for appropriate *or* inappropriate classroom behavior. This basic dictum is frequently overlooked as teachers seek novel and often contrived methods for classroom control. The systematic giving and withholding of attention is probably the single most useful tool available to the teacher, yet it is an extremely difficult tool to use effectively. Several recent studies (10, 11) have indicated that it is not the amount of attention shown students by teachers that predicts high or low disruption rates in classrooms (nor for that matter, the amount of punishment); what appears to be of critical importance is that attention (or any positive or negative stimulus) be given and withheld *systematically* to encourage positive behaviors and discourage negative behaviors (12).

Quite obviously, the extent to which a teacher has established rapport with his or her students and has thus gained power as a rewarding agent, will help determine the effectiveness of this technique. This is not the only determinant, however, since teacher attention, or lack thereof, may cue peer attention and ignoring.

Behaviors which are ignored (or more correctly, extinguished), tend to disappear over time (13). It would seem, then, that the behaviors designated "tolerated" in the Goffman paradigm would be appropriate targets for extinction. Most educators, however, tend *not* to ignore a very wide range of behaviors within the classroom. Indeed, they frequently spend a good part of their day addressing behaviors (through mild or stern reprimands, scowling, etc.) which are mildly annoying or personally distasteful, but which do not actually interfere with the instructional process. This detracts from the more critical duties of encouraging appropriate behavior and, indeed, instruction. For disruptive students, a broader range of minor infractions might be ignored. Figure 1 shows a schematic of this position which might be in operation in a classroom during the earlier part of the school year. This strategy does not require ignoring all disruptive acts; serious misbehavior must be punished. Also, in the proposed program (discussed below), a wider range of behaviors are praised and/or rewarded.

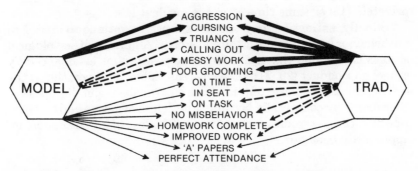

Figure 1. Schematic of hypothetical teacher response to different student behaviors. Bold lines represent punishment; broken lines represent ignoring; thin lines represent praise and reward. Note that in the proposed strategy, the undesirable behaviors which are ignored are indirectly targeted by rewarding incompatible responses whereas the traditional approach frequently emphasizes punishment and does little to encourage marginally positive behavior.

Several points should be kept in mind when attempting to extinguish mild classroom misconduct. First, by the time chronically disruptive students reach secondary schools, they usually have quite a long history of school misconduct. These students, especially those with limited academic and social skills, may have learned that they can solicit teacher attention (albeit negative) and peer attention (often positive) by creating a nuisance. Disrupting the classroom may be very reinforcing to these students. In fact, it has been shown that it often is the reprimands that maintain disruption. While, in the short run, reprimands or threats of punishment can stop much misbehavior, in the long run they tend to have the effect of increasing it (14). It should be anticipated that a substantial decrease in misbehavior may take some time. In fact, in most situations, extinction is accompanied by a sudden and dramatic increase in the behavior ignored (15). If the teacher then decides to abandon the procedure and return to verbal reprimands, she or he may have merely driven up the intensity of the student misbehavior (Note B).

Second, it is not our position that mild forms of misbehavior must be totally left alone. What may be critical is that the immediacy of attention be broken through an extinction procedure.

Several studies (5, 16) have had teachers respond to mild misbehavior by dispassionately stating the preferred behavior or stating the infraction ("Raise your hand before asking a question"; "No talking during tests"). Such procedures minimize the attention and the ability of the student's misbehavior to control the classroom. Others have suggested that teachers frequently give positive feedback ("Everyone has been very good today about waiting their turn in our discussion") (17) or discussing the infraction with the student privately (18) or some time after the incident (19).

Finally, extinction may not work if peers continue to attend to misbehavior in or outside of the classroom. A number of sociological studies have found that status in some peer groups is enhanced by school misconduct (20, 21). It seems reasonable, however, that if the teacher minimizes the extent to which such misbehavior disrupts the classrooms by collaterally becoming both less negative and more rewarding, the classroom environment will be less likely to support inappropriate behavior.

Praise

As seen in Figure 1, the RIP strategy encourages teachers to positively consequate a wider range of behaviors than might be found in most class settings. The studies cited earlier (10, 11) found that in a variety of classrooms negative comments outweighed positive comments by as much as 6:1. Such data make it only too clear why some students find school a highly aversive place.

Teachers on the secondary level, frequently subject specialists rather than generalist educators, often object to praising or rewarding less than exceptional performances. Most disruptive students, typically well behind grade level in achievement, often educationally handicapped, and, in general, from homes where school achievement is not especially valued, are incapable of exceptional achievement when compared to others in their grade. What is suggested is that exceptional performance be rewarded relative to the student's own past performance. Also, disruptive students may not have mastered even the most basic behavioral patterns necessary for success in the secondary classroom (being prepared for class, being able to discuss rather than argue, being consistent school attenders). Unless some-one attends to these behaviors, it is unlikely that they will develop. Classroom teachers may be uncomfortable in positively commenting on an attendance change from 65% to 75% by a student when his attendance is still below most of the others in the class, but such a change may represent as intense a personal effort on the part of that student as a gifted student writing a prize-winning essay.

Praise is not the sole means of positively consequating encouraged behaviors. In fact, the behavior modification literature is characterized by stronger sorts of rewards. One reason for this is that privileges or prizes are able to produce greater results more quickly. Another reason is that teacher praise for disruptive students does not always function as a reward. The most frequently made caveat in the behavioral literature is that one decides what is reinforcing by its ability to increase target behaviors and not on *a priori* assumptions about what should be reinforcing or what is generally reinforcing. Just as teacher reprimands may encourage misbehavior, teacher praise may discourage appropriate behavior.

The underlying plan of attack is to assess the skills of the students and to reward improvement. Such methods have proven successful, even with the most disruptive and academically limited students (22). Thus, rather than rewarding only superior work and making it exceedingly difficult for problematic students in the class to be acknowledged, the teacher provides guidance and encouragement by student-referenced rewards for improvement.

ESTABLISHING INDIVIDUALIZED INTERVENTIONS

Leviton (23) has argued that discipline, like academic achievement, can be enhanced if it is individualized. Such a possibility may be intimidating to some and philosophically repugnant to others. Many believe that there is, or should be, one standard of conduct for the school. The continued successful existence of more authoritarian as well as less structured independent schools suggests that there is no general consensus on what that school-wide disciplinary system ought to be.

Individualized programs have been the hallmark of behavioral interventions. There are several steps involved in developing such programs, which can be subsumed under the topics of 1) selecting target behaviors, 2) developing contingencies, and 3) assessment.

Selecting Target Behaviors

Describing the students in our population by the label "disruptive" may tend to obscure the fact that many of these students have a variety of other problems as well, most notably academic ones. While disruption may well be the most immediate concern of teachers, attending to negative behaviors often increases negative behavior, even when the attention is intended to be aversive (14, 24).

We have advocated the strategy of selecting positive behaviors that are incompatible with misbehavior as targets. Several successful strategies have used academic targets (25, 26). In these studies, when students were rewarded for the amount of work successfully completed, the rate of classroom disruption dramatically declined and academic output sharply increased. When working throughout the period was targeted, more work was accomplished and disruption declined but to a lesser extent. In contrast, when misbehavior was punished, disruption tended to be less frequent, but no effect was observed in academic output. Such data underscore how crucial the selection of target behavior is (15).

Such data do not, on the other hand, suggest that *all* disruptive students be managed by targeting academic output. The teacher who wishes to devise a behavioral intervention must arrive at the individual program empirically. The most effective way of accomplishing this is through a period of systematic observation to determine the typical conditions when disruption occurs and what factors seem to be maintaining disruption. In our observations of disruptive adolescents in mainstreamed classes, individuals may be more disruptive during "dead" time, during unsupervised time, when substitute teachers are present, during class discussions, during certain times of the day, and when unable to carry out assignments. Teacher and peer attention, dismissal from the classroom following aggressive episodes, the ability to disrupt the class, and the verbalizations of argumentative peers, indeed, often serve to strengthen misconduct.

On the basis of observation, a teacher can select promising behaviors to be rewarded, and then can target the more disturbing types of disruptive behaviors for punishment.

Developing Contingency Programs

Once the teacher has defined the behaviors that are to be targeted, the problem is to discover consequences that are appropriate and powerful enough to bring about the desired behavior change and a means of delivering them. Behavior modification has too often been associated in the minds of many members of the educational community with the continuous awarding of tangible rewards, often of dubious value in themselves, such as candy or cigarettes, for any form of positive behavior. In fact, the historical development of many of the techniques was just that, but it should be borne in mind that the earliest studies involved highly disturbed or severely handicapped persons, many of whom had spent years of neglect in the "hopeless" wards of institutions.

The simplest forms of behavioral programs do indeed involve rewards at frequent intervals, often many times within a single instructional period. Teacher approval through positive comments, grades, smiles, or attention are likely to be the least obtrusive in running a classroom and the most readily usable within a secondary school.

The success of classroom management systems may hinge on finding appropriate consequences for behavior. For the majority of students, behavior is maintained by grades, threats of disciplinary action, an acquired enjoyment of the learning process, and encouragement from teachers, peers, and family. For the misbehaving and underachieving students, these consequences are not sufficient.

Punishment   Although not the method of choice, punishment can be effective in eliminating disruptive behavior, provided that what is defined as a punisher is in fact aversive to the student and provided that it occurs consistently and quickly after the infraction (27). Many events conceived of as punishment in the schools are not aversive for the disruptive adolescent. In our work, for example, we have noted many instances of students who will have themselves suspended in order to have a holiday from school. Other students appear to enjoy being sent to the principal's office where they may talk with other students or run errands for staff while waiting for what amounts to little more than a chat with an administrator, which occurs long after the offense. Suspension conferences (attended by the student and his parent) that routinely occur a week after the offense are also unlikely to actually punish misbehavior.

Immediate restitution, time-out, detention, and extra assignments, however, have been shown to be effective punishers in individual instances with disruptive students (28, 29).

Reinforcers   Rewards must also be discovered empirically. One very direct method is to simply observe the frequency with which students engage in certain activities during unstructured periods. Activities which are frequently selected may serve as rewards (Note C). Also, while it might not be wise to ask an adolescent what would be punishing to him, asking the adolescent what is rewarding to him may be of great value. Table 1 shows a reinforcer survey schedule that may be useful to teachers.

Examination of this schedule discloses that many of the items are activities or privileges normally granted all students noncontingently in many classrooms. Such rewards are ideal as they require little financial support and do not afford the disruptive student privileges not granted other students. We strongly advocate the use of such "natural" rewards or rewards that are compatible with the general educational goals of the school (such as books, access to library, and field trips). A recent study (30) has reported, however, that social and other nontangible rewards are preferred more by students who succeed academically than by learning-impaired adolescents. Thus, although we advocate natural and social rewards, tangible rewards may be a necessary starting point with more difficult individuals. In the final analysis, the selection of effective rewards is, within reasonable limits, a practical and empirical matter rather than a philosophical one.

Delivery Systems   Teachers may wish to reward students for more than a single instance of an encouraged behavior. Larger rewards may be given only after a number of instances of the target behavior(s) have occurred (e.g., "You may have a pass to the library on Friday if you have perfect attendance *and* all of your homework and classwork are finished"). The delay between the behavior and consequence may strain the contingency. Thus, systems which provide feedback to the student and intermediate rewards have been developed, such as tokens, point systems, and contracts. These are described in the following chapter.

Other systems have been developed that give rewards occasionally. In one program, students spend accumulated points at weekly

Table 1. Secondary student reinforcement survey schedule

Below are listed some things that we might be able to get for you or let you do if you continue to make progress in school. Circle the number that shows your feelings about each choice. 1, dislike very much; 2, dislike some; 3, don't care; 4, like some; 5, like very much. If you circle a 5 on the items with the stars, write exactly what you would like on the back.

Passes		*Food (besides below)	12345
to library	12345	candy bars	12345
to bathroom	12345	French fries	12345
to smoking area	12345	fruit	12345
to study hall	12345	ice cream	12345
Letters		soft drinks	12345
to parents	12345	milk	12345
job recommendation	12345	hamburger	12345
to probation officer	12345	*Prizes (besides below)	12345
to principal	12345	earrings	12345
to employer	12345	pens	12345
*Activities (besides below)	12345	pencils	12345
play board games	12345	paint	12345
*listen to record	12345	*Craft material	12345
free time	12345	Tickets to dances	12345
use Xerox machine	12345	Tickets to movies	12345
use typewriter	12345	Gym socks	12345
*read a magazine	12345	School T-shirt	12345
use of phone	12345	*Book	12345
set up lab	12345	*Magazine	12345
run movie projector	12345	Plants	12345
*a field trip	12345	Dictionary	12345
longer lunch	12345	*Record	12345
working as teacher aide	12345	Radio	12345
tutoring someone	12345	Calculator	12345
being tutored	12345	Softball	12345
select class topic	12345	Cosmetics	12345
no homework	12345	Sheet music	12345
first to lunch	12345	Better grades	12345
time with teacher	12345	Cigarette lighter	12345
jobs	12345	*Athletic equipment	12345
sports	12345		

auctions where two or three items are sold to about 30 students (16). Lotteries also are used to distribute rewards where each instance of a target behavior earns one ticket and prizes are awarded occasionally (31).

After the students reach initial behavioral expectations, teachers may wish to require more or higher quality work. Teachers may also wish to use more natural rewards. For these reasons, contingencies should be in effect for relatively short periods of time.

The Need for Assessment

Teachers who do not objectively measure the behavioral consequences of their efforts are more likely to fail. Failure can come in
many guises but the most likely are: 1) failure to have an effect but
not knowing it, and 2) failure to recognize a small effect. The cost of
either failure may be serious. In the first case, one may continue an
intervention that is unproductive or even counterproductive. In the
second, one may hastily abandon a productive strategy. Anecdotal
reports of intervention efforts, very frequent in the educational literature, are replete with problems of the first type. Problems of the second type frequently lead to teacher statements such as, "I even tried
behavior modification on Johnny but it didn't work."

The assessment process generally begins well before intervention and continues throughout. Indeed, programmatic assessment
frequently calls for outcome measures that are taken years after program termination. As previously described, well before intervention
objective observation and assessment are involved in selecting and
defining target behaviors, selecting potentially reinforcing events,
and suggesting possible avenues for intervention. Consideration is
then directed toward establishing a baseline for comparison purposes. An objective monitoring system should be chosen that is designed to accommodate the nature and frequency of the behavior(s)
under study. That is, if the behavior is complex and multifaceted
(e.g., school achievement) one may need to analyze a matrix of variables. On the other hand, if it is an easily defined low frequency behavior (e.g., being late to class), it may be monitored on a simple
occurrence/non-occurrence basis. Baselines should be continued until the behavior shows a stable trend. Not infrequently, the act of
monitoring a behavior may have a positive effect on that behavior,
called *reactivity*, which may eliminate the need for any further intervention.

For obvious reasons, objective monitoring should continue
throughout the intervention period. If the behavior change strategy
is working (decreasing undesirable behavior or increasing desirable
behavior), it may be continued or gradually withdrawn. The latter
process, referred to as "thinning" or "attenuation of reinforcement," is often attempted when tangible reinforcers are employed
and the teacher wishes to transfer behavioral control to more "natural" classroom reinforcers such as attention and praise.

If the change strategy is not working (the behavior is not changing in the desired direction relative to baseline or quickly enough to
resolve more serious problems), one may wish to discard the proce-

dure and try a new one or to modify the procedure. Program problems may generally be classified into four separate but related groups: 1) selection of unrealistic or inappropriate goals, 2) selection of inappropriate or inadequate rewards and punishers, 3) infrequent or delayed rewards and punishers, or 4) inconsistent or nonsystematic program implementation. Any or all of these problems can result in program failure although frequently the effectiveness of a strategy will be enhanced with relatively minor modifications.

CONCLUSION

The intent of this chapter has been to provide a general overview of commonly employed behavioral teaching and intervention strategies as well as some basic principles and suggestions for those interested in modifying student behavior. This survey has by no means been exhaustive. More detailed information concerning specific individual treatment of programs is provided in the following chapter.

As a final note it seems imperative to stress the need for objective measurement, although it is often a cumbersome and time-consuming process. This, the most crucial element of an intervention, may be the first to be discarded. We believe this is a mistake for three reasons. First, a lack of accurate assessment necessarily diminishes the quality of student education. Second, in a period in which accountability is increasingly important, precise record-keeping is a must. It is also helpful in sound organizational management. Finally, given that educating disruptive students is generally a slow and painful process, a lack of data may deprive teachers of a valuable source of feedback on their effectiveness.

NOTES

Note A. Terminology in behavior modification has historically been a thorny issue. For the sake of clarity, we have adopted the system of Woods (32), which uses the terms *reward* (the presentation of a positive event), *punishment* (the presentation of a negative event), *relief* (the removal of a negative event), and *penalty* (the removal of a positive event). This avoids the use of the term *negative reinforcement,* which has been used to mean both punishment and relief. This also avoids the general term *reinforcement,* which has a distinctly different use in the educational literature.

Note B. In the pioneering work of John Watson (33), it was noted that the introduction of an extinction procedure is frequently followed by an acceleration of the behavior under study. In studying infant crying, for example, he showed that if the mother ignored this behavior its intensity increased considerably.

If the mother then picked up the baby, subsequent crying episodes would rapidly increase to this new, higher intensity. Conversely, if the mother refrained from picking up her infant, his crying would gradually diminish over time. The tendency for behavior to show a brief increase in rate or intensity following the onset of extinction has more recently been termed an "extinction burst" (27).

Note C. Premack (34) stated that in a given situation a behavior that is more likely to occur can be used to reward a behavior less likely to occur. For example, in the classroom students may prefer to socialize with their peers than to do arithmetic problems. Allowing students to socialize could, therefore, be used to reward a criterion performance on arithmetic problems. There are substantial difficulties in translating this into practice. The more likely behavior of an individual student in a given setting on a given day is extremely difficult to assess. To overcome this, teachers have frequently used free time, when a variety of options are available, to maximize the availability of a preferred behavior.

REFERENCES

1. Nelson, C. M., & Kauffman, J. M. Educational programming for secondary school-age delinquent and maladjusted pupils. *Behavioral Disorders,* 1977, *2,* 102–113.
2. Woody, R. H. *Behavioral problem children in schools.* New York: Appleton-Century-Crofts, 1969.
3. Grossman, J. B. The courts as intervenors. *Education and Urban Society,* 1979, *11,* 567–571.
4. Madsen, C. H., Becker, W. C., & Thomas, D. R. Rules, praise, and ignoring: Elements of elementary classroom control. *Journal of Applied Behavior Analysis,* 1968, *1,* 139–150.
5. Gallup, G. H. The 10th annual Gallup poll. *Phi Delta Kappan,* 1978, *60,* 33–45.
6. Baltimore County Board of Education. *Student behavior handbook.* Baltimore: 1979.
7. Lufler, H. S. Debating with untested assumptions: The need to understand school discipline. *Education and Urban Society,* 1979, *11,* 450–464.
8. Trice, A. D. Unpublished data, 1979.
9. Goffman, E. *Behavior in public places.* New York: The Free Press, 1963.
10. White, M. A. Natural rates of teacher approval and disapproval in the classroom. *Journal of Applied Behavior Analysis,* 1975, *8,* 367–372.
11. Thomas, J. D., Presland, I. E., Grant, M. D., & Glynn, T. L. Natural rates of teacher approval and disapproval in grade-7 classrooms. *Journal of Applied Behavior Analysis,* 1978, *11,* 91–94.
12. Becker, W. C., Madsen, C. H., Arnold, C. R., & Thomas, D. R. The contingent use of teacher attention and praise in reducing classroom behavior problems. *The Journal of Special Education,* 1967, *1,* 287–307.

13. Whaley, D. L., & Malott, R. W. *Elementary Principles of Behavior.* Englewood Cliffs, N.J.: Prentice-Hall, 1971.
14. Becker, W. C., Englemann, S., & Thomas, D. R. *Teaching I: Classroom management.* Chicago: Science Research Associates, Inc., 1975.
15. Bandura, A. *Principles of behavior modification.* New York: Holt, Rinehart, and Winston, 1969.
16. Heaton, R. C., Safer, D. J., Allen, R. P., Spinnato, N. C., & Prumo, F. M. A motivational environment for behaviorally deviant junior high school students. *Journal of Abnormal Child Psychology,* 1976, *4,* 263–275.
17. McAllister, L. W., Stachowiak, J. G., Baer, D. M., Conderman, L. The application of operant conditioning techniques in a secondary classroom. *Journal of Applied Behavior Analysis,* 1969, *2,* 277–285.
18. O'Leary, K. D., & Becker, W. C. The effects of the intensity of a teacher's reprimands on children's behavior. *Journal of School Psychology,* 1968, *7,* 8–11.
19. Scott, J. W., & Bushell, D. The length of teacher contacts and students' off-task behavior. *Journal of Applied Behavior Analysis,* 1972, *5,* 39–44.
20. Willmo, H. P. *Adolescent boys of east London.* Baltimore: Penguin Books, 1969.
21. Yablonsky, L. *The violent gang.* New York: Macmillan, 1962.
22. O'Leary, S. G., & O'Leary, K. D. Behavior modification in the school. In H. Leitenberg (Ed.), *Handbook of behavior modification and behavior therapy.* Englewood Cliffs, N.J.: Prentice-Hall, Inc., 1976.
23. Leviton, H. S. The individualization of discipline for behavior dropout pupils. *Psychology in the Schools,* 1976, *13,* 445–448.
24. Thomas, D. R., Becker, W. C., & Armstrong, M. Production and elimination of disruptive classroom behavior by systematically varying teacher behaviors. *Journal of Applied Behavior Analysis,* 1968, *1,* 35–45.
25. Marholin, D., & Steinman, W. M. Stimulus control in the classroom as a function of the behavior reinforced. *Journal of Applied Behavior Analysis,* 1977, *10,* 465–478.
26. Hay, W. M., Hay, L. R., & Nelson, R. O. Direct and collateral changes in on-task and academic behavior resulting from on-task versus academic contingencies. *Behavior Therapy,* 1977, *8,* 431–441.
27. Kazdin, A. E. *Behavior Modification in Applied Settings.* Homewood, Ill.: Dorsey Press, 1980.
28. Foxx, R. M., & Azrin, N. H. Restitution: A method of eliminating aggressive-disruptive behavior of mentally retarded and brain damaged patients. *Behavior Research and Therapy,* 1972, *10,* 15–27.
29. Drabman, R. S., & Spitalnik, R. Social isolation as a punishment procedure: A controlled study. *Journal of Experimental Child Psychology,* 1973, *16,* 236–249.
30. Serralde de Scholz, H. C., & McDougal, D. Comparison of potential reinforcer ratings between slow learners and regular students. *Behavior Therapy,* 1978, *9,* 60–64.
31. Iwata, B. A., Bailey, J. S., Brown, K. M ., Foshu, T. J., & Alpern, M. A performance-based lottery to improve residential care and training by institutional staff. *Journal of Applied Behavior Analysis,* 1976, *9,* 417–431.

152   *Parker and Trice*

32. Woods, P. J. A taxonomy of instrumental conditioning. *American Psychologist,* 1974, *29,* 584–597.
33. Watson, J. B. *Behaviorism.* New York: W. W. Norton, 1924.
34. Premack, D. Reinforcement theory. In D. Levine (Ed.), *Nebraska Symposium on Motivation.* Lincoln: University of Nebraska Press, 1965.

8

Teaching disruptive youth in the mainstream:
II Beyond the basic strategy

Ashton D. Trice and Frank C. Parker

The preceding chapter described a basic model of classroom management for disruptive secondary school students comprised of stating rules clearly, ignoring nonproductive, nondisruptive behavior, and punishing serious misbehavior. The strategy of positively attending to productive behaviors incompatible with disruption was recommended over negatively attending to misbehavior. Also emphasized was that the intervention be individualized, empirically derived, and continuously assessed.

This model has been shown to be useful for such students (1). There are occasions, however, when teachers need to employ additional means to achieve classroom control. First, there may be instances when these methods may not achieve acceptable levels of conduct with particularly problematic individuals. Second, successful intervention rarely generalizes to other settings (2). Thus, teachers who work diligently to effect behavior change will not be rewarded for their efforts if the student is removed from school for misconduct elsewhere. Third, data suggest that effects will usually not be maintained once intervention is terminated unless specific efforts are made to ensure the maintenance of effects over time. Finally, teachers may wish to use methods that are less intrusive to their normal teaching practices.

This chapter describes a number of techniques that have been designed to address one or more of these issues. These techniques include group contingencies, point and token systems, contracting, and self-control programs. This chapter describes the rationale for each technique, provides examples of the application of the technique, and then evaluates each as it applies to disruptive adolescents in the mainstream.

GROUP CONTINGENCIES

Group contingencies are frequently used when one *or more* members of a class appear unresponsive to the on-going motivational system. They provide a means for the teacher to offer additional incentives without having to construct individual programs, thereby avoiding the situation wherein a single student or a small minority of the class receives special treatment and avoiding using excessive teacher time in creating special individual programs. Four types of group contingencies have been used (Note A).

1. *Independent group contingenices*   Under this type of contingency, each student is rewarded if he or she *independently* meets a specified criterion of performance. For example, students who receive a grade of 90% on a quiz may be relieved of having to do homework that night, or, using a disruptive behavior target, students who have no instances of a rule violation (e.g., no calling out) may be given lottery tickets toward an end of the week raffle. This contingency arrangement is standard practice in many classrooms. It is not, however, typical of the other form of group contingencies in that individuals are rewarded rather than the entire group, thereby minimizing group peer pressure on the behavior of recalcitrant individuals. The term *standardized contingency* might better describe this arrangement.
2. *Dependent group contingencies*   This type of contingency is used primarily to target a single individual's behavior. In this instance, reward for the entire class depends on *all members* meeting the criterion. For example, the teacher may eliminate homework if everyone in the class receives a passing grade on a daily quiz or may give a 10-minute free time period at the end of the lesson if there have been no rule violations. The rationale for this approach is that peer pressure will be exerted on the underachieving or disruptive student to meet the criterion or that peer attention to misbehavior will be curtailed. In instances where this approach has been used, spontaneous tutoring of underachieving students has been noted. Some researchers have used a strategy of giving rewards to the entire group based only on

the performance of a single student, usually the most frequently misbehaving one. Such a situation not only draws excessive attention to the target student's behavior but may undermine the motivation of the rest of the class, and therefore is not recommended, as the process of rewarding all students if all meet criterion will perform the same function.

3. *Interdependent group contingencies* Such arrangements require that a certain group performance be exhibited for group reward (e.g., average grade for academic targets or a specified limit on the number of disruptive behaviors for conduct targets). As in our examples above, homework may be suspended if the average quiz score is 90%, or free time may be given if there are two or fewer instances of rule violation for the entire group. Interdependent contingencies minimize the effects of individuals. Such minimization may be advantageous if one student is likely to deliberately sabotage the system or if certain individuals do not possess the ability to meet the criterion, as may be the case with low achievers.

4. *Competitive contingencies* Competitive contingencies reward a *subgroup* of the class for outperforming other subgroups. The teacher may eliminate homework for the team composed of half of the class that has the higher average score on the quiz. (Both teams, however, may be exempt from homework if both achieve exceptionally well, or both may be required to do homework if both do very poorly.) Again, raffle tickets may be given to the team with fewer rule violations.

One major rationale for competitive contingencies has been to increase cooperation among team members. For example, the consistent findings of the Teams-Games-Tournaments (3) approach which uses competitive contingencies, have been improved race relations in public schools when mixed race teams were employed in large scale efforts of this kind.

Behaviors that have been targeted by group contingencies include noise level, on-task behavior, academic output, aggression, and class preparation (4, 5, 6). The most frequently used rewards are free time, raffle tickets, and suspension of assignments, although with younger students certificates and ribbons are often included (6).

Evaluative Comment

Group contingencies are frequently justified on the basis of their efficiency (7). They require less teacher time than establishing individual programs. In some instances they have been shown to produce as great a change as individual interventions (8), and in these instances the claim for efficiency is warranted. Yet teacher time is only one factor in determining efficiency; the intervention must also be effective. Unless considerable ingenuity is involved in the creation of group programs, the behaviorally or academically deficient student may be little affected by them.

O'Leary and Drabman (9) have pointed out several potential problems of these group-wide programs to which we append a few more. First, peer pressure may become extreme if rewards are powerful and an individual is repeatedly responsible for the group's loss of rewards. Second, under the dependent group contingency, an individual has the ability to sabotage the system. Third, some students may be incapable of meeting criterion because of extreme deficits, and in this instance the continual withholding of rewards (under independent contingencies) or possible excessive peer pressure (under dependent contingencies) may present ethical problems. Fourth, Drabman, Spitalnik, and Spitalnik (10) found rather profound changes in sociometric peer ratings when group contingencies were in effect; these changes need not always be positive. Finally, while spontaneous tutoring has been highlighted as an advantage of this approach, cheating will accomplish the same result.

On the other hand, group contingencies have several advantages. Most obviously they permit the use of a group procedure that actually targets individuals. A group program may draw less attention to the exceptionality of the target child than an individual program in which the student is given rewards (which may not be available to the rest of the class). Also, such programs bring more rewards into the classroom and increase motivation for all students. Finally, they may well work for some of those who have been resistant to the more direct approach and for those whose progress is incomplete.

POINT AND TOKEN SYSTEMS

Point and token systems (together called marker systems) are means whereby rewards are made available following multiple instances of appropriate behavior. Each encouraged behavior is followed by the awarding of a predetermined number of points or tokens, and rewards are granted when a specified number of points or tokens have been accumulated or on some other prearranged basis. In general usage, tokens are tangible markers (e.g., tickets, poker chips) while points are bookkeeping markers (e.g., marks on progress sheets, ledgers, or graphs). Several advantages of point and token systems are detailed below.

1. *Point and token systems delay reward.* Although it has been stressed that rewards are most effective when they occur immediately after the target behavior (and may not be effective at all if the delay is too long), point and token systems prepare students for situations in which rewards must be delayed over lengthy periods of time. Points and tokens are awarded immediately; the prizes, commendations, and privileges for which the tokens and points are markers are made available later.

2. *Points and tokens become secondary rewards.* Students who experience severe school adjustment problems may do so because they fail to find much reward in normal school routine. Grades and other positive evaluations, awards, and the process of learning, all of which motivate most students often fail to effect behavior change in disruptive adolescents who are turned off to school in general or whose skill level is so low that extreme effort would be required to earn these benefits. Thus, in early efforts to help these students, tangible rewards and extraordinary privileges are recommended to begin to build up a repertoire of positive behaviors. Such means are only provisional, however. Behavior modification efforts with maladjusted individuals have as their long-term goals the reintroduction of the individual into the natural community of rewards (11). Within the school, this natural community of rewards includes good grades, social interactions, and mastery of learning. Thus, concurrent with requiring more effort of a higher quality as the intervention continues, teachers should aim for the gradual phasing out of many of the additional incentives. Token and point systems allow for this phasing out. Because tokens and points are cashed in for primary rewards early in the program, they tend to become rewards themselves by nature of their association. Worth nothing in and of themselves, they still function as rewards (secondary rewards). Secondary rewards are able to maintain behavior even when their relationship to the initial primary rewards becomes remote (12).

3. *Points and tokens provide feedback to the student.* Although in the previous chapter we emphasized the importance of direct teacher attention and feedback on student performance, it is not unreasonable that students who find school an intensely unpleasant and unsuccessful situation resist teacher feedback. This, however, can be reversed. By awarding a point or token,

the marker, the teacher's positive evaluation, and the distant primary reward all become associated. Thereby, the point comes to stand for the teacher's *positive* feedback, and the teacher's feedback becomes strengthened by its association with the primary reward.

When the teacher's positive role is not at issue, the token or point system provides a means of automatically providing positive feedback to students. Studies (13, 14) have indicated that the use of token systems increases the likelihood of teachers giving positive feedback more than intensive short-term teacher efforts at direct verbal feedback. Within the normal classroom any number of things distract teachers from attending to the routine good performance of students; token and point systems curtail such lapses.

4. *Comprehensive token and point systems are inherently self-evaluative.* If a substantial sample of all appropriate behaviors are given point credit, records of a point system's implementation will disclose if the system works. If, over time, students accumulate more points, appropriate behavior is increasing. If the point to reward ratio is increased, the effectiveness of the fading procedure will automatically be substantiated (assuming that the number of points earned does not drop).

5. *Point and token systems allow for the use of powerful rewards for long-term goals.* On an ultimately practical level, marker contingencies allow for the use of very large rewards which the direct rewarding of single instances of behavior does not. A student may not value grades, teacher attention, M & Ms, 5 minutes of free time, or any of the rewards that might be applied to single instances of behavior. On the other hand, the student might well be willing to work for the right to take a drivers education class, even if the right to take the class is based on turning in on time 100 passing homework assignments or accumulating 200 positive daily ratings from classroom teachers over a period of 3 months. Quite obviously, the extent to which a student will delay reward and work toward a long-term goal is an empirical question.

Direct Marker Contingencies

This last advantage of point and token systems allows for the establishment of extended control of a particular behavior with the use of one relatively large reward. Marker values are arranged for occurrences of positive behavior or non-occurrences of negative behavior or for a designated level of performance. A certain number of points are required for reward. In many instances this criterion is delimited by constraints (criterion number achieved within a specified time span) or is determined daily on the basis of an improvement from past performance. Three examples of such contingencies are provided.

Trice, Parker, and Furrow (15) awarded points for spelling with a functionally nonreading disruptive adolescent. One point was awarded for each word written in response to ten daily conversational questions. A bonus point was awarded if the word was spelled correctly. If the day's point total exceeded the previous day's, the student was given 10-15 minutes of free time at the end of the period. Over a period of 2 months, length of responses and spelling accuracy increased, and improvement was noted in reading and conduct.

Campbell and Willis (16) awarded points for creativity scores on daily writing exercises which could be cashed in for edibles at an end of the week party. The two students with the highest number of points served as the party hosts. One point was awarded for turning in an excercise, one for reaching a criterion score, and up to three points for improvement over previous levels. The introduction of the direct point contingency produced dramatic increases in the creativity scores of the student compositions. These increases were maintained when the parties were discontinued and also produced a more positive classroom environment.

In a novel application of point systems, Chiang, Iwata, and Dorsey (17) were able to significantly reduce disruption on a school bus by using points. The student studied received a point from the bus driver for intervals of the total trip during which he exhibited no disruptive behavior. Morning trip points could be exchanged for school privileges and afternoon points exchanged for such home privileges as the use of a bicycle. Disruptive bus behavior was virtually eliminated by this procedure.

Direct contingencies are primarily useful in targeting particularly problematic skill deficits and misconduct excesses or in providing motivation along a single dimension. They are not of general usefulness when a wide spectrum of problems are involved. They may be especially useful when the teacher has access to powerful rewards in the school or can arrange home based rewards.

Multiple Behavioral Criteria

It is perhaps more beneficial in the typical case of the disruptive adolescent to award points for more than one behavior, as the student is likely to manifest problems in a number of areas (e.g., inappropriate verbalizations, aggression, off target behaviors, academic under-achievement). Most of the group programs described in this volume have awarded points for a variety of behaviors which were in need of improvement. For the teacher who is creating a program for a particular student in a particular setting, only problematic behaviors need be targeted. In fact, were the teacher to adopt an existing system and award points for behaviors already being maintained at appropriate levels, there is some evidence that the motivation that was maintaining the behavior before the point contingency would be undermined (18).

Again, awarding points for behaviors that are incompatible with disruption or the absence of disruptive behaviors during intervals of the class period is the method of choice, although some systems have included point loss for inappropriate behaviors.

One well substantiated use of multiple behavioral criteria using a single type of reward is the Personalized System of Instruction (19). Grades are awarded on the basis of points, which can be earned in a variety of ways, including tests, quizzes, book reports, papers, and presentations. Beyond basic course requirements (e.g., reading required texts and taking tests on them), students may personalize their course by selecting other means of earning points. Such approaches have repeatedly found that students complete more academic activities under such systems, which results in a substantial increase in learning.

Multiple Back-Up Rewards

The use of more than one back-up reward has been shown to strengthen the secondary reward characteristic of the marker (20). A second factor that recommends the use of more back-up rewards is that rewards may lose their effectiveness with continued use. Finally, a comprehensive set of back-up reinforcers, with each assigned a specific point value, allows students to choose not only *what* rewards they wish, but by selecting to work for rewards of varying point values, *when* they wish reward. Student-selection of academic activities and rewards (within teacher-set limits) has been shown to significantly increase positive performance (21).

Economies

An economy exists when students receive markers for multiple behaviors and spend these markers for a variety of back-up rewards. Economies have been successfully implemented in schools with both normal and special groups and individuals (22). Most often, economies are used for an entire group and focus on a broad spectrum of behavior within the particular setting.

In many respects, comprehensive economies are beyond the scope of the teacher who is looking for means of exerting control over one or two adolescents in a classroom. Less comprehensive sorts of economies can be used, which would not only help to exert control over chronically disruptive students, but which could facilitate normal classroom routine. An example of such a system employed with a remedial 9th grade English class that had several behavior problem students is presented in Table 1.

Table 1. Point and token system used with a 9th grade English class

Behavior	Token value	Points
Attendance		
In seat on time	1	
Daily quiz turned in	1	
A on daily quiz	1	
Daily quiz grade		up to 5
Conduct		
Discussion contribution		1
Raising hand before speaking	1	
Talking out of turn	−1	
No calling out (per period)	1	1
Cheating	−2	−5
Out of seat (without permission)	−1	
Exam (every 3 weeks)	4(A), 3(B), etc.	
up to 100	up to 100	
Book report (every 3 weeks)		
Turned in		5
On time	1	5
Achievement		up to 40
Homework		
Turned in on time		3
Achievement		up to 7
Extra credit		
Extra book report	1	up to 50
Creative writing		up to 25
Short story summary		up to 10
Oral reports	1	up to 10
Being tutored	1	3/15 minutes
Tutoring		3/15 minutes

Grades:	A=600 +	Token exchange:	Bathroom pass	=2
	B=500–599		Library pass	=2
	C=400–499		Homework exemption	=4
	D=300–399		Study hall pass	=4
			Friday treats	=2
			Good notes home	=1

Evaluative Comments

Marker systems are a means of providing secondary or token rewards sufficient to maintain behavior while more immediate rewards used to initiate behavior change are being phased out. Marker systems supplement normal feedback on student performance both to the student and to the teacher.

Group-wide token systems, however, have been rather consistently shown to fail to motivate all students (23). This is not surprising with respect to the need to individualize motivational strategies for individuals who fall in the extreme range on achievement or conduct: if markers are too difficult to come by, students will not work for them; if the rewards are too remote or are not of particular value to the individual, the marker will not become rewarding. Modification of existing classroom marker contingency systems to meet specific individual differences is seen as a very promising strategy for behavior change.

CONTINGENCY CONTRACTING

Simply stated, a contingency contract is a negotiated quasi-legal document that specifies the behavioral expectations and inherent consequences agreed to by two or more parties. As such, contracting is a process rather than the application of a specific technique. That is, the contract offers a framework for the statement of contingent relationships that may involve a broad range of intervention possibilities. Thus contracting, *per se*, cannot be said to be good or bad, effective or ineffective. The strength of a given contract lies in the information conveyed, the contingencies enumerated, and the degree of contract enforcement.

As a delivery system, contracting clarifies arrangements far better than can verbal exchange. It serves as a permanent record of agreements, thus eliminating later confusion and bickering. By requiring specific bits of behavior in exchange for specific consequences, it is an invaluable aid in shaping behavior. In addition, the quasi-legal nature of the document is especially appealing to adolescents and adults, thus promoting compliance with its terms. Thus, while it is not mandatory that special forms be employed in the contracting process, the formalization of the process is worthwhile.

Contingency contracting has been a dominant force in the behavioral literature over the past 12 years. With adults, contracts have been employed in substance abuse (24, 25), in weight management (26), in marital counseling (27, 28), in family therapy (29), and in numerous other problem areas. With younger children, contracting has been used to promote academic achievement, decrease problem classroom behavior (30), and encourage the completion of household chores (31). It is with adolescent populations, however, that contracting may show its greatest utility. Adolescents, generally resenting the dominance of authority figures, appear to particularly appreciate the negotiation process inherent to contract development.

Early studies by Tharp and Wetzel (32) and by Stuart (33–35) were among the first to point to the utility of this technique with adolescent populations (primarily delinquent and predelinquent youth). These authors noted that even with adolescents, parents are the dispensers of a considerable amount of their daily rewards. Allowances, curfew hours, access to the family car, television viewing time, and numerous other privileges and commodities are, to varying degrees, under parental control. In such families, however, relations are often strained. Parents often choose to follow one of two extreme paths: 1) they may simply give up and grant access to all rewards noncontingently, or 2) they may cut off access to rewarding events completely, thus depriving the student of a very powerful and potentially productive source of incentives. Furthermore, given that these parties generally possess few negotiation skills (33), the likelihood of breaking such an impasse is remote. Since contracting usually involves a negotiation process, this can provide an invaluable forum for skill training, theoretically benefiting the family unit far beyond the resolution of the specific problem at hand. Indeed, Alexander and Parsons (36) indicated that families which display appropriate negotiation skills during the contracting process frequently show reduced delinquency recidivism in their adolescent offspring.

Simple two-party contracts have shown promising results in dealing with such problems as truancy, school disruption, and poor academic performance (37, 38). These contracts generally involve a teacher, counselor, or school administrator, and a student. One program (39), for example, used simple teacher-student negotiated contracts as a means of increasing the quality and quantity of academic output. Points and privileges were directly exchanged for meeting certain agreed-upon academic criteria on a weekly basis. These criteria were individualized according to baseline ability levels—a procedure that is commonly employed in special education classrooms but more difficult to implement in the mainstream.

As noted above, however, contracts are optimally employed in systems representing three or more parties. In such cases, a third party (teacher, counselor, administrator, psychologist, etc.) serves as a mediator, consultant, or behavior analyst for the other two parties (frequently a student and his or her guardian). In this role the behavior analyst performs a crucial function in assessing problem areas, identifying and defining prospective target behaviors, overseeing the negotiation process, arranging an exchange system, troubleshooting, and conducting subsequent renegotiation sessions. Further, as noted above, the behavior analyst is in a unique position to demonstrate and model appropriate social behavior, essential in family negotiations.

Components of Typical Classroom Contingency Contracts

While the format for classroom contracts varies widely, there are common elements. Contracts contain specific statements of the behaviors expected of all parties as well as the consequences for meeting and/or failing to meet these expectations. They are typically signed by the involved individuals and may be witnessed by a third person (e.g., the behavior analyst). The duration of the contract period is clearly specified and some provision for renegotiation may be included. Further, some researchers (33) prefer to add some form of long-term bonus or penalty to enhance contract compliance.

A very simple teacher/student contract is shown in Figure 1. Note that while this agreement is basic and informal, it does contain the essential contract elements. A more complex exchange system is

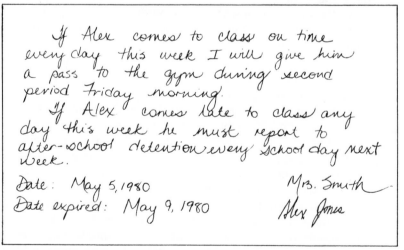

Figure 1.   Informal teacher-student contract.

illustrated in Figure 2. Here, a point system is included, targeting several behaviors throughout the academic day. A guidance counselor is employed in a behavior analyst role to facilitate the contracting process. Parent feedback is arranged through "good day cards," a procedure commonly employed in behavioral efforts to seek parental support for appropriate school behavior (40). Longer term contingencies are also enumerated under the penalty and bonus sections.

The use of clear and verifiable statements of behavioral expectations is well illustrated in both of the above contracts. Statements such as "Bill's behavior (attitude, performance, etc.) must improve next week" are to be avoided. Such imprecision will invariably lead to future problems. When more than two parties are involved, the need for precision is even greater. An important but seldom considered problem area is that of parental compliance with contract terms. It is simply not sufficient to write up a contract and assume that the parental good faith demonstrated during the negotiation session will be translated into steadfast adherence to contract terms. Such behavior must be carefully monitored by the behavior analyst and additional contingencies for *parental* behavior must, at times, be included.

Evaluative Comment

It was stated earlier that the contracting process is, in itself, neither good nor bad, effective nor ineffective. Clearly there are good and bad contracts, given specific circumstances and client characteristics, but the flexibility inherent in this system allows for widely divergent approaches. Virtually any intervention approach that can be stated in a clear and precise manner can be implemented in a contractual agreement.

Nevertheless, some authors have unfortunately reported their failure with contracting systems as an indictment of contracting. In one delinquency study (41), for example, the authors concluded:

> In working with families that are decimated by divorce, crime, drug abuse and woefully inadequate communication and negotiation skills, the introduction of a contingency contract is worth about as much as the paper it is printed on.

Obviously, the utility of any specific approach must be considered in context. In contractual efforts to reduce the longstanding problem behavior of delinquent youth, for example, one must consider how the specified contingencies compete with existing contingencies and

Dates: __May 5/80__ to __May 16/80__   Contract Number: __1__

We, the undersigned, agree to comply with the following contract terms and understand that any term or terms may be renegotiated by mutual consent.

I, the student, agree to:

1. Be on time for all scheduled classes.
2. Hand in classroom and home assignments on time.
3. Avoid asking for passes to bathroom, office, nurse, and counselor.
4. Have Daily Report Form filled out by all five academic teachers and give it to Mr. Harris after 6th period.

In return I, the counselor, agree to:

1. Maintain following point system for behaviors #1–4 above: #1 = 1 pt/class, #2 = 2 pts/class, #3 = 1 pt/class, #4 = 5 pts/day. (25 possible points/day.)
2. 20–25 points for a *good day card.*
3. Fill out *good day card* to be carried home by Alexandra.

We, the parents, agree to:

1. Award 1/5 of current allowance each day Alexandra brings home *good day card.*
2. Restrict TV viewing time to 1/2 hour if no card is brought home.
3. Award $2 extra for 5 *good day cards* per week.
4. Not criticize Alexandra during dinner.

Penalties:

If fewer than 5 *good day cards* earned in next 2 weeks, Alexandra will be assigned to silent study hall for following school week.

Bonuses:

If 8 *good day cards* earned in next 2 weeks, Alexandra can go to party after prom (May 17).

Signed,

Alexandra Johnson	*William Haring*
Student	Counselor
Wilma Johnson	*Fred Johnson*
Parent	Parent

Figure 2. Multiparty contract involving a point and home-based reward system.

outside sources of reward. If the trade-off is not adequate, the contract will fail. Subsequent contracts with more modest goals may, however, be successful.

Fortunately, several researchers (29, 34) have gone a long way in enumerating procedures to maximize contract effectiveness. Blechman (29), for example, in discussing family therapy efforts, noted the importance of reciprocity and self-selection of contract terms in the negotiation process. The need for the establishment of rapport between the family and therapist was also noted as was the need to incorporate measures to monitor and enhance contract compliance. Obviously, contingency contracting is not a panacea and does not preclude the necessity of adhering to the principles of good therapeutic practice.

SELF-CONTROL

Establishing self-control or self-management is frequently a major end point in psychological interventions. External contingencies can influence behavior and maintain change in structured settings, but outside these settings there may be little or no "natural" generalization. Furthermore, external rewards given by others do not directly promote self-control.

Techniques therefore have been devised to facilitate the transfer of the intervention control from the external agent to the student himself. Essentially, the student learns to apply external monitoring and external reinforcement to his own behavior. This learning of self-management skills, some authorities believe, parallels a similar learning process experienced by more successful students (42–44).

Self-control training generally proceeds in four phases: 1) self-selection of goals, rewards, and criteria for reward, 2) self-monitoring, 3) self-evaluation, and 4) self-reward (45). Selection of goals and rewards has been considered earlier. The remainder of this section briefly outlines the remaining three phases.

Self-monitoring

Having students self-record target behaviors appears to have a temporary beneficial effect on classroom conduct (46). If recording is supplemented with consequences for accuracy of recording and for improvement in conduct, the effects are more profound and long-lasting (47).

Several studies have recommended procedures in which student monitoring gradually replaces teacher monitoring. When the teacher is assured that the student is recording accurately, the student continues to self-record. During these self-recording periods, the teacher needs only to make occasional checks for accuracy and assist in the setting of new and tighter reward criteria. (See Chapter 12.)

It is clear that self-recording by disruptive adolescent students will not replace directive teacher management. Nevertheless, a few students who do not respond to direct intervention do appear very responsive to this technique (47). This responsiveness may be partially due to the rebellious postures of many disruptive adolescents who react negatively to demands made by authority figures or who may reject programs devised and supervised by psychologists or other mental health workers as being unnecessary attempts to "shrink their heads."

Simple self-recording has limited effectiveness over time. Working with disruptive adolescents, however, is partly a matter of buying time, and any technique that even temporarily decreases misbehavior and fosters productivity should not be discarded.

Self-evaluation

Self-monitoring is of little benefit unless the student uses the information for behavior change. Generally, recording positive behavior is more beneficial than recording negative behavior. In fact, charting untoward behavior may actually increase misconduct (48). Although self-evaluation *alone* has not been an effective primary intervention with disruptive students, it is of some value as a final phase of a successful intervention program. The procedure then is part of the replacement of continuous monitoring and is described in detail in Chapter 12.

Self-reward

Often, students are encouraged to back up the self-evaluation by rewarding themselves for a good evaluation and penalizing themselves for a poor evaluation. This technique has not been evaluated with disruptive adolescents, but has usefulness with primary school children having adjustment problems (49). Using this procedure, for example, students reward themselves with desirable after-school activities (e.g., sports, television viewing, recreation) on successful days.

Evaluative Comments

The body of information of self-control with disruptive adolescents is slim. Many students have shown disappointing or only marginally successful results (46). It is evident that self-control intervention is not the primary method of choice in most cases, but may be a recommended addition in pursuing generalization and maintenance once a degree of success has been achieved through other means.

CONCLUSIONS: LONG-TERM COMPREHENSIVE INTERVENTIONS

The secondary school teacher who is assigned highly disruptive students is faced with two challenges: maintaining the student's behavior at levels so that teaching is possible and devising interventions that will help the disruptive student become more successful. Fortunately, both challenges often can be met by the same means. Powerful external control procedures appear most productive in bringing disruptive behavior under control. They are, however, fairly time-consuming for the teacher and, in the long term, unlikely to maintain improved levels of behavior after they are abandoned. Thus, for practical as well as treatment efficacy reasons, teachers should shift to a less directive role as soon as possible.

Figure 3 presents a schematic of one such treatment package which successively employs direct management, contracting, self-monitoring, and self-control procedures. Such an intervention may well be spread out over an entire academic year or longer. This is, however, only one possible model, and other components may be added or ordered differently.

These two chapters described systematic behavior management options available to teachers dealing with disruptive adolescents. This presentation cannot, of course, take into account specific student characteristics, teacher strengths, or the restrictions placed on such interventions by schools, school districts, or unique classroom circumstances. It is hoped that these chapters have expanded the teacher's repertoire of possible intervention approaches and have spurred interest in experimentation within the classroom.

NOTES

Note A. This classification is derived from Litow and Pumroy (8) with the addition of a separate category for "competitive contingencies."

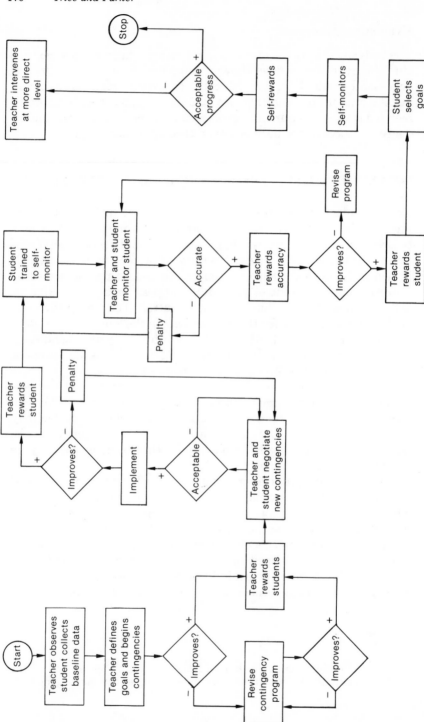

Figure 3. Schematic of a possible long-term classroom intervention package employing successively: direct teacher management, contingency contracting, and self-control procedures.

REFERENCES

1. McAllister, L. W., Stachowiak, J. G., Baer, D. M., & Conderman, L. The application of operant conditioning techniques in a secondary school classroom. *Journal of Applied Behavior Analysis*, 1969, *2*, 277-285.
2. Walker, H. M., & Buckley, N. K. Programming generalization and maintenance of treatment effects across time and across settings. *Journal of Applied Behavior Analysis*, 1972, *5*, 209-224.
3. DeVries, D. L., & Edwards, K. J. Student teams and learning games: Their effects on cross-race and cross-sex interaction. *Journal of Educational Psychology*, 1974, *66*, 741-749.
4. Schmidt, G. W., & Ulrich, R. E. Effects of group contingent events upon classroom noise. *Journal of Applied Behavior Analysis*, 1969, *2*, 171-179.
5. Long, J. D., & Williams, R. L. The comparative effectiveness of group and individually contingent free time with inner-city junior high school students. *Journal of Applied Behavior Analysis*, 1973, *6*, 465-474.
6. Wodarski, J. S., Hamblin, R. L., Beckholdt, D. R., & Ferriton, D. E. The effects of low performance group and individual contingencies on cooperative behaviors exhibited by fifth graders. *The Psychological Record*, 1972, *22*, 359-368.
7. Herman, S. H., & Tramontana, J. Instructions and group *versus* individual reinforcement in modifying disruptive group behavior. *Journal of Applied Behavior Analysis*, 1971, *4*, 113-119.
8. Litow, L., & Pumroy, D. K. A brief review of classroom group-oriented contingencies. *Journal of Applied Behavior Analysis*, 1975, *8*, 341-347.
9. O'Leary, K. D., & Drabman, R. Token reinforcement programs in the classroom: A review. *Psychological Bulletin*, 1971, *75*, 379-398.
10. Drabman, R., Spitalnik, R., & Spitalnik, K. Sociometric and disruptive behavior as a function of four types of token reinforcement programs. *Journal of Applied Behavior Analysis*, 1974, *7*, 93-101.
11. Baer, D. M., & Wolf, M. M. The entry into natural communities of reinforcement. In R. Ulrich, T. Stachnik, & J. Mabry (Eds.), *Control of human behavior* (Vol. 2). Glenview, Ill.: Scott, Foresman, 1970.
12. Kelleher, R. T. Chaining and conditioned reinforcement. In W. K. Honig (Ed.), *Operant behavior: Areas of research and application.* Englewood Cliffs, N. J.: Prentice-Hall, 1966.
13. McNamara, J. R. Behavioral intervention in the classroom: Changing students and training a teacher. *Adolescence*, 1971, *6*, 433-440.
14. Clark, H. B., & Macrae, J. W. The use of imposed and self selected training packages to establish classroom teaching skills. *Journal of Applied Behavior Analysis*, 1976, *9*, 105.
15. Trice, A. D., Parker, F. C., & Furrow, F. Written conversations with feedback and contingent free time to increase reading and writing in a non-reading adolescent. *Education and Treatment of Children*, in press.
16. Campbell, J., & Willis, J. A behavioral program to teach creative writing in the regular classroom. *Education and Treatment of Children*, 1979, *2*, 5-15.
17. Chiang, S. J., Iwata, B. A., & Dorsey, M. F. Elimination of disruptive bus riding behavior via token reinforcement on a "distance-based" schedule. *Education and Treatment of Children*, 1979, *2*, 101-109.
18. Bates, J. A. Extrinsic reward and intrinsic motivation: A review with

implications for the classroom. *Review of Educational Research*, 1979, *49*, 557–576.

19. Lloyd, K. E., & Knutzen, N. J. A self-paced programmed undergraduate course in the experimental analysis of behavior. *Journal of Applied Behavior Analysis*, 1969, *2*, 125–133.

20. Whaley, D. L., & Malott, R. W. *Elementary principles of behavior.* Englewood Cliffs, N. J.: Prentice-Hall, 1971.

21. Glynn, E. L. Classroom applications of self-determined reinforcement. *Journal of Applied Behavior Analysis*, 1970, *3*, 123–132.

22. Rimm, D. C., & Masters, J. C. *Behavior therapy: Techniques and empirical findings.* New York: Academic Press, 1974.

23. Kazdin, A. E. The failure of some patients to respond to token programs. *Journal of Behavior Therapy and Experimental Psychiatry*, 1973, *4*, 7–14.

24. Polakow, R. L., & Doctor, R. M. A behavioral modification program for adult drug offenders. *Journal of Research in Crime and Delinquency*, 1974, *11*, 63–69.

25. Epstein, L. H., Parker, F. C., & Jenkins, C. C. A multiple baseline analysis of treatment for behavior addiction. *Addictive Behaviors*, 1976, *1*, 327–330.

26. Mann, R. A. The behavioral therapeutic use of contingency contracting to control an adult behavior problem—weight control. *Journal of Applied Behavior Analysis*, 1972, *5*, 99–109.

27. Girodo, M., Stein, S., & Dotzenroth, S. E. The effects of communication skill training and contracting on marital relations. *Behavioral Engineering*, 1980, *6* (2), 61–76.

28. Jacobson, N. S., & Martin, B. Behavioral marriage therapy: Current status. *Psychological Bulletin*, 1976, *83* (4), 540–556.

29. Blechman, E. A. Objectives and procedures believed necessary for the success of a contractual approach to family intervention. *Behavior Therapy*, 1977, *8*, 275–277.

30. Homme, L. E., Csanyi, A., Gonzales, M., & Rechs, J. *How to use contingency contracting in the classroom.* Champaign, Ill.: Research Press, 1969.

31. Cantrell, H., Cantrell, C., Huddleston, B., & Woolridge, R. C. Contingency contracting with school problems. *Journal of Applied Behavior Analysis*, 1969, *2*, 215–220.

32. Tharp, R. G., & Wetzel, R. J. *Behavior modification in the natural environment.* New York: Academic Press, 1969.

33. Stuart, R. B. Behavior control within the families of delinquents. *Journal of Behavior Therapy and Experimental Psychiatry*, 1971, *2*, 1–11.

34. Stuart, R. B., & Lott, L. A. Behavior control with delinquents: A cautionary note. *Journal of Behavior Therapy and Experimental Psychiatry*, 1972, *3*, 161–169.

35. Stuart, R. B., Jayaratne, S., & Tripodi, T. Changing adolescent deviant behavior through reprogramming the behavior of parents and teachers: An experimental evaluation. *Canadian Journal of Behavior Science*, 1976, *8* (2), 132–143.

36. Alexander, J. F., & Parsons, B. V. Short-term behavioral intervention with delinquent families: Impact on family process and recidivism. *Journal of Abnormal Psychology*, 1973, *51*, 219–233.

37. Brooks, B. D. Contingency contracts with truants. *Personnel and Guidance Journal*, 1974, *52* (5), 316–320.
38. Diaddigo, M., & Dickie, R. F. The use of contingency contracting in eliminating inappropriate classroom behaviors. *Education and Treatment of Children*, 1978, *1* (2), 17–23.
39. Heaton, R. C., Safer, D. J., Allen, R. P., Spinnato, N. C., & Prumo, F. M. A motivational environment for behaviorally deviant junior high school students. *Journal of Abnormal Child Psychology*, 1976, *4* (3), 263–275.
40. Barth, R. Home-based reinforcement of school behavior: A review and analysis. *Review of Educational Research*, 1979, *49* (3), 436–458.
41. Weathers, L., & Liberman, R. P. Contingency contracting with families of delinquent adolescents. *Behavior Therapy*, 1975, *6*, 356–366.
42. Goldiamond, I. Self-reinforcement. *Journal of Applied Behavior Analysis*, 1976, *9*, 509–514.
43. Skinner, B. F. *Science and human behavior*. New York: Macmillan, 1953.
44. Mahoney, M. J. *Cognition and behavior modification*. Cambridge, Mass.: Ballinger, 1974.
45. O'Leary, S. G., & O'Leary, K. D. Behavior modification in the school. In H. Leitenberg (Ed.), *Handbook of behavior modification and behavior therapy*. Englewood Cliffs, N. J.: Prentice-Hall, 1976.
46. Pressley, M. Increasing children's self-control through cognitive interventions. *Review of Educational Research*, 1979, *49*, 319–370.
47. Seymour, F. W., & Stokes, T. F. Self-recording in training girls to increase work and evoke staff praise in an institution for offenders. *Journal of Applied Behavior Analysis*, 1976, *9*, 41–54.
48. Broden, M., Hall, R. V., & Mitts, B. The effects of self-recording on the classroom behavior of two eighth-grade children. *Journal of Applied Behavior Analysis*, 1971, *4*, 191–199.
49. Bandura, A. *Principles of behavior modification*. New York: Holt, Rinehart and Winston, 1969.

INTRODUCTION TO CHAPTER 9

This relatively small off-site day school for 13- to 15-year old truant youth who are status offenders or delinquents is well described by Lawrence and his co-workers. The Learning Center's emphasis is clearly educational. Its program achieves the following: 1) it keeps approximately 50% of entering, school-aged, chronically truant youth in the program for at least 6 months, 2) it transfers approximately 50% of its graduates back to public school, 3) it transfers its graduates back to public school at a grade level determined by their achievement test score, 4) most of its students make appreciable academic gains in a short period of time, and 5) it provides services at an unusually reasonable price for an off-site day school.

As the authors point out, the program evaluation has some notable limitations. Control group youth are simply age- and sex-matched delinquents; they have only one-half the rate of court appearances of the experimental group and presumably differ measurably on school variables. Furthermore, the authors use only one rather limited measure of delinquency, court appearances. In their analysis of recidivism, they compared a student group that had completed 6 months of the program—certainly the more cooperative segment of the referred population—with a control group which was not self-selected. Lastly, the achievement data presented covers primarily the initial 6 months treatment period for 92 children over the first 5 years of the program's operation.

One should not minimize the great difficulties in running a viable program for truant, court-referred adolescents, and in maintaining funding from year to year with "soft money" grants. The Learning Center's effort is particularly striking because persistent adolescent truants are one of the most formidable treatment challenges and are only rarely the recipients of publicly funded educational services.

9

A day school intervention for truant and delinquent youth

Charles Lawrence, Mark Litynsky,
and
Burton D'Lugoff

The development of an antisocial lifestyle probably begins at home, however unintentionally, but it is usually first noticed by society in the schools. Aggressive, disruptive, and impulsive behavior must be controlled and minimized in the classroom to enable education to take place. Disruptive students are a prevalent feature of public school systems throughout the country and many approaches are currently being tried to ameliorate the problems they present.

However, there is another manifestation of student antisocial behavior that has received less public notice. This is truancy. Perhaps it has received less notice because the participants are less visible, but, like disruptive behavior, it is widespread in public schools, increasing dramatically at the junior high school level.

Truancy can also be related to the other deviant school-related behaviors which are of concern to society. Disruptive or aggressive behavior usually leads to a series of suspensions and other intended punishments of increasing severity that often result in truancy. When excessive, the very existence of truancy can be considered a delinquent act. Failure to attend school constitutes a status offense for those under 16 years of age, although lack of attendance must usually be extreme before it is brought to the attention of the juvenile justice system. Even so, this does occur at a fairly high rate. In the state of Maryland (where our project was based) during fiscal year 1978, 1,100 youth were charged with truancy. This amounted to

177

4% of the total charges filed on persons under 16 (1). These statistics understate the problem considerably because many of those charged for other offenses are also truant and their truancy is addressed by probation officers during the probation supervision that results from the original charges.

From this we see that there are large numbers of youth who are simply not involved in the public schools. These youth may have been suspended or expelled by the school administration. They may not have registered with the school district, or they may be carried on school rolls even though they have not appeared for a single day of school.

Congress recognized the seriousness of the problem posed by out-of-school youth in PL 94-142, which designates them as one of the highest priority groups of "special education" students. Unfortunately this group is one of the most difficult to involve in any form of educational program. They have selected themselves out by the intensity of their dislike of academic situations and their failure to respond to the usual range of in-school alternative programming.

Truants are a high-risk group. They have left the social mainstream, and spend their days wastefully, with few exceptions. They may become involved with drugs or criminal activity. Although one report indicated that being out of school decreased the probability of criminal activity (2), it may actually have decreased only the probability of being caught. There may be less likelihood of having a crime observed or reported on the streets than in the school. In any case, truants are rejecting societal norms early in their lives, and cannot be expected to acquire the social and academic competencies that can lead to active and positive participation in work and other productive social activities.

Early intervention for seriously truant adolescents would seem to be a reasonable strategy. If truants could be induced to participate in a program designed to improve their social and academic skills so that they might become prepared to continue their education, their antisocial inclinations might be altered. The alternative school program described here was such an attempt of early intervention. It used primarily behavioral interventions with inner-city youth who were chronically truant and who had become involved with the juvenile justice system.

Very little is known about the origins of school truancy or the environmental factors that can shape it to a level that brings it to the attention of school administrators and legal authorities. We have employed several assumptions about chronically truant youth and what may be significant influences in the shaping of this behavior. Before going on to the project itself, these assumptions are discussed. Those readers familiar with behavioral principles will find that our analysis holds few surprises.

We start with the assumption that truant behavior, like attendance, is detemined or greatly influenced by current environmental factors which bear on that behavior, and by an individual's unique set of experiences in these and similar situations (the individual's history of reinforcement and punishment). One of the important characteristics of chronic truants is that they are commonly functioning several grades below their expected academic levels in the critical skill areas of reading and mathematics. This situation has significant implications for the understanding and treatment of chronic truant behavior.

As a rule, the chronically truant youth does not possess the academic abilities and competencies to succeed in the public schools. Unless this is understood, there can be a potential misunderstanding on the part of those who work with truant youth. These youth could appear to be self-destructive, to be avoiding participation in what will clearly lead to lasting and powerful reinforcers. That is, regular school attendance leading to high school graduation will in turn lead to better occupational opportunities. However, this usual school-life goal pattern simply does not hold for many chronically truant youth. Before becoming chronically truant, they have acquired a history of academic failure. They need intensive remedial work in basic skills in order to avoid continued failure. The likelihood of a student persevering with little academic success or positive regard by teachers is very small indeed.

Many truants are also socially inept. Even students with adequate academic competence may find the school environment aversive if they cannot develop positive relationships with peers or teachers. They avoid school in order to avoid the unpleasant consequences that result from their misguided social behavior.

Furthermore, family support and encouragement of academic achievement are frequently lacking. In fact, truancy is actually encouraged in some families because the child who remains at home can provide companionship or help with domestic tasks. More often, however, school attendance just holds a low priority in the family.

Briefly, then, we have assumed that for many students truancy is a logical outcome of aversive experiences in school, often coupled with family indifference to school success. Our strategy was based on these assumptions, and therefore included provisions for ensuring positive experiences and feedback in classroom settings along with family involvement in regaining regular school attendance.

We believed it was best to conduct a program for truants in a setting apart from the public schools, partly because a nonschool setting would likely have fewer negative associations, and partly to avoid becoming enmeshed in a public school bureaucracy which could delay or inhibit the use of unconventional methods. We did consult extensively with Baltimore City School administrators in developing the program, and obtained their enthusiastic assistance in setting up the procedures for transferring records and returning program participants to their appropriate public school placement upon separation from our program. This was absolutely necessary because we expected to work with truants for up to 2 years and needed assurance that they could be reinstated in the public schools at their age-appropriate grade, given that it could be shown that they were academically and behaviorally ready to return. Some students, of course, would not ever return to public school and for them some other socially acceptable activity would have to be sought, but our intent was to return as many as possible to public school.

Initial funding came from the Law Enforcement Assistance Administration as a demonstration program in delinquency and drug abuse prevention. This meant that we worked closely with the state Juvenile Services Administration in defining the population to be served and the process of referral for service. It was decided that we would set the age range for entry into the program as 13–15. No exclusions would be made on the basis of sex or race. Further, all referrals would come from the Juvenile Services staff, assuring that those who entered treatment were already having trouble with the law by virtue of truancy or other offenses. The referrals would constitute a high risk group with whom relatively early intervention might alter the course of their educational and social development.

The following description of the program that grew from our assumptions and negotiations suggests objectives that can serve as bases for evaluation. Data relevant to the evaluation are also presented and, in conclusion, a discussion of some issues relevant to the model as well as other aspects of truancy and delinquency.

PROGRAM DESCRIPTION

The program was structured as a day school that students attended in lieu of public school. Although we were not accredited by the state as a school, our arrangement with the city school system permitted us to work with students for a period up to 2 years as long as they had been functionally out of the city system by reason of truancy or multiple suspensions for at least half the previous academic quarter.

The program consisted of two major components: education and counseling. The educational component of the program involved structured classrooms in which clients worked individually or in small groups of similar competencies. The majority of the materials in use were programmed, self-paced instructional materials. These provided frequent opportunities for success and allow the student to begin with very little perseverance and complete tasks without becoming bored or overwhelmed.

The counseling component of the program involved regularly scheduled sessions between each student and one of the project counselors. Although a variety of contingency management and other behavioral counseling procedures have been employed, contingency contracting was the most frequently employed formal procedure. Behaviors targeted in these contracts included school attendance, compliance at home and in school, increased social assertion and self-control/self-management, and adherence to curfews. Consequences included the reinforcers furnished by the project (points, access to preferred staff, selection of academic activities), those furnished by the parents (later curfew hours, control of the television, and selection of activities for the family), and occasionally consequences provided by the students' probation officers (reduction in length of probation or removal of restrictions on the students' activities).

The project employed a token economy (3) as a primary means of encouraging and sustaining attendance and performance. While the token system was designed for use in the classroom, it was also enlarged to include the behavior of students in other areas of the project. In this token system students earned points through successful completion of academic tasks, on-time attendance, and remaining on task for specified periods of time without disruptive behavior. Students accumulated points and exchanged these for desired activities and treats during recreation periods.

The majority of these exchanges occurred in the "Rec Room," a large open area containing a pool table, pinball machine, foosball table, ping pong table, soda machine, and other games. Students using the Rec Room engaged in social interactions in our presence, which would have been impossible for us to observe in the community. This enabled us to model and shape appropriate social behavior and conflict resolution skills in the course of our interactions with students. These observations also served as a partial validation of students' self-reports to their counselors. Because counselors supervised the students in the Rec Room, opportunities for immediate informal counseling also took place.

The opportunity to do paid work on the premises was also made available to students contingent upon appropriate attendance and academic performance.

The intervention program also offered parenting skills training, both in groups and on an individual basis. Most training has been with individual parents because we found it difficult to generate regular attendance at group meetings.

The census of the program varied over the years, but the maximum enrollment was 35 active clients. During the first few years we averaged an enrollment of some 20 students per month, but later it was close to maximum at all times. The program operated year-round, with 2-week breaks in December, June, and August.

The basic goals of the program were:

1. To increase the level of academic competence and of socially desirable behavior. The principle measures in this area have been test scores and program attendance, as these have been recorded regularly for most clients; however, for some individual clients measures such as rate of appropriate assertive behavior, or rate of polite requests of the staff have been used. Herein we report only data on attendance and academic achievement.
2. To place the clients into a public school or other socially acceptable activity upon successful completion of treatment. The measure used here is percent of students so placed.
3. To reduce the frequency of delinquent behavior in the adolescents enrolled in the program. This recidivism is measured in terms of court appearances.

In the next section data are presented on the effectiveness of the program with respect to these goals. The data will not be all from the same group of students. For example, data on attendance are for all students enrolled during the years mentioned, whether they were enrolled for only a month or for the entire year; the recidivism data, however, are based on a specific group of students who had been in the program for a minimum period of time during certain years. The reader should note the characteristics of each group in examining the data presented.

PROGRAM EVALUATION

Recidivism

The least conclusive data, those on recidivism (Goal 3), are reported first. Two serious methodological problems presented themselves in this area. First, there was the constant flow of students in and out of the program, combined with variable durations of enrollment. We did not have a group who all began on one date, departed after a set interval of treatment, and were then in follow-up for a fixed period of time. Second, we did not have random assignment to treatment or control conditions. Therefore a control group was selected retrospectively.

To make the best of the data obtainable, we employed a person-time analysis, a method developed in public health where similar ethical and practical considerations often result in these sorts of dilemmas in making sense of the available data. In using the person-time analysis (PTA) a rate measure is computed in the following manner: The numerator for the rate calculation is the events being recorded or counted during the time span with which one is concerned. In this case it is court appearances. The denominator is the total units of time for all subjects in that period. Simple division yields the person-time rate. This can be expressed in "person months" or "person years." This method balances out the difference in recorded events that may be due to differential durations of experience in a condition. By using PTA we were able to compare data for subjects who had been observed for periods of varying duration. PTA also permitted comparisons of recidivism for the periods before, during, and after treatment, rather than only in the follow-up stage. (For a fuller discussion of person-time analysis, see Colton, 1974, pp. 238–240.)

The recidivism study involved students who had been enrolled in treatment during the years 1973–1977. The criteria for inclusion as a subject were: a) the student had been in treatment for at least 6 months and b) the student had been separated from the program for at least 3 months as of March 31, 1978. Reason for departure from the program was not used as a criterion, so some who did poorly in treatment and were terminated for cause or removed to an institution were included as subjects. (We believed that if treatment were to be fairly evaluated one could not first separate out ostensible failures and successes before taking an independent measure of effectiveness.) Forty-five students met these criteria and constituted the study group (SG).

The students making up the SG were not representative of all the students enrolled in the program. According to an analysis of treatment durations for the years 1976 and 1977, some 50% of students remained 6 months or longer. We felt, however, that 6 months is a minimal treatment period for the expectation of any substantial improvement on academic and social skills, and therefore for an impact on delinquency.

The control group (CG) was selected from the files of the Juvenile Services Administration. We wished to have controls of similar age and date of first court appearance as the SG members, so the method we used was to pick a file drawer arbitrarily and then examine consecutive records until we located a case which matched an SG member on date of first court appearance (± 3 months) and whose birth date fell in the same 3 year period as the SG member (1958–60 or 1961–63). Thus we were able to compare recidivism between juveniles of about the same age over nearly identical intervals of calendar time.

The measure of recidivism we used was court appearance. Most investigators use arrests, but this was unsuitable for our subjects because many were status offenders and were not actually arrested; rather they were summoned to court for offenses such as truancy or ungovernability. We could have used charges, but we observed that a single offense could result in numerous charges, apparently to ensure an adequate prosecution. Therefore the court appearance seemed to be the preferred event to count.

Following the PTA procedure outlined above, we divided each SG member's experience into three periods: before treatment, defined as the period from date of first court appearance to entering the program, during treatment (self-explanatory), and after treatment, defined as the period from date of departure from the program to March 31, 1978. A rate was then computed for each period. (The first court appearance was omitted from the calculations since it did not constitute recidivism.)

CG members were not enrolled in treatment. However, they were matched with the SG members for date of first court appearance and had the same end date (March 31, 1978), so they had similar overall durations of observation. Therefore it was possible to divide each CG member's observation time into three periods corresponding in proportions to the before, during, and after treatment intervals of the matched SG member. We then computed rates for the CG for these arbitrary intervals to compare with the SG rates.

The results of these calculations are plotted in Figure 1. We calculated time in months, and expressed rates in "100 person-months." It is evident that the SG had a much higher rate of recidivism in the pretreatment period, and that the rate dropped during treatment and remained reduced after treatment. The CG rate was lower to begin with and remained about the same through the three periods. An $\chi^2(1)$ test on the before and after rates yields a value of 22.98, $p < 0.001$.

Although these results suggest that treatment had an effect on recidivism, we must be cautious in our interpretations. The controls

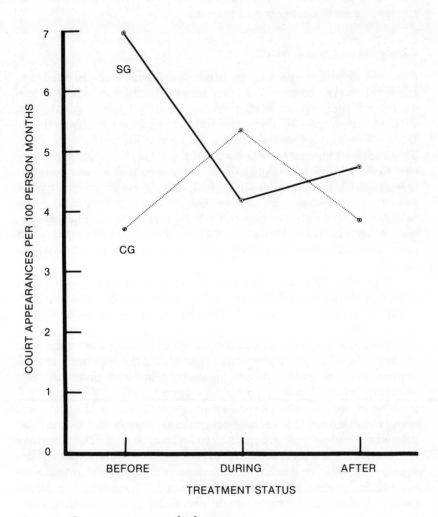

Figure 1. Court reappearances: both groups

were not really a comparable group, as the pretreatment rates indicate. They do not differ significantly from the SG in age ($t=0.4$,
$p>0.5$) or sex ($\chi^2(1)=1.158$, $p<0.25$), but there could have been other
important differences such as truancy or seriousness of first offense
for which there was no matching. It is not possible to know whether a
control group having a similar pretreatment arrest rate would also
have shown a decline over conditions as our SG did. We can be

guardedly optimistic about the program's effect on recidivism, but the results need further corroboration.

Academic and Social Skills

Our results with respect to academic and social skills (Goal 1) are more definitely positive. Our first measure here was school attendance, for that was a basic problem for all of our students and without attendance we obviously couldn't produce any other effects. Daily attendance averaged 82% for the year 1977, and 84% for 1978. This included summer session attendance, which (surprisingly) exceeded 80% in both sessions. We have not counted *excused* days in these figures. Legitimate excuses included illness confirmed by the parent, court appearance, and similar causes. The percentage was calculated as number present/number present + number absent (unexcused absences). However, students were only excused for good cause and rarely were there more than two or three excused absences per day.

This was a dramatic improvement for students who had missed at least 50% of their school days during their previous public school academic quarter, and many of whom had missed an entire academic year or more.

Academic progress in mathematics and reading were measured on the Wide Range Achievement Test (5). This test was always administered to each student upon entering the program, and retesting occurred upon termination, when feasible. We also scheduled testing at 6-month intervals during enrollment in the program. Some results from this testing program are shown in Table 1. The data are from several groups of students as noted. The improvements were impressive, albeit not identical. The different rates of improvement could be due to many factors, including intellectual abilities of the students comprising the groups. These results indicate clearly that academic improvement proceeded at a substantial pace.

Student Placement

The final portion of this evaluation relates to placement of students (Goal 2). In order for a program such as ours to be considered fully successful it should be able to return its clients to an appropriate academic or vocational setting with a reasonable expectation of success. Unfortunately, it was very difficult to obtain data on academic or vocational performance once the students left the program. However, we can present two sets of data that are relevant to measuring the program's effectiveness in this area.

Table 1. Academic progress

	Study I	Study II	Study III[a]
Number in group	26	20	92
Mean progress in grades per year			
Reading	1.7	2.8	1.8
Math	1.8	3.6	1.8
Period covered by study	6/77 to 9/78	9/77 to 6/78	2/73 to 6/79

Academic progress is calculated by summing algebraically the changes which had occurred in grade level scores of the Wide Range Achievement Test. These were divided by the summation of the intervals which had occurred between tests and the result converted to "grades of progress per year enrolled in the project." "1" represents standard (normative) public school progress or one grade level per year.

[a] All students for whom an initial and 6-month test were available.

During the period January, 1976 through June, 1978, 79 students who had been in treatment for at least 3 months departed the program. Of these, 41, or 52%, returned to public school.

A more thorough study was conducted in early 1979. The subjects were those students who had departed the program between June 1977 and August 1978, after being in treatment for at least 6 months. There were 27 subjects who met these criteria. We obtained information from the subjects and their families, probation officers, school records, and juvenile institutions. We then classified the subjects as having a positive or negative outcome, as shown in Table 2.

As can be seen, almost half the subjects have a positive outcome. Actually, over half of the *located* subjects have a positive outcome.

Table 2. Follow-up study of 27 clients

Outcomes		Number
Positive		
Enrolled in public school with satisfactory attendance and grades		7
Involved in a constructive activity such as work or military service		6
	Total	13
Negative		
Institutionalized		6
Idle		3
Enrolled in school, doing poorly		3
	Total	12
Unable to locate		2
	Total	27

Thus we can tentatively estimate on the basis of these data that about 50% of those students who have been in treatment for a substantial length of time can be expected to make a successful adjustment to school or work after leaving. We consider this to be a favorable result given the risk characteristics of those accepted for treatment. Since we do not have any comparison group, however, we cannot determine whether the program has greater or lesser effects than other possible interventions, or even no intervention.

A final consideration in this program evaluation is costs. During the initial three years of operation (1973–76) the annual cost was about $3,300 per student. This was $500 to $1,000 greater than the official cost of special education in the Baltimore public schools. However, the latter figure was computed exclusive of overhead and did not include a summer session. We do not know what special education would cost if overhead were included and a summer session added, but it might well exceed the cost of our program. By fiscal year 1978 the cost of the program had risen to about $4,300 per student, mostly as a result of enlarging the educational staff and adding a research component.

DISCUSSION

The alternative school model that we have described has proven useful in working with truant and delinquent adolescents. When school experience is structured so that students can succeed and receive immediate positive consequences for appropriate behavior, truancy diminishes greatly and learning is enhanced. Students who had constantly avoided public school have become regular attenders and have made substantial academic progress. This has been accomplished without extensive testing for "learning disabilities," or chemotherapy, or residential placement, or other more exotic methods of assessment and intervention. We have simply employed fairly standard behavioral technologies to create an environment that attracts students and promotes learning.

In our program evaluation we examined three important aspects of student behavior: academic and social progress, recidivism, and subsequent school and vocational performance. Of these, the most clearly positive outcome was in the area of academic progress. We believe this is a sufficient basis for concluding that the program has been effective. Students who were doing very poorly indeed have improved considerably in reading and mathematics, basic skills essential to adequate functioning in our complex society. This was our most immediate area of concern, and the results have been favorable.

The results in respect to continued delinquent behavior, recidivism, were inconclusive. There was a significant downward trend, but since the control group did not have as high an initial rate of court appearances there is some ambiguity in interpreting the data.

When we devised this program we felt that it would have beneficial effects in respect to delinquency. It seemed obvious that young adolescents who were out of school and unable to read adequately would have fewer alternatives to antisocial activity than their peers who were functioning adequately in school. If we could promote learning, offer the opportunity to continue in public school, and instill some feelings of competence and self-worth, then it should follow that delinquent behavior would become less frequent. This may, in fact, have occurred, but the data do not yet demonstrate it convincingly.

Several characteristics of the students we have served suggest to us that characteristics other than reading ability or self-confidence may be especially important in respect to delinquency and other antisocial behavior. We had group meetings in which we discussed program rules, recent problems, and other items. Sometimes the problem was theft. Many, perhaps most of the students have outspokenly endorsed the principle that the theft was the fault of the victim: the item should not have been left unguarded. It is very difficult to modify this sort of reasoning, which has strong peer support and probable family concurrence as well.

The absence of parental deterrence of theft was not unusual. Parents routinely reported that their child had a bike or radio which he "found." Occasionally they are even more protective. In one theft incident at our program, a student was observed by a staff member leaving the building with another student's coat. Upon being confronted the student acknowledged the theft and returned the coat. A family meeting was held to determine the punishment for the theft. The mother, however, insisted that her son did not steal. When the counselor asked the student, he said, "Yes, I took the coat." His mother exclaimed, "No, you didn't!"

We now feel that antisocial behavior may be as strongly related to cultural and family mores as it is to basic academic competence. A deficiency in reading ability may contribute to delinquency, but other factors are at least as important, and can be even more difficult to modify.

Later success in public school or on a job is another complicated issue. Although we strongly advocate research in this area, and continue to do such research, we remain uncertain of how much weight should be given to this in program evaluation. As with recidivism, many contingencies beyond the scope of any program bear on these data and may easily overcome the progress that was made in a special program.

A program's cost is certainly relevant to a program's evaluation, especially given the current emphasis on accountability and cost-effectiveness in social programs. Using local public schools' special education costs as a reference, the costs of this program do not seem high. We should point out some complications in using this as an index of program performance: The appropriate reference figure is not easily determined. Should it be the cost of public school special education, which provides little in the way of counseling; residential treatment, which is often recommended for the students we serve; individual psychotherapy; or some other form of special program in the private sector? Another factor to consider is the savings in future costs to the society, such as prevention of institutionalization or other costly, intensive intervention services that might be avoided. As can be seen, both the cost and the cost-effectiveness must be considered when evaluating the functioning of this type of programming.

CONCLUSION

There are several features that we feel have been important, perhaps crucial, in making the program attractive to targeted youth and effective in attaining its goals.

The Token Economy and Recreation Room

These are probably first in importance. These students need, at least initially, some consistent and clear contingencies governing their behavior and its consequences. The token economy serves as the basis for these contingencies.

We have operated the token economy in various ways. Eventually we used dated index cards on which points were awarded by staff using felt tip pens. We purchased pens from an art supply store where we could get uncommon colors. Predictably, one of the greatest problems for any token economy is counterfeiting of tokens or in the case of written point systems, forgery. Frequent shifting of colors, coding systems, or point cards can minimize this.

Positive Point System

In our system points were earned for appropriate or exceptional performance. This emphasized positive contingencies and helped us differentiate the project setting from previous school and counseling experience, much of which had sadly been punitively focused.

We tried point fines in the past. Serious problems occurred when we did. Students became angry when fined, resulting in outbursts of verbal aggression and other problems that could have been avoided. Some students went into point debt. When this happened, students lost their motivation to work in class, as the points they earned could only repay the debt rather than be spent in the Rec Room. The positive point system avoided these problems while rapidly shaping the desired behavior.

Programmed, Self-paced Instructional Materials

The entering reading levels of students referred to the program ranged from total inability through tenth grade reading level, with the mode at the fourth grade level. Knowledge of mathematics varied similarly although no student entered the program with a criterion referenced test score above sixth grade. This wide range of academic skill levels rendered traditional forms of group classroom instruction impossible. Programmed materials allowed students to work in dividually or in small groups of similar skill levels. This individualized instruction has been essential in coping with the wide range of skills and learning rates presented by our students.

The Program Operated Outside of the Public Schools

We were free to employ various procedures that would have been difficult to have approved in a public school setting. We were also able to select and supervise our own staff. Furthermore, many of our students reported that their peers in public school were a major contributory factor in their problems, especially truant behavior, which seemed to be a group activity on most occasions.

Cooperation and Support of Involved Agencies

We enjoyed excellent cooperation and support from both the schools and the Juvenile Services Administration. These were essential. We were very fortunate in having full support for our efforts from both agencies.

Disruptive behavior and truancy are unlikely to be eliminated in the near future. They may be significantly reduced if innovation and research continue. We are, like the other contributors to this volume, continuing our exploration of new methods to improve the effectiveness of the program we have developed.

ACKNOWLEDGMENTS

This project was initiated through a grant from The Law Enforcement Assistance Administration, Project No. 3111-JD4. Continuation funding was arranged through the Maryland State Juvenile Services Administration and the Mayor's Office of Manpower Resources (CETA funds).

REFERENCES

1. Maryland Juvenile Services Administration. *Annual report, fiscal year, 1978.* Baltimore: Maryland Department of Health and Mental Hygiene, 1979.
2. Elliott, D., and Voss, H. *Delinquency and dropout.* Lexington, Mass.: Lexington Books, 1974.
3. Ayllon, T., and Azrin, N. *The token economy.* New York: Appleton-Century-Crofts, 1968.
4. Colton, T. *Statistics in medicine.* Boston: Little Brown & Company, 1974, pp. 238-240.
5. Jastak, J., Bijou, S., and Jastak, S. *Wide Range Achievement Test.* Wilmington: Guidance Associates of Delaware, 1965.

INTRODUCTION TO CHAPTERS 10 AND 11

The school programs of the Institute of Behavioral Research (IBR) in Silver Spring, Maryland, have been one of the largest and most researched for disruptive secondary school students in the United States. IBR certainly has offered the most extensive program of *in-school* alternatives for these students in secondary schools.

Among the many findings and insights described by the IBR team, presently led by Mr. James Filipczak, has been the finding that alternative programs for disruptive youth have to be tailored to the school and to the region. Rural school needs for disruptive students are quite different from those in inner cities; one cannot simply devise one program for all schools. Another particularly useful finding relates to the use of procedures to promote generalization. The behavior of students assigned to a special academic "laboratory" for two periods a day can be monitored and reinforced for the entire school day and the usual result is gains in grades, achievement, and behavior in all classes.

Although the short-term benefits of the IBR program are encouraging, the lack of long-term gains described by Wodarski et al. is sobering. This is not unusual and reflects, as much as anything else, that the follow-up study was honestly done. It also suggests that a 1-year program (for each student) is probably insufficient by itself to produce measurable effects years later. Another sobering and not at all atypical finding is that although Preparation through Responsive Educational Programs (PREP) produced useful school system innovations, only a modest number of these have been incorporated into existing school programs since the federal funding has ceased.

10

Behavioral intervention in public schools:
I Short-term results

James Filipczak
and
John S. Wodarski

The Institute of Behavioral Research (IBR) established and evaluated numerous school programs for disruptive students in Maryland throughout the late 1960s and most of the 1970s, primarily with National Institute of Mental Health (NIMH) grant support. The first IBR venture in this area was an educationally oriented program in a youth correctional institution (1). Following this, an educational laboratory within a junior high school was set up, primarily to develop the academic and social skills of referred disruptive, truant, and failing students. Next, beginning in 1971, a more comprehensive school-based program was implemented for disruptive and alienated students in a number of secondary schools. It was named Preparation through Responsive Educational Programs (PREP), and was instituted in three geographical areas: suburban, urban, and rural. The PREP program ran for a 5-year period and involved 50 to 120 students annually. Each student participated for 1 school year.

PREP

The major components of PREP were

1. Academic training, mostly with self-instructional materials
2. Social skills training, a cognitively oriented group skills class for school credit

3. Parenting skills training using individualized behavior management strategies and contracts
4. A contingency management emphasis
5. Teacher training

The location of the PREP instructional program was a skills center. Between 16 and 24 students came to this center daily during their English and mathematics periods. During their other school periods, their instruction was given by regular teachers within regular sections.

The PREP program used a clear-cut reinforcement (contingency management) system for students and an incentive emphasis for parents and teachers. Student rewards were based on successful academic work and social behavior throughout the entire school day. These included praise, grades, tangible items, and activity options, such as field trips, movies, and game time. Teacher incentives included college credit for training in the program.

At each of its geographical school sites (suburban, urban, and rural), the PREP program had to operate differently and make adjustments. For instance, due to objections from rural school administrators, tangible and edible reinforcers could not be used as student rewards. In the urban PREP programs, objections concerning the evaluation protocol caused a marked alteration in the research design. For the most part, however, program adjustments were made without appreciably altering the major emphasis of PREP.

Program evaluation basically consisted of such measures as: 1) suspensions, 2) grades, 3) office referrals, 4) attendance, 5) achievement, and 6) delinquency. Other measures utilized were sociometric ratings, employment status, and a rating of adult, peer, and family relationships. Control groups were generally used in the evaluations.

SHORT-TERM RESULTS

Initially, the most uniform and large scale gains in PREP were attained in the academic skill areas, as shown by achievement test results (see Table 1). However, these findings were not maintained across all years, particularly at the urban site. Although consistently positive academic findings cannot be reported, academic skill treatment groups generally out-performed nontreatment groups, often at statistically significant levels.

Across program years, there had been clear improvement in results on the measure of attendance. After the first three program

Table 1. Presence of significance in favor of pertinent experimental group on grouped measures, by year in each school setting

Groups of measures	Year 1 Suburban 2 Groups (N=60)	Year 2 Suburban 5 Groups (N=80)	Year 3 Rural 2 Groups (N=78)	Year 4 Rural 3 Groups (N=107)	Year 4 Urban 2 Groups (N=83)	Year 5 Rural 2×2 Factorial (N=96)	Year 5 Urban 2 Groups (N=112)
Academic tests							
Number significant	5**	1** 2*	1** 1*	8**	NA	4** 1*	2**
Number of measures	6	6	2	10	NA	12	12
PREP class grades							
Number significant	1**	1**	1**	2**	1**	2**	4**
Number of measures	1	1	1	2	1	4	6
Other class grades							
Number significant	2**	1*	2**	1**	0	1*	3**
Number of measures	2	2	2	1	1	1	6
Discipline and social							
Number significant	2**	1*	0	0	NA	7** 4*	2** 1*
Number of measures	4	4	2	2	NA	16	5
School attendance							
Number significant	0	0	0	1**	1**	1**	1**
Number of measures	1	1	1	1	1	1	1

*Indicates significance between $P<0.10$—$P<0.06$.

**Indicates significance $P<0.05$ or less.

From: Stumphauzer, *Progress In Behavior Therapy with Delinquents*, 2nd edition, 1979. Courtesy of Charles C Thomas, Publisher, Springfield, Il.

years, significant differences in favor of PREP students were found for 2 consecutive years in both the rural and the urban settings. This seemed to be a particularly important finding for the urban setting, where attendance has characteristically been a major problem. It suggests that PREP's short-term objective of increasing the reinforcing value of school has been at least partially realized.

With respect to student grades, the overall results across years and sites again do not favor treated groups in every instance. Although there was less indication of skill transfer to nonPREP classes in the rural setting the third year, there were strong suggestions that this occurred in the urban site. The findings, in combination with the fact that generalization in grades had been found in five of nine previous comparisons in the first four program years (see reference 2 for a more complete description of these results), do suggest that the benefits of the program are not restricted to the special classes in which it is implemented.

The most encouraging trend in results has come in the area of social behavior. At all sites, highly favorable outcomes were observed. Highly positive change for social treatments was evidenced at the urban site on measures such as suspensions and citizenship ratings, and at the rural site on teacher ratings of classroom social behavior. Before the last reported year, the social behavior outcomes had shown some inconsistency in PREP. Where rather large differences were found on two of five measures during the first year in the suburban setting, a number of treatment and measurement problems had resulted in a failure to replicate these findings. As a result, during the last noted program year, PREP placed greater emphasis on program management in the social performance area, and it appears that this increased focus paid off.

Generally, these results sum to an encouraging multisite and multiyear outcome report. As noted (3), statistically significant ($P<0.1$) differences favoring the pertinent treatment group have been observed in 68 out of 119 (57.1%) measures across the three sites and five years of PREP (see Table 1). Further, only one of the 119 comparisons favored a comparison group, and that difference was not significant. However, equivocal and negative findings cannot be dismissed. Their presence demands future consideration of individual (and site) differences and program development to help ensure the most coherent and productive PREP program that is possible.

Thus, the process embedded in the original planning for PREP has been brought halfway to conclusion. PREP has shown the ability to help students in short-term improvement of their school, home, and community behavior. It may be possible to extend PREP's efforts to the training of other teaching, counseling, and administrative staff where the results of PREP's efforts can be assessed in the arena of daily school practice. However, longer-term follow-up on these efforts is required to identify procedures more resistant to decremental environmental pressures after treatment.

REFERENCES

1. Cohen, H. L., and Filipczak, J. *A new learning environment.* San Francisco: Jossey-Bass, 1971.
2. Friedman, R. M., Filipczak, J., and Fiordaliso, R. Within-school generalization of the Preparation through Responsive Educational Programs (PREP) academic project. *Behavior Therapy,* 1977, 8:986–995.
3. Filipczak, J., Friedman, R. M., and Reece, S. C. PREP: Educational programming to prevent juvenile problems. In J. S. Stumphauzer (Ed.), *Progress in behavior therapy with delinquents* 2nd ed. Springfield, Ill.: Charles C Thomas, 1979.

11

Behavioral intervention in public schools:

II Long-term follow-up

John S. Wodarski
and
James Filipczak

This investigation represents a substantial effort to secure follow-up information about past participants of the school-based social learning program designed for problem adolescents, which is described in Chapter 10. The follow-up occurred approximately 4 years after the students' participation in the program. The behavior of 40 of the original 60 adolescents (identified for the follow-up) was assessed on variables such as their employment and educational status, evaluation of program participation, involvement in leisure time and community activities, self-esteem, aspirations and expectations, involvement in delinquent activity, relationships with family and friends, and anticipated aversive consequences of engaging in criminal acts.

GENERAL BACKGROUND

Recently, many delinquency researchers and therapists have called for the provision of preventive and treatment services to antisocial adolescents on a more rational and theoretical basis. These individuals also ask for the empirical evaluation of available service programs to determine if they are meeting the needs of such youth (1-5).

To evaluate an intervention program adequately, the following items must be specified as concretely as possible: 1) behaviors to be changed with pretreatment baselines of such behaviors, 2) change agent attributes, 3) conceptualization and operationalization of treatment interventions, 4) criteria used for the evaluation of treatment efficiency, 5) mechanism for monitoring the quality of treatment, 6) reliable methods of measuring change, and 7) sufficient follow-up (6–10).

In a previous follow-up investigation concerning 24 past participants of a school-based, social learning program designed for problem adolescents, no long-term maintenance of the behavioral change with this population was observed. However, the follow-up involved only youth exposed to the program, and no comparison data were available (11).

Hence, this study is a report of a second follow-up investigation conducted on a different cohort of adolescents, where comparisons were made between those exposed to an experimental program and those who were not. Such data facilitate a stronger evaluation of the effects of a community-based treatment program on predelinquent students.

DESCRIPTION OF TREATMENT PROGRAM

Preparation through Responsive Educational Programs (PREP), a federally funded and community-based applied research project based on social learning theory, aimed to achieve a number of short- and long-term goals with pre-delinquent adolescents. Each goal attempted to expand students' academic and social skills in order to permit them to function more appropriately within their current school environments. These goals and the means for their achievement are noted in Table 1.

PREP's short-term goals were: 1) the improvement of the participants' academic and social skills, and 2) the development of a school environment that would provide positive incentives for school attendance and participation. Student skill gains and improvement in reinforcing value of their school environments were considered by PREP to be reciprocally related to increasing academic and social skills. Thus, when students achieved short-term objectives, they would be more likely to adopt socially acceptable roles and become involved in mutually reinforcing relationships with prosocial others. It was postulated that each of the foregoing changes would lead to increased incentives for prosocial behavior both within and outside the school environment.

Table 1.   Short- and long-term goals of the PREP project[a]

Short-term goals	Long-term goals
Skill gain(academic and social) Changes in academic skills as shown by achievement tests and attainment of social behavior competence.	*Increased incentive for pro-social behavior* Changes in the extent to which the student selects forms of behavior less likely to yield social trouble.
Gain in school's reinforcement Changes in the student's attitude toward school and things associated with school.	*Decreased juvenile problem behavior* Changes in instances of actual problem behaviors that are viewed by society as highly unacceptable or criminal.
Access to acceptable social roles Changes in the types or number of prosocial roles within which the student is able to function.	
Reinforcing relationships Changes in the type or number of relationships with family and others that are meaningful and satisfying to the student.	

[a] Each of the short-term goals is presumed to affect later components, with significant interaction among and between the first four components. The last two components are seen to act linearly.

The setting for the training program was a suburban junior high school immediately adjacent to a major city on the east coast. In 1971, PREP students (30 experimental and 30 control) were selected from this population on the basis of strong evidence of academic or social problems during the prior year. Participants were matched on criterion measures such as grades, school attendance, in-school behavioral problems, test scores, and family problems and were then assigned randomly to either an experimental or a control group. Each group included approximately 30% girls and 30% nonwhites, and was equally divided between entering 7th and 8th graders. The average age was 13 years, 2 months.

PREP operated as a 1-year intervention for all experimental students. Control students attended the same school with no alteration in curriculum and had contact with the program only for pre-and post-testing. Experimental group students were enrolled in three distinct but interrelated program components: 1) academic training in reading, English, and mathematics; 2) social or interpersonal skills training that facilitated immediate and generalizable social skills for problems inside and outside of school; and 3) family skills training that promoted increased involvement of parents in school activities and programs of family management in the home (see reference 12).

The school-based pre- and post-tested project measures yielded assessment of student change in both academic and social areas. Comparative data on nine measures relevant to the follow-up analysis for the experimental and control students are summarized in Table 2.

As these outcome data suggest, there were significant differ- ences between experimental and control group scores—six favoring the experimental group (reading comprehension, language skills, mathematics computation, mathematics application, number of disciplinary referrals, and class grades), and one favoring the control group (vocabulary development).

1-YEAR FOLLOW-UP

During the school year immediately following their participation in PREP, both experimental and control students were followed up on selected school-based measures. Practical issues limited the number of measures, but analyses were conducted on measures comparable to the program year assessment. The experimental group was found to have a lesser number of suspensions and higher school attendance than the control. On both disciplinary referrals and overall grade point average for English and mathematics classes, the experimen- tal group was found to perform better than the controls. This infor- mation added credence to the original intention to pursue a more long-term follow-up procedure.

METHOD

Design

Follow-up consisted of a randomized experimental/control group design with a follow-up data collection period conducted 4 years after termination of treatment. This design makes the assumption that, because of the procedures of random assignment of par- ticipants to experimental and control groups, pretest data should not be significantly different; posttest comparisons justifiably can then be made (13–17). In many instances, identical measures could not be executed at the 1-year and 4-year periods. Consequently, in addition to parallel or replicated measures, measures were devised to provide a more adequate assessment of participant functioning at follow-up in the areas of personal, academic, family, and community adjustment.

Table 2. Comparison of experimental versus control children on academic and social variables

Measure	Significance	In favor of
Vocabulary development		Control
Reading comprehension	< 0.005	Experimental
Language skills	< 0.001	Experimental
Mathematics computation	< 0.01	Experimental
Mathematics application	< 0.025	Experimental
School attendance	n.s.	n.s.
School suspensions[a]	n.s.	n.s.
Disciplinary referrals[a]	< 0.005	Experimental
Class grades[a]	< 0.025	Experimental

[a] Comparable pre-post data available for 8th graders only.

Final adoption of measures used in the follow-up became a process of compromise because of various bureaucratic constraints (e.g., time-consuming approval procedures, elaborate additional consent protocols, and lack of sympathy for the effort). Direct behavioral measures paralleling those used during the treatment program and cited earlier in this paper proved not feasible. Access to the participants' permanent school records (containing test scores, grades, behavioral data, etc., accumulated during any post-treatment schooling) required cooperation of the school systems, involving several large jurisdictions. Similarly, any information the project wished to obtain from police, juvenile courts, and employers was not available. Therefore, information needed to corroborate self-report data could not be obtained. In selecting the instruments, every attempt was made to use those previously developed and tested by other delinquency researchers and relevant to the evaluation of PREP's objectives. This was done to ensure that reliable and valid measures were employed.

Participants

Follow-up data were collected on 40 youngsters (21 experimental, 19 control) from the original sample of 60. At follow-up, of these students, 21 were juniors and 19 seniors in high school. Their mean age was 17.8. Given that the project dealt with a high-risk population and several years had passed since the treatment phase, sample mortality was anticipated and was in fact found to be 33%. To minimize the rate of dropout, an extensive search strategy was adopted. A telephone canvas was conducted in an effort to verify on-file addresses and phone numbers of participants and their families. Over 60% of the total sample was located through this procedure. Thereafter, address confirmation correspondence was posted to each participant via certified mail, return receipt requested. A stamped, self-addressed envelope was provided for the subject's convenience in returning the enclosed address confirmation form. When a participant could not be located by this procedure, a criss-cross directory, which functioned like a comprehensive telephone book, was used. Information was also sought through the cooperation of informal sources (e.g., school personnel familiar with the program and friends of the participant's family). The collective yield of such search strategies verified current addresses and phone numbers for more than 90% of the participants and gave some concrete explanation for absence for the remainder of the total sample, such as moving to another state or death.

Participants were invited to visit a neutral location, close to their home or school, for the administration of the proposed written interview. The interviews took place over a continuous 6-week period. The group sessions were scheduled on a convenient weekday evening or weekend afternoon. Despite a variety of efforts made to accommodate the participants, some individuals were not available or hesitated to come to the group meetings. Alternate data collection procedures were scheduled to help reduce sample mortality. Among the procedures used were private reception of the participants at the project office, home visits, and questionnaire administration by mail or telephone.

Special efforts were made to secure collaborative data from school and court records. In each instance, the informed consent procedure used to secure the interview data also stipulated that such records would be sought. However, both the schools and the courts required that other specific consent procedures be used with parents and students regarding data from each agency. The school system, for example, required that the investigators develop a special and quite elaborate consent procedure. Finally, because of the school system's reluctance to provide assistance, develop a reasonable consent protocol, and send this form to parents, this aspect of the follow-up investigation was abandoned. Juvenile court requirements were as stringent, and attempts to secure the data were also terminated, thus thwarting this part of the follow-up data-gathering efforts.

Measures

No identical baseline measures existed for self-report inventories noted here. However, they embraced constructs and specific behaviors comparable to those explored at pre- and post-test assessment points.

1. *Student Biographical Questionnaire* is a 17-item multi-faceted inventory that explores the student's family, community, and employment as well as educational history and status, current status of siblings, whereabouts of parents, their occupations, and other demographic information. These biographical data were compared with data secured while the participants were in the program.

2. *Student General Questionnaire* is a multi-faceted, forced-choice inventory of 97 total items exploring the following areas: (a) involvement in leisure-time and community activities, (b) the Rosenberg Self-Esteem Scale (18), (c) an adaptation of the aspiration and expectation measure developed by Elliott and Voss (19), (d) the Nye and Short self-report of delinquency scale (20), (e) involvement with court, police, probation, and correctional institutions, (f) relationship with family and friends, and (g) an adaptation of the items devised by Hirschi, examining anticipated aversive consequences of contacts with authority and severity versus certainty of punishment as a potential deterrent to criminal behavior (21).

3. *The Socialization Scale* was developed independently by Gough in 1975 and later introduced into the California Psychological Inventory (22). The Socialization Scale is a standard, true/false format measure which has seen frequent use in research on troublesome youth. It contains 54 items, has repeatedly demonstrated its reliability and validity in discriminating between delinquent and nondelinquent populations, and has yielded significant reliability coefficients (23, 24).

4. *Student Program Review Questionnaire* is a 22-item, forced-choice response measure intended to secure the student's impression of his participation in PREP. Among the areas explored are the student's perception of his experience in PREP; educational, social, and personal benefits derived from PREP; and what the student anticipates were significant others' impressions of the program. Participants' involvement in any extracurricular or community activities over this time period are also investigated. Premeasures in the above areas were also on file. Specific demand characteristics may have accompanied the administration of the program questionnaire. However, the measure's potential for inviting response bias was outweighed

by the necessity to directly examine the level of consumer satisfaction. Control subjects were administered parallel items that surveyed their general public school experience.

5. *PREP Parental Inventory* paralleled some of the components of the Student Biographical, General, and Program Review Questionnaires. Among the areas it explored were family background, societal attachments, student delinquent behavior, criminal record, as well as school attendance, disciplinary referrals, suspensions, and grade point average. About 20% of the items on the students' inventory were comparable with parental inventory. The interitem reliability agreement was 0.75.

Comparison of Participants versus Dropouts   A critical question to any follow-up investigation centers around whether or not participants in the follow-up are significantly different from the dropouts. In order to answer this question, we analyzed data that were available for baseline measures in terms of the following comparisons: experimental follow-up versus experimental dropout, control follow-up versus control dropout, experimental follow-up versus control follow-up, and experimental dropout versus control dropout. As Table 3 shows, the 64 comparisons executed yielded only four significant differences.

All of these significant differences indicate that the control youth who stayed within the sample were significantly different from the control youth who dropped out. Significant differences were found on the Lorge-Thorndike Verbal IQ, the Lorge-Thorndike Non-Verbal IQ, the Stanford Language Test, and the Rotter Internal-External Locus Control Inventory. In effect, upon inspection of the profiles of the control group, it becomes evident that those who stayed were much higher on the preceding four variables than the controls who dropped out. Thus, in this current follow-up investigation, we stacked the cards against ourselves for the evaluation of the experimental manipulation. The students exposed to the experimental manipulation who participated in the follow-up investigation are representative of the entire population of antisocial students who participated in the community-based program.

RESULTS

Statistical Analysis

The program used for all of the analyses was "subprogram *t*-test: comparison of sample means" from *Statistical Package for the Social Sciences* (25).

Table. 3. Representativeness comparison of experimental and control participants versus nonparticipants

Variable[a]	Significance of control follow-up versus control dropout
Lorge-Thorndike Verbal IQ	S
Lorge-Thorndike Non-Verbal IQ	S
Iowa Vocabulary Subtest	NS
Iowa Reading Comprehension Subtest	NS
Iowa Language Usage Test	NS
Iowa Arithmetic Concepts Subtest	NS
Iowa Composite Score	NS
Stanford Language Test	S
Stanford Arithmetic Computation Test	NS
Attendance for 1970/71 school year	NS
Days suspended during 1970/71	NS
Disciplinary referrals 1970/71	NS
Disciplinary visits 1970/71	NS
Confirmed delinquent acts 1970/71	NS
Rotter Internal-External Locus Control	S
Grade point average	NS

[a] None of these variables showed significant difference in comparison of representativeness of experimental follow-up versus experimental dropout groups.

The data were examined by comparing experimental and control groups across major individual components of PREP's conceptual model, noted in Table 1; 119 comparisons were executed. For the sake of clarity, the significant differences are reported briefly according to PREP's conceptual model. The variables contained within the first two components of the conceptual model—skill gain and gain in school's reinforcement value—are related directly to in-school performance and therefore are not included in the 4-year follow-up. There are also variables within the first two components that are targeted specifically for the 1-year follow-up program and consequently are also unnecessary for the 4-year follow-up study. There were 10 significant differences on the last four components of the model.

Access to Socially Acceptable Roles

Areas of student behavior examined here are those concerned with the individual's proximity to appropriate social vehicles. The control and PREP follow-up participants were examined across 31 variables that indicated the extent of their social involvement. Examples of the particular items that provided the data are: differences between aspirations and expectations, involvement in community activities, and employment and educational status.

The following significant differences for this general category were found. Former controls report that they spent more hours per week in reading for pleasure, $t(38)=2.38$, $P<0.05$. The experimental groups felt that PREP was more advantageous to them as compared to the control group's recollections of their general public school experience, $t(38)=2.63$, $P<0.05$. In addition, parents of PREP students indicated that they believed the program provided beneficial services to their children. This is in contrast to the evaluations given by the parents of the control group of the public school system, $t(38)=2.49$, $P<0.05$.

Reinforcing Relationships

The 25 variables of this component are concerned with measures of family and peer relationships. Examples of the follow-up measures exploring interpersonal relationships are: reported intimacy associated with family members and friends, the number of individuals the student considered to be his friends, and the degree of importance the student attaches to having friends and social interactions.

Program students, as compared to control participants, reported that they consider their early home environment to have been more positive, $t(38)=3.35$, $P<0.05$, and that they would have recommended the PREP program to a friend, $t(38)=2.45$, $P<0.05$. (Controls were asked if they would recommend their school to a friend.) Parents of former PREP students agreed with their children regarding the benefits of the program. They rated the feedback and assistance from the PREP staff as more reinforcing than did control parents, who rated the same variables of the public school system, $t(38)=2.35$, $P<0.05$.

Increased Incentive for Prosocial Behavior

Items of the Student General Questionnaire and the Gough Socialization Scale were used as an index of these 30 variables. Examples of the criteria employed to designate behavior as either prosocial or antisocial include: ratings of the consequences of police contacts in terms of interference with career planning, a subscale score that contains a standardized score relating to the student's self-esteem, an index regarding the student's participation in delinquent behavior and perceived consequences to family and friends, a standardized socialization subtest, and a subscale of career aspirations and expectations.

The experimental and control students did not differ significantly on the subscales, but did exhibit variance on several individual variables. Control students reported feeling that they had done something wrong (i.e., experienced guilt) more often than did experimentals, $t(38)=3.60$, $P<0.05$. The controls also indicated that engaging in aggressive behaviors in order to obtain money would more seriously affect their career goals, $t(38)=2.4$, $P<0.05$).

Decreased Juvenile Problem Behavior

The final component of the PREP model reflects the consequences of implementing the program within an adolescent community, that is, decreased incidence of delinquent behavior. The 33 variables employed to define this component focus on the frequency of student interaction with institutional legal agencies. Specific areas and examples of inappropriate behavior include: subscale and individual items of self-reported delinquent behavior, self-reported incidents of police detention or arrest, and incidence of probation or time served in correctional institutions.

Experimental students reported that they have participated in fewer gang fights since leaving the program, $t(38)=2.5$, $P<0.05$. The former PREP students also indicated that they attempted to avoid trouble more than the controls, $t(38)=2.67$, $P<0.05$.

DISCUSSION

Analyses of self-report data collected from the participants indicate that no substantial differences are present. Actually, of the items that are directly related to the evaluation of the program, three favor the experimental participants. They are: happier home environment, participation in fewer gang fights, and greater avoidance of trouble. Three other items favor the control participants. They are: reading more, experiencing more guilt about engaging in antisocial activities, and having less tendency to engage in aggressive behaviors to secure reinforcers. Thus, data comparisons between experimental and control participants produced no evidence of long-term maintenance of behavioral changes. The results, however, must be interpreted with caution because of the large number of variables studied and the tendency of the data not to yield consistent trends; that is, the significant differences seem to cancel out various components of the conceptual model.

The second cohort follow-up investigation of former program participants was incomplete in two major respects. First, serious practical difficulties were encountered while attempting to develop measures for retrospective follow-up. Second, direct behavioral assessments were not utilized despite the fact that the nature of the treatment dictated their development and use.

The data have implications in five areas for evaluative research on therapeutic services provided to children at risk. First, follow-up evaluation is necessary to determine if therapeutic changes generalize to other contexts and are maintained, and to provide a rationale for the provision of services. Second, the selection or construction of behaviorally based measures for follow-up may be practically impossible because of administrative problems or access to situations where relevant behavior is likely to occur. In this event, self-inventories that have adequate reliability should be employed. Third, follow-up on participants of programs long since terminated is extremely costly in terms of both financial and staff resources, if one desires to locate an adequate follow-up sample. Fourth, ethical and legal problems may be encountered if an attempt is made to solicit information from previous participants who may not be willing to cooperate for nonbeneficial involvement. Such issues become of critical concern when follow-up participants appear to be significantly smaller in number than the original sample group. Fifth, and most important, the type of measures to be used for follow-up should be conceptualized before the treatment program ensues to ensure that comparable measures are employed over time and that they are relevant to the longitudinal statistical analysis of the program.

This study indicates that evaluating a community-based treatment program for delinquents is a complex process. The establishment, implementation, and evaluation of a community-based treatment process are all interrelated. The evaluation component should be considered initially along with the establishment and implementation components. Second, the study raises the issue of what are adequate criteria upon which to evaluate delinquency programs, including self-inventories, behavioral observations, interviews with significant others regarding incidence of antisocial behavior, and contacts with juvenile justice agencies. The primary criteria should be contacts with various juvenile justice agencies after the conclusion of a program. However, securing such data is extremely complicated in terms of energy, access, and qualitative consistency.

ACKNOWLEDGMENTS

Research reported here was made possible through funding from research grants #MH14443 and MH21950 awarded by the Center for Studies of Crime and Delinquency of the National Institute of Mental Health to the Institute for Behavioral Research. Preparation of the manuscript was facilitated by these grants and research grant #MH18813 from the same agency.

The assistance of Dan McCombs, George Koustenis, and Susan Rusilko in this program is deeply appreciated.

REFERENCES

1. Davidson, W. S., II, & Seidman, E. Studies of behavior modification and juvenile delinquency: A review, methodological critique, and social perspective. *Psychological Bulletin*, 1974, *81*, 998–1011.
2. Empey, L. T., & Erickson, M L. *The Provo experiment.* Indianapolis: D. C. Heath and Company, 1972.
3. Lundman, R. J., McFarlane, P. T., & Scarpitti, F. R. Delinquency prevention: Assessment of reported project. *Crime and Delinquency*, 1976, *22*, 297–308.
4. Segal, S. P. Research on the outcome of social work therapeutic interventions: A review of the literature. *Journal of Health and Social Behavior*, 1972, *13*, 3–17.
5. Shireman, C. H., Mann, K. B., Larsen, C., & Young, T. Findings from experiments in treatment in the correctional institution. *Social Service Review*, 1972, *46*, 38–59.
6. Brenner, M. H., & Carrow, D. Evaluative research with hard data. In *Evaluative research in criminal justice.* Rome: United Nations Social Defense Research Institute, 1976.
7. Empey, L. T. *A model for the evaluation of programs in juvenile justice.* Washington, D.C.: National Institute for Juvenile Justice and Delinquency Prevention, 1977.
8. Empey, L. T., & Lubeck, S. G. *The Silverlake experiment.* Chicago: Aldine Publishing Company, 1971.
9. MacIver, A. M. *The prevention and control of delinquency.* New York: Atherton Press, 1967.
10. Rothenberg, J. Cost-benefit analysis: A methodological exposition. In M. Guttentag & E. L. Struening (Eds.), *Handbook of evaluation research* (Vol. 2). Beverly Hills: Sage, 1975.
11. McCombs, D., Filipczak, J., Friedman, R. M., & Wodarski, J. S. Long-term follow-up of behavior modification with high-risk adolescents. *Criminal Justice and Behavior*, 1978, *5*, 21–24.
12 Filipczak, J., Storm, R., & Breiling, J. Programming for disruptive and low-achieving students: An experimental in-school alternative. *Journal of the International Association of Pupil Personnel Workers*, 1973, *17*, 38–42.
13. Bernstein, I. N. Validity issues in evaluative research: An overview. *Sociological Methods and Research*, 1975, *4*, 3–12.
14. Bernstein, I. N. Bohrnstedt, G. W., & Borgatta, E. F. External validity and evaluative research: A codification of problems. *Sociological Methods and Research*, 1975, *4*, 101–128.
15. Campbell, D. T. From description to experimentation: Interpreting trends as quasi-experiments. In C. W. Harris (Ed.), *Problems in measur-*

ing change. Madison: University of Wisconsin Press, 1963.
16. Campbell, D. T. Reforms as experiments. *American Psychologist,* 1969, *24,* 404–442.
17. Campbell, D. T., & Stanley, J. C. *Experimental and quasi-experimental design for research.* Chicago: Rand-McNally, 1967.
18. Rosenberg, M. *Society and the adolescent self-image.* Princeton, N.J.: Princeton University Press, 1965.
19. Elliott, D., & Voss, H. *Delinquency and Dropout.* Lexington, Mass.: D. C. Heath and Company, 1974.
20. Nye, F., & Short, J. Scaling delinquent behavior. *American Sociological Review,* 1957, *22,* 326–331.
21. Hirschi, T. *Causes of delinquency.* Berkeley, Calif.: University of California Press, 1969.
22. Gough, H. G. *Manual for the California Psychological Inventory.* Palo Alto, Ca.: Consulting Psychologists Press, 1975.
23. Severy, L. J., & Elliott, D. S. The dimensionality of the So scale and the prediction of delinquency and high school dropout. *Journal of Research in Crime and Delinquency,* 1975, *12,* 91–98.
24. Stein, K. B., Gough, H. G., & Sarbin, R. T. The dimensionality of the CPI socialization scale and an empirically derived typology among delinquent boys. *Multivariate Behavioral Research,* 1976, *1,* 197–208.
25. Nei, H. N., Hull, C. H., Jenkins, J. G., Steinbrenner, K., & Bent, D. H. *Statistical Package for the Social Sciences* (2nd ed.) New York: McGraw-Hill, 1975.

INTRODUCTION TO CHAPTERS 12 AND 13

The novelty of the Stemmers Run Junior High School program described in these chapters is that it is both multidimensional and operates from within a regular public school building (utilizing regular teachers and regular classrooms). This style of operation is unusual because most secondary school faculties will not tolerate seriously disruptive students in their midst for long. (In one Maryland school district, two small, moderately successful programs begun in the 1960s were terminated in large measure for this reason.) In the case of the Stemmers Run program, faculty flak did indeed cause difficulty. However, this was lessened by the following: 1) strong administrative support; 2) semi-self-containment of the program's classes, along with supervision of program students in the halls and in the cafeteria; 3) assignment of capable regular teachers to the program; 4) removal of enough disruptive youth from other regular sections to offer teachers relief; 5) a tight program structure; and 6) a behavioral resource/holding/time-out room readily available for program youths who misbehave.

The program differs markedly from in-school suspension approaches in its breadth, intensity, and positive emphasis. It is a multidimensional approach offering the following: 1) teacher selection and assignment based on capability and interest, 2) classroom behavior management (a token economy), 3) powerful and varied pupil incentives (such as school play time and early dismissal), 4) parent contracting tied to home reinforcements, 5) small classes with some individualized and small group instruction, 6) built in mainstreaming incentives, and 7) an integrated behavioral resource room. Essentially, the program has the same multidimensional character as most day therapeutic and residential schools. It mainly differs from them in its greater cost-effectiveness and mainstreaming capabilities.

In comparing this program to the IBR program described in Chapters 10 and 11, one must consider that the students identified for the Stemmers Run Junior High (SRJH) program and its control population had *severe* behavior problems in school, meriting multisuspension. Such *extreme* behavioral criteria were not utilized in the IBR project. Consequently, at least 67% of the IBR program and control youth were in the 11th and 12th grades in senior high school at age 17–18, compared to less than 27% for the SRJH program and control groups.

The program summarized by Heaton et al. is a sympathetic report of a moderately successful in-school program. The fact that the Stemmers Run model did not win "hard money" school system budget support in 1981 suggests also that it was not viewed as vital or needed by the school's most influential policy makers.

Technical details of this program are available in a 50-page manual which can be purchased for $4.00 from the Essex Book Service, P. O. Box 7754, Essex, Maryland 21221.

12

A contingency management program for disruptive junior high school students:
I A detailed description

Ronald C. Heaton
Daniel J. Safer
and
Richard P. Allen

PROGRAM INCEPTION

With an enrollment of 1,300 students, Stemmers Run is a crowded junior high school on the urban edge of a large east coast city. The school serves a lower middle-class working population known to have higher rates of crime, drug and alcohol problems, and broken homes than its more affluent suburban counterparts. Nearby to heavy industry, which employs many of the parents, the physical facility is slowly becoming run-down, its student population is increasingly transient, and there are growing problems in maintaining discipline and order.

Stemmers Run's problem with disruptive students was not unique. The administration had to suspend 681 pupils during a 4-year period in the mid-1970s, but this was only moderately above average for the school district. Like other junior highs, the school had made numerous referrals of problem children to school psychologists, truancy officials, and mental health agencies, but for the most part difficult children were returned to the school with little or no change in their deportment. Not that referring a disruptive student to, for example, the local mental health center, did not have any effect; indeed, some benefits to the child often did occur. But the problem of misbehavior in the school usually continued despite the help the student received from counseling (1, 2).

In many cases, the school administrator was told simply that the outside counseling agency did not have adequate staff or programs to deal with these children. Furthermore, these misbehaving students expressed little interest and no need for mental health treatment. They did not want to be perceived as "mental" and resisted treatment programs that could be identified with mental health. They viewed themselves as bad, but not crazy (Note A).

During the 1972/73 school year, one assistant principal of Stemmers Run Junior High had been working closely with psychiatric consultants from the local mental health center. This assistant principal had seen the relative effectiveness of behavioral techniques used in individual cases of school misbehavior. However, it was clear that Stemmers Run had many more cases than the consultants could handle on an individual basis. Therefore, it was proposed that, where possible, the individual cases be combined and handled as a group within the school. It was reasoned that the group approach would be more economical and effective.

After it was decided that the best way of dealing with these misbehaving students was to design a special program for them, the school's administrators had to face certain harsh realities such as: 1) Do we have the space? 2) Will it require extra staff? 3) Who will pay for the extra staff and space? 4) Do we have the experience to manage the program successfully? and 5) Will such a venture be accepted by the other school administrators and faculty members? The administrators realized that if one waits for all obstacles to be removed, programs never materialize.

At Stemmers Run, space was found in a school that was already operating at maximum capacity. The assistant principal correctly assumed that most teachers would not object to trading their worst misbehaving student for two other students not exhibiting such disruptiveness in the classroom. These trades resulted in approximately 15 classrooms receiving an additional student and a single classroom being vacated to be used for the 15 worst trouble-makers at the grade level. It also released the one teacher who would normally be teaching the classroom of 30 so that he would be able to teach the 15 misbehavers. In terms of teaching loads, these trade-offs were made for each of the four traditional subjects (English, math, science, and social studies) so that one teacher in each of these instructional departments was freed for one period to teach in the class containing the disruptive students. One of the incentives for the teachers assigned to the troublemakers was that they would have far fewer students in their class than they would have normally.

The selection of teachers picked to instruct this group of misbehavers is a critical decision. Like Stemmers Run, probably all junior high schools contain some faculty members who have good rapport with disruptive students. We have found these teachers to be self-assured, not easily intimidated, flexible, able to take a joke, and able to take command of explosive situations. They tend to overlook minor disruptiveness rather than make it into a major issue. A few, in fact, had a history of discipline problems when they were in junior high. Although most of the qualifiers are men, we have found a number of women possessing personality characteristics which seem suitable in handling the misbehaving junior high student.

It is very important that the teachers, selected as being qualified to teach such students, be volunteers. Once they have genuinely committed themselves to teach this group, they seem better able to weather the inevitable problems that will arise with this group of students over the year.

The issue of incentives for all program personnel is an important one for success in such a difficult undertaking. In addition to being offered a smaller class size, incentives at Stemmers Run were increased by providing program teachers with an additional free period daily for preparation. This was possible because the program called for limited participation by these students in the minor subjects, and therefore, one of the minor subject teachers could assume their "extra" duties. Thus, the teachers were released from hall and lavatory monitoring duties which are usually disagreeable tasks for school personnel. Also, an attempt was made to increase the status for teachers associated with the program. This was done by providing them more informal and friendly access to the high-status people in the school—the principal and immediate assistants.

Money, of course, is a highly important incentive for teachers, but it was impossible to raise teacher salaries because they were participating in the education of these difficult children. However, it was possible to pay them extra for the time they spent in a workshop in behavior management. As the program progressed in time, it was also possible to pay the experienced teachers for training the newer teachers. Such training funds may come from the local board of education budget or from federal grants (see Chapter 19).

Although you will typically find that nonprogram teaching staff in the school are initially enthusiastic about having the troublemakers removed from their classrooms, their reactions become mixed as the year proceeds. Teachers will feel—and some will complain—about the injustice of doing special things for bad kids. After all, they argue, why should the school reward their misbehavior by allowing them to enter a program where one of the rewards is early dismissal from school. Our answer has been that these students do more work in the new program than they had been doing in their previous classrooms. In substantiating this contention, we can and do display achievement data from standardized tests. The achievement rates for students in the program are compared with their preprogram rates, and the results generally show increased or comparable progress with the special program (3). This type of data can temper the animosity of some ardent detractors of the program.

Other teachers will argue that once nonprogram students observe these troublemakers being placed in a program that offers an early release from school, they will also become discipline problems in order to be admitted and gain the rewards offered in the special program. In our experience over 7 years, however, this happened only very infrequently. Some students did threaten to misbehave in order to be admitted, but few carried out these intentions. We suspect that the stigma of being placed in special programming, however benign, was strong enough to detract students who did not need it for their survival in school.

SELECTION OF STUDENTS

Students selected for the program were nominated by the administrative and guidance staff involved in school discipline. Teachers were also tactfully queried for their choices of the most troublesome students. In this manner, 20–30 students were initially selected at each grade level. All of these students were well known to the assistant principal who handles discipline, all had received numerous office referrals, and most had been temporarily suspended more than two times for major behavior problems.

After careful review of their school histories and achievement data, the worst 15–20 students (per grade level) were selected for inclusion into the program. It is prudent that this review be made by all program personnel in joint consultation so that no one feels "forced" into accepting these students. Although both boys and girls are selected, the boys generally outnumber the girls in ratios sometimes approaching 8:1. It is important, however, that if a girl is to be included in the special class, she not be the only female. We have found that, especially in the early stages of the program, the boys reject the girls. With more than one girl in the class, the girls can form a subgroup for support and survival; with a class size of 15, it is necessary to have at least 2 and preferably 3 girls. This means that some boys with a greater "need" for the program may have to be passed over to achieve a favorable sex distribution in the group.

The Stemmers Run program has not excluded students from being selected because they were "too bad." That, in fact, was the precise criterion for admission.

Following the final selection of students, their parents or guardians were contacted for their permission to enroll the student in the program. This is usually a critical point in determining the child's eventual success or failure in the program. Most of the parents have had a series of negative contacts with the personnel of the child's school. They are defensive, angry, and want to shift the blame for their child's school problems onto the school. They are tired of feeling blamed for the child's difficulties and are usually in a mood to strike back when they receive the school's request that their child be placed in a special program.

It is important that this initial contact with the parents be made by telephone (or in person) rather than by letter. The school administrator who is contacting the parents can begin on a very positive note, stressing the school's increased receptiveness to educating their son or daughter. It must be made clear that the school is ready to accept some of the responsibility for the child's school difficulties, and that this program will provide a *new beginning*—one that will, hopefully, bring the student more success. The school administrator must be willing and able to withstand the parents' initial hostility and distrust without retaliating. The parent will want to be reassured that his child is not being labeled "mental" or "retarded" and that this new program will truly provide the student with a new chance to succeed in school. Usually the parents realize that their child is heading for early school drop-out, but sometimes the administrator must directly suggest the new program as the best alternative to avoid this. The personal contact, with the parent sensing the concerned attitude exhibited by a school administrator, is usually enough to lessen the resistance to the new program.

Just before the start of the school year, parents of the selected students are invited to meet as a group with the program staff. It is at this meeting that the new program is explained and the support of the parents is formally enlisted. The spirit of the meeting is positive and cooperative rather than blaming. At Stemmers Run, we had all the parents give written permission for their child to participate in the program. In the experience of the Stemmers Run staff, approximately 10% of the parents fail to grant permission for their child's inclusion in the program. In some cases, they are yielding to pressure from their child because the majority of these students are not overly enthusiastic about being separated from their classmates with the prospect of being labeled. In other instances, the parents are not convinced that their children need a special program to succeed in school.

PROGRAM STRUCTURE

Essentially, the Stemmers program was a contingency management system operating within a regular junior high school. Such programs can meet with success in solving discipline problems within the school environment (4). An additional reason for choosing a behavioral model was the successful demonstration of a contingency system used with expelled adolescents at the nearby Anne Arundel County Learning Center (5).

The contingencies were carefully established to clearly delineate student responsibilities as well as the behavioral consequences of their actions. In keeping with the behavioral philosophy of the program, the past problems of these students were viewed as a product of their limited social and academic repertoires. We stressed, therefore, the achievement of remedial social and academic tasks within a clearly defined milieu.

At each grade level (7th, 8th, and 9th) the 12–15 students who met the selection criteria and whose parents gave their consent were grouped in one class or section. On the first day of school the students were given material detailing the program's point and reward systems. Good or appropriate classroom and academic behavior were to be rewarded by points, and these points could be exchanged for leisure activities or desirable objects.

STAFF

Program staff for each grade level consisted of a classroom teacher for each of the four major subjects, and one teaching aide to assist them. Although the teachers rotated into the classroom to teach their subject, the aide remained a constant in the classroom providing a "bridge" between teachers to relay instructions and a general description of the day's foregoing events. The aide was also responsible for the afternoon activities and arrangements.

In addition to the classroom staff, the assistant principal and/or one guidance counselor were required to devote some time to handle discipline problems of program students and some parent contacts. Although a bare bones program could possibly operate with only this staff, Stemmers Run found it highly advantageous to also use local mental health consultants. In addition to providing advice at weekly staff meetings, these consultants provided short-term family counseling and managed the bulk of the parent behavioral contracting.

MORNING PROGRAM

The school day was divided into morning and afternoon sessions with the morning period devoted to the four major academic subjects. Because there has been an increasing shift in education toward emphasizing competence in the "basics" (6), these areas received most of the intructional time to the relative exclusion of the minor subjects.

The program seemed to work best when the students were not required to change rooms frequently or to change teachers. Although this was not always practical, we were usually able to arrange for no more than a single room change in the morning. This decreased hall misbehavior, which is a common and serious problem for this type of student. In terms of teacher changes, we had also been able to arrange (for 2 years) for just two teachers to handle the academic instruction, with one teaching math and science and the other teaching reading and social studies. Our experience was that classroom rules and teacher expectations can be made more consistent and hence understandable to these students with fewer teachers dealing with them. Any change in the way they are handled seems to be especially distressing to this type of student.

POINT SYSTEM

The contingency management system was used during the four morning instructional periods with the aim of motivating task-appropriate behaviors and decreasing disruptive behaviors. A point sheet (Behavior Checklist, see Figure 1) attached to a work folder was given to each student at the beginning of the week. The sheet has spaces for 8 points during each of the four academic class periods so that a student can earn a maximum of 32 points each morning

TODAY'S DATE ____________ NAME ______________________________ No. __________

BEHAVIORS THAT EARN POINTS:

1. Being in the assigned seat on time.
2. Having a pencil.
3. Having appropriate folder on desk and opened.

} Preparation behaviors

4. On task behavior.
5. Worked successfully on task.
6. Extra individual behavior: ______________________________.

	MONDAY							
	1	2	3	4	4	4	5	6
Period 1								
Period 2								
Period 3								
Period 4								

	TUESDAY							
	1	2	3	4	4	4	5	6
Period 1								
Period 2								
Period 3								
Period 4								

	WEDNESDAY							
	1	2	3	4	4	4	5	6
Period 1								
Period 2								
Period 3								
Period 4								

	THURSDAY							
	1	2	3	4	4	4	5	6
Period 1								
Period 2								
Period 3								
Period 4								

	FRIDAY							
	1	2	3	4	4	4	5	6
Period 1								
Period 2								
Period 3								
Period 4								

	MONDAY	TUESDAY	WEDNESDAY	THURSDAY	FRIDAY
Previous Cumulative Total					
Today's Total +					
Present Total =					
Today's Expenditure	=	=	=	=	=
Reinforcement Room					
New Cumulative Total =					

Figure 1. Student Behavior Checklist.

with two to four additional points awarded for each required after-noon activity. Teachers or the aide gave points as they were earned by placing their initials on the appropriate spaces. Points were given contingently for starting, maintaining, and completing assigned work as well as for social behavior appropriate to the classroom. At least initially, it was essential to reward even the basic behaviors of having pencils and work papers, and being in the seat at the time the bell rang. Later, it was possible to gradually shift the assignment of points from these essentials to other important classroom behaviors. Ideally, these basic behaviors should not be expected to disappear once they are well established, but at Stemmers Run we found it nec-essary to occasionally return points to these behaviors until they were relearned.

Students earning all but 7 of 34 to 38 points on a given day were awarded a Good Day Slip; if they earned all but 2 of these points, they received an Excellent Day Slip. When a student earned four or more Excellent Day Slips and no less than one Good Day Slip, an Ex-cellent Week Letter was awarded on Friday. A slightly less stringent standard was used for the awarding of Good Week Letters.

The important concept to remember is that the points can be shifted throughout the year so that they can come to control difficult student behaviors. The list of behaviors that earn points, typed at the top of each student's point sheet, must be changed to reflect the behaviors the staff feel are in need of improvement at that time. At each change, the student must be made aware of the change and the reason for it so that he will not have the excuse of "not knowing" the different behaviors which earn points.

Students are responsible for their own Behavior Checklist; if it is lost or stolen, students lose the points they have accumulated. Al-though they become quite upset the first time they lose the checklist, we found that students quickly learn the lesson of being responsible for their school materials.

When points are given by the teacher or aide, they are usually paired with the natural social reinforcers teachers use with students such as praise, smiles, and nods of approval. These are also the most immediate rewards that students are likely to receive on return to the regular classroom.

Another procedure that can be especially beneficial in shaping behavior is the use of extra points. That is, the teacher may "catch" a student performing a sought-after behavior such as holding up his hand when wanting to speak. The teacher simply says, "I like for you to raise your hand (or whatever) when you want to speak so I am go-ing to give you an extra point." This use of extra points can also turn around a student that is off to a bad day and in danger of exploding with anger or frustration. The idea is to catch him "being good."

INDIVIDUAL INSTRUCTION

The assignment of academic tasks is generally done on an individual basis because of the wide disparity in ability level among these students. Although the average grade level for the class has been 3–4 years below their age-expected level, some of the students will actually be functioning near grade level with others behind by 5 or more years.

Early in the school year, pretesting with SRA achievement tests (7) was carried out and a functional achievement level of the student was ascertained in each of the major subject areas. The student was then started on work slightly below his or her achieved level to provide him with early successes in accomplishing his academic tasks. Throughout the school year, each student's expected achievement level was gradually increased with new, more difficult academic tasks being built on to the previously learned simpler ones.

The weekly individual curriculum expectations for each student were established through a contract negotiated by the subject teacher in conjunction with his or her individual student. A student's grades were contingent upon the amount of the contract he or she had fulfilled for that week at an acceptable level of accuracy; accuracy levels were usually set at 90%. Provided that the student was showing a stable work and achievement rate for the personal weekly contracts, these contracts were gradually lengthened to 2-week and then monthly intervals. Unfortunately, this contractual approach to curriculum demanded a high expenditure of time and energy from the staff, and we found that it frequently was not closely adhered to. Perhaps a simpler contract system would have been more acceptable to most teachers and, therefore, more enduring.

RESPONSE TO MISCONDUCT

Throughout the morning academic periods, the emphasis was on motivating academic performance. While the student was involved in completing assignments, these behaviors were largely incompatible with classroom disruption. Inevitably, however, students strayed from their assigned tasks and used the idle time in ways that disturbed others. In these cases of misconduct, the offending student was immediately presented with a Disturbing and Disruptive Behavior Slip (D/D slips). These D/D slips are preprinted with typical infractions encountered in the classroom, such as "disruptive talking" and "wandering around" (Figure 2). There is also a line on the form for writing in a disturbing behavior not listed as such. The appropriate infraction is checked by the teacher or aide and the checked form is handed to the student.

This D/D slip (adopted from the Anne Arundel Learning Center) is intended as a warning to the student that the specified behavior must be stopped. The D/D slip must be delivered with as little negative emotion as possible because strong criticism can lead many of these students to a temperamental flare-up. Teachers and aides must quickly learn to ignore the student's reaction to receiving a D/D slip, which often includes tearing it up, pushing it off the desk, or mumbling something under his breath. Best results are achieved when the teacher can tolerate such a short, angry reaction without becoming emotionally entangled with it. Of course, if the reaction continues too long (e.g., more than 30 seconds) or becomes too intense, the teacher should probably give another D/D slip.

When a pupil receives two D/D slips during the same school period, he or she will immediately be dismissed from class and sent to

Please correct the following serious disturbing or disruptive behavior.

1. Disruptive talking   _____

2. Throwing objects   _____

3. Hitting or pushing   _____

4. Wandering around   _____

5. Noise making   _____

6. Unauthorized area   _____

7. Other   _____

If you receive a second slip, you must report to the office of the assistant principal.

_____

Date _____ Student _____

                 Teacher _____

Figure 2. Disturbing and Disruptive Behavior (D/D) slip.

the office or to a holding room—if one is available. With serious in-fractions, the students may then be temporarily dismissed from the program until a conference can be arranged with the parents. On less serious matters, the student is held in a time-out situation until he or she has cooled off. During the time the student is away from the classroom, all points are lost and hence reinforcers that normally he or she would be working toward. The time-out procedure works best when it is loosely supervised by the assistant principal and the students are given tasks.

AFTERNOON PROGRAM

Cafeteria

Following the four back-to-back periods of academic instruction, the program students were sent to the cafeteria for lunch. It was during such times, when these students had contact with the larger segment of the school population, that most of the problems for the staff occurred. These times were not initially under the control of the point system. In the cafeteria, for example, the program students often harassed other students, clowned, antagonized the cafeteria aides, and generally created a nuisance. Even when they were conducting themselves well, they were often blamed for incidents just because of their well-known reputations as troublemakers.

The most effective way we found for handling these students' problems in the cafeteria was to keep them closely supervised—under the point system— at a separate table. They seemed to do better as a group under the supervision of an aide rather than scattered throughout the room. An adjunct technique used at times was the assignment of group privileges contingent upon the group's performance in the cafeteria. Examples of such privileges included extra auction items and/or the continuation of the early release reward (see below).

Point recording

The points awarded by the teachers during the morning classes were tallied by the aide and were used in determining the individual student's activities for the afternoon. Provided that he or she had earned enough points, the student was eligible for early release from school. In order to be released for the last two periods of the school day, the student must trade a considerable proportion of points acquired. The release followed lunch or the completion of one of the minor subjects (art, music, physical education) if the student had enrolled in one of them.

For legal reasons, the parents of all program students had given their written permission for their child to earn an early release from school, and it was understood that the student was to go directly home. In other words, the parent ostensibly took full responsibility for the student's early departure. Some problems did occur throughout the years with this reward of early release. For one thing, numerous nonprogram teachers resented it because they did not like the idea of these kids not having to go to school for the entire day. Another problem involved the return of some of these students to the school building or the grounds before the end of the last period. When this happened, they disrupted ongoing classes, taunted teachers, and created a potential legal problem for the administration. This problem was dealt with swiftly and severely because it threatened the continued use of the early release reward. Any time a student who used an early release opportunity was found remaining on school grounds, the privilege for this reward was withdrawn for the next two days that it was earned . This was a sufficiently harsh penalty to deter this behavior after it was enforced one or two times. A similar school response was used for those students who left school early without earning the privilege.

Reinforcement room

Early release from school was a popular reinforcer for most of the students, but those not choosing it or not earning the mandatory number of points during the day could "buy" their way into the reinforcement or activity room. Admission to the reinforcement room cost less than purchase of the early release option, and this cost difference was intended to keep students in school as often as possible.

The reinforcement room was a large room used in the morning for audiovisual and music purposes. It was located away from the regular classrooms because program student activities tended to be louder than was normally tolerated in classroom areas. The reinforcement room was staffed with one aide (the morning classroom aide), although having more than one aide proved to be a definite advantage when the number of students using the room was over five.

The primary duty of the reinforcement room aide was to provide activities and maintain some form of order. The students were allowed to choose a variety of games set up in the room such as pool, table tennis, hockey and soccer games, cards, board games, or slot car racers. The aide supervised these activities because they were on a first-come, first-served basis, and sometimes the students would overstay their turn or barge ahead if the aide was not closely observant. In addition to the aforementioned games, which attracted the interest of the boys, a record player with records and magazines were also available—activities which tended to attract the interest of the girls.

The students were allowed to move about at will and were free to talk and have fun as long as they were not disturbing the activities of others. Often the main activity in the room was talking in small groups. We have also found that after the first weeks in the room, the students enjoyed talking to the aide. They teased her by relating their exploits and tried to get a reaction from her. In training the aide for her duties within the reinforcement room, we stressed the importance of not taking too seriously the tales of the students. The aides were also told to ignore bantering and even mild obscenities among the pupils themselves. However, any vulgarity directed to the aide or used in anger was not to be tolerated as it leads to a loss of respect for the aide and also diminishes her authority over the students. Although we stressed the importance of having a loose, relaxed atmosphere in the reinforcement room, it was very important that limits be clearly defined and transgressions never be allowed in order for the aide to maintain control of the situation. Without respect for the aide and firmly adhered to limits, the type of atmosphere established for the reinforcement room could become catastrophic.

While supervising the reinforcement room, the aide was also responsible for tabulating the points earned for the day and the amount used. This was done on the student's weekly Behavior Checklist (see Appendix A) and points were carried over from the preceding week. Maintaining the point economy takes about one-half hour per day for each class of 15 students.

. Admission to the reinforcement room required less than one-half of the points a student could earn during the morning periods. However, the student had to earn that number of points *on that day* in order to go to the reinforcement room for the afternoon. A student was not allowed to use points earned on preceding days for admission to the room. This was also true of the early release reward. These rewards were contingent strictly on the student's performance *of that day* making it impossible to provide a student with a reward on a day when personal behavior or academic performance was not good.

On occasion, a student would not be disturbing or disruptive in the classroom but would still not make enough points to earn admission to the reinforcement room. When this happened, the student was required to stay in a separate room (the holding room) and complete enough academic work to earn his way into the reinforcement area. The staff was lenient with this make-up work and usually the student would earn entrance to the reinforcement room within one-half hour. However, it was necessary to do something on this order for the students to maintain motivation for their morning academic assignments. Although it was not possible at Stemmers Run, the most economical management would be to have the holding room adjacent to the reinforcement room.

Auctions

Immediately after the morning academic sessions on Fridays, a weekly auction was held for the students. The students bid their accumulated (unused) points on a variety of items held up for auction. These included records, tickets for dances, movies, and roller skating, food items (e.g., potato chips, ice cream, gum, and mints), coupons redeemable at fast-food restaurants, and plastic models. Because not all students are interested in all items, it is important to poll them occasionally for suggestions on items they desire to have included in the auction.

The more tangible and immediate reinforcers such as the food items seemed to garner most of the bidding action. However, those students most strongly motivated in their school performance by the auction usually desired some specific, more expensive item such as plastic models, car magazines, or tickets to events. These students were in the minority since most students complied with the morning regimen for the early release reward or the reinforcement room activities. Still, all the students enjoyed the auctions and looked forward to the fun of bidding their points. We were fortunate in having a gifted guidance counselor who served as the auctioneer; his liveliness ensured a good time for all at the auction.

PARENT PROGRAM

Participation in the program by the student's parents was encouraged from the outset. Mention has already been made of the importance of setting a new emotional tone in the relationship between school and home. The parents must believe that the school personnel are trying to establish the best possible program for these misbehaving students. The approach to the parents should be a mixture of sympathetic understanding for what the parents have gone through with these students and an optimistic plan for the future. The parents should see themselves as part of the team attempting to flexibly develop school success for students who have had mostly failure in the past.

The contacts between school and home should be positive whenever possible. This is necessary at the beginning and even then the school staff will have to be exceptionally patient in waiting for a complementary change in the parents' attitudes toward the school. Unfortunately, we have found that no amount of positive outreach will encourage many parents to participate in the program beyond giving their permission for their child's participation and coming to an occasional conference. Judgment must be used in deciding how far to go in encouraging these parents without alienating them.

The major way the parents can support the program is by the use of home-based reinforcers. These are reinforcers delivered by parents to their children contingent upon performance in school. In the week or two following a student's entrance into the program, a meeting is held with each student and his or her parents. One staff member is designated to handle the family unit and ideally this staff person will continue to serve as the liaison between the family and the school. During the first meeting, behavioral concepts and philosophy are discussed with the family and an attempt is made to develop or make use of existing home rewards to motivate school behavior. Asking the parents what they do or allow for their child when he or she is good is one method of identifying potential reinforcers. Asking students what they are willing to work for is another way to develop reinforcers. Popular home-based reinforcers that we often uncover during these meetings include late-hour privileges, allowance adjustments, freedom from chores, dating or socializing privileges, and special gifts. Permission to ride their minibikes seemed to be a very effective incentive for those students having them.

The contingency arrangements regarding school performance and home rewards were formalized in a behavioral contract signed by all parties. Usually, school performance was defined by the student's earning a Good or Excellent Week Letter during the week. The parents used this letter in determining whether the contingency arrangements of the contracts had been met.

Not all of the parents could be persuaded to offer home-based reinforcers for their child's school work. Although we were able to establish initial contracts in over 90% of the cases, only about three-fifths of the families followed through (at least partially) with this part of the program. Those who refused at the very beginning usually did so because of a philosophical disagreement with the idea of rewarding their children "for something they are supposed to do anyway." Others "dropped out" quietly, and our gentle reminders could not influence them to put forth the effort required.

Even those families that were more motivated often gave the rewards before the contingency requirements were met. The staff person constantly had to emphasize the importance of following exactly the provisions of the contract. Gradually, some families caught on to the system, and by the end of their child's participation in the program, a few were using contracts to deal with home problems.

We would estimate that the average family participating in the contracts needed to be seen about every 3 to 4 weeks, but this time interval varied greatly depending upon the problems being experienced by the student at school. Follow-up sessions were used to renegotiate the contracts, to objectively interpret the contract terms, to strengthen the motivation of the parents and student to continue working within the contract system, and to discuss the student's successes or failures since the last conference.

It was the feeling of the staff that the students whose families participated actively in the parent program were more successful in school than students whose families did not participate. Of course, this impression does not necessarily mean that home reinforcement contingencies were responsible because it overlooks the fact that these families were also the best organized and most motivated to help their child succeed in the program. Certainly the students having strong home-based contingencies were perceived to treat the slips and letters they earned at school with care compared with the students not having home contracts.

RETURN TO REGULAR CLASSES

It was always the intention of the program staff to modify the school behavior of these multisuspended adolescents and return them to their usual classrooms as soon as possible. The return was accomplished at Stemmers Run Junior High from 1973–1980 through the use of a transition program designed to provide a gradual re-entry to the regular classroom. The transition period usually began after the student had been in the program for about 1½ years. Because most of the students enter the program in the 8th grade, this meant that their transition period began soon after the Christmas break when they were in the 9th grade.

Specifically, the transition to the regular classroom incorporated several phases designed to achieve generalization of behavior and a successful return to the traditional classrooms. The first of these special methods was that of self-evaluation. The students were told that during this phase of their schooling they would be permitted to specify the number of points they felt they had earned during each class period.

During the first 1–2 weeks using self-evaluation, the teacher or aide continued to independently assign points for each student's performance. At the end of the day, the student would compare his record with that of the teacher or aide. The smaller the point discrepancy between student and teacher evaluation, the more bonus points the student was able to earn and the quicker the student moved to self-evaluation without teacher matching. In the normal course of events, teachers gradually decreased the matching with students. After about 4 weeks of self-evaluation, only those students who were accurately assigning their own points were allowed to attend the auction. The auction was an important enough incentive for most students to learn accurate evaluation of their school performance.

Following self-evaluation, the Behavioral Checklist is replaced by a daily progress report. The progress report is a standard method used in many public schools to give feedback to the student and parent. Students in junior high school are given acceptable or unacceptable marks in conduct and academic performance *for each class period.* Thus, the students were switched to less frequent feedback using a standard method of the regular classroom. The early dismissal reward was now made contingent upon achieving *no more* than one unacceptable mark for the day.

A third method used to prepare the student for the regular school routine was to have nonprogram teachers rotate into the classroom. Exposure to those nonprogram teachers should help prepare the students to work successfully with their future teachers and deal with differences in their teaching styles.

Another technique that served to make the conditions in the program more closely approximate conditions of the regular classroom was the gradual replacement of the individual curriculum with group instruction.

At approximately the 7th week of the fading program, the students began to attend the regular classes. For some students, this was begun by having them assigned to only 1 or 2 courses in which they were doing particularly well. Following a week or two of adjustment in these regular classes, they then began taking all of their courses in the regular classes. For other students who delayed reentry, it appeared that the best procedure was to put them in the regular program all at once.

The next move toward "normalizing" the school program for

these youth consisted of substituting a *weekly* progress card for the *daily* one. Again the reinforcement contingencies were adjusted to meet the change, and the early release was either allowed or disallowed for the entire week dependent upon the weekly progress report of the subsequent week.

Usually at this time in the fading sequence, the early dismissal reward was eliminated while the weekly auction and the home reinforcers were supplemented to offset the loss of this important reward. Approximately 2–4 weeks later the last in-school reinforcer (the auction) is removed leaving only the home-based reinforcers which continue to be contingent upon the weekly progress reports.

We never counsel the discontinuation of the home rewards for good school behavior because we feel they are appropriate for many students, especially for this group of adolescents. Since the weekly progress report is already a standard tool used by the school to monitor the behavior of some students, its continued use serves as a simple, descriptive, and appropriate informational vehicle for parents to use for their home reinforcement efforts.

Our efforts to return this group of seriously misbehaving students to the regular classrooms were modestly successful. Two of the most important factors in predicting successful outcome appear to be high achievement as demonstrated on the Wide Range Achievement Test (8) and above average school attendance.

Certain aspects of the fading program were evaluated in 1975. Trained observers (who achieved an 89% agreement) evaluated the program students for on-task behavior at three time periods: first, before the fading sequence; second, immediately following the fading program; and third, 2½ months after their return to regular classes. As a comparison, a control group of seriously misbehaving junior high students was selected and evaluated at the last two time intervals.

The results of these observations can be found in Figure 3 and clearly show that there was no deterioration in on-task behavior after being returned to regular classrooms. The program students displayed better on-task behavior immediately after fading than did the controls (U (27)=63.5, $P < 0.05$), but this difference was not significant 2½ months later. Although the absence rate increased during the fading and immediate postfading periods (Figure 4), a comparison with the controls suggests that this is primarily caused by a seasonal pattern with attendance decreasing near the end of the school year. At the 1-year follow-up, attendance for the program group now attending high school had returned to the levels achieved while the program was operating. It should also be noted that high

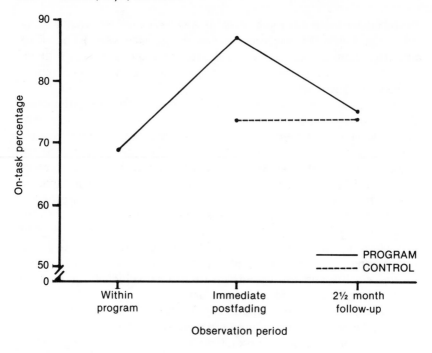

Figure 3.   Observation of on-task behavior of program and control students.

school attendance was better for program than for control students 1 year after the end of the program (t (18)=3.13, $P<0.01$). Finally, teacher ratings of conduct revealed no deterioration in behavior following the fading, with 18 of 23 students receiving the same or better conduct marks after they returned to regular classrooms.

RELATIONSHIPS BETWEEN PROGRAM AND SCHOOL

Important as the above mentioned technology is, the critical element for success of such a program is the way it is perceived by the school's nonprogram personnel. At Stemmers Run, care was taken to prepare the rest of the school for the program's introduction by means of comments during faculty meetings and the enlisting of suggestions on ways of dealing with these disturbing youngsters. The teachers for the program were selected from within the school and were not seen as outsiders by the teaching faculty. The two most respected and powerful members of the faculty (the principal and assistant principal) clearly demonstrated their support for this venture, and the assistant principal, popular with the teaching staff, always

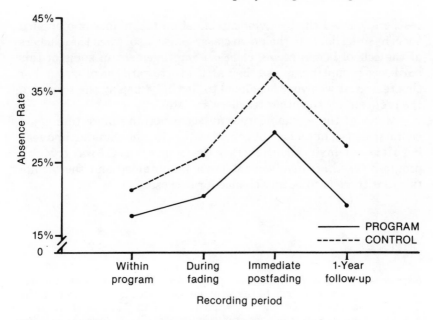

Figure 4. Absence rates for program and control students.

took the lead in introducing elements of the program. The program consultants (the authors) generally took a background position, as they were outsiders.

The rationale for the small class size with the resultant increase in the size of nonprogram classes was carefully explained so as to highlight the advantages of the trade-off for the nonprogram faculty. The assistant principal found time to hear any complaint about the program and to try to work out a solution that would be acceptable to the offended faculty member without sacrificing the program. The mediation role that was assumed by the assistant principal is a tricky but important one and demands a strong, authoritative person who also possesses a great deal of social savvy.

It was also important that the program teachers avoid forming their own social clique within the school. Although we found it helpful for a certain esprit de corps to develop, the program teachers were sensitive to the potential rejection by the rest of the school faculty and very wisely maintained their contacts with staff not involved in the program. By maintaining close relations with the rest of the faculty, our teachers were able to slowly counter some of the initial negative feelings for the program displayed by the nonprogram staff. We found, for example, that the philosophy of how to manage students, and especially disruptive ones, changed as some of these teachers learned the behavior modification techniques and applied them in small doses to their own classrooms. Also, when the teachers of the school began seeing clear-cut improvement in some of this hard-core group, it changed their attitudes toward the program. For this reason, it was very beneficial to tactfully display the results of the program for the other teachers and staff.

Many of these comments may seem nothing more than good common sense, but a lack of consideration for the thinking and feeling of the non-involved members of the faculty is a sure way to sink a program (9). Staff involvement must be obtained and then maintained if there is to be any chance for success.

NOTES

Note A.   In point of fact, a sizable proportion of these misbehaving students were known to the local mental health agencies serving the community. Of the 65 students who in 1974 or 1975 were nominated by their assistant principals as being serious discipline problems (multisuspended), 22 had been admitted to the local psychiatric outpatient facility before 1978. Thus, 34% of these misbehaving students were diagnosed as having a problem suitable for mental health treatment. Of these 22 students who had been seen in a mental health clinic, 41% had not been referred for school problems but rather for other difficulties in their lives. Their clinic records indicated that these other problems largely consisted of disobedience in the home or community and family problems such as running away from home.

REFERENCES

1.   Andrews, W. R. Behavioral and client-centered counseling of high school underachievers. *Journal of Counseling Psychology,* 1972, *18,* 93–96.
2.   Marlow, R. H., Madsen, C. H., Jr., Bowen, C. E., Reardon, R. C., & Logue, P. E. Severe classroom behavior problems: Teachers or counselors. *Journal of Applied Behavior Analysis,* 1978, *11,* 53–66.
3.   Heaton, R. C., Safer, D. J., Allen, R. P., Spinnato, N. C., & Prumo, F. M. A motivational environment for behaviorally deviant junior high school students. *Journal of Abnormal Child Psychology,* 1976, *4,* 263–275.
4.   Becker, W. C. (Ed.). *An empirical basis for change in education: Selections on behavioral psychology for teachers.* Chicago: Science Research Associates, 1971.
5.   Cohen, S. I., Keyworth, N., Kleiner, R. I., & Brown, W. I. Effective behavior change at the Anne Arundel Learning Center through minimum contact interventions. In R. Ulrich, T. Stachnik, and J. Mabry

(Eds.), *Control of human behavior* (Vol. 3). Glenview, Ill.: Scott, Foresman, 1974.
6. Weber, G. Back to the basics in schools: Here's the case for pushing the current trend into a landslide. *American School Board Journal*, 1975, *162*(8), 45–46.
7. Thorpe, L. P., Lefever, D. W., Naslund, R. A. *SRA achievement series.* Chicago: Science Research Associates, 1968.
8. Jastak, J. F., & Jastak, S. R. *The wide range achievement test.* Wilmington: Guidance Associates of Delaware, 1965.
9. Catlin, Glascoe. Personal communication, 1977.

13

A contingency management program for disruptive junior high school students:
II Results and follow-up

Daniel J. Safer
Ronald C. Heaton
and
Frank C. Parker

This report summarizes the results of the first 6-years (1973–1979) of a school-based, combined education and mental health program for disruptive junior high school students, which is described in Chapter 12. The program's first-year results were reported by Heaton et al. (1). Subsequent papers dealt with its evolution (2), its 5-year annual outcome results (3), and a 4-year follow-up of the first three cohorts (4). After a brief introduction, aspects of the program (which were not covered or incompletely covered in Chapter 12) and the evaluation procedures are briefly described. Following this, the annual outcome and long-term results are presented.

GENERAL BACKGROUND

In part because of the increasing amount of violence in public secondary schools (5), programs for seriously disruptive students have increased (6). Nonetheless, most seriously disruptive adolescents never get into alternative or special school programs. They generally follow a downhill school course in their early teens, which includes suspension, truancy, grade retention, and eventually withdrawal from school or expulsion.

Where programs exist for students identified as disruptive, they are mainly at the junior high school level. Smaller scale models usually involve in-school detention or holding rooms. Large-scale programs are few, but are often multifaceted. They can offer work/study opportunities, counseling, behavior management and/or remedial academic assistance. They are often federally funded and located outside the regular school building (7).

Well designed controlled studies or programs for disruptive students have been uncommon. Also, the best designed larger scale studies have had meager results (8–10). However, a sizable number of well-run, small programs have reported areas of success. Positive results from these studies include: improved classroom behavior, decreased suspensions, decreased absenteeism, and higher grades (1, 11–14).

PROGRAM DESCRIPTION

Grade Levels and Subject Selection

The Stemmers Run Junior High (SRJH) School program for multi-suspended students encompassed one 8th grade section in 1973/74, an 8th and 9th grade section in 1974/77, and a 7th, 8th and 9th grade section beginning in 1977/78 (Table I) (Notes A and B).

Students were selected by assistant principals in three adjacent junior highs, one of which was the program school (SRJH), while the other two (for 2 years, it was one) were control schools. The basis of selection was multisuspension and numerous office referrals for misconduct (Note C). Family and school background information for 2 separate years revealed no significant differences between the program and control groups (1, 3). The number of program and control subjects is listed in Table 1.

Staffing: Coordination and Supplementation

Staff from the Eastern Community Mental Health Center (ECMHC) in Baltimore County, Maryland, handled the behavior management training and the evaluation of the program, and the SRJH school staff ran the educational component. Staff meetings were held weekly to coordinate these aspects of the program. Running this pro-

Table 1. Number of students in the program and control groups

Year	Number of students	
	Program	Control
1973/74[a]	14	32
1974/75[b]	32	45
1975/76[b]	29	31
1977/78[c]	48	41
1978/79[c]	46	39

[a]8th graders only
[b]8th and 9th graders
[c]7th, 8th, and 9th graders

gram involved the juggling of staff assignments by administrators in both SRJH school and the ECMHC. From 1973–1977, three ECMHC mental health consultants each averaged five hours/week counseling program students and their parents and consulting with school staff. Also, the ECMHC consultants sought and obtained federal grants to pay one (usually full-time) aide to assist the program teachers. From 1977–1979, approximately $50,000 to 60,000/year was received from an LEAA grant to the ECMHC for the SRJH program and was used mainly to purchase the services of three to four full-time classroom aides and a full-time and part-time mental health consultant.

EVALUATION PROCEDURES

Annual Outcome Measures

At the beginning and near the end of each school year, enrolled and available program and control students were tested on the Wide Range Achievement Test (WRAT) (15). Each year, a composite score was obtained averaging their change scores in mathematics, reading, and spelling. Academic performance was evaluated using student grades. Students with two or more E's in major subjects were– by school policy-judged to be failing. School misconduct was assessed by three measures: school behavioral suspensions, days out of school for disciplinary reasons, and disciplinary withdrawals (expulsions). Because program students were usually disciplined outside the usual school administrative structure for minor classroom misconduct, the statistic "days out of school for disciplinary reasons" was recorded beginning in 1977. It reflects more accurately than the number of suspensions the total extent of disciplinary exclusion. Absenteeism was measured in days absent from school/days officially enrolled. Disciplinary withdrawals (expulsions) included those students who were officially withdrawn from their school for the rest of the term; a small number were subsequently placed on home teaching or transferred to another school.

Follow-up Measures

In 1978 and 1979, the school progress of program students from the 1973/74 and the 1974/75 cohorts was followed. There were 43 program and 55 control students in the follow-up population. School records were obtained for 89% (n=87) of this population. Measures assessed in the follow-up were: absence rate, suspension rate, office referrals for misconduct, classroom conduct ratings, and grades. In addition, educational longevity was assessed. This included number of days attending high school, graduation rate, and frequency of withdrawal prior to graduation. It bears mention that the program and the control students who went into senior high school in 1975 and 1976 did not receive any special program services there. (All the tables and graphs in this chapter are from Reference 3.)

RESULTS

Annual Results

School Misconduct Disciplinary withdrawals (expulsions) were strikingly less frequent from program youth than for controls (Figure 1). An annual average of 7% of program students were withdrawn from school for behavioral reasons, whereas the rate exceeded 29% annually for control youth χ^2 (1)=23.73, $p < 0.001$).

School behavioral suspensions for program students ranged from 0.2 to 1.5/year compared to 1.9 to 2.9/year for control students (χ^2 (1)=38.51, $p < 0.001$) (Figure 2). Days out of school for disciplinary reasons averaged 11/year for program youth compared to the control students' rate of 33 days/year ($t > 3.92$, $p < 0.001$).

Academic Measures The program maintained a high rate of grade promotion since its inception in 1973. Each year at least 80% of its students received passing grades, compared to an average of 48% for the controls (χ^2 (1)=53.78, $P < 0.001$). (See Figure 3.)

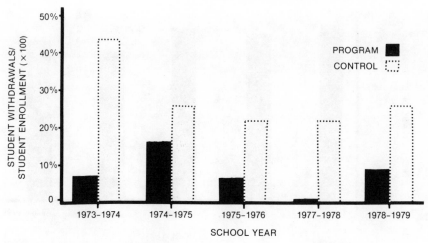

Figure 1. Disciplinary withdrawals.

WRAT tests were complete on only 54% of program and on 36% of control students. The resulting composite average WRAT change scores favored program youth for the first three years (1973–1976), but the reverse was true for the last two (1977–1979) (Figure 4). The results significantly favored program youth in 1974/75 and 1975/76 ($t > 1.88$, $P < 0.05$) (Figure 4). Otherwise, the group differences were nonsignificant (Note D).

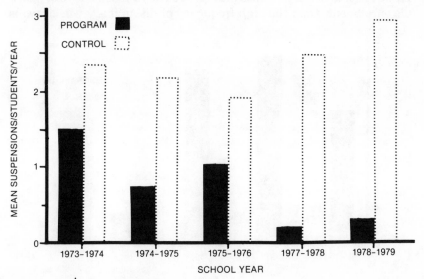

Figure 2. School suspensions.

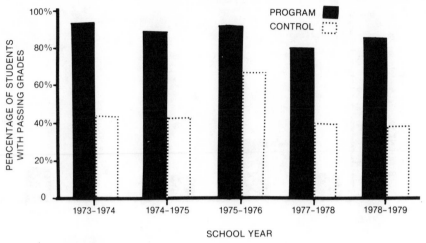

Figure 3. Passing grades.

Absence Rates   Yearly absence rates (days absent/days enrolled) for program youth averaged 27% from 1973–1979, compared to the control average of 32% (Figure 5). Nonetheless, whereas program students maintained a fairly stable attendance pattern, there was a gradual decrease in absenteeism in the control population from 1973 to 1979. By 1977–79, their rate approximated the program level. However, if absence rates are measured as days absent/days of possible enrollment, then the high frequency of disciplinary withdrawals

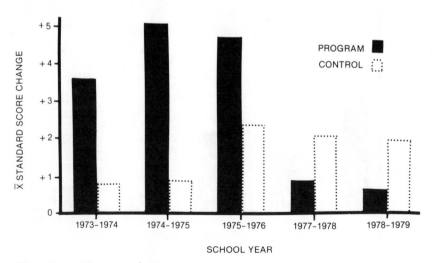

Figure 4. Achievement changes.

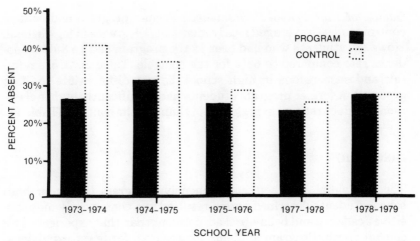

Figure 5. Absence rates.

from the control schools elevates their absence rate considerably above that of program students.

Follow-up Results

Entry into Senior High School A total of 80% of the junior high high school program students entered senior high school versus 40% for the controls (χ^2 (1)=11.82, $P<0.001$) (Table 2). A surprisingly large number of those who did not enter senior high dropped out between the end of junior high school and the fall entrance into the 10th grade.

Senior High School Days Attended Students who had been in the the junior high school program attended high school for a significantly greater number of days than did the controls (t=2.00, $P<.025$) (Table 2). However, when considering only those program and control students who entered senior high school, the difference in high school days attended became no longer significant (Table 2) (Note E).

High School Graduation The rate of high school graduation is limited to only the first cohort since those entering the program in later years were not old enough to graduate. In this analysis, 4/15 (27%) who had been in the junior high school program were known to have graduated high school versus 3/31 (10%) for the control group (Table 2) (Note F).

Quality of High School Performance   Former program and control control students averaged nearly identical D+ grades in high school. However, students who had been in the program had an 80% attendance rate compared to 68% for the controls (Table 2). Office referrals and suspensions in high school did not differentiate the two groups, but former program students had significantly higher classroom conduct ratings in high school than did the controls (Table 2).

DISCUSSION

The behavioral, in-school comprehensive program for junior high school students described herein resulted in a consistently more positive academic and behavioral adjustment than that experienced by control youth. Program students experienced far fewer expulsions, suspensions, days out of school for disciplinary reasons, and grade failures. Also, their attendance and academic achievement were marginally better than the control population. After termination of the program, they entered senior high school in far greater numbers, and in the 10th grade, they stayed somewhat longer, had better attendance, and achieved better classroom conduct ratings. Four years later, they were slightly more likely to graduate.

In considering alternative programs for disruptive youth, administrators in education and mental health are faced with a number of possibilities. They can choose: 1) off-site programs (which are popular with regular teachers but are expensive and low in the rate of return to regular school), 2) special education placement (which is often difficult to obtain for behavior problem youth due to restrictions in PL 94-142), 3) the usual disciplinary approach (e.g., warnings, suspensions, expulsions, grade failure, and drop out; this is by far the cheapest approach, although not the most effective for the involved students), 4) a vocational curriculum (rarely a successful school-based alternative for aggressive youth (8, 16, 17), 5) counseling (a consistently unsuccessful endeavor for disruptive and delinquent youth) (10, 18-20), 6) in-school suspensions (a procedure which has never received a controlled or comprehensive evaluation), 7) an ombudsman program—an untested alternative, or 8) a comprehensive behavioral in-school program meshing mental health and educational services.

The authors feel that option number 8 is attractive for the following reasons:

1. The in-school comprehensive behavioral program described in this paper cost about one-third that of a typical day-therapeutic

Table 2. Four-year follow-up data comparing students from a contingency management system with control students

Follow-up variables	n/N	Program students	n/N	Control students	Difference	$P<$
Educational longevity						
Students entering high school	28/35	80%	20/50	40%	$\chi^2(1)=11.82$	0.001
High school graduates [a,b]	4/15	27%	3/31	10%	$\chi^2(1)=1.14$	0.15
Graduates and transfers	9/19	47%	4/32	12%	$\chi^2(1)=5.91$	0.01
Withdrawn before graduation[a]	22/40	55%	40/54	74%	$\chi^2(1)=2.92$	0.05
	N		N			
X High school days attended/ beginning student	33	153.5	50	85.3	$t(81)=2.00$	0.025
X High school days attended/ student entering high school	25	202.6	24	177.7	$t(47)<1$	n.s.
Performance in high school						
X Grades	25	0.61	23	0.65	$t(46)<1$	n.s.
X Attendance	25	80%	24	68%	$t(47)=6.02$	0.001
X Daily rate of office visits	24	0.05	16	0.19	$t(38)=1.15$	n.s.
X Daily rate of suspensions	24	0.0090	18	0.0111	$t(40)<1$	n.s.
X Classroom conduct ratings	21	0.75	19	0.50	$t(38)=1.97$	0.05

[a]Transfer students not included.
[b]1st cohort only.

cluding all educational and counseling expenses, the cost/student year of this program has (at most) been less than $2,000 above the average cost/student year of public education ($1,953 in Baltimore County in 1978/79).

2. In-school alternative programs can be successful if there is strong administrative support for them and if efforts are made to minimize possible areas of friction between program students and nonprogram teachers. Examples of the latter are separate sectioning for disruptive students and supervision of them in the halls and in the cafeteria.

3. The successful re-entry rate to regular classes and to high school (80%) in this in-school program model is unusually high compared to that of special education and off-site programs. Annual return rates to public school from off-site programs reported in the literature range from 10%–30%. (See Chapter 5.)

4. Behavioral programs in general have had the best reported results for disruptive students (1, 8–14, 17–20).

5. Parent-dispensed home reinforcers based on good school reports are one successful means of motivating disruptive students to improve their classroom conduct (21).

6. Comprehensive programs offer greater options. For example, with a staffed holding-resource room as part of the total program, short classroom exclusions can replace most out-of-school suspensions. Likewise, with the availability of individual educational programming, the academic frustration of most of these low achieving and disruptive youth can be lessened.

The junior high school program described is not without its limitations. The fact that the program and control populations were comparable in attendance and academic achievement in 1977/79 is a disappointment. Even more distressing is the finding that the most former program students drop out of senior high school before the 11th grade. Lastly, programs such as this one for disruptive students, even when partially successful, seem to have only a small impact at best on the overall adjustment of these youth. Their rate of delinquency continues pretty much unabated (8–10, Note G).

CONCLUSION

The comprehensive, behavioral in-school program at SRJH resulted in a far more satisfactory adjustment to a junior high school setting by disruptive youth than was available to controls who received regular educational programming. Also, there was some maintenance of the program's educational benefits into the high school years. The program was the combined effort of education and mental health staff. If mental health personnel maintain only case model services in community mental health centers, they will, in all likelihood, not achieve such broad, system-intervention results.

NOTES

Note A. SRJH assigns students to tracked classes based upon their academic level. For example, in the 7th grade, there are approximately 13 sections arranged consecutively from the 3rd to the 8th grade achievement level. To establish one section for the behavior modification program, one of these sections was separated off from the others, given a small student enrollment, scheduled for a morning-only/major subjects program, given an aide, assigned 2-4 motivated teachers, provided with outside consultants, and set up with a token economy format. The section was thus a modified regular education section which can be called semi-self-contained.

Note B. The SRJH program utilized, in behavioral terms, a token economy. It was modelled after an off-site program, the Anne Arundel County Learning Center (AACLC). The two programs have in common a similar behavioral and procedural emphasis, student-teacher contracts, parent contracts, disciplinary practices, and many reinforcement options. However, they differ in a number of respects. Some major program differences—aside from general off-site versus on-site ones described in Chapter 5—are: 1) entrance requirements (AACLC requires expulsion; SRJH requires multisuspension), 2) reinforcement options (AACLC has an available gym and its own grounds and, therefore, has more athletic options; SRJH is a neighborhood school and can use early release as a reward option), 3) parent contracts (AACLC has more leverage over parents; if the parents don't cooperate, their child can be expelled. SRJH depends upon voluntary parent support which is often less reliable).

Note C. Multisuspension for misconduct did not include suspensions for smoking and truancy.

Note D. Although the SRJH program students scored less well than control students on individual achievement tests in 1977-1979, this was not representative of the entire experimental group during that period. In 1977/78, indeed, the control group had a nonsignificant advantage. (Such variations are reported by others; see Chapter 10). However, during the years 1978/79 and 1979/80, program students in the entire 3-school program population had significantly greater ($P < 0.05$) achievement gains on the WRAT than did the control population (22).

Note E. It must be stressed that the majority of the control students dropped out of school by mid-9th grade and that most of the program youth dropped out before or in the 10th grade (4). In SRJH, multi-suspended students had a tightly structured program tailored more to their interests, abilities, and needs. In such an environment, they survived and did relatively well on average. When multisuspended students went to senior high school (before 1977), no such program existed there. Thus, the attrition rate in senior high school was great. (With the advent of the senior high school resource program, the rate of high school drop-out from program youth has significantly decreased (see Chapter 18).

Note F.   One second cohort student had been skipped and was thus added to the original first cohort of 14 students. Subsequent data (4) led to a composite, three-cohort, average high school graduation rate by program students of 26% (10/39), compared to 17% (10/60) by control students (χ^2 (1)=0.69; n.s.). The analysis of the first three cohorts on percent entering high school was virtually the same as the two-cohort data presented in Table 2; 77% (33/40) of program youth entered senior high school versus 41% (25/61) for the controls (χ^2 (1)=11.67; $P<0.001$).

Note G.   The SRJH program was evaluated for its impact on delinquency during the 1977 to 1980 period. The results show that it did not decrease recidivism, but that it did decrease first offenses from 1977 to 1979, though not from 1979/80. The total difference for first offense rates between the controls and experimentals was not significant.

REFERENCES

1. Heaton, R. C., Safer, D. J., Allen, R. P., Spinnato, N. C., & Prumo, F. M. A motivational environment for behaviorally deviant junior high school students. *Journal of Abnormal Child Psychology,* 1976, *4,* 263–275.

2. Trice, A. D., Parker, F. C., Safer, D. J., Iwata, M. M., & Marriott, S. A. *Teaching bad boys: Perspectives on an in-school program for disruptive adolescents,* Baltimore: American Young Company, 1982.

3. Safer, D. J., Heaton, R. C., & Parker, F. C. A behavioral program for disruptive junior high school students: Results and follow-up. *Journal of Abnormal Child Psychology,* 1981, *9,* 483–494.

4. Heaton, R. C., & Safer, D. J. Secondary school outcome following a junior high school behavioral program, *Behavior Therapy,* in press.

5. National Institute of Education, DHEW. *Violent schools—safe schools: The safe schools study report to Congress* (Vol. I). Washington, D. C.: Author, January, 1978.

6. Garibaldi, A. M.. (Ed.). *In-school alternatives to suspension: Conference report.* Washington, D. C.: National Institute of Education, April, 1979.

7. Pennsylvania Department of Education. *Alternative Disciplinary Programs and Practices in Pennsylvania Schools.* Harrisburg, Pennsylvania: Author, 1977.

8. Ahlstrom, W. M., & Havighurst, R. J. *400 losers: Delinquent boys in high school.* San Francisco: Jossey-Bass, 1971.

9. Reckless, W. C., & Dinitz, S. *The prevention of juvenile delinquency: An experiment.* Columbus, Ohio: Ohio State University Press, 1972.

10. Berleman, W. C., Seaberg, J. R., & Steinburn, T. W. The delinquency prevention experiment of the Seattle Atlantic Street Center: A final evaluation. *Social Service Review*, 1972, *46*, 323–346.
11. Cohen, S. I., Keyworth, M., Kleiner, R. I., & Brown, W. I. Effective behavior change at the Anne Arundel Learning Center through minimal contact intervention. In R. E. Ulrich, T. Stachnik, & J. Mabry (Eds.), *Control of Human Behavior* (Vol. 3). Glenview, Ill.: Scott, Foresman, 1974.
12. Friedman, R. M., Filipczak, J., & Fiordaliso, R. Within school generalization of the Preparation through Response Education Programs (PREP) academic project. *Behavior Therapy*, 1977, *8*, 986–995.
13. Long, J. D., & Williams, R. L. The comparative effectiveness of group and individually contingent free time with inner-city junior high school students. *Journal of Applied Behavioral Analysis*, 1973, *6*, 465–474.
14. Kent, R. N., & O'Leary, K. D. A controlled evaluation of behavior modification with conduct problem children. *Journal of Consulting and Clinical Psychology*, 1976, *44*, 586–596.
15. Jastak, J. F., & Jastak, S. R. The Wide Range Achievement Test. Wilmington, Del.: Guidance Associates of Delaware, 1972.
16. Jeffery, C. R. *Crime prevention through environmental design.* Beverly Hills, Ca.: Sage, 1977.
17. Longstreth, L. E., Shanley, F. J., & Rice, R. E. Experimental evaluation of a high school program for potential drop-outs. *Journal of Educational Psychology*, 1964, *55*, 228–236.
18. Meyer, H. J., Borgatta, E. F., & Jones, W. C. *Girls at vocational high: An experiment in social work intervention.* New York: Russell Sage Foundation, 1965.
19. McCord, J. A thirty-year follow-up of treatment effect. *American Psychologist*, 1978, *33*, 284–289.
20. Sarri, R. C., & Vinter, R. D. Group work for the control of behavior problems in secondary schools. In D. Street (Ed.), *Innovation in mass education.* New York: Wiley-Interscience, 1969, pp. 91–119.
21. Bailey, J. S., Wolf, M. M., & Phillips, E. L. Home-based reinforcement and the modification of predelinquent classroom behavior. *Journal of Applied Behavior Analysis*, 1970, *3*, 223–233.
22. Freeman, L. Unpublished data, 1980.

IV

Specific nonbehavioral program interventions

INTRODUCTION TO CHAPTER 14

The Kansas City project described by Ahlstrom and Havighurst broke new ground in the early 1960s. It was a 7-year, systematic, controlled, well staffed, well organized, large-scale effort that included a work/study program for all experimental youth, community employment opportunities (with remuneration), major classroom curriculum modifications, counseling, and a continuous program assessment. It aimed to demonstrate that a primarily school-based, work-experience program could decrease the delinquency and likelihood of drop-out of alienated, maladjusted adolescent youth from the inner city.

Of the nearly 200 students assigned to the work/study program, approximately 45 had a positive experience that they would have not otherwise had at that time. Nonetheless, analyses of comparative group data revealed that the intervention did not significantly benefit social adaptation, reduce delinquency, or increase the rate of high school graduation.

A full description of the project in the book "400 Losers," contains depressing details about the neighborhoods, schools, homes and personal backgrounds of most of these youth (1). To intervene measurably in such an environment required stronger medicine than was available to the program staff. Furthermore, the point is amply documented that adolescents in the worst social circumstances (having disorganized family patterns, little educational support, unstable living arrangements, poor neighborhoods, and cultural disadvantages) had the worst educational and vocational outcomes.

This study should be compared and contrasted with that of Reckless and Dinitz (summarized in Chapter 15). Although the Reckless-Dinitz project was more systematically evaluated, the Ahlstrom-Havighurst program was a far more intensive intervention effort. Willing students were given a multitude of support services for up to 3 to 5 years, whereas in the Reckless-Dinitz project, students received an alternative school program for only 1 year.

The two projects also studied different youth populations. In the Reckless-Dinitz project, the identified high risk 7th graders had achievement score averages only 1 year below grade level; their absenteeism rate never exceeded 10% in junior high school; their grades averaged C and D throughout junior high school; their average rate of police contacts by age 16 was less than half that reported generally for inner city youth (2); and their known dropout rate at age 16 was only 21%. Disruptive students in the Ahlstrom-Havighurst project were much like others in the literature (see Chapter 2) and were on average two to three times more deviant than the Columbus population.

1. Ahlstrom, W. M., & Havighurst, R. J. *400 losers: Delinquent boys in high school.* San Francisco: Jossey-Bass, 1971.
2. Wolfgang, M. E., Figlio, R. M., & Sellin, T. *Delinquency in a birth cohort.* Chicago: University of Chicago Press, 1972.

14

The Kansas City work/study experiment

Winton Ahlstrom
and
Robert J. Havighurst

Inner city boys screened as socially maladjusted in the 7th grade were placed in a work study program at the beginning of the 8th grade. The project was a carefully designed control group experiment that continued through high school and on into late adolescence. The experiment featured a work-experience program combined with a modified academic program. It was expected that the boys in the experimental program would show better social adjustment and early adult competence than those youth in the control (regular high school) program. In general, these expectations were not fulfilled.

The target group was composed of 13- and 14-year-old boys screened in 1961 and 1962 as socially, behaviorally, and educationally maladjusted from among all 7th grade inner-city classrooms in Kansas City, Missouri, public schools. The ratio of black to white youths was three to two. The boys were divided into experimental and control groups. Experimental boys, beginning in the 8th grade, received special attention through half days of classroom work geared to their abilities and their assumed needs, interests, and personal orientations and half days of supervised work experience; these boys had their own teachers and work supervisors. Control group boys were enrolled in regular school programs and their progress was followed. The study was longitudinal and complete records were maintained on the school, work, community, and family adjustment of the boys, both while they were in school and up to the age of 18 or 19. Work experience, as the independent variable, included three different developmental stages involving different kinds of work experience, supervision-guidance, and rewards.

In stage one, beginning in the 8th grade, the boys worked half of each school day in group work under the supervision of work supervisors, men who knew how to use tools, could manage difficult boys, and could serve as models for the boys.

The students attended a special study class the other half day. This first stage included various group work projects around the schools and in the community, for which the boys received token pay of a dollar a week. The focus was on learning to work with others, following instructions, using and caring for tools, and developing good work habits and attitudes. In substance, stage one was designed to develop a work orientation that would permit boys about 15 years of age to move into stage two, part-time paid employment with private employers, while continuing the half day of classroom study. In stage two, a full-time employment coordinator sought out and developed job openings in the community, assisted boys in finding suitable work, helped them with adjustment problems, and observed and recorded their progress. The boys continued to spend half days in school.

In stage three, boys moved out of school completely, into full-time work in the community. This stage extended through the 17th and 18th years or even longer, during which time the employment coordinator worked closely with the boys, observing and recording progress and problems as entry was made into the adult world of work. At the termination of stage three, boys who remained in the program received high school certificates, authorized by the board of education, certifying that they had successfully participated in a program of supervised and graded work experience sponsored by the Kansas City, Missouri, public schools.

THE POPULATION

Approximately 400 youth were selected from the 7th grades of inner-city schools, half in the spring of 1961 (group 1) and half in the spring of 1962 (group 2). Selected youth had to meet the multiple criteria of average or below average (but not retarded) intelligence, above average aggressive maladjustment scores on peers' and teachers' ratings, and below average achievement in 6th and 7th grades.

Groups 1 and 2 were each made up of about 200 youth with experimental and control groups about the same size at the beginning of the study. Within the first few months, however, group size varied somewhat because some youth were overaged and were dropped from the program, other youth were withdrawn from the experimental group by their parents, several boys moved to other schools, and a few were committed to institutions for delinquency during the first few weeks.

The assignment of boys to experimental and control groups was different for group 1 (1961) than for group 2 (1962). In the former, the assignment was done by a matching procedure that used a combination of scores on the screening instruments but also included nomination by school personnel. This procedure, it was found, heavily weighted the experimental relative to the control group with more severely maladjusted youth from the very beginning of the work/study program. A sizable number of experimental group 1 boys had already been in trouble with police before the 8th grade and several had already experienced institutional confinement. In contrast, while showing predelinquent characteristics, most of the control group 1 youth had not been in any serious difficulty with the police prior to selection. For group 2, the assignment of youth to experimental and control groups was done by a random sampling procedure, which resulted in the research groups being more comparable in terms of the amount of social and school adjustment represented in each.

The Work Experience Program

The first group work assignment in stage I was landscaping at various schools and in city parks. It varied from raking leaves to cleaning out flower beds, transplanting, trimming hedges, and making pathways. This work was not generally liked by the boys, mainly because much of it was done in full view of their schoolmates, who teased them a good deal. Some of the boys objected to the work on the ground that it was mainly busy work, of little value to them or to the community. The work supervisors at this time were trying to create work attitudes and to teach the care and use of hand tools. For the first time in the lives of many of the boys, they were confronted with the need to use tools properly. The tools were simple ones—rakes, shovels, small hand sickles, and garden hoes. The boys immediately became aware that if they destroyed or misused the tools, they would not have to work until replacement tools could be obtained. Some of the boys would deliberately strike their rakes or hoes on cement curbs or blunt their sharp tools.

There was some fighting among the boys. The first task of the work supervisor was to control aggression among these aggressive boys; each supervisor worked out his own methods of control. Of the group of 20 to 25 boys, at least half were outspokenly aggressive, both in words and action. In the early phases of group work it was very difficult to get the boys to work together. They threw rocks, dirt, and tools at each other. In many cases the boys would not work with each other and would purposely do the opposite of what the supervisor told them to do. In each group there seemed to be at least one boy, and in some cases more than one, whom the group liked to pick on. They would usually make life miserable for him. In spite of all the aggressive behavior among the youngsters in the work groups, there were very few injuries and no serious ones.

With the coming of cold and wet weather at the end of autumn, inside work became necessary. On the whole, this went better than the yard work. Some jobs, such as moving and storing materials, were found in the warehouse of the school system. The principal job, and one that grew in importance, was the refinishing of school furniture, mainly old wooden tables and desks whose surfaces were deeply scarred. These had to be sandpapered and surfaced with shellac or varnish. Principal tools were hand sanders, power sanders, and paintbrushes. During this phase of work, many boys began to develop some skill and to take pride in their work. They particularly liked to use power sanders, and some of them enjoyed the varnishing and shellacking.

The 8th grade boys needed to pay a good deal of attention to the details of their work. For the most part, they could not follow complex directions. They had no mental grasp of a two- or three-step operation. They would do one phase of an operation and then stop and wait for directions. For example, if they were sanding desks with coarse sandpaper, someone had to tell them when to change to finer sandpaper, and once the sanding was completed they had to be told to wipe off the dust before putting sealer or varnish on the wood. There was constant bickering among the boys as to who was and who was not doing his share of the work. If one boy sat down and stopped work for a minute, the others would be after him. Some boys complained that they were not paid adequately. One group, led by a smart and aggressive youngster, tried to strike for more pay. Yet the dollar a week was appreciated, and absences were very few on Fridays, which were paydays. It was difficult to get the boys to wear work clothes. If they had good-looking clothes they wanted to wear them no matter what kind of work they were doing. It was found that the boys tended to work better in pairs than alone or in large groups.

Despite all these initial difficulties, as time went on one-half to one-third of the boys followed directions well, showed respect for their work supervisors, and gained in self-confidence. The matter of self-confidence was important for boys with rather severe academic disabilities which placed them at the bottom of their school classes. By spring the first year, and for the next 2 years, the group work was chosen and organized with much greater success. A most successful work project was carried on at the Rotary Club camp. This camp for disadvantaged children was used mainly in the summer. Its cabins were badly in need of repair, and road-building, fence-repairing, and general landscaping were needed. The boys of one work group were bussed to the camp five mornings a week. Their academic instructor came with them, and they did classwork with him a half of each day. This situation had two distinct advantages. The group was undisturbed by their schoolmates, and they could see themselves completing a job. They could celebrate when they finished work on a particular cabin, and they could see the entire camp take on a new appearance as they worked.

Another away-from-school project was carried out at a county park. Ten 9th grade boys were assigned to do landscaping, grass-cutting, and so forth. They were paid 50 cents an hour at first. Their work was continued during the summer when they were paid $1.25 an hour. The park supervisor commented that these boys did as good work as had the high school graduates and college boys who had formerly worked on this job at $1.65 an hour. This group of boys showed almost no delinquency or police contacts during the summer work periods.

As soon as boys reached the age of 15 they pressed for paid part-time jobs. They were anxious to earn money. The work supervisors, however, felt that many of them were not mature enough to be placed on competitive employment and to hold jobs. Furthermore, the number and variety of available jobs were small at first because the boys were under 16 years of age. This barred them from most work. An employment coordinator was employed to seek out jobs and connect boys with jobs. This was a key role because it required introducing the project to employers and convincing them it was socially useful even though the boys might not add much profit to their businesses. Several men filled this role effectively.

One major problem was finding employment for black boys, especially in 1963 and 1964. It became somewhat easier later, although the type of work experience for black boys remained more limited than for white boys. The jobs generally available to the former were as busboys and kitchen workers in restaurants and cafeterias. A few additional jobs appeared later in automobile service stations, in stockrooms of wholesale houses, for trainees in automobile body and fender work, and for delivery boys.

Not all the boys in the work/study program got part-time jobs, but the majority of them did. Some dropped out of the program in stage 1 or early in stage 2.

One hundred forty-six out of 178 boys secured paid work. However, most boys had difficulty working consistently; it did not come naturally to them. For instance, James was placed in a body shop in a garage. This was the result of some 20 hours of the work supervisor's time spent in arranging for the job; clearances with the union and resolving insurance problems took considerable time before the placement was made. After James had worked a few days in the garage the employment supervisor noticed James' fellow workers were beginning to take a personal interest in him. In fact they began pooling their surplus tools to give James a set of his own. On later visits to the garage the employment supervisor received favorable remarks about the boy from the employer and the men with whom he worked. "He's doing a fine job," "He's a good boy; we like him," and "He tries hard," were some of the comments made. This led the supervisor to believe James was doing very well on the job. After several weeks of work, when James had received a few pay checks, the employment supervisor observed that James had bought some new clothes, a bicycle, and many other things. He realized that the purchases might have been hastily made, yet he felt they were not out of the ordinary for a boy James' age and temperament. After another week, James quit his job without notice. The employment supervisor was surprised, because James had said he enjoyed his job very much. When asked why he had quit, James' only reply was, "I didn't like the work."

Another boy was employed in a shop where glass was replaced in automobile windows. Joe was learning the job of glass-setting while doing other small jobs in the business. After the first week on the job, the employer asked Joe to work on Saturday, explaining that Saturday was usually a busy day. The boy did report for work on the following Saturday, but at ten o'clock instead of seven o'clock, the usual starting time. The employer approached Joe again, pointing out the importance of Saturday's work and of being on time. Joe came to work 3 more days and then quit, telling his employer he had too many things to do on Saturdays. Talking to the employment supervisor, Joe commented, "I didn't like the job, and besides I don't want to work on Saturday."

These kinds of experiences were also learning situations for other boys in the group. It provided the classroom teacher with an opportunity to discuss the meaning of jobs from various points of view, including the employer's. These job discussions were held during a portion of each day to review various phases of work experience. These periods additionally provided time for role-playing episodes in which one boy would take the role of an employer while another boy took the role of an employee. In these role-playing sessions the boys treated "employees" much more severely than they themselves were treated while working on the job. There also developed a group feeling among work/study boys regarding the obligations connected with job placement and job retention. One teacher, for example, told of a boy who was truant from his work as an attendant in a service station. The boy called his employer one day at the time he was to report for work saying he had a blister on his heel and wanted to be excused for the afternoon. After permission was granted, Bill met a friend and played most of the afternoon on the school's playground. Other boys in Bill's group, finding this out, brought it up for job discussion the following morning. The group severely criticized Bill for his actions, saying that such actions on his part cooled their chances for job placement. Bill reported to the group the following day with his uniform saying, "See, I'm going to work today." There was no further trouble from this boy, and it seems likely that the group peer pressure was more effective than a lecture from the employment coordinator would have been.

The importance of finding the right job for a boy is illustrated by the experience of Tony, who was hired as a helper in a greenhouse. He seemed so interested in his work that the employer decided to teach him the complete operation of a greenhouse and florist shop. The teacher reported Tony as very enthusiastic about his new job and that he was banking a portion of his money in order to some day own his own greenhouse and florist shop. Tony's parents expressed to the employment supervisor their happiness with the boy's job, saying, "Tony has found something he is interested in for the first time in his life."

Another youth, Marvin, was placed in a wholesale grocery firm taking orders. He was provided a private desk and a telephone. His behavior and dress changed remarkably in a very short period of time. Marvin had always dressed in a careless, slovenly way at school; after he was employed he became conscious of his clothes and personal cleanliness at school and work. His clothes were neatly pressed, and his hair was cut and combed in a conventional manner. The academic teacher reported that "Marvin can now sit in a classroom without interrupting other people—a habit which used to cause a lot of trouble. I feel this is partially due to the environment in which he finds himself at work. The association with adults and their actions have, in my opinion, been very helpful to this boy."

A part-time job was a source of prestige among many work/ study boys and proved one of the more constructive experiences. One group contained several boys who tended to boast about their drinking and their sexual experiences while less experienced boys listened eagerly. As some of the boys got jobs, the teachers noticed that the jobholders became the center of attention; boys clustered around them asking how much money they earned last week, what kind of boss they had, and whether they knew of other jobs. The most frequent jobs in stage 2 were in the food services and stockrooms. Black boys were more likely to work in the food services and white boys in stockrooms.

The work/study program definitely gave most of the boys a great deal more work experience than they would otherwise have obtained. The boys were interviewed when they were just under 16 years of age and were asked to describe their work experience. Of the first 75 boys interviewed, 40% of those in the experimental group had had paid work with regular hours and regular pay, while only 15% of the control group reported such experience.

Stage 3 was for youth ready for full-time jobs. Some youth did not move into Stage 3 because they decided to stay in school and graduate. Ninety-seven experimental boys were placed in full-time jobs. Again, black boys were hard to place. Only 45% of those available in each group were placed. Also, white boys held jobs longer than black boys. Full-time jobs were more easily available than part-time jobs when boys were over 16, with the most frequent placements made in such jobs as stock clerks, delivery boys, food service workers. Some youth were placed in jobs where they received training in special skills. One youth was trained as an audiovisual equipment repairman. Another was placed in a print shop, and one in a motorcycle repair shop. Other youth placements were as janitors, a baker, a wholesale grocery clerk, and a truck driver. Several boys entered the military service at age 17 or 18, where they learned job skills that helped them find employment on discharge from the service. The black boys were still overwhelmingly located in food service. About 50% of their job placements were in this area.

Problems still existed in the placement of boys in stage 3. There was still considerable job turnover. Horace tried 18 different jobs in stage 3 and then went into military service. Another youth had 17 jobs before entering military service. Many boys were unrealistic about the type of work they were qualified to do or the jobs they might hold. Many felt that their wages were too low.

In contrast, a number of boys did quite well. Jerry tried a number of jobs, but then he got married, had a child, and settled down to a single job as a janitor. Will took over his father's chili parlor when his father became ill and ran it quite successfully. Another youth started out as a messenger boy with an audiovisual firm and was trained as a technician by the firm.

A boy who started out as a busboy in a restaurant chain was promoted to supervisor and then to night manager after two years. The proportions of experimental youth showing such patterns of success and unsuccess in late adolescence are identified in the research summary that follows.

RESEARCH SUMMARY

It was clear initially, though more so later, that the youth screened for the work/study program represented a diverse and heterogeneous population. Youth showed sizable differences in their adolescent patterns of responses to school and to the work/study program.

Control youth also differed in their responses to school, their interests in work and in their adolescent work experience. In both groups, big differences were observed in adjustment to community and family life, particularly as reflected in their arrests by police, their juvenile court experiences, and commitments to institutions.

To represent these differences, subgroups of students were pragmatically identified in mid-adolescence (ages 15½ to 16) using school data, police and juvenile court records, and information from interviews with boys during this period. In the experimental group, one subgroup appeared to be profiting from their work experience in the work/study program. A few control group youth were showing some interest in work and in holding part-time jobs. In both experimental and control groups other youth showed some signs of adapting to school (attending) although with relatively little progress in academic achievement. Another relatively large subgroup was showing various degrees of maladjustment both in school and in the community.

Adjustment Patterns in Late Adolescence

During the final 2 years of the study when most experimental and control youth were 17 to 19 years old, an assessment was made of each individual's adjustment pattern, independent of the earlier mid-adolescent assessment. Several kinds of data collected during this late adolescence period were used for this assessment including interview, police, family, and school status data. For youth in the experimental group, ratings of work adjustment and daily work records maintained by employment coordinators, work supervisors, and employers in stage 2 (part-time) and stage 3 (full-time) employment were used as part of the assessment.

On the basis of these data, experimental and control youth were divided into five subgroups: 1) seriously maladaptive, 2) marginal, 3) erratic, 4) work adaptive, and 5) school adaptive. Each of these subgroups represented a distinct type of outcome for experimental and control youth in late adolescence.

Of the original 422 7th grade youth screened for the program, about 87 were not assigned ratings of adjustment in late adolescence. Sixty of this group did not have sufficient data to be rated. Another 10 had been killed by violence or accidents prior to this late adolescent period. The remaining unassigned youth could not be located. Table 1 shows the distribution of the late adolescent adjustment ratings across experimental and control groups 1 and 2.

As Table 1 shows, late adolescent rating for group 1 significantly favor control youth. However, the biased sampling noted earlier mitigates use of group 1 data for comparing program outcomes. Any further examination of differences in adjustment between groups uses data from group 2 experimental and controls, which as noted previously were much more comparable in terms of screening criteria.

In group 2, experimental and control groups showed a relatively similar distribution of late adolescent adjustments although the former showed a slightly higher percentage of adaptive youth (48%, combining work and school adaptive) than controls (44%).

Experimental and Control Group Delinquency Rates

Police reports of late adolescence arrests (see Table 2) indicate that differences in the relative numbers of experimental and control youth arrested were minimal (59% to 61% respectively), with control youth showing a slightly higher percentage of repeat arrests (38%) than experimental youth (33%). Both groups showed a similar percentage of youth with arrests for serious offenses (51%).

When arrest records for experimental and control youth are contrasted for the earlier adolescent period (ages 13 through 16), experimental youth showed much more involvement with the police than did the controls (51% to 36%, respectively). Experimental youth

Table 1. Late Adolescent Adjustment (Youths ages 17–19)

		Maladaptive			Adaptive	
		Serious	Marginal	Erratic	Work	School
Research groups	Number identified	(%)	(%)	(%)	(%)	(%)
Group 1	139					
Experimental 1	85	33	16	21	20	10
Control 1	54	24	15	13	5	43
Group 2	167					
Experimental 2	95	19	16	17	31	18
Control 2	72	15	18	22	26	18

From: Ahlstrom & Havighurst, *400 losers: Delinquent Boys in High School,* Jossey-Bass, San Francisco, 1971.

with arrests during this period were more likely to be arrested more than once (28%) than control youth (21%) and for serious offenses (42% to 31%).

For both experimental and control youth, the number of youths arrested during the late adolescent period (ages 17 to 19) increased substantially over that of the earlier adolescent period. The rate of increase was significantly greater for the control group although, as noted above, in late adolescence the relative numbers of youth with arrests were similar for both groups. For controls, the percentage of youth with arrest records increased from 36% to 61%, indicating a rate of increase of about 70%. The experimental group, on the other hand, increased from 51% to 59% of youth with arrests, an increase of less than 20%.

In substance, the work/study program in the schools during the 8th, 9th, and 10th grades did not reduce the rate of delinquency among experimental youth, which had been one goal of the program. In fact, there is some evidence to suggest that in some schools grouping delinquent and predelinquent youth in experimental work and classroom settings may have actually accelerated delinquent activity.

On the other hand, the evidence indicating an accelerated arrest rate during late adolescence for the control group suggests that while the regular school program may have acted as a suppressor of delinquent behavior during the earlier adolescent period, this influence diminished markedly during late adolescence.

Description of Late Adolescent Adjustment Types

Work Adaptive Almost one-third of experimental youth (31%) and slightly over one-fourth (26%) of control youth were rated "work

Table 2. Late adolescent adjustment and police records for the experimental and control Group 2

| | Maladaptive | | | | | | | | Adaptive | | Total Group | |
| | Serious | | Marginal | | Erratic | | Work | | School | | | |
	X2	C2	X2	C2	X2	C2	X2	C2	X2	C2	X2	C2
Youth with arrests	N=18 *n*(%)	11 *n*(%)	15 *n*(%)	13 *n*(%)	16 *n*(%)	16 *n*(%)	29 *n*(%)	19 *n*(%)	17 *n*(%)	13 *n*(%)	95 *n*(%)	72 *n*(%)
Arrests prior to 8th grade	12 (67)	6 (55)	8 (53)	2 (15)	5 (31)	5 (31)	7 (24)	5 (26)	1 (6)	3 (23)	33 (35)	21 (26)
Arrests ages 13 through 16	17 (94)	10 (91)	9 (60)	5 (38)	7 (44)	4 (25)	10 (34)	6 (32)	5 (29)	1 (8)	48 (51)	26 (36)
For more than one offense	14 (78)	9 (82)	4 (27)	2 (15)	4 (25)	1 (6)	2 (7)	2 (11)	3 (18)	1 (8)	27 (28)	15 (21)
For serious offenses	15 (83)	9 (82)	8 (53)	5 (38)	5 (31)	4 (25)	8 (28)	3 (16)	4 (29)	1 (8)	40 (42)	22 (31)
Arrests ages 17 through 19	18 (100)	11 (100)	10 (67)	8 (62)	12 (75)	12 (75)	12 (41)	10 (53)	4 (24)	3 (23)	56 (59)	44 (61)
For more than one offense	14 (78)	10 (91)	4 (27)	5 (38)	6 (38)	7 (44)	7 (24)	5 (26)	0 (0)	0 (0)	31 (33)	27 (38)
For serious offenses	14 (78)	11 (100)	6 (40)	7 (54)	9 (56)	9 (56)	6 (21)	8 (42)	3 (18)	2 (15)	38 (40)	37 (51)

adaptive" in late adolescence. For experimental youth these ratings were based on demonstrated ability to obtain and hold jobs in late adolescence and upon ratings by employment coordinators indicating that they were showing real progress in moving toward adult work role identity.

For the controls, "work adaptive" ratings were based mainly on late adolescent interview data concerning their job histories. Factual records of the amount and quality of work experience and work adjustment for these youth were limited. Their self-reports on their late adolescent work history in conjunction with interview ratings on their attitudes toward work, their knowledge, planning, and expressed goals relevant to work provided the basis for designating a control youth as showing or not showing a work adaptive orientation.

Generally, youth rated work adaptive had fewer arrests during late adolescence than other adjustment subgroups, with the exception of the school adaptive youth. Among the total work adaptive group, 54% had no records of arrests during late adolescence. Of the remaining 46%, those in the experimental group had relatively fewer of their number arrested than in the control group (41% to 53%), had fewer youth with repeated arrests (24% to 26%) and had considerably fewer youth with arrests for serious offenses (21% to 42%).

School Adaptive   Youths rated "school adaptive" (18% for both experimental and control groups) either were in school and showing signs of staying in and adapting sufficiently to meet at least minimal requirements of attendance, or had already graduated. Although most in this group had low academic achievement they had managed to stay in school and achieve some success in certain of their school experiences. A few showed successful adaptation to both academic and social-athletic aspects of high school.

Among school-adaptive youth, only one in four had police arrests during late adolescence. None of these youth had more than one arrest and less than one-fifth of those arrested were charged with serious offenses. Among this group, the major contacts with police in late adolescence were for traffic violations.

The 18 % of experimental youth rated school adaptive in late adolescence represent the remainder of an experimental subgroup who transferred out of the work/study program into the regular school program sometime during the first 3 years of the project (8th, 9th, 10th grade) or had completed a 3-year work/study program and then decided to continue school in the regular program. The 18 percent of control youth rated school adaptive represent the control group students still in school or graduated who had been enrolled in the regular school curriculum since the 8th grade.

School adaptive ratings in late adolescence were not based upon a youth's individual classroom achievement or conduct, but rather on whether they were in school attending school regularly, expressed positive attitudes toward school in interviews, had graduated, or had received a certificate of attendance.

Erratic Adjustment   Experimental and control youth who showed both adaptive and maladaptive behaviors in school, work, or community life were identified as the *erratic* subgroup (17% experimental and 22% control). Many of these youths were still in school in late adolescence and showed some progress at times but also were in frequent difficulty with the police and sometimes with school authority. Some showed the ability to find jobs and to do satisfactory work for a while, but then were involved in various delinquent pursuits outside work which created problems on the job through absences for frequent court hearings.

Control and experimental youth identified in this category were similar in the numbers of those with arrests during late adolescence (75% each) and in the number of youth with arrests for serious offenses (56% each). The control group showed a slightly higher percentage of youth with more than one arrest during this age period (44%) than the experimental group (38%).

Marginal Adjustment   Youth who in late adolescence were high school drop-outs, were out of work and/or had held only very few menial part-time jobs and showed little initiative in seeking employment were identified as the marginal subgroup (16% experimental, 18% controls). A large portion of these youth (67% experimental and 62% controls) had been arrested during late adolescence with 27% and 38% of experimental and control youth respectively having been arrested more than once during late adolescence. Mainly these arrests were for misdemeanors, such as drinking in public, disorderly conduct and fighting, but 40% of experimental and 54% of control youth rated marginal adjustment were arrested for serious offenses. Some of them spent time at the county farm or in the city jail. However, the predominant characteristic of this group was a kind of aimless drifting without apparently much thought of the future or even of their current life situation.

Seriously maladaptive   Experimental and control youth who were rated seriously maladaptive (19% and 15%, respectively) were clearly identified by their record of arrests for serious offenses and by their records of commitments to correctional institutions. They were recidivists. Only a few had held jobs and these were for brief periods of time. In both experimental and control groups all of these youth had dropped out of high school by late adolescence and appeared to be hard-core delinquents with values and a way of life differing markedly from those of the larger society and from those of their work and school adaptive peers.

FAMILY AND SOCIAL BACKGROUND FACTORS

The considerable heterogeneity among youth screened for the work/study program in their responses to this program and to the high school academic program appeared due in large part to differences in family background and local neighborhood experiences.

In describing the typical unsuccessful and the typical successful work/study youth, we use longitudinal data collected on experimental youth in group 2. As noted earlier, it was this group of youth screened for study who were randomly assigned to experimental and control groups. Thus experimental group 2 youth were more representative of those youth for whom the program was designed.

The typical unsuccessful work/study youth had a childhood police record (64% had arrests before the 8th grade) with the average age at first arrest being 11 years. He frequently came from a family in which considerable tension, conflict, or indifference characterized the family relationship (40% of families). The unsuccessful youth usually came from a large family (6 or 7 people on the average) and his father generally was unskilled (50%) or semiskilled (37%). During his childhood he and his family moved about from one inner city neighborhood to another, and he attended several different elementary schools. He usually came from the most delinquent neighborhoods in the inner city and the physical environment of his home was inadequate for his family's needs. He typically began showing signs of serious school maladjustment not later than the 3rd grade, and his elementary teachers saw him as particularly limited in self-control and regard for school rules and regulations.

The typical successful work/study boy did not have an early childhood police record (17% had records). He more frequently came from a cohesive family situation (92% versus 60% for the unsuccessful boy) and his father was semiskilled or skilled (90%). During childhood he moved once or twice with his family and attended only one or two elementary grade schools. In general, he had a much more stable family life than did the unsuccessful youth. The successful boy's neighborhood was usually less delinquency-prone and his family dwelling was somewhat more adequate. In the early elementary grades he generally did very poor school work and was consistently rated low on work habits and other traits important to organizing and doing his school work. He typically was seen by his teachers as showing fair self-control but was rated low on responsibility, initiative, work habits, and personal habits.

IMPRESSIONS

A fairly thorough examination of these boys as they moved through adolescence has helped us to understand the problems they faced in trying to grow up. There seemed to be six main aspects of the problem. The first was lack of successful male role models. Most of these boys seemed to have been blocked in their efforts to grow up by lack of models of successful manhood. Many boys did not have fathers in their homes. The fathers who were at home were often examples of failure, as were many male adults in the neighborhoods where boys lived.

Secondly, most boys were handicapped by inadequate basic reading and arithmetic skills to support a semiskilled job or to permit high school graduation.

Inadequate family support was the third aspect of the problem. Some parents were indifferent and hostile toward school and did not insist that their children attend school regularly. Some parents changed homes so frequently that their children had to adjust to new schools continuously. Others were so involved in trying to provide for large families that they had insufficient time and energy to provide help and emotional support to children having difficulty in school.

The fourth aspect of the problem was neighborhood settings that exposed boys to trouble. Just happening to be at a place where there was trouble seemed to account for many of the episodes that got the boys into police difficulty. This resulted in public police records, an increasing sense of alienation, and a forced association through confinement with severely maladjusted youths at an early age. Having to get along with tough boys singly and in gangs often meant adopting the behavior of these boys.

The fifth contributing factor was lack of a sense of control over the environment. Although this often reflected an accurate appraisal (e.g., work opportunities were relatively limited for these boys), most youth saw the world around them as operating either by chance or under the control of powerful people alien to them. This limited them in studying a situation, deciding how to act rationally and effectively, and then acting with the expectation that they could produce the desired effect.

The sixth aspect of the problem was the prevalence of delinquency in the lives of many of these boys. Their delinquency was different from the "normal" delinquency of adolescent boys. Many research studies have shown that the majority of boys commit delinquent acts during adolescence. But most boys do this very seldom. Many are caught and punished or warned by parents or police. Many come from families which have taught them to feel guilty about delinquency. To them, adolescence brings only a temporary disruption of their formerly docile and self-controlled behavior. The boys in our study had a very different experience with delinquency. They did not feel guilty over their delinquent behavior. They obtained rewards from it, and what little punishment they received was unsystematic and may have been seen by them as a source of prestige with their peers, as was the case with commitment to the county correction institution in many instances.

These sources of the problem, particularly those limiting both work opportunity and adequate adult male models and those contributing to development of a pervasive sense of helplessness in controlling their destiny, seemed most evident among the black youths in our sample. Among white youths who were most seriously socially and economically disadvantaged, however, these sources of problems also appeared predominant. As we followed these youths through adolescence, it became increasingly clear that the study group was having difficulty with their development of identity for all of the reasons outlined above. It also became evident that progress and adjustment in school and work experience could not be understood and evaluated unless they were seen as segments of the total life space of individual boys.

INTRODUCTION TO CHAPTER 15

The program of Reckless and Dinitz, described by Dinitz is the best designed, large-scale, controlled study of a comprehensive school program planned to lessen disruptive behavior in adolescents. Few before and fewer since have used random selection to study this issue in public schools. The results are described clearly and simply.

The study, however—like all studies—does have its limitations and does not support the "nothing works" theory as well as it seems to. The major limitations of the project, as recognized by Dinitz in the chapter, were its limited treatment intensity, duration, and scope. The students were given a special self-contained class, concerned teachers, a time-out procedure in the classroom when they misbehaved, and a modified curriculum which was designed to increase academic motivation, improve reading skills and promote positive social goals. The students each stayed only 1 year in the program and returned to regular classes. There was no parent involvement, with the exception of teacher initiated phone calls to parents during the last year of the project.

The program was devised in the late 1950s and early 1960s when special education for learning disabled and emotionally deviant children was just getting off the ground in suburban schools, when all male schools and all male classes were not unusual, and when informed consent was not necessary. It was a time when there was more optimism among the well read that counseling, educational, and recreational efforts for disruptive youth could favorably affect delinquency proneness. The beliefs then were that self-contained classes would (almost by themselves) improve the milieu for remediation, a role model educational focus would have both an immediate and a prolonged effect on school behavior, and good results in achievement and behavior would naturally generalize into the community sphere.

I have to agree with Dinitz that nothing much has been shown to reduce delinquency and recidivism in the United States, but would disagree if Martinson's catch phrase "nothing works" (1) is applied generally to all outcomes of programs for disruptive youth. Successful results are indeed not generally maintained for years after intervention ceases, but many short-term results in schools (see Chapter 4), in motivated families, and in group homes (see Chapters 3 and 5) have been documented well enough to be believed. Intermediate range achievements are now in sight.

1.   Martinson, R. What works—questions and answers about prison reform. *Public Interest*, 1974, *35*, 32–54.

15

A school-based prevention program to reduce delinquency vulnerability

Simon Dinitz

The conventional wisdom of the 1970s concerning the prevention and treatment of both juvenile delinquency and adult criminality is the now famous dictum of Martinson that "nothing works" (1-3). This refrain, neither new nor wholly accurate, has caught and reflected the prevailing climate of public and professional opinion, including that of the courts and the legislatures. State after state is revising its juvenile codes and procedures regarding waiver to adult jurisdiction, trial and due process, age of majority, and disposition (Note A). The trend is clearly to "scare them straight" by getting tough, tougher, and still tougher (4). As we enter the 1980's, the immediate preoccupations are the identification and incapacitation of the hard-core offenders (variously estimated to constitute from less than 1% to more than 6% of all juveniles), who presumably account for the majority of juvenile crimes and an even greater disproportion of all violent offenses (5, 6).

Furthermore, much more is heard about imposing penalties than about reforming or rehabilitating delinquents. Juvenile law, in the mid and late 1980s, will involve the following: imposing a fair and equitable sanction on each and every offender apprehended for a non-status crime, imposing the least restrictive penalty consistent with the severity of the offense and the history of the offender, tightening the sanctions if the antisocial behavior continues, and restricting juveniles in those instances that require heroic responses from the criminal justice system (7). Primary and secondary prevention of delinquency has also come to mean the hardening of targets (e.g., using security personnel to reduce violence in schools), the increased reliance on psychoactive drug treatment, greater community vigilance and surveillance, and a renewed emphasis on work and work training programs (8). Most of these more recent efforts are concentrated in the schools—at least in terms of school security, antivandalism and anti-drug abuse programs, and the identification and management of special problem children (such as the learning disabled, hyperactive, and aggressive). Because the school is still the central or focal social institution affecting the daily lives of all children and all adolescents (even the truants), it remains the most logical point to introduce delinquency programs. Even with the legitimate, if often excessive, strictures in obtaining informed consent in introducing prevention programs, the school remains the single best outreach setting in the U.S. (9).

The school program devised by us (Reckless and Dinitz, 1972) was predicated on a variety of assumptions and propositions (10). None was more important than our consistent finding over the years that predelinquent and delinquent boys were more likely than their counterparts from the same tenements and areas to have poor self-concepts, to think of themselves as worthless, unproductive, and unimportant, nameless and faceless, and without much future (11). Our prior research in Columbus, Akron, Brooklyn, and elsewhere around the country, had led us to conclude also that the poor self-concepts of the boys were both cause and reflection of the esteem in which they were held by their mothers, peers, and teachers. By age 12 or probably earlier still in their lives, the common-usage tag of "loser" had been successfully applied to them and stuck. However, some of the boys with poor self-concepts who remained in school to high school graduation were free of legal and court entanglements and went on to become skilled and semiskilled workers, economically independent, and more or less stable in their marriages. These were the boys among the vulnerable ones who had managed to reverse the process, to destigmatize themselves, and develop a sense of self-worth and personal esteem (12–18).

After many years of observing and following "good" and "bad" boys, we were asked by officials in the Columbus, Ohio school system to devise and implement a school-based delinquency prevention program. Our only nonnegotiable demands were that this program be experimental (random selection of vulnerable subjects) and that we would be permitted to follow-up (with the school, police, and courts) all treated and untreated subjects in the study to determine case outcome. The project was conducted in all inner city junior high schools from 1963–1966 and the follow-up of subjects was completed in 1970.

PROJECT DESIGN

The investigators asked teachers and principals in 44 elementary schools in the inner city of Columbus, Ohio, to evaluate all of their male 6th grade students as candidates for delinquency status using three categories: 1) unlikely, 2) possible, and 3) likely. "Good" boys obviously constituted the first category, "vulnerable" and "bad" boys the last two.

Teachers and principals were also asked to indicate the likelihood of each 6th grade boy's finishing high school. Previous experience with 6th grade teacher evaluations indicated that such ratings were quite realistic. The 6th grade teacher, who had the boy in class the whole school day for the entire school year, had become well acquainted with his development and was a good predictor of his behavioral and school outcome.

The 6th grade teacher's rating list was reviewed by the principal in each elementary school. He or she usually confirmed the rating, not just as a procedural matter but as one based on personal knowledge of the boy. (See references 9, 19–21 for material on teacher prediction.) Differences between the ratings of principal and teacher appeared in only a very few instances. In the three cohort years, teachers and principals disagreed (likely–unlikely or unlikely–likely) in from two to seven cases of an average of 600 boys rated yearly (Note B).

The investigators also asked the 6th grade teachers to indicate those boys on their class lists with IQ test results lower than 70 as well as the boys who showed obvious emotional disturbances and serious physical handicaps. These boys were eliminated from the samples.

The rating lists of the 6th grade teachers were turned over to the staff of the project. The investigator and the project director made random assignments of the vulnerable boys who were to be placed in the all-boy experimental self-contained 7th grade classes, of the vulnerable boys who were to be placed in the regular self-contained 7th grade classes, and of the good boys (not headed for trouble) who were to be assigned to the regular self-contained classes and followed as a special comparison group.

These random assignments were made from cards with name identifications, obtained from the 6th grade teachers. However, because of class sizes of the elementary schools that fed the junior high

schools and the requirements in the eight junior high schools to assign as close to 35 boys as possible to the experimental classes, it
was necessary to assign randomly almost two-thirds of the vulnerable boys to the experimental classes. It was only possible to approximate a 50–50 split of the bad boys (those boys likely to become
involved in law-violating activity) in the final year (1965/66).

It was decided to select the project teachers for the experimental
self-contained classes from the male teachers who ordinarily taught
self-contained classes in the 7th grade. The assistant superintendent
in charge of instruction of the Columbus public schools suggested
several male 7th grade teachers who might well qualify for the task.
After a personal interview with each prospect, four men became the
project teachers.

The four teachers selected joined in a training seminar at the
Ohio State University over a 2-week period. Discussions were held
on topics pertinent to the project and to the understanding of the
particular types of boys on whom the experimental classes would
focus. Suggestions for effective topics and methods of presentation
as well as approaches to the behavior problems of the boys and their
level of comprehension were discussed. One of the main results of the
daily seminar sessions was the development of a close group identification—a sort of "in-group" feeling. The consulting psychiatrist also
held a preliminary session with the four project teachers.

Arrangements were made with the principals of each of the eight
junior high schools to place the incoming 7th grade boys according
to assignments decided upon by the project staff. Case folders were
prepared for each boy assigned to the experimental class, to a regular
class, and also for the sample of the good-boy comparisons who also
received the regular 7th grade self-contained curriculum.

The same assignment procedure was followed in September of
three consecutive school years beginning in 1963, 1964, and 1965.
Consequently, the project had three yearly cohorts and three subgroups in each yearly cohort: the randomly selected bad boys who
were assigned to the all-boy experimental self-contained class; the
bad boys who were assigned to the control group, receiving the regular material of the self-contained class; and a randomly selected sample (about 15%) of the good boys who were also assigned to a regular
self-contained class. Students remained in their program for one entire school year.

It was agreed by the project teachers, the staff, and the principals that inquiries from boys as to why they were assigned to the experimental class would be answered by the following statement:

"Mr. Jones wanted to have an all-boy class, and he picked you." This seemed to allay the suspicions of the experimental boys and certainly answered the questions, "Why are we here? Are we hoods?"

During the first part of the demonstration, the project director visited each junior high school at a teachers' assembly or meeting and presented a statement of the design and purpose of the project and the experimental class. This did much to improve understanding and to further cooperation.

By arrangement with the Columbus school authorities, including the principals of the junior high schools, each of the four project teachers was assigned to handle the experimental all-boy self-contained class in two junior high schools. He handled the all-boy experimental class in one junior high school in the morning and in another in the afternoon. The staff made certain that each project teacher was able to identify with each of his two junior high schools, so as not to be considered a part-time outsider. The morning assignment consisted of conducting the all-boy experimental self-contained class for three class periods (120 minutes) plus other teaching duties that were assigned at that particular junior high school. The afternoon assignment in a different school duplicated the morning assignment.

Daily After School Sessions

The four project teachers met with the project director in a 2-hour discussion session at the end of each school day. The project teachers received an overtime stipend for this after school assignment. At these daily sessions, difficulties were presented and recommendations made. Proposals for presentation of role models and related materials were discussed, and agreements were reached on what content to present and in what form. In other words, lesson plans were produced. Agreement was also reached as to on what day a particular lesson plan was to be offered in each experimental self-contained class. The supplemental curriculum content consisting of the role model lesson plans was a product of these daily after school sessions, particularly in the first year of the project.

The training-teaching also included a 2-hour morning session with the project's consulting psychiatrist attended by the project director and the four project teachers. Discussion focused on the behavioral problems that arose in the experimental self-contained classes, and suggestions were developed as to how to handle these problems in the classroom and how to approach the special problems of individual boys.

Classroom Discipline

In particular, a plan of classroom conduct regulation was developed in the initial sessions. This was called, in the words of the consulting psychiatrist, "respecting the rights of others" (22). According to this plan, a boy in any of the eight experimental classes whose behavior was disturbing or rule-violating was asked to leave the group and to sit in front of the classroom door until he felt he was ready to join the class again and to respect the rights of others. Under this plan, no boy was sent to the principal's office for misconduct. The project teachers and the staff of the project were convinced that the mutual respect approach to classroom discipline worked very successfully, that it enhanced learning on the part of the pupils, and that it increased the effectiveness of the teachers.

Most of the decisions on the content and the form of presentation of models of behavior (lesson plans) were made the first year by the project teachers and the staff of the project. However, the lesson plans were improved in content and presentation during the second year in the daily after school sessions. During the third year, the afternoons of the project teachers were in large part devoted to home calls on the families of the individual boys in the project classes. This was looked upon as adding an extra reinforcement to the content of the role model supplement of the self-contained classes.

Remedial Reading

Very early in the first year of the project, the teachers and the staff became increasingly concerned with the fact that the experimental boys were behind in reading ability. They averaged 1.05 years below grade level. At the end of the 6th grade, they ranged in reading achievement level all the way from 2.6 to 10.1 grade level. (IQ levels averaged 93.96 and ranged from 65 to 140 (23).) During the first year, the project purchased an ample supply of paperback novels, biographies, and histories, which were placed in the classroom library and made readily available to the boys in the experimental class. The two most popular books were found to be H. G. Wells's *The Time Machine* and Don K. Stanford's *The Red Car*. These two books were adopted as texts, and exercises were developed covering various pages (23).

After examining many workbooks, the staff discovered that the Turner-Livingston Reading Series dealt with topics closely paralleling the project's five curriculum topics for role model building, and the series was adopted. The staff also used a third set of remedial reading materials from the Reader's Digest Reading Skill Builder Series (23).

A series of shotgun exercises that focused on nearly every type of reading problem was developed during the second year of the project. Each project teacher was given a set of exercises and a handbook with instructions on how to teach the particular principle involved. When he discovered a commonly shared reading difficulty in his class, he pulled the appropriate exercise from the file and did remedial work then and there (23). The experimental classes, beginning in the second cohort year (1964/65), devoted four 40-minute periods per week to this remedial reading program. One final resource was used: the experimental classes received copies of the morning newspaper twice a week. The pupils read, orally or silently, news items of interest to them and then discussed the contents.

Content of the Role Model Supplement

In addition to the project teachers' approximating the role of a significant other in the lives of the experimental boys, the interaction of an all-boy class, the measures taken to improve reading, and the development of a special classroom discipline system (respecting the rights of others), the main thrust of the experimental program consisted of the presentation of role model material to the pupils.

The director of the project and the project teachers agreed on the general topics to be contained in the role model supplement. There were five main topics: 1) The World of Work, 2) The School and You, 3) The House We Live In (a presentation of government services), 4) Getting Along with Others, and 5) The Family. In each section, acceptable role models were presented, for example, the legitimate worker, teacher, physician, crane operator, judge, father, and son. The lesson plans that were generated under each topic were presented in this sequence during the school year (24).

Data Input and Evaluation

A case folder was kept on each vulnerable boy assigned to the experimental class as well as on each vulnerable boy assigned to the regular self-contained classes (constituting the control group) and on each so-called good-boy comparison also assigned to the regular self-contained classes in the eight junior high schools. Information obtained on each boy, beginning with the ratings by the 6th grade teachers, was kept and filed in his folder. Subsequent school clearances regarding attendance information, conduct reports, and school performance were obtained in June of each year. The police clearance, indicating which boys had been referred to, or arrested by the police, was made in August of each year. The clearances, of course, were made by name for each member of the 1963, 1964, and 1965 cohorts, but were classified by case-folder information as experimentals, bad-boy controls, and good-boy comparisons.

In addition to the initial case information and the school and police clearances, the staff administered certain pre- and posttests. The first cohort of boys was administered a battery of tests while still in the 6th grade, which included selected items from the following sources: the Socialization Scale of the California Psychological Inventory, the significant self-concept items developed previously by us, and an interpersonal-competence items checklist. In May, toward the end of the first cohort year, the same battery of tests was administered to the boys.

It was found that the battery of tests used the first year was not satisfactory for measuring possible change in direction of behavior or in outlook (25). Consequently, the staff developed a different battery of tests that would be more sensitive to the kinds of changes the project was trying to produce in the experimental boys. These tests were to be administered at the beginning and at the end of the school year (referred to hereafter as pretest and posttest). An instrument was developed and pretested that, according to Guttman's method of scaling, had six subscales dealing with the boy's outlook on school and teachers (26), and 9 subscales dealing with the boy's outlook on the law, the courts, the police, and probation officers (27). These two sets of Guttman subscales were used for the last two cohorts (1964/65 and 1965/66) as pretests at the beginning of the school year and as posttests at the end of the school year. In addition, the second and third cohorts were also administered (at the beginning and end of the school year) a value orientation instrument (28) that attempted to measure the extent to which a youth subscribed to certain social values.

As a special input into the data bank of the project, the investigators and the director decided to make a follow-up study of the experimental and the bad-boy controls in the second cohort (1964/65) in the spring of 1967, which was 2 years after the school year that contained the role model supplement for the boys assigned to the experimental all-boy self-contained class. This particular follow-up information consisted of a structured interview of the boy by the former teacher and of an inventory of self-report items (filled out by the boy).

THE HUMAN MATERIAL

In summary form, the vulnerable boys were about 13.25 years of age upon entering the project, and the good boys were 12.8 years of age on the average. About half, just over 50%, of the vulnerables were white as against 62% of the comparison or good boy subjects. In terms of family composition, some 55 percent of the vulnerables were from intact families as opposed to more than two-thirds of the nominated good boys. (For a more complete description, see Chapter 5 of reference 10.)

The school achievement data reflect the general difference in group composition. The comparisons are up by nine points on mean IQ (100.4 versus 91.2), by one full grade level in mean reading achievement (6.7 to 5.7), and by almost a grade level in mean arithmetic achievement level (7.1 to about 6.2). In mean grade point, the comparisons were at 2.5 (B−), the vulnerables at 1.5 (C−). The percentage of school days present also favored the comparisons and by a comfortable margin.

Almost one in five vulnerables was previously known to the police (19.5 percent), although only 5.1 percent of the nominated good boys had a record of some type with the local police. The record could be for dependency, neglect or delinquency, as well as for such status offenses as truancy (school or home) and incorrigibility. Our subjects reflected the generally lower rates of school drop-out and delinquency in Columbus compared to other communities. This is evident when the program is compared with those in cities like Cleveland, Brooklyn, or Philadelphia. The rapid growth of Columbus since the inception of the program has altered the picture materially. While still no Detroit, our crime and delinquency rates have ballooned in the last decade.

FINDINGS

The result of this experimental in-school delinquency prevention program were disappointing. For the most part, the vulnerable boys left much as they entered our program—potentially or actually delinquent, unlikely to complete high school, candidates for loser status in life. Likewise, the nominated good boys (comparisons) continued their more socially satisfactory adaptations to the economic, social, and personal deprivations endemic in the inner city and in the disorganized areas in which all our subjects were residing at the time of the study (9).

To recap the design briefly, this program was conducted in the 7th grade of all inner city junior high schools in Columbus, Ohio, during three school years. The experimental and control subjects (boys) had been nominated by their 6th grade teachers and their elementary school principals as headed for trouble with the law; the good boy comparisons had been judged as not headed for trouble.

In a special sense the study is the culmination of 15 years of systematic research on the role of the self-concept in the identification, prevention, and control of juvenile delinquency.

A varied and seemingly inexhaustible supply of data was accumulated on each of the 1,726 subjects of the study. This information included three time periods: before the 7th grade, during the 7th grade, and 3 years after the 7th grade. When these data were analyzed the following results were evident:

1. On none of the outcome variables were the experimental subjects significantly different from the controls. This was especially and most painfully evident in the school performance and police contact data. There were no significant differences in the number of boys who experienced contact with the police, the frequency of such contact, or the seriousness of the unreported behavior. In regard to the school data, the rate of drop-out, attendance, grades, and school achievement levels of experimental and control groups of boys were very much alike. (See Tables 1–3.)

2. The police involvement of both the experimentals and controls increased with age as did the seriousness of the offenses. By the end of the 10th grade, approximately 47% of all nominated bad boys (experimental as well as controls) had become known to the

Table 1. School status of experimental, control, and comparison subjects at the end of the project[a]

School status	Experimentals	Controls	Comparisons
	(632)[b]	(462)[b]	(632)[b]
In school	56.6	51.3	77.1
Dropout	19.1	22.7	6.2
Moved away	18.6	20.8	16.1
In custody	5.7	5.2	0.6
Total	100.0	100.0	100.0

[a]Reprinted with permission from Reckless, W. C., and Dinitz, S. *The prevention of delinquency: An experiment.* Ohio State University Press, 1972.
[b]Denotes total number of subjects.

Table 2. Attendance ratios of experimental, control, and comparison boys from the sixth through the tenth grade[a]

Attendance ratio[b]	Experimentals	Controls	Comparisons
Sixth grade	.937	.936	.961
Seventh grade	.929	.927	.955
Eighth grade	.908	.913	.951
Ninth grade	.906	.906	.944
Tenth grade	.866	.869	.919

[a]Reprinted with permission from Reckless, W. C., and Dinitz, S. *The prevention of delinquency: An experiment.* Ohio State University Press, 1972.

[b]Attendance ratios computed on basis of ratio of days attended to total number of school days.

police; mostly, however, for relatively minor violations of municipal ordinances or commonplace misdemeanors. (See Table 4.)

3. The school performance of the experimentals and controls deteriorated with age. This was evident in attendance, drop-out, and school grades.

4. Racial differences were highly significant in the areas of criminal involvement and school performance variables. On both counts, the white subjects in the experimental and control groups fared better than their black counterparts.

5. Although the same trends toward greater delinquency involvement and poorer school performance with age characterized the good boy comparison group, these boys continued to maintain their superiority on these measures in every time period; before the 7th grade, during the 7th grade and 3 years thereafter. This finding provides additional confirmation for our general thesis concerning the relative insulation of good boys in high delinquency areas.

Table 3. Mean grade-point averages of experimental, control, and comparison subjects, before, during, and after the program[c]

Grade average[a]	Experimentals	Controls	Comparisons
Pre-program (6th grade)	3.29	3.36	2.54
During program (7th grade)	3.33	3.48	2.93
Post-program (8th, 9th, and 10th grades)	3.64	3.55	3.11

[a]A=1, B=2, C=3, D=4, and F=5.

[b]Attendance ratios computed on basis of ratio of days attended to total number of school days.

[c]Reprinted with permission from Reckless, W. C., and Dinitz, S. *The prevention of delinquency: An experiment.* Ohio State University Press, 1972.

Table 4. Distribution of experimental, control, and comparison subjects who had recorded contacts with police for serious, moderate, and slight offenses during three time periods of the project[a]

Type of offense	Experimentals				Controls				Comparisons				Total
	Pre [b](632)	During (536)	Post (536)	Total	Pre (461)	During (379)	Post (379)	Total	Pre (632)	During (535)	Post (535)	Total	
Serious													
Aggravated assault	0	0	4	4	1	0	2	3	0	0	1	1	8
Armed robbery	0	0	1	1	0	0	2	2	0	0	0	0	3
Arson	1	0	0	1	1	0	0	1	1	0	0	0	2
Assault and battery	2	2	16	20	1	2	17	20	1	0	9	10	50
Assault with a deadly weapon	4	0	0	4	0	0	0	0	0	0	0	0	4
Auto theft	2	13	80	95	4	15	47	66	0	0	16	16	177
Breaking and entering	6	7	17	30	4	2	13	19	1	0	5	6	55
Burglary	14	7	24	45	8	5	21	34	4	2	6	12	91
Escape from custody	0	0	0	0	0	0	2	2	0	0	0	0	2
Felonious assault	0	0	0	0	0	0	1	1	0	0	0	0	1
Forgery, fraud	0	0	2	2	0	0	1	1	0	0	0	0	3
Grand larceny	3	3	7	13	1	1	8	10	0	1	2	3	26
Hit and run	0	0	1	1	0	0	1	1	0	0	0	0	2
Housebreaking	10	3	3	16	4	3	9	16	2	0	1	3	35
Influencing a minor	0	0	1	1	0	0	1	1	0	0	1	1	3
Molesting	3	2	4	9	0	1	2	3	0	0	1	1	13
Murder	0	0	1	1	0	0	0	0	0	0	1	1	2
Purse snatching	0	0	3	3	0	0	3	3	0	0	0	0	6
Receiving and concealing stolen property	2	1	7	10	3	1	5	9	0	0	4	4	23
Theft from mail	0	0	0	0	1	0	0	1	0	1	0	1	2
Unarmed robbery	4	1	12	17	1	0	4	5	0	0	1	1	23
Vandalism	1	0	0	1	1	0	0	1	1	0	0	1	3
Sodomy	0	0	0	0	0	0	0	0	1	0	0	1	1
Embezzlement	0	0	1	1	0	0	0	0	0	0	0	0	1
Total	52	39	184	275	30	30	139	199	10	4	48	62	536

Moderate

Offense												Total
Any serious offense attempted investigated	24	36	49	109	20	24	28	72	4	1	13	18	199
Carrying a concealed weapon	1	3	7	11	0	0	6	6	0	0	0	0	17
Glue sniffing	0	0	3	3	0	0	2	2	0	0	0	0	5
Impersonating a police officer or member of armed forces	0	0	1	1	0	0	1	1	0	0	0	0	2
Malicious destruction of property	24	5	13	42	14	4	9	27	5	3	5	13	82
Petit larceny	66	34	53	153	42	12	36	90	7	6	14	27	270
Shoplifting	2	1	0	3	1	2	0	3	0	0	1	1	7
Riding in stolen car	0	0	1	1	0	0	0	0	0	0	1	1	2
Starting careless fire	0	0	1	1	1	0	0	1	0	0	0	0	2
Illicit sex with consent	0	0	0	0	0	0	0	0	1	0	1	0	2
Car tampering or stripping	2	0	7	9	1	0	3	4	1	0	4	2	18
Resisting arrest	0	0	3	3	0	0	3	3	0	0	1	5	7
Obscene literature	0	0	1	1	0	0	0	0	0	0	0	1	1
Total	119	79	139	337	79	42	88	209	18	10	40	68	614

Slight

Offense												Total
Curfew violation	5	2	70	77	4	0	57	61	0	0	19	19	157
Discharging firearms in city limits, BB gun	1	1	3	5	0	2	3	5	1	0	4	5	15
Disorderly conduct	3	1	8	12	0	0	9	9	2	0	5	7	28
False fire alarm, false report	3	0	0	3	2	0	2	4	1	0	0	1	8
Fighting	2	0	5	7	2	0	5	7	0	0	1	1	15
Improper language	1	0	2	3	0	0	0	0	0	1	0	1	3
Incorrigibility	11	15	66	92	5	15	42	62	0	0	12	13	167
Intoxication	0	1	10	11	0	0	9	9	0	0	5	5	25
Menacing threats	1	1	0	2	0	0	1	1	0	0	0	0	3
Pointing firearms	0	0	0	0	0	1	0	1	0	0	0	0	1

—continued

Table 4. *continued*

Type of offense	Experimentals				Controls				Comparisons				Total
	Pre	During	Post	Total	Pre	During	Post	Total	Pre	During	Post	Total	Total
Possession of fireworks	0	2	4	6	0	0	0	0	0	0	0	0	6
Obstructing justice	0	0	0	0	0	0	1	1	0	0	0	0	1
Suspicious person	0	0	14	14	0	0	5	5	0	0	4	4	23
Swimming in an unguarded area	0	3	0	3	0	0	0	0	0	0	0	0	3
Throwing missiles	1	1	2	4	0	1	2	3	1	0	1	2	9
Trespassing	2	2	9	13	5	2	12	19	4	1	3	8	40
Truancy from home	19	7	36	62	6	3	27	36	1	0	12	13	111
Truancy from school	4	2	9	15	2	3	5	10	1	0	5	6	31
Violating probation	0	1	1	2	0	0	1	1	1	0	1	1	4
Gambling	0	0	3	3	3	0	3	3	0	0	0	0	6
Delinquency	2	0	3	5	0	0	2	5	0	0	0	0	10
Indecent exposure	0	0	0	0	0	0	0	0	0	0	1	1	1
Riding double on a bicycle	1	0	0	1	0	0	0	0	0	0	0	0	1
Failure to appear in court	0	0	1	1	0	0	0	0	0	0	0	0	1
Misrepresentation of minor status	0	0	1	1	0	0	0	0	0	0	0	0	1
Shooting pool	0	0	0	0	0	0	1	1	0	0	0	0	1
Unlawful assembly	0	0	1	1	0	0	0	0	0	0	0	0	1
Total	56	39	248	343	29	27	187	243	11	2	73	86	672
Grand Total	227	157	571	955	138	99	414	651	39	16	161	216	1,822

[a] Reprinted with permission from Reckless, W. C., and Dinitz, S. *The prevention of delinquency: An experiment.* Ohio State University Press, 1972.

[b] Denotes total number of subjects

6. The findings on the attitudinal dimensions paralleled those on the behavioral data. In the first cohort (1963/64), no significant attitude change was observed at the end of the 7th grade when compared with the end of the 6th grade. When improvement did occur on the tests (the socialization and self-concept scales) used on the first cohort (1963/64), it was no greater for the experimental than for the control subjects. The improvement could be attributed, in most part, to the test-retest learning situation rather than to genuine alterations in self-perceptions and other perceptions.

7. Similarly, despite the rigorousness of the methods used in developing nine Guttman-type subscales on perception of law, police, and courts and six Guttman subscales on school, teacher, and education dimensions, no marked differences were found between the pre- and postprogram responses of the experimental and control subjects tested in the second (1964/65) and the third (1965/66) cohorts.

8. Personal interviews were conducted, whenever possible, with former experimental and control subjects of the 1964/65 cohort in the spring of 1967. According to the teacher interviewers, the experimental boys were doing very much better than their control counterparts. This was particularly evident in the section on demeanor, which included cooperativeness, ease of interaction, honesty, and delinquency assessment. The teacher interviewers were also confident that fewer of the followed-up experimentals than control interviewees would become school drop-outs or police blotter statistics. In short, the three project teacher interviewers were impressed by the positive gains made by their former charges in comparison with the controls. Unfortunately, the hard data do not reflect this improvement or optimism. The attitude responses noted above and the answers to the specific interview questions covering progress in school, after school activities, interpersonal relationships, self-reported activities, and self-reported misconduct likewise do not reflect the optimism of the project teachers concerning the greater improvement of the experimental boys.

9. Last, when questioned about their reactions to the Youth Development program in the 7th grade, the interviewed experimental subjects were overwhelmingly favorable to the program. They were pleased to have been in this special type of class and thought that many of their friends could have benefited from it and that it merited extension to include all 7th grade boys in the school. This enthusiasm for the program, like that of the

teachers, was impressive. Still, it would have been more impressive if this indication of favorable impact could have been translated into behavioral terms, such as better school performance and fewer police contacts.

DISCUSSION

There are certain assumptions inherent in every strategy of delinquency prevention. The theory behind the approach of this project was that the inner city boy at the threshold of adolescence needed to internalize models of behavior and perceptions of self that could build up some inner self-control, which in turn would help him withstand the circumstances of his family, neighborhood, and companions. We still believe this to be the case and subscribe to the control or containment model of delinquency prevention (29). Perhaps Martinson is correct in his overblown claim that "nothing works" (1). And perhaps, after decades of research, Sheldon and Eleanor Glueck could really offer no more than the advice that maturation (whatever it is) is the best hope in turning youth away from conventional delinquency, much as age is said to cure acne.

Our school program failed because it was too limited in scope, intensity, and duration. We also did nothing about the home, the play groups, the neighborhood, the influence of the media, or the many other impacts (many negative) on deprived youth. If this project, and the 17 years devoted to our action research programs, taught us anything at all, it is that alternative school programs as described are not a force powerful enough to counter delinquency trends. We still need to learn how to develop positive self-concepts in youth who have every reason to feel as worthless and inconsequential as their circumstances teach them to be.

NOTES

Note A. A major investigation of state-by-state practices and proposed or effective changes in these areas is being conducted by Joseph L. White at the Academy for Contemporary Problems, Columbus, Ohio. This study on Major Issues in Juvenile Justice is sponsored by the Office of Juvenile Justice and Delinquency Prevention of LEAA.

Note B. In some instances this agreement occurred because the principal saw those students sent him by the teachers for disciplinary reasons. For the most part, the judgments were not based on this type of contact.

REFERENCES

1. Martinson, R. What works? Questions and answers about prison reform. *Public Interest*, 1974, *35*, 32–54.
2. Lipton, D., Martinson, R., and Wilks, J. *The effectiveness of correctional treatment*. New York: Prager, 1975.
3. Palmer, T. Martinson revisited. *Journal of Research in Crime and Delinquency*, 1975, *12*, 133–152.
4. Scared Straight: The myth that roared. Institutions, ETC., April 1979, *2*, 1–9.
5. Hamparian, D., Schuster, R., Dinitz, S., and Conrad, J. *The violent few*. Lexington, Mn.: Lexington, 1978.
6. Van Dine, S., Conrad, J., and Dinitz, S. *Restraining the wicked: The incapacitation of the dangerous criminal*. Lexington, Mn.: Lexington, 1979.
7. National Advisory Committee on Criminal Justice Standards and Goals. *Juvenile justice and delinquency prevention*. Washington, D. C.: 1976, pp. 11–30.
8. Klockars, C. B. The time limits of effectiveness of correctional treatment. *The Prison Journal*. Spring/Summer, 1975, *55*, 53–64.
9. New York State Youth Commission. *Reducing juvenile delinquency*. Albany, N.Y.: Author, 1952, pp. 7, 12, 13.
10. Reckless, W. C., and Dinitz, S. The prevention of delinquency: An experiment. Ohio State University Press, 1972.
11. Reckless, W. C. *The crime problems* (4th ed.). New York: Appleton-Century-Crofts, 1967, pp. 475–478.
12. Reckless, W. C., Dinitz, S., and Murray, E. The good boy in a high delinquency area. *Journal of Criminal Law, Criminology, and Police Science*, 1957, *48*, 17–25.
13. Reckless, W. C., Dinitz, S., and Murray, E. Self-component as an insulator against delinquency. *American Sociological Review*, 1956, *21*, 221–223.
14. Reckless, W. C., Dinitz, S., and Kay, B. The self-component in potential delinquency. *American Sociological Review*, 1957, *22*, 566–570.
15. Dinitz, S., and Kay, B. Self-gradients among potential delinquents. *Journal of Orthopsychiatry*, 1958, *28*, 598–601.
16. Dinitz, S., Scarpitti, F. R., and Reckless, W. C. Delinquency vulnerability: A cross group and longitudinal analysis. *American Sociological Review*, 1962, *27*, 157.
17. Donald, E. P. Self concept of sixth grade boys: A study of delinquency proneness. Doctoral dissertation, Ohio State University, 1963.
18. Donald, E. P., and Dinitz, S. Self concept and delinquency proneness. In W. C. Reckless and C. L. Newman (eds.), *Interdisciplinary problems in criminology: Papers of the American Society of Criminology*. Columbus, Ohio: Ohio State University Press, 1964.
19. West, D. J., and Farrington, D. P. *The delinquent way of life*. London: Heineman, 1977, pp. 156, 159.
20. Havighurst, R. J. *Growing up in River City*. New York: Wiley, 1967.
21. Craig, M., and Glick, S. School behavior related to later delinquency. *Criminilogica*, 1968, *5*, 17–27.
22. Missildine, W. H. The mutual respect approach to child guidance: A

report of 97 cases from private practice. American Journal of Diseases of Children, 1962, *104,* 116-121.

23. Hall, N. E., and Waldo, G. P. Remedial reading for the disadvantaged. *Journal of Reading,* 1967, *11,* 81-84.

24. Hall, N. E. et al. Youth development project: Curriculum guide, lesson plans, and supplementary materials. Columbus, Ohio: Ohio State University Research Foundation, 1964.

25. Zahn, M. A. An evaluation of an experimental delinquency prevention program. Master's thesis, Ohio State University, 1964, pp. 45, 46, 65-69.

26. Hall, N. E., and Waldo, G. P. School identification and delinquency proneness. *Journal of Research in Crime and Delinquency,* 1967, *4,* 234-235.

27. Waldo, G. P. Boys' perceptions of outer containment and delinquency potential. Doctoral dissertation, Ohio State University, 1967, pp. 46-48, 81-106, 124-125, 154-171.

28. Landis, J. R. and Scarpitti, F. R. Delinquent and nondelinquent value orientation and opportunity awareness. In W. C. Reckless and C. L. Newman (Eds.), *Interdisciplinary problems in criminology.* Columbus, Ohio: Ohio State University Publication Service, 1965, 67-68.

29. Reckless, W. C. A new theory of crime and delinquency. *Federal Probation,* 1961, *25,* 42-46.

V

Small-scale interventions

INTRODUCTION TO CHAPTER 16

In-school suspension (ISS), in association with counseling opportunities, is viewed positively (though cautiously) by Garibaldi as a useful administrative option. His survey of eight well staffed, primarily state and federally funded programs, indeed supports his position. However, *most* ISS programs in this country are far more limited in scope and generally emphasize strict discipline and partial exclusion. Their major value then, if carefully supervised by a conscientious and concerned administrator, lies in providing the school staff with a discipline option between detention and the out-of-school suspension.

The results reported by the proponents of ISS programs almost entirely emphasize their effect in decreasing out-of-school suspensions. Although there have been dozens of reports on this school-based alternative, no one has reported that ISS also improves attendance, grades, academic achievement and prospects for graduation. Thus, although ISS provides the school with another mild punishment option and occasionally some related counseling, its overall effectiveness is limited.

Nevertheless, if one wants to build a comprehensive program for disruptive students, an ISS room can provide a useful component. In a multi-option setting, it serves the total program as a behavioral resource room, a crisis center, a half-way station, a cooling off place, a holding room, and an alternative learning center.

16

In-school suspension

Antoine Garibaldi

With the recent emphasis on the high cost of living and inflationary prices, one might expect the public to have rated increased taxes to support public schools as the major problem facing public education. Instead, in eight of the nine Gallup polls taken between 1969 and 1977 (1) the public rated discipline the most crucial issue demanding attention and change. Parents expressed concern that administrators and teachers were not strict enough and that public schools allowed students too much freedom. They charged schools with being both academically lax and unable to enforce behavioral standards and have pressured administrators to make school rules more stringent.

At the same time, recent concerns with the rights of youth have also led to new Supreme Court decisions limiting school administrative authority in dealing with student misconduct. These decisions include: 1) the need for an informal due process hearing before school removal (*Goss* vs. *Lopez*, 1975) and 2) the liability of principals if they deprive students of their civil rights (*Wood* vs. *Strickland*, 1975). In effect, conflicting pressures have spurred principals to become not only more zealous but also more cautious. To resolve this dilemma, some have experimented with new, in-school disciplinary alternatives. This chapter focuses on a description of various models of in-school suspension currently being used around the country.

The views expressed here are solely those of the author and do not reflect the policy or opinion of the National Institute of Education.

EFFECTS OF SUSPENSION

Before discussing the alternatives now available to school administrators, it is worthwhile to describe the effects of out-of-school
suspension. Students lose valuable instruction time when suspended
and are usually not offered the opportunity to make up missed
assignments. They may lose credit for an exam or homework which
may substantially affect their end of term grades. Secondly, most
students suspended out of school are left unsupervised for the rest of
the day. Many families today have two working parents and many
students come from single parent homes. Thus, the student when
suspended has no place to go until his or her parents return home and
may loiter in the community. It is not unreasonable to assume that
the student may then get picked up by the police for truancy or
juvenile delinquency. Third, local districts whose daily operating
budgets are based on average daily attendance (ADA) formulas lose
money each day for every student not attending classes. In both
large and small districts, this loss of revenue has a measurable impact on the school budget. Fourth, school suspension may produce a
ripple effect in the lives of students by provoking the phenomena of
dropping out, poor work opportunities or unemployment,
demoralization, a sense of failure, and occasionally criminal activity.
Moreover, there is evidence that most students who are or will be
suspended are already lagging academically or possess undiagnosed
learning disabilities. And finally, suspending students from school
may decrease their self-concept, provoke taunting by other students,
and cause the faculty to expect more of the same type of misconduct
(a self-fulfilling prophecy).

IN-SCHOOL ALTERNATIVES

A way to remedy some of these problems, while still using the policy
of exclusion for misbehavior, has been the implementation of day-
time suspension centers inside or adjacent to the school building. In
a survey by the National Association of Secondary School Principals
(NASSP) (2), administrators were asked to list those procedures
which they used before out-of-school suspension. Approximately
34% said that they used in-school suspension. In a similar survey by
the New York Statewide Youth Advocacy Project (3), 33% of the
principals said that they used some form of in-school alternative.

In-school programs offer a variety of different emphases, although all provide for student confinement away from the classroom
for a few hours to a few days. A number stress this confinement and

give the student an isolated, generally unpleasant experience in a controlled environment (4–6), hoping this will deter future misconduct. Many offer services to students during their confinement, particularly academic support. Counseling is also frequently provided. This can be in the form of individual counseling, teaching students salient aspects of developing self control (7), supporting the development of coping strategies through "school survival" courses (8), and providing counseling to parents to get them positively involved in the school process or to improve their child-rearing practices at home (9). Very little solid research has been conducted on the success of these different types of in-school programs, but the literature reveals a sizable number of articles by principals describing their schools' individual centers (10–14).

As might be expected, each school administrator evaluates the worth of his or her program on different criteria (e.g., financial economy to the school, positive faculty involvement, decreases in out-of-school suspension). Hayes Mizell, a major proponent and advocate of positive and effective alternatives to suspension and expulsion, found it very easy to identify in-school alternatives to suspension in South Carolina but difficult to summarily evaluate their effectiveness because of different philosophies and theoretical orientations, management systems, goals, and diverse staffs. As a guidepost, Mizell (15) suggested the following criteria for assessing the value of using in-school alternatives to out-of-school suspensions.

1. Is there real evidence over a period of time that the number of suspensions are actually reduced by the use of the alternative program or technique?
2. Does the alternative program or technique truly help to meet the needs of the student who would have been suspended? Does it help solve the problem that led to the disciplinary action?
3. Is the student making genuine academic progress at a level which is appropriate for him/her if participating in an alternative program?
4. As a result of the use of the alternative program or technique, does the student begin to develop greater self-discipline?

Using Mizell's basic criteria, this author set out to identify in-school alternatives during the 1977/78 school year. Though the goal of formulating an "exact" taxonomy of progress was not realized, the primary characteristics of eight well organized in-school suspension programs and of similar programs described in the literature were delineated. The following sections more explicitly describe these.

CHARACTERISTICS OF IN-SCHOOL SUSPENSION PROGRAMS

School Level

Data on suspensions indicate that junior high school students are suspended most frequently. In junior highs, most suspensions are in the 7th and 8th grades and in senior highs in the 9th or 10th grades. A common explanation for the predominance of suspensions at these grades is that students encounter difficulties in making the transition from elementary school to junior high and from junior high to senior high. After the elementary school child enters the junior high, he or she must quickly adapt to a much larger school, interact with peers from other schools, work within a more impersonal atmosphere, and be more independent. In junior high, probably for the first time, the student is confronted with drugs, 6-foot bullies, smoking in lavatories, noisy halls, and strong peer pressure. Students soon also realize that there are more rules to follow and that teachers will more readily refer students to the office for school rule violations.

As would be expected, in-school alternatives are most commonly offered at the junior and senior high school level, although two of the eight programs (listed in Table 1) also operate in elementary schools (K–6). In these elementary schools, the majority of the suspensions and referrals come from the 6th grade.

Reasons for Referral

Most students are suspended from school for absenteeism, tardiness, smoking, and insubordination, which includes disrespect for teachers. The majority of in-school programs cite class cutting and tardiness as the most common reasons for referral (14). A short-term (1–2 day) in-school suspension can be required for class cutting or truancy, whereas a longer term (e.g., 3 days) stay is generally used for more serious problems, such as insubordination, vandalism, drug usage, and excessive classroom disruption. Most schools automatically suspend students for fighting, although some teachers see a value in putting the two students in the same room to resolve their differences with the help of a counselor or a teacher.

Process of Referral

The preferred method of referral to an in-school detention center is through the assistant principal, not directly from the teacher. Someone has to serve as a "gatekeeper" (16) or the program will suffer from flooding, inappropriate referrals, and the abdication of responsibility by some classroom teachers. The gatekeeper must know the faculty and be able to screen the incoming referrals very carefully. He or she must consider other resources, inquire if other milder interventions were exhausted, and determine the potential value of the referral. In schools where there is no gatekeeper and teachers refer directly, the addition of an in-school program can increase the total number of suspensions (in-school plus out-of-school) to a striking degree (e.g., fourfold).

The gatekeeper must discuss the plan with the parents after a due process procedure. His or her referral to the in-school suspension room should be accompanied by suitable documentation to justify the referral (16).

Length of Placement

The average amount of time spent by a student in an in-school program varies according to the projected goal of the program, the offense committed, the individual needs of the student, and the student's cooperation during the suspension. Time-out or holding rooms generally limit daily participation from one to three class periods since they serve to temporarily remove the student for a nonviolent offense, such as refusing to do classwork, persistent minor misbehaviors, or cutting class. In-school centers usually retain students for 1 to 5 days. Although they are most frequently used for truancy (14), they can also be used for more serious offenses. Most programs add days in in-school suspension for students who refuse to do the work there and require make-up days for school absences (14, 17, 18). Counseling alternatives have only a small influence on the length of time a student is required to participate. However, serious infractions of school policies or repeated peer conflicts may require more use of the time-out situation for counseling and/or parent meetings.

In some school programs, the administrative and project staff prefer to retain their options and not establish any fixed placement time. However, they are cognizant of both state and local regulations that restrict the amount of time for suspension and demand a documented due process procedure in instances of extended removal of students from classes. In most states, 10 days is usually considered a maximum for suspension. If school officials anticipate placement lasting longer than that, they are quick to place students in a resource or learning center.

Placement time may depend upon who has the authority to dismiss a student from the program. Administrators often wish to reserve this right for themselves, although many others are willing

Table 1. Analysis of 13 characteristics of eight in-school suspension programs

Name and location of school program	School levels	Major reason for referral	Mean length of placement	Staff size per school	Students served daily	Students served annually	Location in building
Student Referral Center (Houston, Texas)	6 junior and senior highs	Classroom misbehavior Truancy	1.5 days	3 (teacher, counselor, social worker)	10–15	750	Annex to school
In-School Correction Room (Albion, New York)	2 middle schools, 1 senior high	Absenteeism Tardiness	1.9 days	1 (teacher)	15	350	Remote area in building near other classrooms
Minority Suspension Reduction Program (Jefferson, Louisiana)	4 middle schools	Classroom misbehavior	1 class period	3 (teacher, social worker, counselor)	15	Data unavailable	Adjacent to principal's office
Behavior Modification Center (Chicago, Illinois)	1 elementary (K–8)	Tardiness School misbehavior	1.5 days	1 (teacher)	10–15	350	Central
Positive Alternatives to Student Suspension (St. Petersburg, Florida)	12 senior highs	Classroom misbehavior Truancy	2.5 class periods	1 teacher (plus psychological team for all schools)	10–15	12,000	Central
Cope (Wexford, Pennsylvania)	1 senior high (in 2 schools)	Truancy Misbehavior	3 days	1 teacher-counselor (plus parent volunteers and interns)	20	200	Central
Contractual Opportunities Program Education (Los Angeles, California)	165 elementary, 75 junior highs	Truancy Tardiness Misbehavior	1.5 days	1 teacher (plus 12 advisors and 1 coordinator)	Varies by school	Varies	Varies by school
Comprehensive Guidance Center (Montclair, New Jersey)	1 senior high, 2 middle schools	Truancy Tardiness Misbehavior	2 class periods	2 counselors	15–20	750	Near guidance office

Table 1. Analysis of 13 characteristics of eight in-school suspension programs

Name and location of school program	Parent participation	Percentages of males and females	Recidivism rate	Lunch with other students	Intervention approach used	Funding source
Student Referral Center (Houston, Texas)	Yes	81% males 19% females	17%	No	Reality therapy Values clarification	Federal and local district
In-School Correction Room (Albion, New York)	Yes	82% males 18% females	64%	No	Combination	Local district
Minority Suspension Reduction Program (Jefferson, Louisiana)	Yes	68% males 32% females	Unknown	Yes	Reality therapy Transactional analysis	Federal
Behavior Modification Center (Chicago, Illinois)	Yes	60% males 40% females	5%	Yes	Behavior modification	Local district
Positive Alternatives to Student Suspension (St. Petersburg, Florida)	Yes	50% males 50% females	Unknown	Yes	Transactional analysis Reality therapy Behavior modification Values clarification	Federal, state, and local district
Cope (Wexford, Pennsylvania)	Yes	60% males 40% females	10%	Yes	Adlerian counseling Peer tutoring/counseling Reality therapy	State and local district
Contractual Opportunities Program Education (Los Angeles, California)	Yes	Varies	Unknown	Yes	Confluent education (Affective strategies and transactional analysis)	Local district
Comprehensive Guidance Center (Montclair, New Jersey)	Yes	65% males 35% females	13%	Yes	Reality therapy Behavior modification through counseling	Federal and local district

to delegate that authority to a member of the program staff. Another impact on placement time is "earning your way out." When this is applied, student behavior and academic effort are evaluated and the accumulated positive rating permits a return to classes.

PROCEDURES IN IN-SCHOOL SUSPENSION

Most in-school programs have a tight discipline policy. No talking is allowed in the room and rules are strictly enforced. Rule violations can lead to either longer stays or to an out-of-school suspension, depending upon the persistence and severity of the infraction.

In the room, doing academic work is required, often in accordance with an individual contract. Generally, academic assignments come from the regular teachers (6, 10, 17, 19). Not infrequently, however, such assignments are delayed, which causes both interstaff and staff-pupil tensions. In other in-school centers, the program staff give their own assignments, usually using programmed materials. On occasion, group discussions or films are available in the afternoons (17).

Students in the room are generally not allowed to be involved in the school's extracurricular activities (14) or to attend school assemblies, and they are frequently escorted as a separate group to lunch (3, 6, 19, 20). Some staff even escort the students individually to the lavatory (21, 22).

Staff Size and Expertise

The number of staff used in an in-school suspension program is dependent upon funding and the focus of the alternative. Most time-out rooms have one staff person (usually a teacher); in-school centers retaining students longer than a day have one full-time teacher, occasionally an aide, and some part-time staff members (a counselor, psychologist, social worker, and/or a community advocate to establish contact with the parents). In smaller districts staff potential is maximized by using more part-time persons (e.g., parent volunteers, college students, and fellow students as peer tutors). The use of parent and college student volunteers also serves the useful purpose of bridging the gap between the school and the community.

The expertise of the staff is quite critical. The teacher in charge must be capable of being firm, must not be noticeably uncomfortable when verbally challenged by hostile adolescents, and must be able to recognize the special needs of some students. He or she should like most of these students as well (16).

Number of Students Served

In-school alternative programs avoid serving more than 10 students at any one time. If students are given much individual attention in academic and counseling sessions, then the teacher-pupil ratio must be small. Thus, referrals should be processed cautiously by administrators who are cognizant of the number and needs of students in the classroom at particular times.

Formal data on the annual number of clients served by an in-school program is necessary for evaluative and administrative purposes. Each student who is referred and all inquiries for referral (for whatever reason) should be separately recorded. Because some students are allowed to use the counseling or academic services of the centers during their "free" time, data on the number of students referred annually can be easily confounded unless separately categorized. Another issue in interpreting yearly figures is the fact that often over 25% of program students are repeaters (23).

A careful observer of the in-school suspension data in Table 1 can ask this question: Are the number of students sent into the program centers those who would normally be suspended during the course of the school year? The answer to this question is partially yes, in that in-school suspension programs generally decrease out-of-school suspensions annually by about one-third (3, 5, 14, 20). However, many of the totals on in-school suspensions are misleadingly high because 1) students can be referred to the center for insignificant reasons, and 2) students who are having personal and academic problems are usually also allowed to consult with the in-school suspension team.

Location of Program in School

One concern expressed by critics of in-school detention programs is that problem students are further alienated by being placed in a room away from the normal flow of school activities. The table shows that at least five of the eight programs are centrally located or near the administrative offices of the school. Personnel in some of these programs suggest that the shifting of students away from the regular classroom area considerably limits the amount of distraction students may encounter and offers a more conducive environment for learning and counseling. The program's location is important for a number of other reasons. Students, and teachers as well, may feel that displacement from homerooms and from peers is a form of punishment. Also one must recognize that a program which is isolated from the regular school environment (e.g., in a portable classroom or at the extreme end of a wing in a school building) limits its accessibility to regular teachers who should be familiar with the operation of the program and be in frequent contact with its staff. Conversely, a program centrally located near the principal's office is susceptible to being an unintended "display showcase" where students and visitors can see who is being "punished" on a particular day. Stigma and low self-perceptions of students are inevitable in either case. Therefore, individual schools must select the optimal location in an effort to lessen these potentially negative effects. The location of special programs should not be based upon accidental circumstances or be primarily dependent upon available space. Rather, site selection should be based on conscious decisions made by administrators and other school personnel. In one large survey of "in-school" suspension centers (14), 11 of 24 programs were within the school building, 10 were in a separate adjacent structure, and 3 were "off campus."

Parent Participation

An essential ingredient of each of the eight programs listed in Table 1 is parental involvement. At least three of the programs have professional support staff who establish regular contact with the parents of assigned students. One of the programs employs trained paraprofessional counselors to bridge the gap between the families of the students and the school personnel. In another alternative program, parents participate in biweekly workshops on efficient ways of managing discipline at home, using an Adlerian perspective. Such participation transcends the normal and perfunctory types of communication initiated by schools. Utilization of counseling may be the first time parents have come to the school for a reason other than a discipline crisis involving their son or daughter. Moreover, their familiarity with the in-school suspension team may lead to a more positive relationship with other school staff.

Student Characteristics

The only index of student characteristics provided in Table 1 is the ratio of males and females in the programs. The average male/female referral ratio to these programs is 2:1. Programs rarely maintain accurate ISS records on students by race, but it would be interesting to see whether referrals by race to in-school detention centers are similar to published figures on out-of-school suspensions.

Intervention

Each in-school suspension program, irrespective of type, usually incorporates one or more theoretical models of intervention. Glasser's Reality Therapy model is the most popular method, with variations of behavior modification strategies ranking a close second. Very few program directors rigidly state that they use only one method; they prefer to consider themselves as eclectic. In addition to behavior modification and reality therapy, values clarification, transactional analysis, Adlerian psychology, and other types of humanistic approaches (e.g., positive peer culture and confluent education) are also used. The choice of one model of intervention over another seems to be primarily dependent upon the proficiency of the program staff with a particular therapeutic approach.

Recidivism

Rates of return by students to in-school programs are not generally reliable due to poor record keeping and the self-referral process in most centers. Where the latter is allowed, a student who has been positively affected by a warm and sensitive staff person is more likely to come to the center on a regular basis. This person should not be classified as a "recidivist" in the literal sense of the word. Another example of misleading data is the instance of a student in need of counseling daily for an extended period of time. Though the student may be counted as a daily participant, he is not a recidivist.

The data on use of the center, in cases where actual figures are reported, could be more valuable if one were able to identify the referring teacher for each student. When individual referral rates are extreme, such details may identify teachers who need additional support in handling discipline problems in their classrooms.

DISCUSSION

It seems important to include some caveats here about the implementation of these programs. The comments are designed to encourage some administrators while discouraging others.

1. The purpose of an in-school alternative must be precise, realistic, and justifiable. If a secondary school is under parent, faculty, or school board pressure because of high rates of student disrup-

tion, an in-school suspension plan should not be the initial response. Rather, the primary emphasis should be directed to determining the cause of the problem. First responses could be faculty meetings on the issue or a consideration of administrative changes.

2. Although many alternative programs for disruptive youth have been initiated with federal and state funds (see Chapter 19), hiring a separate, full-time staff to run an in-school detention program room is not a prerequisite for a good program. Presently employed full- and part-time school staff (e.g., teachers, aides, counselors, psychologists) can work as a team to run such a program cooperatively assisted with local support money. Also, members of such a team can be economically shared among several schools. The point here is that outside grant funding is not required. Alternatives funded by local districts have additional flexibility in that they can meet their local needs rather than being constrained by the exigencies of a federal program.

3. Student restrictions within in-school detention rooms should be reasonable rather than harsh and students should know the rationale for imposed limitations. Programs perceived by students as serving a punitive function may create unduly negative attitudes. On the other hand, program staff who attempt to produce an environment that is better than the regular class may establish an atmosphere so comfortable that the student does not want to leave.

School personnel should seriously consider all the ramifications before setting up an in-school detention center. They should consider whether a teacher's expectation of a pupil is negatively affected by the student's participation in the program. Do students become labeled or stigmatized by their peers when they return? How informed is the regular teaching staff about the program and do they offer to work collaboratively with the center's staff on the serious problems of some students? Will the detention room be viewed only as a method of punishment? Will the program staff make a valiant effort to get at the heart of the student's behavioral difficulties? Once again, before putting the onus exclusively on the disruptive student and excluding him, other possibilities must be explored. These include the teacher's inability to manage the class, inflexibility in the school rules, and a lack of interest by school administrators to work with particular students. When the school staff is willing to modify its educational climate to better deal with disruptive youth, then an in-school alternative can indeed help it serve its purpose more effectively.

REFERENCES

1. Gallup, G. H. Ninth annual poll of the public's attitude toward the public school. *Phi Delta Kappan*, 1977, *59*, 33–48.
2. *NASSP Bulletin*, January 1977, *61*.
3. Block, E. E., Covill-Servo, J., & Rosen, M. F. *Failing students—failing schools: A study of dropouts and discipline in New York State.* Rochester, N.Y.: New York Civil Liberties Union, 1978.
4. McClung, M. Alternatives to disciplinary exclusion from school. *Inequality in Education*, July 1975, *20*, 58–73.
5. White, B. In school suspension: No panacea but the impact's positive. *Phi Delta Kappan*, 1977, *58*, 497–498.
6. O'Brien, D. M. In-school suspension: Is it the new way to punish productively? *American School Board Journal*, March 1976, *163* (3), 35–37.
7. Fagen, S. A., & Long, N. J. Before it happens: Prevent discipline problems by teaching self-control. *Instructor*, January 1976, *85* (5), 42–47; 95–96.
8. Bailey, R., & Kackley, J. *Positive alternatives to student suspension.* St. Petersburg, Fla.: Pinellas County Schools, 1977, Mimeo.
9. Boyle, T. J. Early detection and treatment of school maladjustment. *Catalyst for Change* (Journal of the National School Development Council), Fall 1977.
10. Meares, H. O., & Kittle, H. A. More advantages: In-house suspension. *NASSP Bulletin*, February 1976, *60*, (397), 60–63.
11. Harvey, D. L., & Moosha, W. G. In-school suspension: Does it work? *NASSP Bulletin*, January 1977, *61*, 14–17.
12. Bettker, D. F. Suspensions: Get rid of EM! *Thrust for Educational Leadership*, October 1975.
13. Maynard, W. Working with "disruptive youth." *Educational Leadership*, 1977, *34* (6), 417–421.
14. Neill, S. B. *Suspensions and expulsions: Current trends in school policies and programs.* Arlington, Va.: National School Public Relations Association, 1976.
15. Mizell, M. H. Alternatives to suspension. *Your Schools*, May 1975.
16. Mizell, M. H. Designing and implementing effective in-school alternatives to suspension. In A. Garibaldi (Ed.), *In-school alternatives to suspension.* Washington, D.C.: U.S. Government Printing Office, 1979, pp. 133–150.
17. Bornmann, S. An in-school suspension program. *School and Community*, May 1976, *62*, 36.
18. *Alternative disciplinary programs and practices in Pennsylvania schools*, Harrisburg, Pennsylvania: Pennsylvania Department of Education, April 1977.
19. *An Alternative Learning Center.* Manchester, Missouri: Parkway

South Junior High School, 1977, Mimeo.

20. Winbourne, C. R. In-school suspension programs: The King Williams County model. *Educational Leadership*, 1979, *37*, 457–458.

21. Quonset hut becomes "jail" for junior high, reducing suspensions. *New York Times*, December 2, 1979, p. 44.

22. Rakowsky, S. G. Alternative classrooms for disruptive students. *NASSP Bulletin*, March 1979, *63*, 122–123.

23. Kelly, N., & Kinky, E. R. An alternative to suspension. *School and Community*, April 1974, *60*, 9.

INTRODUCTION TO CHAPTER 17

There is no doubt that peers have a major impact on the behavior of adolescents. They strongly affect motivation in school, probably more so than do teachers (1), and they clearly affect the propensity of adolescents to commit delinquent acts (2). One certainly cannot ignore the fact that 60% to 90% of delinquency is group delinquency (2).

Thus, a therapeutic intervention for disruptive adolescents using peer influence positively is both appropriate and attractive. This point is made strongly by Dr. Garner, a firm and unswerving believer in positive peer culture (PPC). Compared to the common, adult-managed, disciplinary emphasis present within most secondary public schools, the reliance on peer influence characteristic of PPC represents a radical approach. PPCs group method of stressing individual student responsibility is likewise quite novel in American schools.

However, before getting too carried away, one must also consider the note of caution made by Dr. Garner. Data-based, controlled assessments supporting the use of PPC in secondary schools are minimal. Hopefully, future clinical outcome studies will fill this gap.

1. Coleman, J. S. *Equality of educational opportunity.* Washington, D.C.: U.S. Government Printing Office, 1966.
2. Empery, L. T. Delinquency theory and recent research. *Journal of Research on Crime and Delinquency*, 1967, *4*, 28–42.

17

Positive peer culture programs in schools

Howard Garner

Teachers and principals who daily confront acting out and hostile youth see the adolescent peer group as a negative support system for behaviors that can make the teaching/learning process impossible. Some behavior managers suggest that educators should isolate the disruptive student from the support of his or her classmates before attempting disciplinary action, assuming that the peer group will usually support the student against the teacher. Guidance counselors have shared the disheartening experience of having a deeply moving counseling session with a repentant student who, in tears of remorse, promises never to misbehave again, only to be referred a few days later for a more serious infraction. Apparently, promises made in the security of the one-to-one counseling session are difficult to keep in the real world where the peer group exerts its influence. Teachers now report that students who are achieving in their classes request in private that their good grades not be announced in front of classmates. It seems that the peer group for certain youth plays a more dynamic role in shaping their behavior than the family, schools, or other institutions such as the church. The pervasive need of adolescents to conform to peer group norms has been called the "tyranny of adolescents" (1).

The power of the adolescent peer group to influence values, attitudes, and behaviors has increased during the past decade (2, 3, 4). During the 1950s and early 1960s peer influence was seen in teenage fads such as white socks, rock music, and hot rod cars. During the late 1960s and early 1970s a youth culture emerged full-blown with marijuana, long hair, acid rock, work shirts, and the hippie movement as the symptoms of an underlying rejection of the prevailing adult value system. The attitude that "you can't trust anyone over thirty" was translated into behaviors that said "adults don't deserve the right to tell us what to do." Because schools were the obvious place where adults attempted to teach, socialize and control youth, conflict between students and school personnel increased (5, 6). In the 1970s the adult-student tensions were undergirded by almost universal support for disruptive students given by their adolescent peers.

The widespread negative behaviors in many schools are clearly the result of more than isolated individuals attacking our educational system. They are the result of factors that deeply affect many youth of our country. Consequently, interventions that hope to change these student values and behaviors must focus on their underlying support system. Merely removing and counseling relatively few students who exhibit extreme expressions of hostile youth values misses the opportunity to influence many students, even those who are not showing disruptive behavior. Thus, paralleling the growth of the peer group as a significant factor affecting student behavior in secondary schools has been the development of treatment approaches for hard-to-manage youth that actually use the peer group as the focus of the intervention strategy.

POSITIVE PEER CULTURE AND GUIDED GROUP INTERACTION: A BRIEF HISTORY

The history of this radical approach to dealing with disruptive youth can be traced back to the 1950s and the application of guided group interaction (GGI) at a residential treatment program for juvenile delinquents at Highfields Residential Treatment Program in Hopewell, New Jersey. Here McCorkle, Elias, and Bixby (7) began applying strategies with youthful offenders that had been developed for use with incarcerated soldiers at the end of World War II (8).

Harry Vorrath served an internship in social work at Highfields and saw the potential of guided group interaction for serving problem youth. He took GGI to Minnesota and implemented the program in the Red Wing Training School. Later, Vorrath extended GGI to a program called positive peer culture (PPC) (9). Reacting to the proliferation and diversification of GGI, Vorrath and Brendtro re-emphasized the power of caring and helping while being opposed to peer coercion and peer punishment. Thus, PPC emphasized the development of trust and positive helping as well as group service projects in the community.

PPC and GGI have a number of similarities, especially in the structure of the daily group meetings. Some professionals today use the terms interchangeably. Because of the author's greater familiarity with programs using the name PPC, this term will be used here except where other writers have specified GGI as the program descriptor.

Although positive peer culture began as a means of working with incarcerated delinquents, it has been successfully adapted for use in public schools. As other adult-centered programs for managing disruptive youth failed to accomplish substantial changes in student attitudes and behaviors, certain public schools courageously tried a more radical approach. The Omaha, Nebraska public schools began a PPC program in one junior high school in 1973. Since that time they have expanded the program to six schools in 1979/80. The Lansing Public Schools in Michigan utilized a GGI Program in four secondary schools. Another public school program using PPC was in Rock Island, Ill. Applications of positive peer culture in still other public schools have also been reported in the educational literature (10, 11).

BASIC CONCEPTS OF POSITIVE PEER CULTURE

PPC in a secondary school has as its goal the creation of a helping and caring environment for all those involved: students, teachers, and administrators. This goal is achieved through a direct attack on the negative peer culture that appears in many classrooms today. Instead of removing the negative leaders who "call the shots behind the scenes," PPC views these strong leaders as resources in changing the life of the entire school.

The basic concepts of PPC are as follows

1. Adolescents are commonly more responsive to the values of peers than to those of adults.
2. Most negative behaviors emerge from individuals (and groups) who feel badly about themselves and who feel weak and unsuccessful.
3. Adolescents are strong resources of idealism and caring and can be assisted to responsibly take charge of their own lives.
4. The most powerful experience that can change a person's self-concept and life is helping and being of service to another person.

Positive peer culture uses the peer group as the agent of change. The same dynamics that allow negative student leaders to adversely influence their peers can work to produce a school environment that values human beings, promotes learning, cares about people with problems, and protects property and people. The process of reversing a negative peer culture and developing a positive one obviously requires great skill and understanding. Unsuccessful attempts to apply the PPC model are almost always related to the use of untrained adult leadership.

Building a Positive Peer Culture

The first step in implanting PPC is securing trained, experienced personnel. Some schools have hired group leaders from other programs. Others have purchased consultant services to work with students and to train their own staffs. Experience with untrained leaders attempting to start PPC groups has shown that the situation frequently gets worse instead of better. The process of shifting responsibility and power from adults to the adolescent peer group is a delicate and sometimes fiery one. Untrained leaders frequently give up at crucial stages of group development thus increasing the frustration and sense of failure on the part of the youth. Trained leaders are able to use the dynamics of group development to create a degree of tension and discomfort that promotes change in the group and in individual lives.

When a trained leader goes into a large secondary school, the first stage is the orientation of the teachers, counselors, and administration. The school faculty must, at a minimum, understand the goals of the PPC program. In the early stages of the program, school personnel are asked to continue their normal procedures in responding to behavior problems. Once the PPC groups begin to function, these procedures will be modified because the young people themselves will be taking more responsibility for student misconduct.

Initially, the trained PPC leader asks teachers to identify the student leaders in their school. They are asked to name both positive and negative leaders, students whom others look to for approval and direction. In identifying the true student leaders, the students are also asked whom they see as the most influential individuals. Each trained PPC leader will then form two groups of nine student leaders. These group members are carefully placed in groups to balance positive and negative leaders, assertive and quiet personalities, and individuals with different types of problems. These groups will meet once a day during a regular school period, and the students generally receive social studies credit for a unit in leadership skill development.

The focus of these group meetings is not on the teacher or on cognitive theories of leadership. The groups instead focus on problem solving, dealing first with the problems of the group members. A structured agenda based on the principles of guided group interaction asks each member to report all of the problems they have had since the last meeting. A problem list is used to educate the youth to the types of problems experienced by human beings in daily life. The twelve problems include: low self-image, inconsiderate of others, inconsiderate of self, authority problem, misleads others, easily misled, aggravates others, easily angered, stealing, alcohol or drug problem, lying, and fronting (putting up a false front).

The reporting of problems serves several purposes. First, it establishes the point that sharing your problems allows you to begin solving them. Second, it builds trust in the group with confidentiality being a basic expectation for group members. Third, it establishes the idea that it takes courage and strength to face your own problems and to take responsibility for them. Finally, reporting problems runs directly counter to the youth culture's attitude of hiding your problems and helping others to cover up their weaknesses and mistakes. In a mature PPC group, members will remind each other of problems they forget to report. This is encouraged and accepted as a form of caring since unreported problems cannot be solved.

The second part of the PPC leadership class involves a group decision regarding which group member most needs the meeting to work on his or her problem. Each member initially states whether or not they would like their problem to be the focus of the meeting. Then each member indicates whom he or she believes most needs and can use the problem solving portion of the meeting. This process continues until all group members agree to devote the rest of the session to one individual. This decision-making process is important training, for it shows the youth the value of input by each person in the group and requires compromise, understanding, and insight.

Once the focus of the meeting has been awarded to a group member, problem solving begins. The person who was "given" the meeting explains the problem as he or she sees it. The other eight members ask questions and offer their perspective on the problem. Adolescents can quickly learn the difference between giving advice and true problem solving. A major part of the helping process is the group's insistence that individuals assume the responsibility for their own behavior and problems. The PPC group is trained to recognize the defense mechanisms used to explain and rationalize problems. When a student excuses disruptive behavior by claiming the teachers are unfair, the PPC group might respond, "Do you mean that unfair people control you and make you act in ways that hurt others?" As the individual confronts his or her own responsibility for a problem, the group offers to assist and support the attempt of the student to gain self-control and awareness.

During the group meeting, the adult leader of the PPC groups sits behind a desk with the group members seated in a semicircle in front of the desk. This physical arrangement is designed to communicate the leader's role as helper, facilitator, and teacher. The adult is not a member of the group. Rather he attempts to enhance the group's effectiveness and power. As the groups meet and focus on individual problems, the members begin to experience and know their collective power to affect behavior. This power was there all along, and for some was being used to lead others into negative behavior. The training provided in the PPC group shows the youth how to use their collective influence to help instead of hurt. The effects of one's helping another human being to cope better can be "life changing" for the helper. PPC believes that the act of helping another person is an event that reverses a negative self-concept. A person who feels worthless cannot maintain that belief after he has participated in helping another person to deal with a drug problem, to be less inconsiderate of others, and to handle anger better. Young people have a tremendous ability to care for each other, but the current value system of the youth culture sees caring as weakness. In PPC, caring is the highest value and requires strength and courage.

During problem solving, the leader supports and praises youth who risk trying to help another person. A keen knowledge of group dynamics assists the leader in confronting indirectly those youth who are reluctant to be of service to others. The same power of peer pressure that has made the negative peer culture such a potent force in adolescent misbehavior can be used to influence hostile leaders, and later the whole atmosphere of the school.

The final event of each leadership class consists of a short summary by the leader. This allows the leader to emphasize the important issues that emerged during the meeting, to praise the group for its efforts in helping, and to challenge the group to higher levels of functioning. The summary may include participation by the youth, as the leader involves the students in understanding their own motivation.

Leadership classes can form a nucleus of student leadership in a large high school and are the beginning points of a change effort focused on the whole student body. As these groups grow in their ability to recognize and solve real human problems, their focus gradually shifts from personal problems to those of the entire school and student body. Hurting of any kind can become an issue within these leadership groups. Students who get in legal trouble and are placed on probation by the juvenile court often become a special concern of the leadership classes. The student leaders have actually gone to juvenile judges to request a chance to work with youth who otherwise might have been committed to a state correctional facility. These leaders have been able to keep a fellow student in school, to provide tutoring, and to support this student to help others.

Following a 3- to 4-month period of training, the leadership groups are usually functioning as strong units of helping, confronting, supporting, problem solving, and caring. The young people develop an understanding of their collective power and the degree to which peer pressure influences the behavior and values of their friends and classmates. Once a leadership group develops this level of maturity, the members are ready to use their abilities and skills with problems outside their group. In some projects, trained student leaders form advisory groups to serve students from their own neighborhoods. These advisory groups receive referrals from administrators, teachers, and other students. Individuals who are experiencing problems such as fighting, truancy, shop-lifting, or school failure are asked to attend student-led sessions in which the problems can be faced directly and appropriate help initiated. Students who are on the verge of being suspended or expelled from school are of particular concern. Youth who are on probation from the juvenile court need help in maintaining themselves in school. Leadership groups have also been instrumental in diffusing potentially explosive crises involving racial tensions, gangs, and student violence. The success of these programs, however, depends on factors beyond the PPC group members and their adult leaders.

As PPC has been extended to public schools, several key variables affecting the program's effectiveness have emerged. It is clear that the faculty of the school must be supportive of the concept of increased student involvement in managing behavior. Also, teachers must understand the goals and processes of the groups in order to encourage and allow their working in the classroom. The faculty needs to be informed of the groups' stages of development, their successes, and their stresses. The total school needs to feel a degree of ownership and pride in their peer culture program.

In addition to faculty support, PPC programs need administrative assistance in key areas. First, the teachers who become group leaders should be relieved of one class assignment rather than sacrificing their planning period. Second, students need to be given credit for participating in the leadership classes. A negative leader who must volunteer to join the leadership class will be more likely to say yes if credit toward graduation can be earned. Those who have observed these groups have no problem justifying the academic credit once they see the insight into human behavior and group dynamics that the youth develop. Third, flexibility is needed in changing student schedules allowing important leaders to be in the appropriate PPC group and ensuring that group members have some classes together. This would allow the group's influence to extend beyond the leadership class and into other classrooms. Finally, teachers who serve as group leaders need support from a coordinator, consultant, and each other. Running PPC groups is a very challenging job and requires opportunities to receive help and feedback from others who understand the process they are using. Time is needed for these leaders to meet with others during staff development activities. In short, PPC works best where the participants are valued and supported by the total school community in tangible and intangible ways.

Research on PPC and GGI

Research studies on the effectiveness of PPC have been conducted in several projects. These studies have shown positive changes in the lives of youth who previously engaged in disruptive and frequently delinquent behaviors in schools and communities. The research studies have most often been conducted in residential settings rather than in public schools. Recently, however, several public school projects have reported their evaluations of PPC and GGI.

Gerrard compared parole revocation rates of graduates of a PPC program and a behavior modification program in the same institutions in Nebraska (12). The results showed a parole revocation rate of 42.2 percent for the behavior modification unit and of only 14.3 percent for the positive peer culture unit.

Lybarger studied the effects of PPC in several residential facilities and found an increase in self-esteem after 120 days of treatment. Lybarger also showed positive changes in behavior associated with changes in self-esteem (13). In another field study, Wasmund found similar changes in the self-concept in institutionalized delinquents following their admission to a program emphasizing PPC (14). In a later study, Wasmund focused on the self-concept scores of 103 students in a Woodland Hills residential program in Duluth, Minnesota, where PPC was used. Here again significant increases in self-concept scores were commonplace. Wasmund claims that the only other residential programs for delinquents to report positive changes in self-concept were Highfields and the Michigan State youth corrections programs, both of which utilize the power of peers as the primary agent of behavior and attitudinal change (15). In all the above studies on self-esteem and self-concept, changes in scores between the time of commitment and after a period in residence were measured. None of the studies utilized a control group.

Pilnick reported that the boys who completed the Essexfields program had only a 12 percent recidivism rate compared to the normal 50 to 75 percent rate for other programs (1). The Minnesota Department of Corrections reported that between 1970 and 1972 there were 845 boys who experienced the PPC program and were subsequently released on parole. By March, 1973, 71.4 percent of these young men had not had their paroles revoked. This 28.6 rate of revoked paroles compares with a 50 percent rate prior to the institution of the PPC program.

It was the success of PPC in residential programs that led to its application to behavior management problems in public schools. Although PPC has been used in schools in Nebraska, Michigan, Minnesota, Illinois, and Canada, the total amount of published research has been minimal. Two well researched programs were a PPC project in Omaha, Nebraska, and a GGI project in Lansing, Michigan.

The Omaha Public Schools in Omaha, Nebraska have utilized PPC groups perhaps to a greater extent than any other. Beginning in 1973 with Monroe Junior High School, which was going through the desegregation process, the school system has in 1979/80 spread this program to three junior highs and three senior high schools. The school division has evaluated the effects of this program over time.

At the end of the first year the principal reported several significant changes, which he attributed to the PPC program. These included the following (16):

1. A decrease in the number of failing grades with percentages of change ranging between 3% and 80% in various subject areas.
2. A decrease in staff turnover at the end of the year.
3. A decrease in the number of discipline suspensions from 364 in 1972/73 to 205 in 1973/74.
4. The return of stolen items such as watches, purses, and shop tools in 10 cases where the PPC groups were asked to help.
5. Positive changes in 100 of the 114 students who had direct contact with PPC leadership, help, or core groups.
6. Support from 31 of 45 teachers to continue the PPC program a second year.

In 1976, the Omaha Public Schools released Instructional Research Report #1975–10 in which 8th graders ($N=90$) who had participated in the PPC groups were compared with 8th graders ($N=62$) who were not involved in the program. Although statistically significant differences were generally not found, the consistency of the trends listed below is important to note (17).

1. PPC students suspension rates declined after 1 year: 0.31 to 0.26. Control students suspension rates rose after 1 year, 0.07 to 0.15.
2. Tardy rates declined for PPC students from 3.2 to 2.7. Tardy rates rose for control students from 2.4 to 4.3.
3. Absence rates rose for both groups of students. For PPC students from 7.5 to 10.3, and for control students from 10.5 to 13.0.
4. Grades earned by both groups were almost identical during the 7th and 8th grade.
5. Problem-solving abilities stressed in PPC were enhanced by students who participated in the PPC program and were better than those of students who were not involved in the program.
6. Attitudes of students toward school for the PPC group remained constant from fall to spring testing.

In 1978, the Omaha Schools published Instructional Research Report #1977–3 which updated the PPC evaluation. In a controlled study of student attitudes, 142 7th and 8th graders who had been PPC participants were compared with a randomly selected control group of 78 students. Students in both groups were enrolled in three different schools. Three measures were administered to both groups including the Attitude Toward School Learning questionnaire, the Attitude Toward School questionnaire, and a situations questionnaire that measured the application of PPC problem solving to hypothetical conflicts. The PPC group scored significantly higher ($P<0.05$) than the control group on the Attitude Toward School Learning questionnaire and on the Situations measure. In addition to these measures of attitudinal change, the report cited lower tardy and absence rates for the PPC group, as well as better grades in reading and mathematics over a 2-year period. The suspension rates were lower for the PPC group in 1976/77 and for the control group in 1977/78 (18).

Omaha's use of PPC to confront the problems of disruptive behavior, racial desegregation, and drug abuse has received national attention. This program was highlighted in the January 1978 edition of *Creative Discipline* (19). The continued use of this program in Omaha after 6 years is clear evidence that its effects have been important to this school division. The fact that the program has been continued through the local monies since 1976 after federal funding expired is perhaps the most impressive endorsement. The local funding of the program occurred in spite of a strict ceiling on the school board's budgets.

In Rock Island, Illinois, a peer group counseling program based on PPC was developed in four junior high schools and one senior high school (20). The goal of the program was the reduction of the incidence of violence, disruption, truancy, drop-outs, and referrals to juvenile court. In a student population of 4,712, approximately 15% of the student body were regular participants. Another 5 percent were occasional participants. The results of the program were measured primarily in rates of disciplinary action. Suspensions decreased by 55.7 percent from 253 to 112 between the 1972/73 and 1973/74 school years. Expulsions declined from 7 to 2 over the same period. Overall, there was a 51.6 percent decrease in disciplinary incidents.

Petrock studied the effects of a GGI program in four Michigan secondary schools. This project was sponsored by the State of Michigan's Departments of Social Services and Education to reintegrate Department of Social Service Wards in the community, to assist school personnel in managing and preventing behavior problems, and to prevent delinquency in the community (8). Although the study was modified due to funding problems, several interesting findings emerged.

First, Petrock found statistically significant changes in self-concept as measured by the Rotter I-E Scale in the locus of control of youth who participated in the GGI groups. The movement from an external to an internal orientation was seen as resulting from giving students more control of their lives in school (8). Petrock states that this finding seems "to support Wittes hypothesis that locus of control in public school students is more a function of belonging to a peer group with power than a function of individual personality characteristics" (p. 84). The school administration's legitimizing the power and responsibility of students for the quality of life in the school was seen as a prerequisite for this shift of locus of control.

An interesting negative effect Petrock encountered was the perception by teachers that the GGI group members showed less eagerness, self-confidence, stability, considerateness, and sensitivity over time. Petrock speculated that this effect might be caused by teacher resistance to student control, teacher's not valuing GGI learned behaviors of speaking up, getting involved, and confronting others, or the tendency of teacher morale to decrease near the end of the year when the post-test data were collected. It is clear that greater teacher involvement and staff training are needed for the GGI program to be maximally effective.

Finally, Petrock's study produced three important recommendations for other public school programs using GGI and PPC. These recommendations were to ensure the inclusion of positive student leaders in the groups, to schedule group members into some of the same classes to ensure daily interaction outside the group meetings, and to include a number of students in the program sufficient to have an impact on the entire school.

A need exists for continuing research on the effectiveness of student peer groups to control and prevent disruptive behavior in public schools. Clearly, PPC and GGI can produce positive effects. Therefore the research studies should now move into more specific questions such as

1. What types of problems are best handled by student peer groups?
2. Which students respond best to direct experience in the leadership classes?
3. What are the characteristics of students who become the most effective in helping others?
4. What are the characteristics of students who do not respond to peer influence and who therefore may need some other intervention?
5. What types of teachers make the most effective group trainers?
6. What degree of faculty support for such a program is a prerequisite for its initial success?
7. What benefits occur in the community as a result of successful programs in the public schools?
8. Are certain types of schools (urban/suburban, large/small, etc.) more appropriate for these programs?
9. What ratio of students in leadership classes to total school enrollment is optimal for having total school effects?

Certainly this list of research questions is not complete. However, it does point to the specificity needed in future research to aid school officials in selecting the interventions most appropriate to their respective situations. More schools would be willing to choose PPC as their planned response to disruptive behavior in schools if these questions were more completely answered.

REFERENCES

1. Pilnick, S., Elias, A., & Clapp, N. The Essexfields concept: A new approach to social treatment of delinquents. *Journal of Applied*

Behavioral Science, 1966, *2* (1), 109–125.
2. Pilnick, S. et al. *Collegefields: From delinquency to freedom.* U.S. Department of Health, Education and Welfare Office of Juvenile Delinquency, 1967.
3. Chesler, M. Student and administrative crises. *Educational Leadership*, October 1969, *27*, 34–42.
4. Bayh, B. (Chairman). *Our nation's schools—A Report Card: "A" in school violence and vandalism.* Washington, D.C.: Committee on the Judiciary, 1975.
5. Bidwell, C. E. The school as a formal organization. In J. March (Ed.), *Handbook of organizations.* Chicago: Rand McNally, 1965.
6. Sexton, P. *The American school.* Englewood Cliffs, N.J.: Prentice-Hall, 1967.
7. McCorkle, L., Elias, A., & Bixby, L. *The Highfields Story.* New York: Henry Hold, 1958.
8. Petrock, F. *Guided group interaction in public schools: Managing student behavior through peer group advocacy.* Doctoral dissertation, University of Michigan, 1976.
9. Vorrath, H., & Brendtro, L. *Positive peer culture.* Chicago: Aldine Publishing Company, 1974.
10. Giles, J. Positive peer culture in the public school system. *NASSP Bulletin*, January 1975, *59*, 22–28.
11. Roffers, D. The development of a model for implementing the Positive Peer Culture Program in an inner-city high school. *Resources in Education*, October 1976, *11*, 190.
12. Gerrard, J. *An evaluation of the positive peer culture program in a boy's correctional school.* Master's thesis, University of Nebraska, 1975.
13. Lybarger, W. The effect of positive peer culture on the self-concept and rate of exhibition of inappropriate behavior of the emotionally disturbed adolescent male. *Dissertation Abstracts International*, September/October 1976, *37*.
14. Wasmund, W. *Behavioral and self conceptional differences among delinquents at two Minnesota institutions.* Master's thesis, University of Minnesota, 1977.
15. Wasmund, W. *Woodland Hills Tennessee self concept scale research project report.* Duluth, Minnesota, 1979, Unpublished report.
16. Bathke, R. *Principal's evaluation of positive peer culture program.* Monroe Junior High School, Omaha Public Schools, Omaha, Nebraska, June 1974.
17. Instructional Research Report #1975-10, *Evaluation: Positive peer culture program.* Omaha Public Schools, Omaha, Nebraska, August 1976.
18. Instructional Research Report #1977-3, *Evaluation: Positive peer culture program.* Omaha Public Schools, Omaha, Nebraska, June 1978.
19. Southeastern Public Education Program. *Positive peer culture. Creative Discipline*, November 1977 to January 1978, *1*, 1–3.
20. Edelman, M., Beck, R., & Smith, P. *School suspensions: Are they helping children?* Cambridge, Mass.: Children's Defense Fund, 1975.

INTRODUCTION TO CHAPTER 18

This well done, comparative, classroom study by Trice et al. is uncommon in secondary school educational research. Many more studies of this kind are needed, even though the results of such evaluation typically have little impact on the decisions of educational administrators (who are far more influenced by faculty, parent, and community pressures than by scientific assessments).

For those planning school programs for disruptive adolescents, the chapter provides the following: 1) a model *high school* study wherein resource programming was found to be more effective than a self-contained program for equivalent populations of disruptive adolescents, 2) evidence that a less restrictive educational environment, in addition to being more cost-efficient, can also be more effective and durable than a more restrictive intervention, and 3) additional data that school programs for disruptive youth (see Chapters 2, 10, and 13) can improve specific educational and behavioral outcomes.

The results described in this chapter provide one answer to the cynicism which in part characterized Chapter 6 and suggests that all schools might do well to have all-purpose, flexible resource services for those students in their midst who, for whatever reason, do not succeed.

18

A comparison of
senior high school interventions
for disruptive students

Ashton D. Trice
Frank C. Parker
and
Daniel J. Safer

A majority of programs for disruptive adolescents exist in junior high schools (1) because more behavior problems occur at that level (2) and because repeatedly aggressive adolescents do not generally remain in school beyond the 9th grade (see Chapter 13). Some disruptive students do, however, enter the senior high, and for these students programs are needed.

Such a need was obvious when a large percentage of disruptive students from an alternative junior high school program (see Chapters 12 and 13) entered senior high school. Without intervention, the senior high school experience for these behavior problem youth in a great many instances resulted in a short 10th grade stay. Worse yet, this brief period was characterized by academic failure, misconduct, and drop-out, accompanied by faculty hostility.

At the junior high school, the program had aimed at keeping misbehavior at a manageable level, increasing basic academic skills and sheltering students from the normal consequences of their misbehavior (such as long suspensions and expulsion) by attaching additional educational and therapeutic services to tightly structured mainstream education so that disruptive students did not disrupt very many. Such an approach appeared less feasible at the senior high level. Senior high schools are, generally, more orderly and quieter. They are larger. There is more reluctance to pass students in senior high school because of "trying hard" or "making progress." Instruction is much more geared to the various academic disciplines, and progress is based on the accumulation of Carnegie units. For example, the shortened day offered at the junior high would not permit the senior high school student to earn enough units to graduate at the usual time.

Misbehavior by a 16- or 17-year-old is a much more serious threat than that by a younger student; they are larger and stronger and readily perceived as adults. They are expected to behave as adults. Importantly, students at the senior high level are old enough to leave school voluntarily. Programs developed at this level must therefore appeal to the student in order to succeed.

INTERVENTIONS

Following years of no special programs for entering disruptive students at the receiving senior high school, two different models were developed for these 10th grade students during two successive years. As a result, we were able to compare mainstream (no special program) intervention with the self-contained and resource programs that followed. Identified disruptive students each year were equivalent in terms of 9th grade standardized achievement tests and attendance, and the three groups were similar in mean age at entry and sex composition. Although the self-contained group had a somewhat higher 9th grade suspension rate than either the mainstream or the resource group, the differences were not statistically significant. (See Table 1.)

Mainstream Students

During the 2-year period 1975–1977, no special program at the 10th grade was available. Thus, all students were enrolled in four major academic subjects (English, math, world history, and biology), physical education, and one or two minor subjects. Students attended a full seven-period day and were assigned to sections by achievement levels according to regular board of education procedures. Normal attendance, guidance, and administrative services were available.

Self-contained Program

The initial model employed was devised (for 1977/78) to mesh with another ongoing, self-contained work-experience program for students with poor academic motivation. Also it took into account

Table 1. Mean values of relevant pre-intervention variables

Variable	Mainstreamed (N=23)	Self-contained (N=17)	Resource (N=22)
Age at entry	16:4	16:3	15:11
Percent male	88%	78%	83%
9th grade attendance	78%	74%	73%
9th grade suspension rate	0.78	1.51	0.99
Pre-WRAT standard scores	83.1	85.8	84.3

the reluctance of school staff to keep disruptive students in regular school classes. The program featured a small self-contained section in which students received their major subject instruction. One teacher and an aide were responsible for academics and discipline with part-time consultation provided by a Ph.D. psychologist and a bachelor's level behavioral consultant. Points were awarded for being prepared for class, remaining on task, and work completion. Points were exchanged for weekly prizes and activity reinforcers (such as bowling and skating passes and field trips), and daily progress reports were sent to parents. Besides the normal disciplinary procedures of suspension and referral to school administrators, the teacher and the consultant could initiate short-term removal of students from school pending conferences with parents. These conferences were used to find specific solutions to immediate problems, often using contingency contracting with home-based reinforcement of the daily reports home. During the afternoon, all students received vocational instruction in carpentry and related areas for credit in an off-site workshop. They received pay for this training during the second semester.

Resource Program

During the 1978/79 school year, all high school entrants were placed in regular sections and a resource program was available within the school, staffed by a teacher/counselor and two aides. The resource program monitored students on disciplinary and academic matters and provided services when problems were noted. Students were also referred to the resource program by teachers for tutoring, individual instruction, counseling, and in-school detention. The majority of staff time was spent in relatively long-term (2–3 month) academic instruction. Students were referred for this service because of academic difficulty or persistent behavior problems. Although board of education curricula were followed, the one-to-one nature of the majority of this instruction also permitted intensive remedial work. Students themselves often solicited academic assistance and counseling.

Ten of the 22 students participated in a modification of the vocational program. Students were paid for work throughout the school year, and access to work experience was granted only upon receiving favorable daily reports from their four major subject teachers. Students who were eligible to go to the work site could opt to leave school after lunch. Students who received unfavorable reports remained in the resource center for detention but could earn an earlier dismissal by completing academic tasks.

Dependent Measures

Program outcomes were assessed by determining the percentage of students remaining on roll throughout the year and 2 years hence, the percent of students re-enrolling the following year, attendance and suspension rates (suspensions/100 school days attended), final grade point averages based on major subjects, and achievement changes on Wide Range Achievement Test (WRAT) standard scores. All data were collected from school files except for scores on the WRAT, which were administered by program personnel during the self-contained and resource program years only.

RESULTS

Table 2 displays the 10th grade school outcome measures for the three models under consideration. The resource program resulted in the greatest school longevity (completing the year, re-enrolling, and remaining in school 2 years hence), the highest attendance, the lowest rate of suspensions, the highest grades, and greater achievement test gains than during the self-contained program. In general, the self-contained program impacted least on these measures.

School longevity is a particularly sensitive measure of program outcome in that students over 16 can legally withdraw from school. The finding that 64% of the resource program students remained for the entire 10th grade, that 82% of the original group enrolled at the beginning of the following year, and that 59% were on the roll 2 years hence (as opposed to 50% or less during the mainstreamed and self-contained programs) suggests strongly that a variety of positive changes in the school lives of these students occurred then.

Although 9th grade attendance had been slightly lower for the resource group than for both of the others, it had the highest atten-

Table 2. 10th grade follow-up school outcome measures for mainstreamed, self-contained, and resource programs

Variable	Mainstreamed ($N=26$)	Self-contained ($N=18$)	Resource ($N=22$)	Test	Level of significance
10th grade measures					
Attendance	76%	68%	86%	χ^2	$P<0.05$
Suspension rate	1.68	3.11	0.52	F	$P<0.05$
Final GPA	1.04 ($N=12$)	0.73 ($N=8$)	1.34 ($N=14$)	F	$P<0.05$
WRAT change	(unavailable)	-1.3 ($N=8$)	$+4.3$ ($N=9$)	F	$P<0.01$
Follow-up measures					
Completing year	46%	44%	64%	χ^2	n.s.
Re-enrolling	42%	50%	82%	χ^2	$P<0.05$
On roll 2 years hence	31%	33%	59%	χ^2	$P<0.05$

dance rate during the 10th grade. Several special incentive programs for truants were undertaken during that year for the resource room group, which would have been somewhat more difficult to manage under the other programs, including daily contacts with parents and special contracts. The 10th grade suspension rate doubled over 9th grade rates for both the mainstreamed and self-contained groups, but was cut in half among resource students. However, the self-contained program students did have a higher rate of suspensions prior to entry into the program. Finally, grades and WRAT score changes indicate greater academic achievement for the resource room program.

PROGRAMATIC CONSIDERATIONS

The resource program had the advantage of being more varied. It had a similar staff: pupil ratio to the self-contained (3.0 staff persons for 22 students versus 2.4 staff persons for 18 students in the self-contained option), but it was not burdened by classroom instruction on a continuous basis. It could offer more as-needed services and a greater variety of interventions, including more individualized academic instruction, teacher consultation, and drop-out prevention. In addition, the resource program staff provided services for over 20 additional students who were not formally identified as disruptive students.

The format in the resource operation was not fixed. Some of its students had relatively little contact with the program staff aside from monitoring and occasional tutoring and counseling. Other students spent up to 2 academic periods/day in the resource center for lengthy periods (3–4 months) and participated in the afternoon vocational class. In practice, then, the resource option served to remove some problem students from classrooms until the students were better able to cope in them. The resource program also offered an early release from school option, which the self-contained program did not. However, among resource room students, this privilege was used on less than 15% of the occasions when it was earned.

DISCUSSION

The study's comparative data analysis revealed that the resource program in senior high school resulted in better school adjustment for disruptive youth during the 10th grade and 2 years hence than did the self-contained and the mainstream programs. We are unsure if these findings apply primarily at the senior high school level or if they are applicable at all grade levels. Obviously, replication and comparative program implementation at various grade levels are required.

However, there is a sizable body of evidence in the literature showing that at the elementary school level, self-contained classes do *not* produce significant benefits, whereas resource programs frequently achieve *short-term* results (see Chapter 6). The evidence on resource programs is for emotionally disturbed and learning-disabled students (3-5), while the evidence for the limitations of self-contained educational programming comes mainly from studies on educable mentally retarded children (6-12).

This report supports these conclusions at the senior high school level. Not only was the resource program the most effective model, but it was more in keeping with the least restrictive environment requirement written into PL 94-142. Compared to the self-contained classroom, the resource option offered the following least restrictive benefits: 1) a greater degree of contact between special students and their regular classroom peers, 2) more regular academic content, and 3) a better chance of success within the usual school environment.

Resource programs for disruptive adolescents offering a variety of academic and behavioral supports at the senior high school level have not often been reported in the literature. The results of this study indicate that the resource model is a readily available and viable option. The relative success of this program seems to be attributable to the variety of services available, and to its flexible crisis-oriented structure. The resource program was also quite cost-efficient, requiring an excess outlay of funds averaging no more than $1,200/program student per year.

REFERENCES

1. Pennsylvania Department of Education. *Alternative disciplinary programs and practices in Pennsylvania schools*, 1977.
2. National Institute of Education. *Violent schools—safe schools: The safe school study report to the Congress* (Vol. 1). Washington, D.C.: Author, 1978.
3. Glavin, J. P., Quay, H. C., Annesley, F. R., & Werry, J. S. An experimental resource room for behavior problem children. *Exceptional Children*, 1971, *38*, 131-137.
4. Glavin, J. P. Behaviorally oriented resource rooms: A follow-up. *Journal of Special Education*, 1974, *8*, 337-347.

5. Sindelar, P. T., & Deno, S. L. The effectiveness of resource programming. *Journal of Special Education*, 1978, *12*, 17–28.

6. Budoff, M., & Gottlieb, J. A. A comparison of EMR children in special classes with EMR children who have been reintegrated into regular classes. *Studies in Learning Potential*, 1974, *3*, 50.

7. Budoff, M., & Gottlieb, J. A. Special class EMR children mainstreamed: A study of an aptitude (learning potential) × treatment interaction. *American Journal of Mental Deficiency*, 1976, *81*, 1–11.

8. Egeland, B., & Schrimpf, V. Approaches to the understanding and treatment of learning-disabled children. In A. P. Goldstein (Ed.), *Prescriptions for child mental health and education*. New York: Pergamon, 1978.

9. Gampel, D. H., Gottlieb, J. A., & Harrison, R. H. Comparison of classroom behavior of special class EMR, integrated EMR, low IQ, and non-retarded children. *American Journal of Mental Deficiency*, 1974, *79*, 16–21.

10. Gorman, C., & Gottlieb, J. A. Mainstreaming mentally retarded children: A review of research. *International Review of Research in Mental Retardation*, 1978, *9*, 251–275.

11. Haring, N. G., & Krug, D. A. Placement in regular programs: Procedures and results. *Exceptional Children*, 1975, *41*, 413–417.

12. Macy, D. J., & Carter, J. L. Comparison of a mainstream and self-contained special education program. *Journal of Special Education*, 1978, *12*, 303–313.

VI

Funding sources

INTRODUCTION TO CHAPTER 19

Innovative school projects can be usefully begun on a small scale primarily with local funds. Additional money from outside sources enables a school district to enlarge the project, expand it to other schools, and improve the quality and scope of the evaluation. The additional money is clearly useful if there is a likelihood of continued funding from local monies or other grants after the initial outside funding ceases.

There are a number of potential drawbacks to receiving outside funds for innovative projects. First, the grant can lead to administrative headaches, increased interagency friction, bookkeeping mazes, and political quagmires. Second, a primary reliance on outside funding for innovative projects can indirectly stifle initiative for useful projects within the budget.

Grantsmanship in a social service or an educational setting is a challenging enterprise. Very industrious and productive individuals can obtain "soft" money funding for years and build their own "empire." However, like the survival of new business ventures, survival in this field is low (1).

Those seeking grants are advised to make sure of all the details in advance from the granting agency—*before* writing the grant—and to spend more time on arrangements, contacts, and the set-up than on writing the proposal.

1. Whittington, R. R., & Brand, C. R. Defunct grants—Special considerations for termination effectiveness. *Adolescence*, 1980, *57*, 201-210.

19

Funding sources for
alternative programs
for disruptive youth

Ashton D. Trice
and
Daniel J. Safer

In evaluating the availability of funding for programs for disruptive students, it is fair to say that the disruptive student is, per se, a very low priority. Unless disruptive students can be classified under another rubric, they are without a federal department, office, or agency, that includes them as one specific focus of concern.

Recent research addressing the issue of disruptive adolescents in the schools has obtained funding by characterizing the population as disadvantaged, educationally handicapped, culturally divergent (such as non-English speaking or of a racial minority), emotionally disturbed, delinquent, pre-delinquent, or vocationally handicapped. Even though most seriously disruptive students are also likely to be classified under one or more of these categories, special funding for the *specific problem of school misbehavior* is justifiable.

First, disruptive student behavior seriously interferes with the educational process and is on the increase. During the 1960s, school violence rose over 100% (1). Furthermore, between 1970 and 1973, assaults against teachers and students increased over 80%, and between 1969 and 1975, the rate of school fires nearly tripled (2).

Second, the classification of students for special intervention that does not target the presenting problem is contrary to good practice. The establishment of pseudotreatment categories (such as predelinquent) may represent a benign bureaucratic response to include an unpopular problem (unruly students) under a funded category to which the presenting problem is correlationally related (delinquency). Aside from the caveat that correlation does not demonstrate causation, several flaws exist in this procedure. By including discipline problem students in a statistically related category, those aspects of the problem that most closely relate to the funding category may receive priority over the aspects of the problem more relevant in the school setting. Programs funded under delinquency prevention monies may focus on determinants of crime more than on an examination of the contingencies within the school that influence misbehavior.

Moreover, the referral of students who have school behavior problems to programs that target other behaviors may have deleterious effects if the programs to which students are referred are not appropriately validated. Among other concerns expressed by the independent evaluator of the Rahway Lifers' Juvenile Awareness Project (*Scared Straight*) was that nondelinquent adolescents, specifically disruptive and truant students, were frequently being sent to a program which was found to *increase* delinquency significantly (3, 4).

Third, chronic school misbehavior is a problem significant enough in itself to warrant attention, in that 1) chronic school misbehavior may be exhibited by as many as 8% of primary and secondary school students (5), 2) school misbehavior is a frequent precursor of community misbehavior and other social adjustment problems (6), and 3) the resort to final exclusion from school has a disadvantageous effect on adult vocational and economic adjustment. Solving the school's problem in the short run may create more serious and more costly problems for the larger society later.

In any event, because funding is generally not available for programming for disruptive students, seeking funds by way of other classifications appears presently the most useful and pragmatic approach to establish alternative programs. Furthermore, such programs should have a remedial focus on academic deficiencies as well as on classroom misbehavior. The discussion below includes only funding sources that target both these program goals.

GENERAL CONSIDERATIONS

At present, the Departments of Labor, Justice, Education, and Health and Social Services provide most funding for disruptive student programs. Many disruptive student programs, though, require no additional cost at all (Note A). In-school suspension, remedial tutoring, and problem solving counseling can, for example, be supported by changes in administrative policy, alternative deployment of staff (e.g., assigning teachers to in-school suspension areas from other non-classroom duties) and by using volunteers from the community, college students, and parents. Other innovative programs have used peers as counselors, monitors, tutors, and as contact agents to inform parents of problems such as class cutting and truancy (7, 8).

Additionally, alternative programs may be funded by grants from private philanthropic and research sources. The experience of the authors and an examination of the recent literature suggests, however, that public school programs are highly unlikely to receive such support. Several excellent resources, though, on private grants can be recommended (9, 10).

The remainder of this paper examines the funding for alternative programs from the four departments mentioned. The dispersion of funds takes a variety of forms. In some instances, funds are applied for directly at the federal level. This is most likely to occur when the technique to be used is new, the population to be served is large, and the project is to be framed experimentally. When methods are taken directly from other models or only slightly adapted to meet local situational demands, or when funds are sought to continue an existing program or expand services in a traditional manner, federal funds are more likely to be channeled through state and local governmental agencies by means of "formula grants" (Note B). Applications for these grants are made directly to the state and local agencies. Often formula grants also require some local funding. This may present problems because the continued presence of disruptive students in public schools is one of the least popular ideas in education today (11). In fact, the experience of many workers in the field is that local elected officials are extremely reluctant to support the expenditure of even modest amounts of money for disruptive student programs.

Funding, however, does exist, and the 1978 fiscal reports of the agencies described disclose that in some instances a relatively large percentage of available funds were not allocated because of a lack of a sufficient number of sound local proposals.

Department of Labor

The Department of Labor has shown some concern for the development of stable and appropriate vocational careers by high-risk older adolescents. Only a small number of seriously disruptive adolescents graduate high school (12), and high school graduation is increasingly becoming a minimum prerequisite for entry into the job market at even a semiskilled level. Jobs that are still available for drop-outs include service station attendants, restaurant and fast-food workers (without advancement), toll booth attendants (10th grade minimum education), waiters and waitresses, janitorial and sanitation workers, and low-paying jobs in small businesses owned by local residents (13).

Furthermore, disruptive students are unlikely as a group to maintain job continuity. Ahlstrom and Havighurst (14) report a high job turnover among their work experience program students, and national statistics indicate that this trend continues into young adulthood. Robins (6) notes a similar finding through middle age. The routine and low paying nature of the jobs available may interact with the impulsivity of these individuals to bring about frequent switching and quitting of jobs. Collateral problems such as substance abuse, poor attendance, poor fiscal management, and irresponsible behavior also lead to frequent job firings.

The primary focus of most programs in the Department of Labor is not formal schooling or school conduct. Most funds are available to adolescents who have been out of school for a long enough period to be classified unemployed or unemployable. Two acts, however, have funds especially for adolescents who are still in school.

1. The Comprehensive Employment and Training Act of 1973 (CETA) supplies funds directly to states or local governments of 100,000 or more persons to increase employment or employability in areas demonstrating a 6.5% or higher unemployment rate. Disadvantaged, native American, non-English speaking, and delinquent youth are specifically targeted. Age limitations are 16 and above. In 1977 over 2,000,000 persons between the ages of 16 and 23 were served by CETA. Typical programs were Youth Work Incentive Projects which provided, in some instances, part-time paid job training for students likely to drop out of school; Job Corps, which currently serves over 80,000 youths 16–21 by providing short-term job training in residential settings; and the School to Work Transition Programs, which combine work experience and G.E.D. classes for young drop-outs.

    CETA can also be an invaluable indirect funding source for alternative programs in that unemployed adults may be given salaries and training funds to function as clerical assistants and teacher aides.

In 1981, recommendations to significantly decrease the scope of CETA have been made concurrently with proposals to do away with the program entirely. Congressional testimony suggests that the scope and nature of programs under CETA will be quite different within the forseeable future.

2. The Youth Employment and Demonstration Projects Acts (YEDPA) of 1977 provide a limited amount of funding for low income students under three of the four programs legislated. Importantly, although the act has primary responsibility for the age group 16–21, the Secretary of Labor is empowered to extend the lower age limit to 14.

Twenty-two percent of the monies of the Youth Employment and Training Programs are designated to create programs for adolescents still in school. These funds are to be used in programs developed in cooperation with local educational agencies. Typical programs have included training for nontraditional jobs and remedial educational support services in high unemployment areas.

The Youth Incentive Entitlement Pilot Projects (YIEPP) have sponsored 17 large innovative programs for students in school or drop-outs who agree to return to school. These 17 projects, each receiving substantial funding (the average over 5 million dollars), emphasize vocational training and school attendance and performance, and all have served sizable populations. At present, this project has the expressed purpose of disseminating successful models to other locations: no monies are available for the creation of new programs under YIEPP.

Youth Community Conservation and Improvement Projects have typically served drop-outs by employing them in local conservation projects. Adolescents remain in their home community. Students in school or G.E.D. programs may qualify for these funds, although only a small proportion of those served were thus enrolled.

Justice Department

The concerns of the Justice Department with disruptive students are that school disruption is a likely sign of delinquency-proneness and that the chronic delinquent who is out of school is at high risk for developing an adult criminal career, as well as the parallel concern that students who are conduct problems in school be afforded their due-process rights. Through a number of programs in the Law Enforcement Assistance Administration's (LEAA) Office of Juvenile Justice and Delinquency Prevention (OJJDP), school programs that can demonstrate an impact on school achievement and conduct, as well as delinquency, are funded. This same office funds advocacy programs to watch for illegal exclusion of students from school (e.g., unwarranted and arbitrary suspensions).

Through formula grants to states to develop state-wide delinquency prevention plans, the LEAA disperses funds that may be granted to local agencies to create programs for disruptive students. The emphasis in these grants is keeping youths within their communities, their homes, and whenever possible, their normal schools. Although these OJJDP funds can be used for all minors, the majority of these grants have been developed for youths aged 13–17.

Special emphasis programs, grants applied for directly at the federal level, have been available during the 6 years from 1974 to 1980. Monies are currently available to fund rather large projects ($150,000– $350,000) in the areas of 1) school crime, especially vandalism, 2) drug and alcohol education, 3) the advocacy programs mentioned above, and most recently, 4) novel school programs for problem students. The aims of this last program are the reduction of delinquent acts in and around schools, a reduction of drop-outs, suspensions, expulsions, and referrals to the juvenile justice system, and an increase in attendance, achievement, employment after graduation, and higher education.

Finally, the LEAA's National Institute for Juvenile Justice and Delinquency Prevention is the repository for information gained under OJJDP. One of the recent functions of the institute is to make funds available to communities that are willing to adopt a model developed under formula grants or special emphasis programs for the purpose of scientific validation. Several models that showed special promise have been advertised for such replication.

The LEAA's initial legislative mandate stressed innovation, and the history of the agency has been that a variety of approaches have been funded, including counseling, behavior modification, and work-experience models. In the past, community-based, alternative school, and in-school interventions have been funded, but at the present, only the community-based and in-school emphases are clear.

Department of Education

During 1980, the Department of Health, Education, and Welfare became the Department of Education and the Department of Health and Human Services. It is unclear what effect this split will have on services and funding, although for the present it appears that few differences will be noted, as the enabling legislation for most programs is unchanged. Some observers of the transition, however, have noted a trend to more bureaucracy, more intramural research, and less autonomy for formerly independent agencies, such as the National Institute of Education (15).

Within the Department of Education, four pieces of legislation may be relevant to the issue of disruptive students: the Elementary and Secondary Education Act (ESEA), the Emergency School Assistance Act (ESAA), the Teacher Corps, and the Education for All Handicapped Act.

1. Under several titles, The Elementary and Secondary Education Act channels considerable funds to local school districts. Title I disseminates funds to all school districts to supplement educational programs for disadvantaged students. Title VII competitively makes monies available to districts to create programs for students for whom English is not the primary language. As culturally disadvantaged and divergent groups are at risk to develop disruptive behavior, the special needs of these groups may be met under these titles.

   Under Title IV-C, special programs may be developed specifically aimed at increasing the number of students completing secondary schools. Awards are made to state Title IV Advisory Councils for dispersal and to local districts based on their proposals. Each state must create a state-wide plan, and funds are available without a local or state matching requirement. Fifteen percent of the funds must go to establishing programs for handicapped students, although it should be noted that Title IV-C's definition of handicapping conditions is somewhat different from the more widely known use under the Education for All Handicapped Act (PL 94-142).

   A number of discipline focused programs have been developed under Title IV-C although traditional counseling, curriculum change, and community service work experience programs have been favored by this agency.

2. The Emergency School Assistance Act provides funds to districts that are desegregating under court order. Special programs may be developed within the framework of the court decree and the district's desegregation proposal, requiring substantial community involvement. Additionally, grants are available to public agencies other than the schools to study the effects of the desegregation order on minority achievement and

disciplinary actions. Funding for similar projects in desegregating districts can also be obtained through Title IV of the Civil Rights Act.

3. The Teacher Corps provides monies to universities for paid internships for teacher trainees who are interested in disadvantaged students. Special concerns are youth who are re-entering school from correctional facilities and schools in high crime/low employment areas. Continued funding for the Teacher Corps is doubtful.

4. The Education for All Handicapped Act (PL 94-142) is the largest single fiscal effort to include all students in educational programs, guaranteeing a free public education to all students who can be classified handicapped from age 3 to 21. The act has initiated a large number of programs that provide monies to school districts, states, community organizations, and other educational institutions to increase services, to set up innovative programs, to develop early identification procedures, to create barrier-free educational facilities, and to do research. To date the emphases have been learning disabilities, developmental delay, orthopedic handicap, visual and hearing impairment, and multiple handicaps. Moreover, funds are being specifically loaded to emphasize services to youngsters in the 3–7-year-old age range. The law additionally restricts funds away from those whose handicaps can be attributed to cultural disadvantages.

Although some disruptive adolescents will no doubt receive support under the provisions of the act, the emphasis on early childhood programs and the exclusion of cultural disadvantage make the law an unlikely funding source, at present, for programs that are primarily interested in disruption. Also, the most likely category, emotional handicaps, is severely restricted in its definition to include only serious problems, such as childhood schizophrenia. No large-scale emphases on the entire category of emotional handicaps have yet been announced and no awards have been made thus far in this category under the field-initiated research grants.

Department of Health and Human Services

Like the Department of Education, the Department of Health and Human Services is undergoing transitions as it becomes independent. Funding for various large-scale research efforts and staff training is available under several study groups within the National Institutes of Mental Health, Alcohol Abuse and Alcoholism, and Drug Abuse. Each of these Institutes also provides small grants that can be used for program evaluation. Additionally the department provides monies for programs under the Social Security Act, but school-based efforts are being de-emphasized.

Priorities

Historically, as federal criteria have been announced to identify persons who can receive funds, services for these persons have dramatically increased along with estimates of the incidence of the problem in the general population (16). Thus, were major funding made available on the federal level specifically for adolescent school disruption, it would be predicted that a large number of students whose primary problem was school misconduct would be discovered and new programs would be created. Perhaps the end result would be that more of these students would remain in school and adjust better socially and economically in adulthood.

NOTES

Note A. To give a specific idea of which funds support school programs for disruptive youth, the funding sources revealed in two recent surveys are listed. In Pennsylvania in 1977, out of 19 alternative disciplinary (school) programs, 10 had local funding, three received LEAA support, three received Title IV–C aid, two had Title I funding, and one received vocational educational financing (17). In the NIE 1978 survey of eight comprehensive, in-school suspension programs, their funding sources were as follows: LEAA, 1; local, 3; vocational education, 1; Title IV–C, 1; and ESAA-Title VII, 2 (18).

Note B. Important funding sources and addresses for program information about these programs are given below.

Department of Labor

YEDPA

Office of Youth Programs
Department of Labor
601 D Street, N.W.
Washington, D.C. 20213

CETA

Local

Justice Department

LEAA

Office of Juvenile Justice & Delinquency Prevention
Law Enforcement Assistance Administration
Washington, D.C. 20531

Local

354   *Trice and Safer*

Department of Education

Department of Education
Washington, D.C. 20202

Department of Health and Human Services

National Institute of Mental Health
5600 Fishers Lane
Rockville, Maryland 20852

REFERENCES

1. McGowan, W. N. Crime control in public schools: Space age solutions. *NASSP Bulletin*, April 1973, *57*, 43–48.
2. Neil, S. B. Violence and vandalism: Dimensions and correctives. *Phi Delta Kappan*, January 1978, *59*, 302–307.
3. Finckenauer, J. O., & Storti, J. R. *Juvenile Awareness Project HELP*, Evaluation Report No. 1. Newark, N.J.: Rutgers University, 1979.
4. Finckenauer, J. O. *Juvenile Awareness Project*, Evaluation Report No. 2. Newark, N.J.: Rutgers University, 1979.
5. Woody, R. H. *Behavioral problem children in the schools*. New York: Appleton-Century-Crofts, 1969.
6. Robins, L. N. *Deviant children grown up*. Baltimore: Williams & Wilkins, 1966.
7. Robertson, S. J., DeReus, D. M., & Drabman, R. S. Peer and college student tutoring as reinforcement in a token economy. *Journal of Applied Behavior Analysis*, 1967, *9*, 169–177.
8. Bolds, G. S. Reducing truancy by using student aides in the attendance office. (ERIC Document Reproduction Service No. ED 146 493).
9. The Foundation Center. *The foundation directory* (7th ed.). New York: Author, 1979.
10. Marquis Academic Media. *Annual register of grant support*. Chicago: Author, 1980.
11. Gallup, G. H. The 10th annual Gallup poll. *Phi Delta Kappan*, 1978, *60*, 33–45.
12. Safer, D. J., Heaton, R. C., & Parker, F. C. A behavioral program for disruptive junior high school students: Results and follow-up. *Journal of Abnormal Child Psychology*, 1981, *9*, 483–494.
13. Parrish, J. S. P., & Trice, A. D. Unpublished data.
14. Ahlstrom, W. M., & Havighurst, R. J. *400 Losers: Delinquent boys in high school*. San Francisco: Jossey-Bass, 1971.
15. McNett, I. New dept., same old NIE. *APA Monitor*, 1980, *11* (2), 1, 7.
16. Gallagher, J. J., Forsythe, P., Rengelheim, D. & Weintraub, F. J. Funding patterns and labeling. In N. Hobbs (Ed.), *Issues in the classification of children* (Vol. II). San Francisco: Jossey-Bass, 1975.
17. Pennsylvania State Department of Education. *Alternative disciplinary programs and practices in Pennsylvania schools*. Harrisburg, Penn., 1977.

18. Garibaldi, A. M. *In-school alternatives: The state of the art.* Read at National Institute of Education Conference on In-School Alternatives to Suspension, Washington, D.C., April, 1978.

Index